GOTTLOB FREGE
COLLECTED PAPERS ON MATHEMATICS, LOGIC, AND PHILOSOPHY

GOTTLOB FREGE

Collected Papers on Mathematics, Logic, and Philosophy

Edited by
BRIAN McGUINNESS

Translated by
MAX BLACK
V. H. DUDMAN
PETER GEACH
HANS KAAL
E.-H. W. KLUGE
BRIAN McGUINNESS
R. H. STOOTHOFF

Basil Blackwell

© in the English edition Basil Blackwell Publisher Ltd 1984

This collection includes most of the papers which appeared in German as *Kleine Schriften*, edited by I. Angelelli (Olms and Wissenschaftliche Buchgesellschaft, Hildesheim, 1967)

First published 1984

Basil Blackwell Publisher Ltd
108 Cowley Road, Oxford OX4 1JF, UK

Basil Blackwell Inc.
432 Park Avenue South, Suite 1505,
New York, NY 10016, USA

British Library Cataloguing in Publication Data
Frege, Gottlob
   Collected papers on mathematics, logic, and philosophy.
   1. Philosophy   2. Mathematics—Philosophy
   I. Title   II. McGuinness, Brian
   III. Kleine Schriften. *English*
   193   B3245.F2

ISBN 0-631-12728-3

Library of Congress Cataloging in Publication Data
Frege, Gottlob, 1848–1925.
   Collected papers on mathematics, logic, and philosophy.

   Translation of most of the papers which appeared in: Kleine Schriften.
   Includes index.
   1. Mathematics—Collected works.   I. McGuinness, Brian.   II. Title.
   QA3.F732513 1984   510   84-12490
   ISBN 0-631-12728-3

Typeset by Bell and Bain Ltd., Glasgow
Printed in Great Britain by Bell and Bain Ltd., Glasgow

TABLE OF CONTENTS

sphere from a point on the sphere which is neither the nearest nor the furthest. In that case there is no difference in projection between proper points and points at infinity. In what follows we shall attempt to do the same for imaginary forms. By a geometrical representation of imaginary forms in the plane we understand accordingly a kind of correlation in virtue of which every real or imaginary element of the plane has a real, | intuitive element corresponding to it. The first advantage to be gained 7 by this is one common to all cases where there is a one–one relation between two domains of elements: that we can arrive at new truths by merely carrying over known propositions. But there is another advantage peculiar to this case: that the non-intuitive relations between imaginary forms are replaced by intuitive ones. The meaning of imaginary forms comes out equally whether they are considered metrically or projectively. We shall, however, confine ourselves to metrical relations and only indicate at the end a way of generalizing our method of representation which might be more suitable for projective propositions.

1 REPRESENTATION OF IMAGINARY POINTS

For the sake of brevity and precision of expression in what follows, we introduce the following designations:

The plane whose forms we represent shall be called the base plane. The points, straight lines and curves to be represented shall always be distinguished by the addendum 'real' or 'imaginary' from those forms that serve to represent them and which are always to be regarded as real. Further, the real shall in general be subsumed under the imaginary. Now if we want to represent imaginary points on the base plane, it seems appropriate that we start with the way they are defined in algebraic analysis, because this allows us to describe them in their entirety in the most general way. Accordingly, we think of | imaginary 8 points as given by their rectangular coordinates

$$x = \xi + i\xi', \qquad y = \eta + i\eta'.$$

We could now represent the imaginary points (x, y) by the two points (ξ, η) and (ξ', η'). However, this would not enable us to tell which one of the two was to express the real parts. We therefore displace the point (ξ', η') onto a special plane which is parallel to the base plane and contains the rectangular axes of ξ' and η'. We call this plane the plane of the imaginary. The base plane considered as the locus of the points (ξ, η) may be called the plane of the real. In order to characterize as such those points on these planes that belong together, we connect them by a straight line, and we regard this as a representation of the imaginary point. If a straight line passes through the origin of coordinates in the plane of the imaginary, it represents a real point. For the sake of brevity we will call the origin of these coordinates the point of origin of the imaginary.

2   IMAGINARY CURVES AND IN PARTICULAR THE IMAGINARY STRAIGHT LINE

Let some curve be given by the equation

$$S(x, y) = 0.$$

This breaks down into

$$\varphi(\xi, \xi', \eta, \eta') = 0, \qquad \psi(\xi, \xi', \eta, \eta') = 0. \tag{1}$$

Each system of values ξ, ξ', η, η' which satisfies equations (1) gives us an imaginary point of the curve. | There is a doubly infinite set of such points, if we call the multiplicity of real points on a straight line a singly infinite set. If we solve equations (1), we obtain

$$\xi' = f(\xi, \eta), \qquad \eta' = f_1(\xi, \eta)$$

and these functions give us a mapping of the plane of the real to the plane of the imaginary.

Suppose first that the curve is a straight line given by the equation

$$ux + vy + 1 = 0,$$

where

$$u = \rho + i\rho', \qquad v = \chi + i\chi'.$$

The mapping functions are then:

$$\xi' = \frac{\chi + (\rho\chi + \rho'\chi')\xi + (\chi^2 + \chi'^2)\eta}{\rho'\chi - \chi'\rho}$$

$$\eta' = \frac{-\rho - (\rho^2 + \rho'^2)\xi - (\rho\chi + \rho'\chi')\eta}{\rho'\chi - \chi'\rho} \tag{2}$$

or in the case of the inverse solution:

$$\xi = \frac{\chi' - (\rho\chi + \rho'\chi')\xi' + (\chi^2 + \chi'^2)\eta'}{\rho'\chi - \chi'\rho}$$

$$\eta = \frac{-\rho' + (\rho^2 + \rho'^2)\xi' + (\rho\chi + \rho'\chi')\eta'}{\rho'\chi - \chi'\rho} \tag{3}$$

The mapping is one–one.

Not every pair of linear functions

$$\xi' = A + B\xi + C\eta, \qquad \eta' = D + E\xi + F\eta$$

can occur in formulae (2). The following conditions must first be satisfied:

$$F + B = 0, \qquad BF - EC = 1. \tag{4}$$

In order to investigate what special kind of mapping may be given in this way, we effect a rotation of the coordinate system in both planes by putting: |

$$x = x_1 \cos\alpha - y_1 \sin\alpha, \qquad y = x_1 \sin\alpha + y_1 \cos\alpha. \qquad 10$$

We then obtain the new mapping functions

$$\xi'_1 = A_1 + B_1\xi_1 + C_1\eta_1, \qquad \eta'_1 = D_1 + E_1\xi_1 + F_1\eta_1.$$

Here

$$B_1 = B\cos^2\alpha + F\sin^2\alpha + (E + C)\sin\alpha\cos\alpha$$

or

$$B_1 = B\cos 2\alpha + \frac{E + C}{2}\sin 2\alpha$$

$$F_1 = -B\cos 2\alpha - \frac{E + C}{2}\sin 2\alpha.$$

We can now determine α in such a way that $B_1 = 0$ and $F_1 = 0$. We then have

$$\operatorname{tg} 2\alpha = -\frac{2B}{C + E}.$$

From this we can infer two values for α itself which differ from each other by $90°$. We now have

$$\xi'_1 = A_1 + C_1\eta_1, \qquad \eta'_1 = D_1 + E_1\xi_1. \tag{5}$$

Equation (4) can be transformed into

$$E_1 C_1 = -1. \tag{6}$$

Now what is the geometrical meaning of this? To a parallel to the ξ_1-axis corresponds a parallel to the η'_1-axis, and to a parallel to the η-axis a parallel to the ξ'_1-axis. Up to now we have made no stipulations about the respective positions of the coordinate systems in the planes of the real and the imaginary. We now stipulate that the coordinate system in the plane of the imaginary has been rotated through $90°$

6   *Imaginary Forms in the Plane*

relative to the one in the plane of the real, so that the ξ'-axis is parallel to the η-axis, and the η'-axis to the negative side of the ξ-axis. The same holds then for ξ_1' and η_1' with respect | to ξ_1 and η_1. The advantage to be gained by this is that the parallels to the ξ_1- and η_1- axes become parallel to their images. It is now possible to carry out the mapping by means of a simple geometrical construction. For if we place a plane through each pair of parallels to the η_1- and ξ_1'-axes, then all these planes intersect in a common edge NR (figure 1), because in virtue of (5) the distance between two parallels in the plane of the real has a constant relation to the distance between their images. In the same way, all of the planes placed through each pair of parallels to the ξ_1- and η_1'-axes intersect in a common edge QM. These edges are parallel to the base plane and perpendicular to each other. In virtue of equations (5) and (6), and because the axes of η_1' and ξ_1 are opposite whereas those of η_1 and ξ_1' have the same direction, the edge QM must be at the same distance from the plane of the real as the edge RN is from the plane of the imaginary, but in the opposite direction. The mapping is given by the edges RN and QM; for every straight line which connects a point on NR with a point on QM cuts the two planes at corresponding points. Since the two edges yield in this way all the

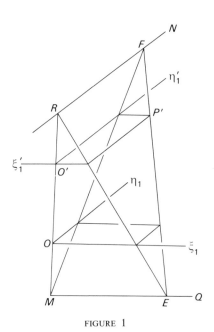

FIGURE 1

imaginary points on the imaginary straight line, we regard them as a representation of the latter. For a pair of straight lines to represent an imaginary straight line, they must be perpendicular to each other and parallel to the base plane, and one of them must be just as distant from the | plane of the real as the other is from the plane of the imaginary, 12 but in the opposite direction. We will call such a pair of straight lines the guide lines of an imaginary straight line. The special case of a real straight line still remains to be considered. An imaginary straight line has only one real point, for through the point of origin of the imaginary we can in general place only *one* straight line intersecting the two guide lines. Only when one of the guide lines itself passes through the point of origin of the imaginary do we have infinitely many real points. These are represented by the straight lines which connect them with the point of origin of the imaginary. Since one of the guide lines lies in the plane of the imaginary, the other must lie in the plane of the real, and consequently it must coincide with the real straight line to be represented. In addition to the real points, we have in this case a doubly infinite set of imaginary points, which are represented by the lines connecting other points on the guide line in the plane of the imaginary with points on the guide line in the plane of the real. We cannot properly speak of a mapping in this case, as is clear from the disappearance of the denominator in (2) and (3) and is also geometrically self-evident. This happens whenever the guide lines lie in the planes of the real and the imaginary, or in analytical terms, when the denominator $\rho'\chi - \chi'\rho$ of formulae (2) disappears. The two conditions are clearly identical; for if there is no possibility of a mapping, each of them | is necessary and sufficient. When $\rho'\chi = \chi'\rho$, we can put 13

$$u = \rho + i\rho' = Q(\cos \gamma + i \sin \gamma)$$

$$v = \chi + i\chi' = R(\cos \gamma + i \sin \gamma).$$

The coefficients u, v of the equation $ux + vy + 1 = 0$ have therefore the same amplitude. We will call such an imaginary straight line a purely imaginary one. Considered metrically, such straight lines are closer to real lines.

3   THE IMAGINARY CONNECTING LINE

Suppose we are given two straight lines (g, h) which represent imaginary points, and we are to construct the guide lines of their imaginary connecting line.

We first exclude the case where g or h is parallel to the base plane and assume that the two intersect. Then the guide lines we are seeking must either lie in the plane of g and h or pass through their point of intersection. Both guide lines cannot lie in the plane of g and h, because they would then be parallel to each other. Hence one at any rate passes through the point of intersection. But then the other cannot in general pass through that point as well, because of the condition that must be satisfied by the distances of the guide lines from the planes. The second guide line lies therefore in the plane of g and h. This and the other restrictions to which it is subject determine its position completely. This also gives us the direction | of the guide line which passes through the point of intersection of g and h. The only cases where neither of the guide lines needs to lie in the plane of g and h are those where the point of intersection of g and h is equidistant from the planes of the real and the imaginary, and hence, where it lies either in the middle between the two or at infinity. In these cases, both guide lines pass through the point of intersection and their direction becomes indeterminate. In the second place, if the straight line g is parallel to the base plane, it evidently represents an imaginary point at infinity. We do not assume that g is cut by h, but that g lies neither in the middle between the planes of the real and the imaginary nor in the plane at infinity. If we now place through g a plane F parallel to the base plane and draw in it a guide line which intersects g and h, then the other guide line cannot also lie in this plane. If it is nevertheless to intersect g and at the same time to be parallel to the base plane, it must be assumed to be parallel to g. This and the other conditions determine it completely. From this it follows that the first guide line intersects g at a right angle; it too is completely determined by this. g represents the imaginary point at infinity on the straight line whose guide lines we have just drawn. If g is displaced on the plane F parallel to itself, the construction remains unchanged. All those parallels represent accordingly the same imaginary point at infinity. If we place a plane F' parallel to the base plane through the other guide line and draw in | it lines perpendicular to it, or what comes to the same thing, perpendicular to g, then these perpendiculars together with h yield the same imaginary point at infinity. Such a point is therefore represented by two singly infinite families of parallels which are perpendicular to one another and which lie in two planes which are parallel and symmetrical to the planes of the real and the imaginary. The case where g lies either parallel to and in the middle between the plane of the real and the imaginary or in the plane at infinity will be considered later on.

If h is also parallel to the base plane, then the imaginary line connecting the imaginary points at infinity represented by h and g is the line at infinity of the base plane. This is therefore one of the guide lines. The question about the other one must remain unanswered for the time being. We here exclude the cases where, according to the results obtained above, g and h represent the same point at infinity.

Finally, if g and h are neither parallel to the base plane nor intersect each other, then we project everything on a plane which lies in the middle between the planes of the real and the imaginary and parallel to them, and which will subsequently always be designated by E. Let the lines of projection be parallel to a straight line g. This is then mapped as the point G (figure 2). Let the point of intersection of the straight line h with the plane E be H and its projection h_1. Further, let GA and GB be the projections of the guide lines we are seeking. | Then   16 $HA = HB = Hg$. We thus obtain A and B by marking off HG from H to h in both directions. The projections GA and GB we have found can then be moved to their positions in space by parallel displacement along g.

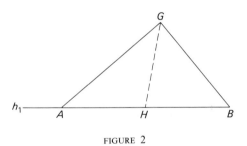

FIGURE 2

4   THE DISTANCE BETWEEN IMAGINARY POINTS

The expression

$$r = \sqrt{(x_1 - x_0)^2 + (y_1 - y_0)^2} \qquad (1)$$

expresses the distance between two points when x_0, y_0 and x_1, y_1 are the real coordinates of these points. Every proposition which states a relation between lengths and does not merely contain an inequality follows from the foundations of analytic geometry and can be derived analytically from (1) by operations and inferences which are equally applicable to complex numbers. These relations obtain therefore also among the values of r for complex coordinates. If we now take the view that what is essential to the concept of distance is not the intuitive character of a straight line but conformity to the laws of algebraic analysis, then we can apply the name 'distance' also where the end points are imaginary. We shall henceforth speak of 'distances' in this sense.

If we now introduce into (1) the values

$$x_0 = \xi_0 + i\xi_0', \qquad y_0 = \eta_0 + i\eta_0'$$

$$x_1 = \xi_1 + i\xi_1', \qquad y_1 = \eta_1 + i\eta_1',$$

we obtain |

17

$$r = \sqrt{\begin{array}{c}(\xi_1 - \xi_0)^2 + (\eta_1 - \eta_0)^2 - (\xi_1' - \xi_0')^2 - (\eta_1' - \eta_0')^2 \\ + 2i[(\xi_1 + \xi_0)(\xi_1' - \xi_0') + (\eta_1 - \eta_0)(\eta_1' - \eta_0')]\end{array}}$$

or, by introducing

$$\xi_1 - \xi_0 = \sigma, \qquad \eta_1 - \eta_0 = \tau$$

$$\xi_1' - \xi_0' = \sigma', \qquad \eta_1' - \eta_0' = \tau',$$

$$r = \sqrt{\sigma^2 + \tau^2 - \sigma'^2 - \tau'^2 + 2i(\sigma\sigma' + \tau\tau')}. \tag{2}$$

To simplify the calculation, we place the coordinate system in such a way that its axes becomes parallel to the guide lines of the imaginary connecting line between (x_0, y_0) and (x_1, y_1). As in section 3, we again project everything on the plane E in the way indicated in that section. The straight line g, which represents the imaginary point (x_0, y_0), is mapped as the point G (figure 3). Let h_1 be the projection of h, the straight line that represents the imaginary point (x_1, y_1). GB and GA are the projections of the guide lines. C and D are the images of the intersections of h with the planes of the real and the imaginary. Then $CA = DB$. If we now draw $CK \| DJ \| AG$, then

$$GJ = \xi_1 - \xi_0 = \sigma$$

$$DJ = \eta_1 - \eta_0 = \tau$$

$$GK = -(\eta_1' - \eta_0') = -\tau' \tag{3}$$

$$CK = \xi_1' - \xi_0' = \sigma'.$$

Further, $\dfrac{DJ}{JB} = \dfrac{CK}{BK}$ or $\dfrac{DJ}{GK} = \dfrac{CK}{GJ}$ or

$$\frac{\tau}{-\tau'} = \frac{\sigma'}{\sigma}. \tag{4}$$

18   If for σ in (2) we introduce the value $-(\tau'/\tau)\sigma'$, | we obtain for the real

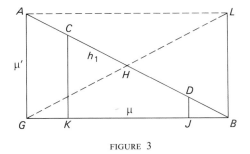

FIGURE 3

part of the expression under the root sign

$$A = \frac{(\sigma'^2 - \tau^2)(\tau'^2 - \tau^2)}{\tau^2}$$

and as the factor of i

$$B = -\frac{2\tau'}{\tau}(\sigma'^2 - \tau^2).$$

Now if

$$r = \rho + i\rho' = \sqrt{A + iB},$$

then

$$\rho = \sqrt{\frac{\sqrt{A^2 + B^2} + A}{2}}, \qquad \rho' = \sqrt{\frac{\sqrt{A^2 + B^2} - A}{2}}.$$

Here $\sqrt{A^2 + B^2}$ is always to be taken as positive, and ρ and ρ' have the same sign if $B > 0$ and the opposite sign if $B < 0$. By substituting the values of A and B we get

$$\rho = \sqrt{\tau^2 - \sigma'^2}, \qquad \rho' = \frac{\tau'}{\tau}\sqrt{\tau^2 - \sigma'^2},$$

if $\sigma'^2 < \tau^2$, or

$$\rho = \frac{\tau'}{\tau}\sqrt{\sigma'^2 - \tau^2}, \qquad \rho' = -\sqrt{\sigma'^2 - \tau^2},$$

if $\sigma'^2 > \tau^2$.

The case where $\tau^2 > \sigma'^2$ can always be reduced to the case where $\sigma'^2 > \tau^2$ by rotation of the coordinate system through $90°$. Such a rotation does not disturb the assumed parallelism between the axes and the guide lines. If we distinguish the new σ and τ by a subscript, then |

19

$$\tau = \sigma_1$$

$$\sigma' = -\tau_1'$$

$$\sigma = -\tau_1$$

$$\tau' = \sigma_1'.$$

Thus if

$$\tau^2 > \sigma'^2 \quad \text{or}$$

$$\tau^2 \sigma^2 > \sigma^2 \sigma'^2$$

or

$$\tau'^2 \sigma'^2 > \sigma^2 \sigma'^2$$

$$\tau'^2 > \sigma^2,$$

then

$$\sigma_1'^2 > \tau_1{}^2.$$

We can therefore always presuppose the case where $\sigma'^2 > \tau^2$. Then

$$r = \sqrt{\sigma'^2 - \tau^2} \left(\frac{\tau'}{\tau} - i \right).$$

This leads us to compare the real and imaginary parts of this formula with the segments $GB = \mu$, $GA = \mu'$ on the guide lines. Then (figure 3)

$$\mu = GJ + GK, \qquad \mu' = KC + DJ$$

or by (3)

$$\mu = \sigma - \tau', \qquad \mu' = \sigma' + \tau$$

and in the light of (4)

$$\mu = -\frac{\tau'}{\tau}(\sigma' + \tau).$$

Accordingly

$$\rho = -\mu \sqrt{\frac{\sigma' - \tau}{\sigma' + \tau}}$$

$$\rho' = -\mu' \sqrt{\frac{\sigma' - \tau}{\sigma' + \tau}}.$$

Consequently

$$r = \pm \sqrt{\frac{\sigma' - \tau}{\sigma' + \tau}} (\mu + i\mu'), \quad | \tag{5}$$

where the sign of the root depends on arbitrary assumptions. Given our 20
assumption that $\sigma'^2 > \tau^2$, the root is always real. It assumes a simple
form when the connecting line is a purely imaginary straight line. Then
the guide lines lie in the planes of the real and the imaginary. If we
assume the ξ-axis to be parallel to the guide line in the plane of the
real, then the condition that $\sigma'^2 > \tau^2$ is satisfied, since $\tau = 0$. Formula (5)
then becomes

$$r = \mu + i\mu'.$$

This leads one to conjecture that the factor

$$\sqrt{\frac{\sigma' - \tau}{\sigma' + \tau}}$$

depends on the distance of the guide lines from the planes of the real
and the imaginary. For the sake of symmetry we determine the distance
N of the guide lines from the plane E and call $2d$ the distance of the
planes of the real and the imaginary from each other. Then (figure 4)

$$\frac{N+d}{N-d} = \frac{CD}{AB} = \frac{\xi'_1 - \xi_0}{\eta_1 - \eta_0} = \frac{\sigma'}{\tau},$$

where the plane of the drawing has been placed through the η- and ξ'-
axis. From this we can infer the following relationship between the

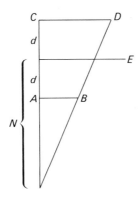

FIGURE 4

distances:

$$\lambda = \frac{N}{d} = \frac{\sigma' + \tau}{\sigma' - \tau}.$$

Formula (5) becomes

$$r = \frac{1}{\sqrt{\lambda}}(\mu + i\mu').$$

If we consider once more the projection on the plane E (figure 3), we notice that, according to Gauss's way of representing complex numbers in the plane, the diagonal GL of the rectangle constructed from the sides

$$GB = \mu, \qquad GA = \mu' \mid$$

21   gives us the distance we are seeking up to a real factor, if we assume the axis of the real to be parallel to the one guide line and the axis of the plane of the imaginary to be parallel to the other guide line. The same holds also for GH, the distance between the points of intersection of the straight lines g and h with the plane E, because $GH = \frac{1}{2}GL$. It still remains to be investigated to which of the two guide lines the axis of the real is to be made parallel. It is to be made parallel to that guide line to which we had to make the ξ-axis parallel, in order to satisfy the condition

$$\sigma'^2 > \tau^2;$$

for this assumption lies at the bottom of all our considerations. Now according to (3) this inequality is identical with $CK^2 > DJ^2$. In view of figure 3 we can substitute for it

$$DB^2 > CB^2. \tag{6}$$

Now DB and CB are related in the same way as the distances between the guide line which is parallel to the ξ-axis and the planes of the real and the imaginary. Accordingly the inequality (6) expresses that we must assume the ξ-axis to be parallel to that guide line which is nearer in the absolute sense to the plane of the real. Accordingly we obtain the proposition:

If the imaginary points γ and δ on the imaginary straight line ε are represented by the straight lines g and h, then the connecting line GH of the points of intersection of g and h with the plane E, multiplied by a real constant $2/\sqrt{\lambda}$ dependent only on ε, $\mid$ gives us an intuitive representation of the imaginary

22

distance between γ and δ, on the assumption that the axis of the real is parallel to that guide line of ε which is nearer to the plane of the real.

We therefore call the guide line of an imaginary straight line which is nearer to the plane of the real the guide line of the real, and the other one the guide line of the imaginary.

It is now also easy to specify what it means for two straight lines which represent imaginary points to intersect. As can be inferred immediately, the distance between the two imaginary points is then either purely real, in case the point of intersection lies nearer to the plane of the imaginary, or purely imaginary, in case it lies nearer to the plane of the real.

5 POINTS OF INTERSECTION AND ANGLES OF
IMAGINARY STRAIGHT LINES

Suppose we are given two imaginary straight lines by their guide lines, and we are to find the straight line which represents their imaginary point of intersection.

The straight line we are seeking must intersect the four given guide lines. In general four straight lines are intersected jointly by·two others. Since all four guide lines are here parallel to the same plane, one of those two straight lines is in every case the line at infinity of that plane. Because this may be disregarded, the straight line we are seeking must be the other one. |

As for the meaning of an angle of imaginary straight lines, we only 23 need to recall what was said in the beginning of section 4. This can, essentially, be applied to the present case. We reduce the definition of an angle to the concept of distance by means of the formula

$$a = \arcsin(\tfrac{1}{2}s) \tag{1}$$

Here s means the chord in the circle described by radius 1. The function arc sin may be defined purely analytically.

Suppose we are given two imaginary straight lines by their guide lines, and we are to find an intuitive meaning for the angle defined by (1).

The general case where the corresponding guide lines cross can be constructed from two special cases. In the one case the guide lines intersect and are equidistant from the plane E; in the other they are parallel and at different distances from the plane *E*. To construct the general case, all we need to do is introduce an imaginary auxiliary line whose guide lines intersect the guide lines of the first imaginary straight line and are parallel to the corresponding guide lines of the second. The angle we are seeking is then the sum of the separate angles. The first case has the peculiarity that the one pair of guide lines turns into the other simply by rotation; peculiar to the second case is that the second pair of guide lines arises from the first simply by parallel displacement. In order to apply our definition (1) to the first case where the guide lines intersect, we must mark off distance 1 on both sides of the angle. |

24   Translated into our representation this means that, starting from the point of intersection *C* of the guide lines of the real (figure 5), we must mark off the distance $CD = CG = \sqrt{\lambda}$, where λ has the meaning given in the previous section. If we connect the points *D* and *G* which we have found in this way with the point of intersection *H* of the guide lines of the imaginary, then the straight lines *GH* and *DH* represent the imaginary points which lie on the imaginary sides of the angle at distance 1 from the vertex. The distance between the imaginary points is real: it is equal to $GD/\sqrt{\lambda}$. Now let the guide lines of the real combine to form the angle α. Then

$$GD = 2CD \sin \tfrac{1}{2}\alpha = 2\sqrt{\lambda} \sin \tfrac{1}{2}\alpha$$

and the angle of the imaginary straight lines

$$2 \arc \sin \tfrac{1}{2} \frac{GD}{\sqrt{\lambda}} = \alpha.$$

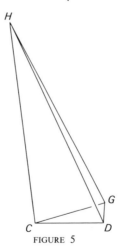

FIGURE 5

Thus when the guide lines intersect, the angle of the imaginary straight lines is equal to the angle of their guide lines. In the second case, where the corresponding guide lines of the two imaginary straight lines I and II are parallel and at different distances from the plane E, we must mark off on the guide lines of the real (figure 6) the lengths

$$DG = \sqrt{\lambda_1}, \qquad CF = \sqrt{\lambda_2} \qquad (2)$$

where the meanings of λ_1 and λ_2 for the two guide lines correspond to that of λ above. Now if DK represents the imaginary point at the vertex and if J and K are the points where this straight line is cut by the guide lines of the imaginary, then the straight lines FJ and GK represent the imaginary points which delimit the line segments of ∣ length 1 on the imaginary sides of the angle. The distance between 25 these points is purely imaginary because the point of intersection H of the straight lines FJ and GK lies nearer to the plane of the real, as can easily be found. In order to determine this imaginary distance, we calculate the distance VW between the intersections of the straight lines JF and KG with the plane E. Thus

$$VW = RW - RV = \tfrac{1}{2}(DG - CF)$$

$$VW = \tfrac{1}{2}(\sqrt{\lambda_1} - \sqrt{\lambda_2}).$$

This, multiplied by $2i/\sqrt{\lambda_3}$, gives us the imaginary chord, where λ_3 is

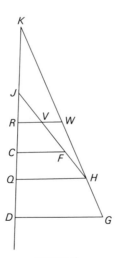

FIGURE 6

the value of λ to be assigned to it. Now

$$\frac{RC}{\lambda_2} = \frac{RD}{\lambda_1} = \frac{RQ}{\lambda_3} \tag{3}$$

and
$$\frac{CF}{CJ} = \frac{QH}{QJ}, \qquad \frac{DG}{DK} = \frac{QH}{QK}.$$

From this we get, by elimination of QH and in the light of formulae (2) and (3),

$$\lambda_3 = \sqrt{\lambda_1 \lambda_2}.$$

The imaginary chord is therefore

$$\frac{i\sqrt{\lambda_1} - \sqrt{\lambda_2}}{\sqrt[4]{\lambda_1 \lambda_2}},$$

and the imaginary angle we have been seeking is

$$2\arcsin\left(\frac{i}{2} \frac{\sqrt{\lambda_1} - \sqrt{\lambda_2}}{\sqrt[4]{\lambda_1 \lambda_2}}\right) = \pm\frac{i}{2}\lg\left(\frac{\lambda_1}{\lambda_2}\right). \tag{4}$$

In order to determine the sign, we stipulate that the direction of rotation from the ξ-axis to the η-axis | is to be positive. We further see to it that in equating an infinitely small purely imaginary angle with its sine we remain in accord with our previous stipulations. If we now follow the motion of the point W (figure 6) in the case of positive rotation and its motion as DG approaches the plane E, we find that the latter direction is related to the former as the axis of the imaginary ξ' is related to the axis of the real ξ. It follows from this that in making the transition from I to II we must choose the positive sign in (4), for $\lambda_1 > \lambda_2$ when the guide line of II is nearer to the plane E than the guide line of I.

In the general case a complex angle is composed of these two special cases. Thus

$$\alpha = \alpha + \tfrac{1}{2}i\lg\left(\frac{\lambda_1}{\lambda_2}\right) \tag{5}$$

where α is the angle formed by the two guide lines when the direction of transition is from I to II.

In order to obtain another geometrical interpretation for this, we interpolate the following digression.

On Representing Complex Numbers by Magnitudes of Angles in the Plane

A magnitude can in many cases be conceived as a way and means or operation by which one element A is transformed into a second B. A length can thus be regarded as a motion by which one end point is translated into the other. | An angle thus appears as a rotation by 27 which one of its sides – thought of as unbounded – turns into the other. Just as Gauss represented complex numbers by straight line segments in a plane, taking into account also the direction in which the one end point had to be moved if it was to get to the place of the other, so we now want to try to generalize the concept of an angle, taking into consideration the sides of an angle not just according to their direction but at the same time according to their length. Thus what we call an angle in this general sense is the way in which a bounded straight line turns into another which has one end point in common with it. This kind of transition consists of a rotation and an increase at a certain rate. These ideas, which are still indefinite, gain a firmer foundation by the following considerations. Let a_1 and a_2 be complex numbers, namely:

$$a_1 = r(\cos \rho_1 + i \sin \rho_1)$$

$$a_2 = r(\cos \rho_2 + i \sin \rho_2).$$

Let them be represented in Gauss's manner by two line segments of equal length. Let the angle they form between them be given by

$$a = \rho_2 - \rho_1 = i \lg \frac{a_1}{a_2}.$$

Generalizing this definition to cover line segments of unequal length, we call

$$\alpha = i \lg \frac{a}{b} \qquad (6)$$

the complex angle formed by the line segments represented by

$$a = r(\cos \rho + i \sin \rho), \qquad b = s(\cos \psi + i \sin \psi) \quad |$$

By separating real and imaginary parts in (6) we get 28

$$\alpha = \rho - \psi + i \lg \frac{r}{s}.$$

The real part is accordingly the rotation, and the factor of i is the negative logarithm of the rate of increase at which the first line segment is transformed into the second. From this it is easy to get geometrical constructions for the sums, differences, multiples and halves of such angles, which can all be carried out with ruler and compasses. We shall, however, content ourselves with pointing out that, when we construct the multiple of such a complex angle, one of its sides is fixed while the end points of the other lie on a logarithmic spiral whose polar equation has the form

$$r = ae^{b\varphi}$$

and which takes the place of a circle here. Finally, we want to show how to construct the trigonometric lines of this complex angle. Thus

$$\sin\left(\psi + i\lg\frac{1}{b}\right) = \frac{\frac{1}{b} + b}{2}\sin\psi + i\frac{\frac{1}{b} - b}{2}\cos\psi.$$

The modulus of this is

$$r_1 = \tfrac{1}{2}\sqrt{\frac{1}{b^2} + b^2 - 2\cos 2\psi}.$$

This admits of the following interpretation. Let BAC be our complex angle and $BA = 1$ (figure 7). Then $AC = b$. If we mark off the same angle on the other | side of AB, so that $\angle DAB = \angle BAC$, then it follows that $AD = 1/b$. If we connect C with D, then DC is equal to the double of our modulus above. The amplitude χ_1 of

$$\sin\left(\psi + i\lg\frac{1}{b}\right) = r_1(\cos\chi_1 + i\sin\chi_1)$$

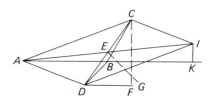

FIGURE 7

is

$$\text{tg}\,\chi_1 = \frac{\left(\dfrac{1}{b}-b\right)\cos\psi}{\left(\dfrac{1}{b}+b\right)\sin\psi}.$$

By comparing this with ω, the angle formed by DC with the direction AK of the real, we get

$$\text{tg}\,\omega = \frac{\left(b+\dfrac{1}{b}\right)\sin\psi}{\left(b-\dfrac{1}{b}\right)\cos\psi} = -\frac{1}{\text{tg}\,\chi_1}.$$

That is to say: we must rotate $EC=\frac{1}{2}DC$ through $90°$ if EG is to be the geometrical representation of the sine of our complex angle.

Further

$$\cos\left(\psi+i\lg\frac{1}{b}\right) = \frac{\dfrac{1}{b}+b}{2}\cos\psi - i\frac{\dfrac{1}{b}-b}{2}\sin\psi.$$

The cosine is represented with respect to both length and direction by AE. For if we complete the triangle ACD so as to get the parallelogram $ACJD$, then

$$AE = \tfrac{1}{2}AJ$$

$$AK = \left(\frac{1}{b}+b\right)\cos\psi, \qquad JH = -\left(\frac{1}{b}-b\right)\sin\psi,$$

which makes our assertion immediately evident. It remains to be mentioned that the points D, B and C lie on the | above-mentioned 30 spiral, and hence, that DC is one of its chords. Accordingly, the sine is represented by half the chord of the double angle rotated through $90°$, and the cosine by the line connecting the vertex with the point bisecting that chord when the bisecting side of the double angle is made equal to 1. The relationships among ordinary angles are merely special cases of this.

Application to the Angle of Imaginary Straight Lines

We make use of the ideas we have acquired to obtain a geometrical representation for formula (5). Let QC represent the imaginary point at

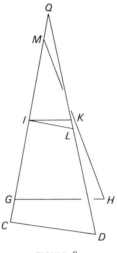

FIGURE 8

the vertex (figure 8). We mark off the lengths $GH=\sqrt{\lambda_2}$ and $CD=\sqrt{\lambda_1}$ on the guide lines of the real, as we did before, and draw DQ and HM to represent the imaginary points lying on the sides of the angle at distance 1 from the vertex. The straight lines CQ, MH and QD then cut the plane E at the points I, K and L. The real angle KIC is then equal to the angle α formed by the guide lines, and

$$IK=\tfrac{1}{2}GH=\tfrac{1}{2}\sqrt{\lambda_2}$$

$$IL=\tfrac{1}{2}CD=\tfrac{1}{2}\sqrt{\lambda_1}.$$

Accordingly, formula (5) becomes

$$a=\alpha+i\lg\frac{IL}{IK}.$$

That is to say, the figure KIL represents the complex angle.

31   In conclusion let it be remarked that purely imaginary | straight lines differ from the rest by forming real angles with real straight lines.

6   IMAGINARY CURVES

Let

$$S(x,y)=S(\xi+i\xi',\eta+i\eta')=0$$

be the equation of an imaginary curve. By separating real and imaginary parts, we break it down into

$$\varphi(\xi, \xi', \eta, \eta') = 0, \qquad \varphi_1(\xi, \xi', \eta, \eta') = 0.$$

By solving for ξ' and η', we get the mapping functions

$$\xi' = f(\xi, \eta) \tag{1}$$

$$\eta' = F(\xi, \eta). \tag{2}$$

If we solve for η' and η, we obtain the equations

$$\eta = \Phi(\xi, \xi'), \quad \eta' = \Phi_1(\xi, \xi'),$$

for which the following differential equations hold:

$$\frac{\partial \Phi}{\partial \xi} = \frac{\partial \Phi_1}{\partial \xi'}, \qquad \frac{\partial \Phi}{\partial \xi'} = -\frac{\partial \Phi_1}{\partial \xi}. \tag{3}$$

From this it follows that the functions f and F are not independent of each other either. In order to obtain these restrictions, we differentiate (1) and (2) with respect to ξ while supposing ξ' to be constant. This gives us

$$0 = \frac{\partial f}{\partial \xi} + \frac{\partial f}{\partial \eta} \frac{\partial \Phi}{\partial \xi}, \qquad \frac{\partial \Phi_1}{\partial \xi} = \frac{\partial F}{\partial \xi} + \frac{\partial F}{\partial \eta} \frac{\partial \Phi}{\partial \xi}. \tag{4}$$

Further, if we differentiate with respect to ξ' while letting ξ be constant, we can infer from (1) and (2) |

$$1 = \frac{\partial f}{\partial \eta} \frac{\partial \Phi}{\partial \xi^1}, \qquad \frac{\partial \Phi_1}{\partial \xi^1} = \frac{\partial F}{\partial \eta} \frac{\partial \Phi}{\partial \xi^1}. \tag{5}$$

32

If we take

$$\frac{\partial \Phi}{\partial \xi}, \frac{\partial \Phi}{\partial \xi^1}, \frac{\partial \Phi_1}{\partial \xi}, \frac{\partial \Phi^1}{\partial \xi_1}$$

from equations (4) and (5) above and substitute them in (3), we get the differential equations

$$\frac{\partial f}{\partial \xi} + \frac{\partial F}{\partial \eta} = 0 \tag{6}$$

$$\frac{\partial f}{\partial \xi} \frac{\partial F}{\partial \eta} - \frac{\partial F}{\partial \xi} \frac{\partial f}{\partial \eta} = 1, \tag{7}$$

which must be satisfied by the mapping functions f and F.

We saw in the special case of an imaginary straight line that for any point of the plane of the real there are two mutually perpendicular directions which are parallel to the corresponding directions in the plane of the imaginary. We shall now investigate whether this proposition can be generalized. As we move from a point in the plane of the real in a certain direction, the direction of our simultaneous motion in the plane of the imaginary is given by

$$\frac{\partial \xi^1}{\partial \eta^1} = \frac{\partial f}{\partial F} = \frac{\dfrac{\partial f}{\partial \xi} + \dfrac{\partial f}{\partial \eta}\dfrac{\partial \eta}{\partial \xi}}{\dfrac{\partial F}{\partial \xi} + \dfrac{\partial F}{\partial \eta}\dfrac{\partial \eta}{\partial \xi}},$$

where

$$\frac{\partial \xi^1}{\partial \eta^1}, \frac{\partial f}{\partial F}, \frac{\partial \eta}{\partial \xi}$$

do not really mean differential quotients, but are only supposed to determine the directions of our movement. If we now recall the stipulated position of the ξ^1- and η^1-axis as against the | ξ- and η-axis, we will see that the parallelism of corresponding motions is expressed by

$$\frac{df}{dF} = -\frac{d\eta}{d\xi}.$$

We thus obtain the quadratic equation in $\dfrac{d\eta}{d\xi}$:

$$\left(\frac{d\eta}{d\xi}\right)^2 - \frac{\dfrac{\partial f}{\partial \eta} + \dfrac{\partial F}{\partial \xi}}{\dfrac{\partial f}{\partial \xi}} \frac{d\eta}{d\xi} = 1 \tag{8}$$

or

$$\operatorname{tg}\gamma = \frac{d\eta}{d\xi} = \frac{\dfrac{\partial f}{\partial \eta} + \dfrac{\partial F}{\partial \xi}}{2\dfrac{\partial f}{\partial \xi}} \pm \sqrt{\left(\frac{\dfrac{\partial f}{\partial \eta} + \dfrac{\partial F}{\partial \xi}}{2\dfrac{\partial f}{\partial \xi}}\right)^2 + 1} \tag{9}$$

or if we substitute the expression $1 - 2\dfrac{\operatorname{tg}\gamma}{\operatorname{tg}2\gamma}$ for $\operatorname{tg}^2\gamma$:

$$\operatorname{tg} 2\gamma = -2\,\frac{\dfrac{\partial f}{\partial \xi}}{\dfrac{\partial f}{\partial \eta}+\dfrac{\partial F}{\partial \xi}}.$$

For any point of the plane of the real there are therefore two mutually perpendicular directions to which the corresponding directions in the plane of the imaginary are parallel. We will call them the distinguished directions. Now if a point in the plane of the real moves in such a way that it always follows a distinguished direction, it describes a curve. Through any point of the plane pass one or more pairs of such curves, each member of which is perpendicular to the other. We thus obtain two systems of curves which intersect at right angles. | The same holds 34 for the plane of the imaginary and any parallel plane. To get the equations for these curves, we integrate (9) after representing the right-hand side as a function of ξ and η. An individual curve is characterized by the constant of integration.

If we connect two corresponding points of the planes of the real and the imaginary by a line, and if we let the point in the plane of the real move on one of our curves, which also causes the corresponding point in the plane of the imaginary to move, then the line connecting the points describes a developable surface and envelopes a curve, which is the edge of regression of the developable surface. If we now let our curve in the plane of the real turn into another by making every point move on a curve of the other system, then the developable surface moves at the same time, and its edge of regression describes a surface which we call the guide surface of the imaginary curve. Every point of the space curve describes another curve as it moves. We thus have two systems of curves on the guide surface, which correspond to the systems of curves in the planes of the real and the imaginary. The lines that connect corresponding points in these planes touch the guide surface, for they are tangents of curves on that surface. If we now interchange the systems of curves in the plane of the real, we arrive in the same way at a second guide surface, which does not exclude the possibility that both guide surfaces may be merely envelopes of a single surface. A family of common tangents to the guide surfaces enables us | to map 35 the planes of the real and the imaginary to each other and to the guide surfaces. We still need to mention the special case where all edges of regression meet at one point. In that case they describe a guide curve instead of a guide surface as they move. This is what happened in the case of the imaginary straight line. In such a case cutting the guide curves takes the place of touching the guide surfaces.

We have seen that the guide lines of an imaginary straight line are equidistant in opposite directions from the plane E. In order to decide whether something like this happens in general, we look for the quotient

$$q = \frac{ds'}{ds}$$

of the corresponding motions along curves in the planes of the real and the imaginary. If $\eta' = \psi(\xi)$ specifies the connection between η' and ξ for corresponding points of a curve in the plane of the real and the corresponding ones in the plane of the imaginary, then

$$q = \frac{d\psi}{d\xi} = \frac{\partial F}{\partial \xi} + \frac{\partial F}{\partial \eta} \, \text{tg} \, \gamma.$$

From this we can infer the value of

$$\text{tg} \, \gamma = \frac{d\eta}{d\xi},$$

and if we substitute this value in (8) and refer back to (6) and (7), we obtain the following quadratic equation for q:

$$q^2 + \left(\frac{\partial f}{\partial \eta} - \frac{\partial F}{\partial \xi} \right) q + 1 = 0,$$

one of whose roots is the reciprocal of the other. From this it follows that the two points of contact | of a line of projection with the guide surfaces are equidistant in opposite directions from E. The one guide surface is situated wholly on the one, and the other on the other side of the plane E. To be able to express ourselves more conveniently with respect to curves and surfaces, we lay down the following designations:

The guide surface situated on the same side of E as the plane of the real shall be called the guide surface of the real S. The other shall be the guide surface of the imaginary S'. The curves along which we must move in the plane of the real in order to envelop a curve on S by the line of projection shall be called s_i and the corresponding curves in the plane of the imaginary s_i', on S σ_i, and on S' σ_i'. On the other hand, the curves along which we must move in order to envelop a curve in S' shall be designated by s_r and the corresponding ones in the plane of the imaginary by s_r', on S by σ_r, and on S' by σ_r'.

All other planes in space are also mapped to one another by the lines connecting corresponding points. The plane E and the plane at infinity U are distinguished among them since they are equidistant from the

36

planes of the real and the imaginary. It now appears that the mapping of these two planes one to the other deserves to be investigated more closely on its own. We assume that the coordinate system in the plane E with the axes $w\|\xi$, $z\|\eta$ is such that

$$w=\frac{\xi-\eta'}{2}, \qquad z=\frac{\eta+\xi'}{2}. \tag{10}$$

In place of the plane at infinity we substitute | a plane U' which is 37 similar to it and which arises when we draw a parallel to every line through an arbitrary point P and cut the resulting pencil of lines by a plane U' which is parallel to the plane E and just as distant from P in the same direction as E is from the point of origin of the imaginary. The axes $u\|\xi$, $v\|\eta$ of the coordinate system in the plane U' may be assumed to be such that

$$u=\frac{\xi+\eta'}{2}, \qquad v=\frac{\eta-\xi'}{2}. \tag{11}$$

From equations (10) and (11) it follows that

$$\begin{cases} \xi=u+w, & \eta=z+v, \\ \xi'=z-v, & \eta'=u-w. \end{cases} \tag{12}$$

If we regard u and v as functions of w and z, we get from (12) by partial differentiation

$$\frac{\partial\Phi}{\partial\xi}=\frac{2\dfrac{\partial v}{\partial w}}{M}, \qquad \frac{\partial\Phi_1}{\partial\xi'}=\frac{2\dfrac{\partial u}{\partial z}}{M},$$

$$\frac{\partial\Phi}{\partial\xi'}=\frac{\left(1+\dfrac{\partial v}{\partial z}\right)\left(1+\dfrac{\partial u}{\partial w}\right)-\dfrac{\partial v}{\partial w}\dfrac{\partial u}{\partial z}}{M},$$

$$\frac{\partial\Phi_1}{\partial\xi}=\frac{\left(\dfrac{\partial u}{\partial w}-1\right)\left(1-\dfrac{\partial v}{\partial z}\right)+\dfrac{\partial u}{\partial z}\dfrac{\partial v}{\partial w}}{M},$$

$$M=\left(\frac{\partial u}{\partial w}+1\right)\left(1-\frac{\partial v}{\partial z}\right)+\frac{\partial u}{\partial z}\frac{\partial v}{\partial w}.$$

By substituting these values in (3) we get

$$\frac{\partial v}{\partial w}=\frac{\partial u}{\partial z}, \qquad \frac{\partial u}{\partial w}=-\frac{\partial v}{\partial z}. \quad |$$

38   Hence $v+iu$ is a function of $w+iz$. Accordingly, if we put

$$\begin{cases} w=\alpha, \ z=\alpha', \quad v=\beta, \ u=\beta', \\ \alpha+i\alpha'=a, \qquad \beta+i\beta'=b, \end{cases} \tag{13}$$

then the following equation must hold:

$$W(a,b)=0.$$

And this equation is easy to find; for because of (12) and (13)

$$\begin{cases} \xi=\beta'+\alpha, \ \eta=\beta+\alpha', \quad \xi'=-\beta+\alpha', \ \eta'=\beta'-\alpha \\ x=a-ib, \ y=b-ia \end{cases} \tag{14}$$

and therefore

$$0=W(a,b)=S(a-ib,b-ia), \tag{15}$$

where $S(x,y)=0$ is the equation of our imaginary curve. The plane E is mapped to the plane U' by the same lines that map the plane of the real to the plane of the imaginary. But there is the noteworthy difference between these mappings that in the latter case the real and imaginary parts (ξ and ξ') belonging to the same variable, e.g. x, are represented in different planes, whereas in the former case each of the variables a and b occupies a special plane.

From what we have determined about the coordinate systems it follows that

$$\xi\|-\eta'\|\alpha\|\beta', \ \eta\|\xi'\|\alpha'\|\beta.$$

The plane U' is therefore turned over relative to the plane E. As a consequence of this, when we let an infinitely small motion **da** rotate about a point a_0 of the plane E, the corresponding motion **db** in the

39   plane U' rotates in the opposite direction with the same | angular velocity, as long as db/da is neither 0 nor ∞. We start from position I (figure 9), where the direction of **db** bisects the right angle of the coordinates. Then **db** and **da** form between them the angle 2ε, which they would continue to enclose if the plane U' was rotated through $180°$ about the line bisecting the angle of the coordinates. Since

$$\frac{db}{da}=\frac{\partial\beta}{\partial\alpha}+i\frac{\partial\beta'}{\partial\alpha},$$

therefore

$$\operatorname{tg} 2\varepsilon=\frac{\dfrac{\partial\beta'}{\partial\alpha}}{\dfrac{\partial\beta}{\partial\alpha}}.$$

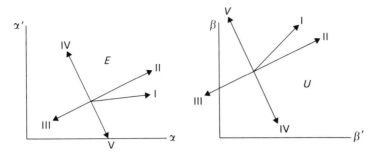

FIGURE 9

There are four positions, II, III, IV and V, in the rotation of **da** where **da** and **db** become parallel. In II and III **da** and **db** have the same direction, and in positions IV and V, which are perpendicular to them, the opposite direction. These directions must coincide with the distinguished directions in the plane of the real. We therefore call γ, as above, the angle formed by **da** in position II with the α-axis. Then $\gamma = 45° - \varepsilon$,

$$\operatorname{tg} 2\gamma = \operatorname{ctg} 2\varepsilon = \frac{\partial \beta}{\partial \alpha} \Big/ \frac{\partial \beta'}{\partial \alpha}$$

$$\operatorname{tg} \gamma = \frac{-\dfrac{\partial \beta'}{\partial \alpha} \pm \sqrt{\Delta}}{\dfrac{\partial \beta}{\partial \alpha}} \tag{16}$$

$$\Delta = \left(\frac{\partial \beta}{\partial \alpha}\right)^2 + \left(\frac{\partial \beta'}{\partial \alpha}\right)^2. \ \big|$$

In each of the planes E and U' there are also two systems of curves, 40 which will be designated respectively by p_r, p_i, q_r, q_i, so that the indices will agree with those of the corresponding curves s, s', σ, σ'.

Finally, we want to determine the point of a guide surface which corresponds to a given point of the plane E. As we move along a curve p_i, the increments of ξ and η' are

$$d\xi = d\beta' + d\alpha, \qquad d\eta' = d\beta' - d\alpha$$

according to (14). The motions along curves s_i' and s_i are then related as follows:

$$\frac{ds_i'}{ds_i} = \frac{-d\eta'}{d\xi} = \frac{-d\beta' + d\alpha}{d\beta' + d\alpha}.$$

Now if λ represents the distance from E of the point we are seeking on the guide surface and the plane of the real (cf. section 4), then

$$\frac{\lambda+1}{\lambda-1}=\frac{ds_i'}{ds_i}=\frac{d\alpha-d\beta'}{d\alpha+d\beta'},$$

$$\lambda=\frac{d\alpha}{d\beta'}=-\frac{1}{\dfrac{\partial\beta'}{\partial\alpha}+\dfrac{\partial\beta'}{\partial\alpha'}\,\mathrm{tg}\,\gamma}.$$

After introducing the value of $\mathrm{tg}\,\gamma$ given by (16), we obtain

$$\lambda=\frac{1}{\pm\sqrt{\Delta}}. \tag{17}$$

The double sign corresponds to the two guide surfaces. We see once more that the two points are equidistant in opposite directions from the plane E. We see further that $\lambda=\infty$ when $db/da=0$ | and only then, and that $\lambda=0$ when $db/da=\infty$. The planes E and U have only individual (real) points in common with the guide surfaces, and these are the branch points of one plane when it is mapped to the other by $W(a,b)=0$.

7 THE IMAGINARY CIRCLE

Let the equation of an imaginary circle be

$$S(x,y)=(x-m^2)+(y-n)^2-r^2=0. \tag{1}$$

Instead of x and y we introduce the variables a and b (as in section 6, equation 15):

$$(a-ib-[a_0-ib_0])^2+(b-ia-[b_0-ia_0])^2=r^2, \tag{2}$$

where a_0 and b_0 are formed from the coordinates m, n of the centre in the same was as a and b from x and y. Equation (2) becomes

$$4i(a-a_0)(b-b_0)+r^2=0.$$

If we put

$$\alpha-\alpha_0=\alpha_1,\ \alpha'-\alpha_0'=\alpha_1',\ \beta-\beta_0=\beta_1,\ \beta'-\beta_0'=\beta_1',$$

we get, by separating real and imaginary parts,

$$\begin{cases} -4\alpha_1\beta_1-4\alpha_1'\beta_1'=\rho'^2-\rho^2 \\ 4\alpha_1\beta_1-4\alpha_1'\beta_1'=-2\rho\rho', \end{cases} \tag{3}$$

where $r = \rho + i\rho'$. It follows from this that

$$\frac{\partial \beta}{\partial \alpha} = \frac{\partial \beta_1}{\partial \alpha_1} = \frac{2\rho\rho'(\alpha_1{}^2 - \alpha_1'^2) - 2\alpha_1\alpha_1'(\rho^2 - \rho'^2)}{4(\alpha_1{}^2 + \alpha_1'^2)^2}$$

$$\frac{\partial \beta'}{\partial \alpha} = \frac{\partial \beta_1'}{\partial \alpha} = \frac{(\rho^2 - \rho'^2)(\alpha_1'^2 - \alpha_1{}^2) - 4\alpha_1\alpha_1'\rho\rho'}{4(\alpha_1{}^2 + \alpha_1'^2)^2}$$

$$\sqrt{\Delta} = \frac{(\rho^2 + \rho'^2)(\alpha_1{}^2 + \alpha_1'^2)}{4(\alpha_1{}^2 + \alpha_1'^2)^2}.$$

From this we get for $\operatorname{tg}\gamma$ either |

$$\operatorname{tg}\gamma = \frac{\rho\alpha_1 + \rho'\alpha_1'}{\rho'\alpha_1 - \rho\alpha_1'} \tag{4}$$

or

$$\operatorname{tg}\gamma = -\frac{\rho'\alpha_1 - \rho\alpha_1'}{\rho\alpha_1 + \rho'\alpha_1'}. \tag{5}$$

The curves p_r have the differential equation

$$(\rho'\alpha_1 - \rho\alpha_1')\,\mathrm{d}\alpha_1' = (\rho\alpha_1 + \rho'\alpha_1')\,\mathrm{d}\alpha_1,$$

whose integral is

$$\rho' \operatorname{arc tg}\frac{\alpha_1'}{\alpha_1} - \frac{\rho}{2}\lg(\alpha_1{}^2 + \alpha_1'^2) = c_r$$

or, after we introduce the polar coordinates $\operatorname{arc tg}\alpha_1'/\alpha_1 = \varphi$, $\alpha_1{}^2 + \alpha_1'^2 = R^2$,

$$R = \exp\!\left(\frac{\rho'}{\rho}\varphi - \frac{c_r}{\rho}\right). \tag{6}$$

For the curves p_i we likewise get the polar equation

$$R = \exp\!\left[\frac{\rho}{\rho'}\!\left(\frac{\pi}{2} - \varphi\right) - \frac{c_i}{\rho'}\right]. \tag{7}$$

The constants of integration c_r and c_i characterize the individual curves. The curves p_r and p_i are congruent with one another and arise from one another by rotation about the pole. These logarithmic spirals are the same as the ones we have already encountered when considering the complex angle. By making very similar calculations, we could also obtain the curves q_r and q_i and would arrive at analogous results. However, we content ourselves with deriving the guide surfaces, since these are best suited for giving us an intuitive picture of the system of

43   straight lines that represents an imaginary circle. For this purpose we
assume a spatial | coordinate system whose X-axis coincides with the
α_1-axis, whose Y-axis coincides with the α'_1-axis and whose Z-axis
coincides with the straight line that represents the imaginary centre, so
that the positive direction is from the plane of the imaginary to that of
the real. If (X_0, Y_0, Z_0) and (X_1, Y_1, Z_1) are two points in space, it is
easily found that their connecting line is characterized by

$$\alpha_1 = \frac{Z_1 X_0 - Z_0 X_1}{Z_1 - Z_0}, \qquad \alpha'_1 = \frac{Z_1 Y_0 - Y_1 Z_0}{Z_1 - Z_0},$$

$$\beta_1 = \frac{Y_1 - Y_0}{Z_1 - Z_0} d, \qquad \beta'_1 = \frac{X_1 - X_0}{Z_1 - Z_0} d,$$

where d means half the distance between the planes of the real and the
imaginary. If we introduce these values into equations (3), we obtain

$$0 = Z_0(Y_1^{\,2} + X_1^{\,2}) - Y_0(Z_1 - Z_0)Y_1 - X_0(Z_1 - Z_0)X_1$$

$$+ (Y_0^{\,2} + X_0^{\,2})Z_1 + \frac{\rho^2 - \rho'^2}{4d}(Z_1 - Z_0)^2. \qquad \text{(I)}$$

$$0 = (Z_1 - Z_0)\left(X_0 Y_1 - Y_0 X_1 + \frac{\rho\rho'}{2d}(Z_1 - Z_0) \right). \qquad \text{(II)}$$

If we regard X_0, Y_0, Z_0 in I and II as constant, then these equations
represent a cone and a pair of planes. The line of intersection of the
pair of planes passes through (X_0, Y_0, Z_0) where the vertex of the cone
is located. For $Z_0 = 0$ the cone degenerates likewise into a pair of
planes, one of which is the plane $Z_1 = 0$. The straight lines in which the
cone I intersects the pair of planes II are straight lines of its generating
system. It is now easy to see that in general the plane $Z_1 - Z_0 = 0$ meets
the cone only at its vertex. The plane $Z_1 - Z_0$ can therefore be left
44   entirely out of our considerations | because imaginary points are
represented only by real lines of intersection. The only exception occurs
when $Z_0 = 0$. In that case the two planes $Z_1 = 0$ coincide, which means
the same as that they touch each other. The plane E is therefore a
component of the guide surface; for all of its straight lines are straight
lines of the generating system. Through any point (X_0, Y_0, Z_0) in space
pass in general two lines. These coincide when the plane

$$X_0 Y_1 - Y_0 X_1 + \frac{\rho\rho'}{2d}(Z_1 - Z_0) = 0$$

touches the cone. But in that case (X_0, Y_0, Z_0) is a point of the guide
surface.

Thus if we set up the conditions for the plane and the cone to touch, we get the equation of the guide surface. Instead of the plane and the cone we can also consider their intersections with an arbitrary plane, say $Z + Z_0 = 0$. These intersections are

$$X_1{}^2 + Y_1{}^2 = X_0{}^2 + Y_0{}^2 + \frac{\rho'^2 - \rho^2}{d} Z_0$$

$$X_0 Y_1 - Y_0 X_1 = \frac{\rho \rho'}{d} Z_0.$$

The condition for this circle and this straight line to touch is

$$\frac{\rho \rho' Z_0{}^2}{d^2 (X_0{}^2 + Y_0{}^2)} = \frac{\rho'^2 - \rho^2}{d} Z_0 + Y_0{}^2 + X_0{}^2.$$

This equation breaks down into

$$X_0{}^2 + Y_0{}^2 + \frac{\rho'^2}{d} Z_0 = 0, \qquad X_0{}^2 + Y_0{}^2 - \frac{\rho^2}{d} Z_0 = 0.$$

These are paraboloids which are cut in circles by planes parallel | to 45 the plane E. They touch each other and the plane E at the point $X = 0$, $Y = 0$, $Z = 0$, where the straight line representing the imaginary centre cuts the plane E. This straight line, which we will call the centre line, is a diameter of both paraboloids and passes through the centres of the circular sections we have just mentioned. The plane of the real cuts the guide surface of the real in a circle

$$X^2 + Y^2 = \rho^2,$$

whose radius is equal to the real part of the complex radius. In the same way the plane of the imaginary cuts the guide surface of the imaginary in a circle

$$X^2 + Y^2 = \rho'^2,$$

whose radius is equal to the imaginary part of the complex radius. Besides the plane E and the two paraboloids, we can also count the plane at infinity as a part of the guide surface; for where $Z_1 = Z_0 = \infty$, I becomes $Z_1 - Z_0 = 0$, so that I and II are satisfied. If we put $\rho' = 0$, equation (6) becomes

$$R = \exp\left(-\frac{c_r}{\rho} \right).$$

This is a circle. We first raise equation (7) to the ρ'-th power and then obtain for $\rho'=0$

$$1=\exp\left[\rho\left(\frac{\pi}{2}-\varphi\right)-c_i\right]$$

or

$$\varphi=\frac{\pi}{2}-\frac{c_i}{\rho}.$$

46   This is a radius. Our systems of curves p_r, p_i | consist therefore of concentric circles and their radii.

The systems of curves in the planes of the real and the imaginary have a similar make-up. The guide surface of the real cuts the plane of the real in the real circle which is to be represented. The guide surface of the imaginary contracts into the centre line. The imaginary points of the real circle are represented by the tangents of the paraboloids which cut the centre line.

We will now show by a few examples how our method can be used to represent non-intuitive relationships.

We will represent first the points of intersection of a real straight line and a real circle for the case where the points of intersection are imaginary. The guide lines of the imaginary for the two real figures intersect at the point of origin of the imaginary. Now the straight lines we are seeking, those representing the imaginary points of intersection, must either pass through the point of intersection of the guide lines of the imaginary or lie in their plane. If the former case they would represent real points, a possibility we have excluded. We therefore choose the plane of the guide lines of the imaginary as the plane of the drawing (figure 10). This plane cuts the guide surface of the real in a parabola and the guide line of the real for the real straight line at a point A. The straight lines P_1, P_2 we are seeking must pass through A and touch the parabola. Our task therefore amounts to drawing

47   tangents from a point to a parabola. The tangents | AC and AD represent the imaginary points of intersection we are seeking. Further, it is easy to see that $O'C=O'D$ and that it is equal to the tangent which can be drawn from A to the circle. This provides us with an easy method of constructing the straight lines AC and AD. As A approaches the circle, the straight lines P_1 and P_2 approach each other until they coincide as A moves into the circumference of the circle, and they then represent the real point of contact. As A continues to approach the centre, P_1 and P_2 separate again, but in such a way that their point of intersection is now situated at the point of origin of the imaginary and

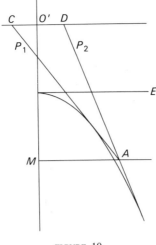

that they pass through the real points of intersection which they represent. On the other hand, as A moves farther and farther away from the centre, P_1 comes nearer and nearer to the plane E, while P_2 and at the same time A move to infinity. The circular points at infinity are therefore represented by two straight lines, one of which lies in the plane E while the other lies in the plane at infinity. But now it is easy to see that every straight line in the plane E represents the one imaginary circular point, while every straight line of the plane at infinity represents the other one. For in the first place their direction cannot make any difference because it depends on the direction of the straight line which we let move to infinity. In the second place, as we have seen above, when a straight line represents an imaginary point at infinity, all of its parallels which are equidistant from the plane E represent the same imaginary point. The circular points at infinity are therefore distinguished by the fact that they are represented by a | doubly infinite set of straight lines, whereas all other points at infinity   48 are represented in each case only by a singly infinite family of straight lines, and each point in the finite domain only by *one* straight line. In what follows, the circular points at infinity shall always be designated by E and U, depending on whether the straight lines that represent them lie in the plane E or in the plane at infinity.

We will carry out a few more constructions relating to imaginary circular points.

In section 3, where we were dealing with the connecting line between imaginary points, we provisionally excluded the case where the straight lines which represented imaginary points lay in the planes E and U. In such a case they represent the circular points at infinity. There are only two cases where the guide lines of an imaginary straight line intersect: either when they lie in the plane E or when they lie in the plane U. In either case the imaginary straight line passes through one of the circular points at infinity. Thus if we want to connect an imaginary point A within the finite domain with E, we must draw in the plane E two straight lines intersecting at right angles through the point where the straight line representing A intersects the plane E. The direction remains arbitrary. In all subsequent constructions too, all that matters is the point of intersection of the guide lines, and we can therefore say:

49   An imaginary straight line which passes through E is | represented by a point in the plane E or by the pencil of lines originating at that point.

The same holds for the imaginary point U and the plane at infinity, and we can therefore say:

An imaginary straight line which passes through U is represented by a direction or a pencil of parallel lines.

Thus if we are to represent the intersection of an imaginary straight line g which passes through E and another, h, which passes through U, we must draw a straight line through the point in the plane E which represents g in the direction which represents h.

To give an example of the application of these propositions, we construct a complete quadrilateral for the case where two of its corners are the imaginary circular points E and U. Figure 11 gives a general view of the construction, on the assumption that all is real. In figure 12,

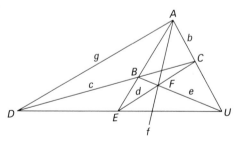

FIGURE 11

which represents our case, the corresponding elements are designated by the same letters as in figure 11. The guide lines of the imaginary for the imaginary straight line have been marked with a superscript. The arrows indicate the directions which represent the imaginary straight lines which pass through U. We first take A arbitrarily and connect A with E and U. a is represented by a point in the plane E and by a direction. We then take an imaginary point F, connect it likewise with E and U, and let e and a intersect in B, and further b and d in C, so that $A\|C$ and $B\|F$ (figure 12). | If we then connect B with C by an   50
imaginary straight line whose guide lines are c and c', then the parallels to E which pass through c and c' are cut by the straight lines A, B, C and F at the corners of two congruent parallelograms. These must be rhombuses if c' is perpendicular to c. Finally we connect A with F. If we go through the same considerations for the guide lines f and f' as

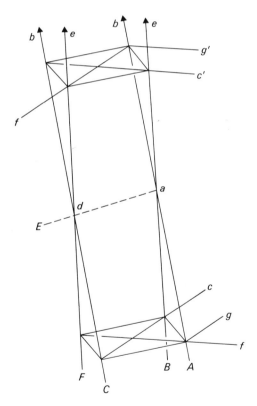

FIGURE 12

we did for c and c', we can conclude that the planes parallel to the plane E which pass through f and f' cut the straight lines A, B, C and F at the corner points of congruent rhombuses. From this it follows that f lies in a plane with c, and f' with c', and that c is perpendicular to f, and c' to f', while constituting the diagonals of a rhombus. The imaginary straight lines c and f are then themselves perpendicular to each other. The same holds accordingly for g and f as well, since D is a point at infinity. Now g and f are harmonic to a and b; we thus obtain the proposition that two straight lines are perpendicular to each other when they are harmonic to the straight lines that go in the direction of the circular points at infinity. This proposition, which is elsewhere derived analytically, results here from purely elementary geometrical propositions. We can still go one step further. If f coincides with a, then g also coincides with a, and according to the proposition stated above, a must be perpendicular to itself. This riddle too is solved by our method of representation in an extremely simple way. We have seen already that the guide lines of a lie in the same plane E. Since they are, moreover, perpendicular to each other, | we will be correct in saying that a is perpendicular to itself.

These examples may suffice to show how propositions of plane geometry can be translated into our method of representation, and how relations which are quite non-intuitive, or even in conflict with all our intuitions, are made visible by this method in a very simple way.

8   ON TANGENCIES

In order to find the tangents of a curve for a point P, we connect it with another point of the curve and determine the limiting position which this straight line approaches as the second point moves towards the first. Now where the curve is an imaginary one, there are infinitely many ways in which the second point can be made to approach the first. Yet in all of these ways we must always arrive at the same tangent, as can be inferred from the proposition that the differential quotient of a function of a complex variable is independent of the direction of the increment we assign to the independent variable. If we now imagine the approach to take place in such a way that the straight line B, which represents the second imaginary point, evolves from a curve σ_r' (section 6), then the guide line of the imaginary for the imaginary tangent passes through the point of intersection of B with A, where A represents the fixed imaginary point of the curve. As it reaches the limit, this point of intersection turns into the | point of contact of A

with S'. The guide line of the real lies in the plane of A and B, which S touches. By interchanging σ'_r with σ_i and S' with S, we arrive at an analogous result in which the guide lines of the real and the imaginary are interchanged. By taking both results together, we recognize that the guide line of the real touches the plane S, and the guide line of the imaginary surface S', at the same points where the straight line A, which represents the imaginary point of contact, touches the surfaces S and S'. Since the guide lines of an imaginary tangent are perpendicular to each other, we get the following proposition:

> If the perimeters of the guide surfaces are projected from an arbitrary point P on the plane E, then the resulting curve intersects itself at right angles as often as the lines of the generating system pass through P.

The guide lines of the imaginary tangent are parallel to the principal directions of the corresponding point in the plane of the real, and the guide line of the real in particular is parallel to the directions of ds_r, ds'_r, dp_r and dq_r.

Two curves touch in the first degree when they have a point and a tangent at that point in common. The straight line A, which represents the imaginary point of contact, and the guide line L of the common tangent determine a plane which touches the guide surfaces S_0 and S_1 of the two imaginary curves at the intersection of A and L. An exception could occur if one of the guide surfaces had a cusp at the point in question. We exclude this case. The guide surfaces of the real therefore touch | in the first degree, and the same holds for S'_0 and S'_1. 53 The line connecting the points of contact between the surfaces represents the imaginary point of contact.

Now if $Z = \chi(X, Y)$ is the equation of the guide surface of an imaginary curve, then $\partial Z/\partial X$ and $\partial Z/\partial Y$ can be represented generally by ξ, ξ', $\Phi(\xi, \xi')$, $\Phi_1(\xi, \xi')$ and by the first partial differential coefficients of Φ and Φ_1, if we assume that the equation of the imaginary curve is, as above,

$$\eta + i\eta' = \Phi(\xi, \xi') + i\Phi_1(\xi, \xi');$$

for if two imaginary curves have the same η and η' and the same $\partial\Phi/\partial\xi$ and $\partial\Phi/\partial\xi$ and so on for the same ξ and ξ', then they touch each other, and consequently, their guide surfaces also have the same $\partial Z/\partial X$ and $\partial Z/\partial Y$ at the point in question. From this we can infer further that the nth partial derivative of Z with respect to X and Y cannot depend on partial derivatives of Φ and Φ_1 higher than the nth. In geometrical terms this means that when two imaginary curves touch in the *n*th degree, then so do their guide surfaces.

9   ON THE COMPLEX LENGTH OF A CURVE

In section 4 we found a geometrical meaning for the length of an imaginary straight line. Let us now try, with the help of this proposition, to do the same for imaginary curves. |

54   We first consider an element **dr** of the length of a curve. This can also be regarded as an element of the tangent. According to section 4

$$dr = \frac{2}{\sqrt{\lambda}}(d\alpha + i\, d\alpha'), \qquad (1)$$

if the axes of α and α' are parallel to the guide lines of the imaginary tangent. If this is not the case, then

$$dr = \frac{2}{\sqrt{\lambda}}\, d\alpha\,(\cos(-\gamma_0) + i\sin(-\gamma_0)), \qquad (2)$$

where γ_0 is the angle formed by the guide line of the real for the imaginary tangent with the α-axis, so that according to section 6, equation 16,

$$tg\,\gamma_0 = \frac{-\dfrac{\partial \beta'}{\partial \alpha} + \sqrt{\Delta}}{\dfrac{\partial \beta}{\partial \alpha}}.$$

As a result of the rotation indicated by the factor

$$\cos(-\gamma_0) + i\sin(-\gamma_0)$$

every element of a curve p_r is made parallel to the α-axis and every element of a curve p_i to the α'-axis. Accordingly, if the plane E is mapped to a plane R by means of a function $R(a)$ which gives the length of the curve, then all curves p_r are transformed into parallels to the ρ-axis and all curves p_i into parallels to the ρ'-axis, if we assume that the points of the plane R are determined by $r = \rho + i\rho'$. It is easy to prove that the length of the curve can be represented as a function of a. For through any point of the plane E pass as many straight lines of the generating system as there are degrees n of the imaginary curve; for each one represents a point of intersection of the imaginary straight line

55 | which is represented, according to section 7, by the point in question

of the plane *E*. Now if we have chosen a fixed point of origin, then the length of the curve depends only on the end point, though it does so in general in more ways than one. The imaginary end point in turn depends on *a* in *n* ways, so that the length of the curve is a many-valued function of *a*. Thus as we move along a curve p_r, we describe at the same time a multiplicity of parallels to the ρ-axis in the plane *R*. The analogue holds for the curve p_i and the ρ'-axis. Accordingly, if

$$R(a) = P(\alpha, \alpha') + iP_1(\alpha, \alpha'),$$

then

$$P_1(\alpha, \alpha') = \rho_1'$$

is the equation of a curve p_r and

$$P_1(\alpha, \alpha') = \rho_1$$

the equation of a curve p_i, where ρ_1' and ρ_1 are constants. These are therefore the integrals of differential equations (17) in section 6. If we regard the constants ρ_1' and ρ_1 as rectangular curvilinear coordinates, we can also express the result as follows:

> The imaginary length of a curve is given by the differences of the curvilinear coordinates of the points at which the straight lines representing the imaginary end points cut the plane *E*.

It should be noted in this connection that every curve p_r or p_i corresponds to a multiplicity of constants and that every straight line which passes through a point a_0 of the plane *E* corresponds to only one pair of curves p_r and p_i which pass through a_0.

The curves p_r and p_i contain all points of the | plane *E* which 56 correspond to those imaginary points of a curve that delimit between them a purely real or, respectively, a purely imaginary length of an arc.

We obtain the function $R(a)$ when in place of *x* and *y* we introduce the quantities $a - ib$ and $b - ia$ into the integral $\int \sqrt{dx^2 + dy^2}$ according to section 6, equation 14, thus turning this integral into

$$R(a) = 2\sqrt{-i} \int \sqrt{da\,db} = 2\sqrt{-i} \int \sqrt{\frac{db}{da}}\,da,$$

where the relation between *a* and *b* is expressed by the equation

$$W(a, b) = 0.$$

It is worth noting that the curves p_r and p_i, which are connected with this integral in the way we stated, can be generated geometrically by connecting corresponding points in the planes E and U so as to make them the bearers of the variables a and b, and by then moving in the plane E so that the straight line generates a developable surface.

10 ON SOME PROPERTIES OF THE GUIDE SURFACES

The method we made use of in section 7 to determine the equation of the guide surface can be applied generally. If the substitutions we carried out one after the other are made all at once, we obtain

$$\xi = \frac{X_1(Z-d) + X(Z+d)}{2Z}$$

57

$$\xi' = \frac{Y_1(Z+d) + Y(Z-d)}{2Z}$$

$$\eta = \frac{Y_1(Z-d) + Y(Z+d)}{2Z}$$

$$\eta' = \frac{-X_1(Z+d) - X(Z-d)}{2Z}.$$

If we substitute these values into the equations

$$\varphi(\xi, \xi', \eta, \eta') = 0, \qquad \varphi_1(\xi, \xi', \eta, \eta') = 0$$

and regard X_1, Y_1 alone as variable, we obtain the equations of two curves (C_1, C_2) of the same degree as the imaginary curve to be represented. The condition for these curves to touch is the equation of the guide surface in X, Y, Z.

We can thus set up the guide surface of an imaginary conic without difficulty with the help of the known formula which expresses the point of contact of two conics. In this way we obtain not only the guide surface, but also parts that do not belong to it. The reason is that for a real point (X, Y, Z) the curves C_1 and C_2 may touch each other at an imaginary point. In this case (X, Y, Z) does not belong to the guide surface in spite of the contact, because the straight lines of the generating system must always be real. In addition we obtain the plane E as a superfluous component, because in this plane the curves C_1 and C_2 necessarily decompose into a number of straight lines all of which pass through one point.

From the equation of an imaginary curve in line coordinates we can find in the following way the orthogonal projection of the perimeter of its guide surface on an arbitrary plane perpendicular to E. For this purpose we take as the | coordinates of the imaginary straight line the   58 vertical distance from the point of origin

$$r = \rho + i\rho'$$

and the angle

$$c = \gamma + i\gamma',$$

which it forms with the x-axis. We determine the guide line of the real for such an imaginary straight line by the angle $\psi = \gamma$ which it forms with the X-axis and by the rectangular coordinates Z and W of its intersection with a plane which is placed perpendicular to it through the Z-axis, where the line of intersection of this plane and the plane E (X, Y) is taken as the W-axis. Then, according to sections 4 and 5,

$$\rho = \sqrt{\frac{d}{Z}}\, W,$$

$$\gamma = \psi, \qquad \gamma' = \tfrac{1}{2}\lg\left(\frac{d}{Z}\right),$$

and further:

$$\sin c = \frac{(d+Z)\sin\psi}{2\sqrt{Zd}} + i\,\frac{(d-Z)\cos\psi}{2\sqrt{Zd}},$$

where $2d$ means the distance between the planes of the real and the imaginary. If we substitute these values in the equation of the imaginary curve and separate real and imaginary parts, we obtain two equations from which we eliminate ρ'. This equation represents in Z and W the projection of the perimeter of the guide surface on a plane which is determined by the angle ψ which it forms with the XZ-plane. |

Many properties of the guide surface can be derived immediately   59 from the properties of its imaginary curve. The real points of a real curve are represented by the generators of a cone whose vertex lies at the point of origin of the imaginary and whose guide line is the real curve itself. From this it follows that the point of origin of the imaginary is a cusp of the guide surface and that the real curve is the intersection of the guide surface with the base plane. If an imaginary curve can be transformed into a real one by a linear complex transformation, then its guide surface must have a cusp to which the point of origin of the imaginary is mapped by the transformation. The cusp can be found in this way.

The two points of contact of a straight line G which represents a point of a curve may coincide. They then lie in the plane E or U. The straight line then makes four-point contact at this point. The guide lines of the imaginary tangent must also pass through this point and touch the guide surface at that point. The guide surface must therefore touch three lines at the same point even though they do not in general lie in one plane. This is possible only because the guide surface has a cusp at P and approximates the straight line G. The number of individual points at which the guide surface forms a cusp and cuts into the plane E is equal to the class of the imaginary curve to be represented; for every cusp corresponds to a tangent from the imaginary circular point E. We have seen above (section 6) that these cusps

60   are branch points of the plane E with respect to the | plane U. In a similar way we find that the guide surface approaches asymptotically an equal number of straight lines as it approaches infinity through the cusps it forms. Two of these cusps or prolongations can coincide only if the imaginary curve passes through one of the circular points at infinity E and U, in which case its cuspidal character is lost and its asymptotic behaviour is replaced by a parabolic approach to infinity.

Thus the guide surface of an imaginary conic cuts into the plane E in two cusps and approaches asymptotically two straight lines. If we draw parallels to the asymptotes of the guide surface through the two cusps in the plane E, we obtain four straight lines which represent the focal points. From this it is easy to get the result that for a real ellipse

$$\left(\frac{x}{A}\right)^2 + \left(\frac{x}{B}\right)^2 - 1 = 0$$

the cusps in the plane E are situated at the points C and D (figure 13) with the coordinates

$$X_0 = +\tfrac{1}{2}\sqrt{A^2 - B^2}, \quad Y_0 = 0, \quad Z_0 = 0$$
$$X_1 = -\tfrac{1}{2}\sqrt{A^2 - B^2}, \quad Y_1 = 0, \quad Z_1 = 0$$

and that the straight lines g and h represent the real focal points G and H while i and k represent the imaginary focal points.

It appears from this that it would be possible to decide by mere intuition of a guide surface to what class an imaginary curve belonged: all we would need to do is count the cusps in the plane E. Its degree could also be recognized at once by counting the number of times the

61   guide surface on each side of E | runs parallel to the base plane; for each such position corresponds to an imaginary point of intersection

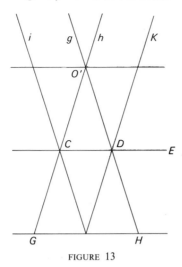

FIGURE 13

with the line at infinity. For if we represent the imaginary points at infinity and the corresponding imaginary asymptote, then we have on each side of the plane *E* two straight lines which intersect at right angles, are parallel to the base plane and must touch the guide surface at their point of intersection.

These hints may suffice to give a general idea of the nature of guide surfaces and how they can be investigated. It cannot be denied that these figures are usually so complicated that the aim of making imaginary relationships intuitable can be achieved only to a very imperfect degree, at least without models. This desire can be completely fulfilled only in the case of the simplest and most elementary, but for this very reason also most important, relationships. However, in the case of these more complicated figures another use comes to the fore: it is possible for us to take the properties of very simple figures of one or two dimensions and by mere translation use them to investigate the nature of far more complicated figures of a higher dimension. However, for this purpose it might be more advantageous to have a more general way of representing imaginary elements, and it is to this that we will now turn. |

11 A MORE GENERAL WAY OF REPRESENTING IMAGINARY ELEMENTS OF THE PLANE

We have up to now represented an imaginary point by a straight line. 62

The possibility of representing it in this way rests on the fact that the multiplicity of the imaginary points in the plane as well as of the straight lines in space is a quadruply infinite one. And we have up to now represented an imaginary straight line by a pair of straight lines which had to fulfil certain conditions, whereby their multiplicity was restricted likewise to a quadruply infinite one. But in representing the two in these heterogeneous ways we have evidently failed to observe the principle of duality which holds between straight lines and points in the plane. It is impossible to represent an imaginary straight line as well as an imaginary point by a straight line in space. An imaginary straight line would not then be determined by two imaginary points, nor, conversely, would an imaginary point be determined by two imaginary straight lines. However, there would remain the possibility of representing imaginary points as well by two straight lines each. The four straight lines of two imaginary points would then determine two other straight lines, which could then represent the imaginary connecting line. This has actually been the case all along; for the four guide lines of two imaginary straight lines determine not only the straight line by which we represent their imaginary point of intersection, but in

63   addition the line at infinity $|$ of the plane E. But this is where we come in conflict with the principle of duality, in that the line at infinity is the same for all imaginary points, whereas in the case of an imaginary straight line both guide lines are variable. Now if the multiplicity of the figures which are to represent imaginary points is not to exceed the quadruply infinite, it is necessary to place restrictions on the arbitrariness of the guide lines. Closer reflection shows that it is not possible to fix a guide line also for an imaginary straight line, nor is it possible to subject the guide lines of an imaginary point to the condition that they cut a given straight line. The simplest thing to do is therefore to pair off the straight lines in space and to stipulate that such a pair will represent either a point or an imaginary straight line.

To carry out this idea, we assume a tetrahedral coordinate system with one of its sides falling in the base plane where it forms the triangle of coordinates. The complex point coordinates of the base plane will be designated throughout by lower-case letters in the following manner:

$$x_1 = \xi_1 + i\xi_1', \qquad x_2 = \xi_2 + i\xi_2', \qquad x_3 = \xi_3 + i\xi_3'.$$

The complex line coordinates in the plane will be named as follows:

$$u_1 = \varphi_1 + i\varphi_1', \qquad u_2 = \varphi_2 + i\varphi_2', \qquad u_3 = \varphi_3 + i\varphi_3'.$$

Let the point coordinates in space be

$$X_1, X_2, X_3, X_4$$

or their analogues in Y or Z, so that the point $X_1, X_2, X_3, X_4 = 0$ is identical with |

$$x_1 = X_1, \; x_2 = X_2, \; x_3 = X_3. \qquad\qquad 64$$

The plane coordinates shall be

$$U_1, U_2, U_3, U_4$$

or their analogues in V or W. Finally, the line coordinates in space shall be designated in the following manner:

$$\rho p_k = X_k Y_4 - Y_k X_4 \qquad (k = 1, 2, 3)$$

$$\rho \pi_1 = X_2 Y_3 - Y_2 X_3$$

$$\rho \pi_2 = X_3 Y_1 - Y_3 X_1$$

$$\rho \pi_3 = X_1 Y_2 - Y_1 X_2,$$

if the straight line is determined by the points X and Y, or by

$$\rho g_k = U_k V_4 - V_k U_4 \qquad (k = 1, 2, 3)$$

$$\rho \gamma_1 = U_2 V_3 - V_2 U_3$$

$$\rho \gamma_2 = U_3 V_1 - V_3 U_1$$

$$\rho \gamma_3 = U_1 V_2 - V_1 U_2,$$

if the straight line is determined by the planes U and V.

Now let

$$u_1 x_1 + u_2 x_2 + u_3 x_3 = 0 \qquad\qquad (1)$$

be the equation of an imaginary straight line. This breaks down into

$$\varphi_1 \xi_1 + \varphi_2 \xi_2 + \varphi_3 \xi_3 - \varphi_1' \xi_1' - \varphi_2' \xi_2' - \varphi_3' \xi_3' = 0$$
$$\varphi_1' \xi_1 + \varphi_2' \xi_2 + \varphi_3' \xi_3 + \varphi_1 \xi_1' + \varphi_2 \xi_2' + \varphi_3 \xi_3' = 0. \qquad (2)$$

If we now substitute

$$\xi_1 = p_1, \quad \xi_2 = p_2, \quad \xi_3 = p_3 \qquad\qquad (3)$$
$$-\xi_1' = \pi_1, \; -\xi_2' = \pi_2, \; -\xi_3' = \pi_3,$$

we obtain the equations of two linear Plücker complexes. But if this interpretation of ξ is to be possible, it is necessary that

$$\xi_1 \xi_1' + \xi_2 \xi_2' + \xi_3 \xi_3' = 0. \qquad\qquad (4)$$

But this can always be achieved; for if | the coordinates of a point were   65
originally $\gamma_k = \eta_k + i\eta_k'$, then we could multiply them all by the same

quantity $e^{i\varepsilon}$ and obtain

$$\xi_k = \eta_k \cos \varepsilon - \eta'_k \sin \varepsilon; \qquad \xi'_k = \eta_k \sin \varepsilon + \eta'_k \cos \varepsilon. \tag{5}$$

If we substitute these values in (4), we get

$$\operatorname{tg} 2\varepsilon = -2 \frac{\eta_1 \eta'_1 + \eta_2 \eta'_2 + \eta_3 \eta'_3}{\eta_1{}^2 + \eta_2{}^2 + \eta_3{}^2 - \eta'_1{}^2 - \eta'_2{}^2 - \eta'_3{}^2}. \tag{6}$$

From this we can find two values for ε. The problem is identical with the following:

Find the guide lines of a congruence which is given by the equations

$$\begin{aligned}
\eta_1 g_1 + \eta_2 g_2 + \eta_3 g_3 - \eta'_1 \gamma_1 - \eta'_2 \gamma_2 - \eta'_3 \gamma_3 &= 0 \\
\eta'_1 g_1 + \eta'_2 g_2 + \eta'_3 g_3 + \eta_1 \gamma_1 + \eta_2 \gamma_2 + \eta_3 \gamma_3 &= 0.
\end{aligned} \tag{7}$$

For $\operatorname{tg} \varepsilon$ is the factor by which we must multiply the second before we add it to the first if we are to obtain the equation of the guide line.

Now let ε_0 and $\pi/2 + \varepsilon_0$ be the two values we have found for ε, and let p and p' be the guide lines corresponding to them. Then

$$\begin{aligned}
p_k &= \eta_k \cos \varepsilon_0 - \eta'_k \sin \varepsilon_0 = \xi_k \\
\pi_k &= -\eta_k \sin \varepsilon_0 - \eta'_k \cos \varepsilon_0 = -\xi'_k \\
p'_k &= -\eta_k \sin \varepsilon_0 - \eta'_k \cos \varepsilon_0 = -\xi'_k \\
\pi'_k &= -\eta_k \cos \varepsilon_0 + \eta'_k \sin \varepsilon_0 = -\xi_k.
\end{aligned} \tag{9}[1]$$

The straight lines p and p' are interdependent in the following manner:

$$p'_k = \pi_k, \qquad \pi'_k = -p_k. \tag{10}$$

This relation between straight lines in space is one–one.

The results of our considerations up to now are as follows: |

66   I. If the real and imaginary parts of the coordinates of an imaginary point $y = \eta + i\eta'$ are turned into coefficients of the equations of a congruence, as indicated in formulae (7), then their guide lines are paired in an invariant way, as expressed by formulae (10).

II. If the coordinates of one of these guide lines are equated according to formulae (3) with the real and imaginary parts of the coordinates of an imaginary point, or with the part multiplied by (-1), then this imaginary point is identical with the imaginary point y from which we started.

---

[1][A formula (8) is lacking. (*Ed.*)]

We regard these guide lines, which are always real, as a geometrical representation of the point x.

If we now return to the imaginary straight line and introduce p and π in place of ξ and ξ' in equations (2), we obtain

$$\varphi_1 p_1 + \varphi_2 p_2 + \varphi_3 p_3 + \varphi_1' \pi_1 + \varphi_2' \pi_2 + \varphi_3' \pi_3 = 0,$$
$$\varphi_1' p_1 + \varphi_2' p_2 + \varphi_3' p_3 - \varphi_1 \pi_1 - \varphi_2 \pi_2 - \varphi_3 \pi_3 = 0. \tag{11}$$

These are the equations of a congruence. It is easy to see that the straight line p' belongs to it if the corresponding p belongs to it. A comparison of (11) and (7) shows that the problem of finding the guide lines of this congruence coincides with the one already solved above. Let g and g' be the guide lines; then, analogously to the above,

$$g_k = \varphi_k \cos \delta_0 - \varphi_k' \sin \delta_0$$

$$\gamma_k = \varphi_k \sin \delta_0 + \varphi_k' \cos \delta_0,$$

where δ_0 is determined by

$$\text{tg } 2\delta = -2 \frac{\varphi_1 \varphi_1' + \varphi_2 \varphi_2' + \varphi_3 \varphi_3'}{\varphi_1{}^2 + \varphi_2{}^2 + \varphi_3{}^2 - \varphi_1'^2 - \varphi_2'^2 - \varphi_3'^2}. \tag{12}$$

67

The coordinate of the other guide line are

$$g_k' = -\varphi_k \sin \delta_0 - \varphi_k' \cos \delta_0$$

$$\gamma_k' = \varphi_k \cos \delta_0 - \varphi_k' \sin \delta_0.$$

This gives us the following relation between straight lines in space:

$$g_k' = -\gamma_k, \qquad \gamma_k' = g_k,$$

which we recognize to be identical with the one we found above if we remember that g is defined by plane coordinates whereas p is defined by point coordinates. If the φ satisfy the equation

$$\varphi_1 \varphi_1' + \varphi_2 \varphi_2' + \varphi_3 \varphi_3' = 0,$$

then

$$g_k = \varphi_k, \, \gamma_k = \varphi_k', \, g_k' = -\varphi_k', \, \gamma_k' = \varphi_k.$$

We have accordingly the following:

All straight lines in space are paired. Every pair represents an imaginary point. The imaginary points of an imaginary straight line are represented by a congruence whose guide lines are also paired.

It is easy to see that the guide lines of an imaginary point x cut the base plane at two points, one of which is given by the real and the other by the imaginary part of the coordinates of x, when

$$\xi_1\xi_1' + \xi_2\xi_2' + \xi_3\xi_3' = 0.$$

We likewise have the proposition that the guide lines of an imaginary straight line u, when projected from corner IV of the tetrahedron of coordinates on the base plane, produce images on the base plane whose 68   coordinates are equal to the real or, respectively, | imaginary parts of the coordinates of u, when

$$\varphi_1\varphi_1' + \varphi_2\varphi_2' + \varphi_3\varphi_3' = 0.$$

From these propositions it follows further that a real point is represented by two straight lines, one of which connects corner IV of the tetrahedron with the real point itself, while the other lies in the base plane. One of the guide lines of a real straight line coincides with the real straight line itself, while the other passes through corner IV.

Every pair of straight lines in space represents an imaginary point as well as an imaginary straight line. This gives us a one–one relation of imaginary points and straight lines in the base plane. The straight line with the coordinates

$$\rho p_k = \gamma_k, \qquad \rho \pi_k = g_k$$

together with its conjugate represents the imaginary point

$$x_k = p_k - i\pi_k$$

and the imaginary straight line

$$u_k = \rho(\pi_k + ip_k)$$

and thereby determines the relation in the following way:

$$u_k = \sigma x_k.$$

This relation is that the pole and polars with respect to the conic

$$x_1^2 + x_2^2 + x_3^2 = 0 \tag{13}$$

or $$u_1^2 + u_2^2 + u_3^2 = 0,$$

which is imaginary. In order to represent it, we separate real and imaginary parts: |

69              $$\xi_1^2 + \xi_2^2 + \xi_3^2 - \xi_1'^2 - \xi_2'^2 - \xi_3'^2 = 0$$

$$\xi_1\xi_1' + \xi_2\xi_2' + \xi_3\xi_3' = 0$$

or

$$p_1{}^2 + p_2{}^2 + p_3{}^2 + \pi_1{}^2 - \pi_2{}^2 - \pi_3{}^2 = 0 \tag{14}$$
$$p_1\pi_1 + p_2\pi_2 + p_3\pi_3 = 0.$$

This last is identically true. Our conic is the only imaginary curve which is represented by only *one* equation between the line coordinates and therefore the only one which is represented by a triply infinite set of straight lines. As can easily be seen from (10) and (14), these straight lines are all those that meet their conjugates.

The pairing of straight lines in space is the kind of relation that is given by a second-degree surface

$$X_1{}^2 + X_2{}^2 + X_3{}^2 - X_4{}^2 = 0 \tag{15}$$

or
$$U_1{}^2 + U_2{}^2 + U_3{}^2 - U_4{}^2 = 0$$

when the pole moves along the one straight line as the polar rotates about the other. The surface is real and without real generators. Its self-polar tetrahedron is the tetrahedron of coordinates. Its intersection with the base plane is the imaginary conic (13). Now since this surface and the imaginary conic are given along with the coordinate system, all further investigations will have to be based on them, and they will therefore be called the fundamental surface and the fundamental conic. But it is to be noted that the equations need not necessarily have the forms (13) and (15); for if we alter the coordinate system in such a way that corner IV remains fixed | and only the triangle in the base plane is 70 displaced, then the fundamental surface and curve, the pairing of the straight lines and the representation of the imaginary elements of the base plane all remain unchanged; the only change is in the form of the equations that express this. Every second-degree surface without real generators which has no real point of intersection with the base plane can be turned into the fundamental surface if the pole of the base plane is taken as corner IV of the tetrahedron of coordinates, because a coordinate system and the constants connected with it can always be chosen in such a way that the equation of the surface takes on the form (15). If we base our work on the more general form of the equation of the fundamental surface

$$\alpha_1{}^2 Y_1{}^2 + \alpha_2{}^2 Y_2{}^2 + \alpha_3{}^2 Y_3{}^2 - \alpha_4{}^2 Y_4{}^2 = 0, \tag{16}$$

then the equation of the fundamental curve is

$$\alpha_1{}^2 y_1{}^2 + \alpha_2{}^2 y_2{}^2 + \alpha_3{}^2 y_3{}^2 = 0. \tag{17}$$

The representation of the imaginary points is then given by the equations

$$\rho \alpha_k \eta'_k = \alpha_k \alpha_4 p_k = -\frac{\alpha_1 \alpha_2 \alpha_3}{\alpha_k} \pi'_k$$

$$\rho \alpha_k \eta'_k = -\frac{\alpha_1 \alpha_2 \alpha_3}{\alpha_k} \pi_k = -\alpha_k \alpha_4 p'_k,$$

where η is subject to the condition

$$\alpha_1{}^2 \eta_1 \eta'_1 + \alpha_2{}^2 \eta_2 \eta'_2 + \alpha_3{}^2 \eta_3 \eta'_3 = 0.$$

Every point y of the fundamental curve is represented by a pencil of lines. For the equation

$$\mathrm{tg}\, 2\varepsilon = -2 \frac{\eta_1 \eta'_1 + \eta_2 \eta'_2 + \eta_3 \eta'_3}{\eta_1{}^2 + \eta_2{}^2 + \eta_3{}^2 - \eta_1'^2 - \eta_2'^2 - \eta_3'^2} \quad |$$

71   becomes indeterminate due to the simultaneous disappearance of numerator and denominator, which is why every straight line with the coordinates

$$p_k = \rho \eta_k - \sigma \eta'_k, \qquad \pi_k = -\rho \eta'_k - \sigma \eta_k$$

represents the point y, where ρ and σ are arbitrary. These straight lines form the pencil of tangents of a point on the fundamental surface.

12   THE CONNECTION BETWEEN THE TWO WAYS OF REPRESENTING IMAGINARY ELEMENTS

If we compare the two ways of representing imaginary points, we are easily led to conjecture that the planes E and U correspond to the fundamental surface. We will therefore investigate the case where the fundamental surface degenerates into a pair of planes whose line of intersection coincides with side III of the triangle of coordinates; for this is how we must conceive of the line at infinity of the base plane.

We start our investigation with the general formulae (16), (17) and (18) in section 11. Hence, necessarily

$$\alpha_1 = \alpha_2 = 0,$$

and

$$\alpha_3{}^2 Y_3{}^2 - \alpha_4{}^2 Y_4{}^2 = 0$$

is the equation of the fundamental surface, which breaks down into

$$\alpha_3 Y_3 + \alpha_4 Y_4 = 0, \qquad \alpha_3 Y_3 - \alpha_4 Y_4 = 0.$$

The equation of the fundamental curve is

$$\alpha_3{}^2 y_3{}^2 = 0. \quad |$$

Every point of this real straight line is represented by a singly infinite 72
family of straight lines. If we let side III of the triangle of coordinates
move to infinity, then our fundamental curve is the line at infinity.
Plane III of the tetrahedron becomes parallel to the base plane. We
turn the angle at corner III of the triangle of coordinates into a right
angle and take the line of intersection of planes I and II of the
tetrahedron to be perpendicular to the base plane, so that

$$\sigma y_1 = x, \ \sigma \eta_1 = \xi, \ \sigma \eta_1' = \xi',$$

$$\sigma y_2 = y, \ \sigma \eta_2 = \eta, \ \sigma \eta_2' = \eta',$$

$$\sigma y_3 = 1, \ \sigma \eta_3 = 1, \ \sigma \eta_3' = 0,$$

$$\sigma Y_1 = X, \ \sigma Y_2 = Y, \ \sigma Y_3 = 1 + Z, \ \sigma Y_4 = Z.$$

The coordinates of the connecting line between two points Y and Y'
are then expressed by

$$\sigma^2 p_1 = XZ' - ZX'$$

$$\sigma^2 p_2 = YZ' - ZY'$$

$$\sigma^2 p_3 = Z' - Z$$

$$\sigma^2 \pi_1 = Y - Y' + (YZ' - ZY')$$

$$\sigma^2 \pi_2 = X' - X - (XZ' - ZX')$$

$$\sigma^2 \pi_3 = XY' - YX'.$$

But now also (section 11, equation 18)

$$p_1 = \tau\xi, \qquad \pi_1 = -\tau \frac{\beta_1 \alpha_4}{\beta_2 \alpha_3} \xi'$$

$$p_2 = \tau\eta, \qquad \pi_2 = -\tau \frac{\beta_2 \alpha_4}{\beta_1 \alpha_3} \eta'$$

$$p_3 = \tau, \qquad \pi_3 = \frac{0}{0},$$

where

$$\frac{\beta_1}{\beta_2} = \mathrm{Lim} \frac{\alpha_1}{\alpha_2}. \quad |$$

If we assume that Y' is in the plane of the imaginary (III of the 73 tetrahedron) and Y in the plane of the real, so that

$$Z' = -1, \qquad Z = 0,$$

then

$$\sigma^2 \tau \xi = -X, \qquad -\sigma^2 \tau \frac{\beta_1 \alpha_4}{\beta_2 \alpha_3} \xi' = -Y',$$

$$\sigma^2 \tau \eta = -Y, \qquad -\sigma^2 \tau \frac{\beta_2 \alpha_4}{\beta_1 \alpha_3} \eta' = X',$$

$$\sigma^2 \tau = -1$$

or

$$\xi = X, \qquad \frac{\beta_1 \alpha_4}{\beta_2 \alpha_3} \xi' = -Y'$$

$$\eta = Y, \qquad \frac{\beta_2 \alpha_4}{\beta_1 \alpha_3} \eta' = X'.$$

This coincides in effect with our previous method of representation if we put

$$-\lambda = \frac{\beta_1 \alpha_4}{\beta_2 \alpha_3} = \frac{\beta_2 \alpha_4}{\beta_1 \alpha_3} = -1$$

or

$$\beta_1{}^2 = \beta_2{}^2, \qquad \alpha_3{}^2 = \alpha_4{}^2.$$

The fundamental surface then reduces to

$$-(1+Z) + Z = 0, \qquad (1+Z) + Z = 0,$$

i.e., to the plane at infinity and the plane E. From this it appears that we can conceive of an infinite number of other methods of representation where the fundamental surface reduces to two parallel planes and where the fundamental curve is the line at infinity. E.g., we only need to assign to

$$\lambda = -\frac{\beta_1}{\beta_2} \frac{\alpha_4}{\alpha_3}$$

a value other than 1, which would mean that the lengths in the plane of the imaginary would be measured on a different | scale than in the plane of the real. Among these possible methods of representation may well be some that are no less favourable to metrical relationships than the one we singled out for special consideration.

In the case of the general way of representing an imaginary curve we also have a guide surface, as can be seen by representing an imaginary point and the imaginary tangent that corresponds to it. We then get four straight lines which intersect at four points. These points must belong to the guide surface because two infinitely near lines of the generating system intersect at each of these points. These four points are the corners of a self-polar tetrahedron of the fundamental surface. The four lateral planes touch the guide surface at one corner point each. Thus if a point on the guide surface moves, its polar envelopes the guide surface. One family of bitangent lines of the guide surface represents the imaginary points and another the imaginary tangents. It should finally be noted that Gauss's representation of complex numbers can be generalized. One of the two guide lines of every imaginary point always cuts the fundamental surface. To every imaginary point corresponds therefore a pair of points on that surface. Now if we determine the imaginary points of an imaginary straight line by means of a complex parameter, we can regard the pairs of points on the fundamental surface as representing these complex numbers. Every plane placed through the guide line of the imaginary straight line which cuts the fundamental | surface divides the fundamental surface into two parts, which represent the complex numbers in one-to-one fashion. It can be seen that Gauss's representation is the special case where the fundamental surface reduces to the pair of planes E and U.

The conics generated on the fundamental surface by pencils of planes whose axes are the imaginary straight lines correspond, according to the way they are generated geometrically, to the parallels to the axes of the real and the imaginary in Gauss's representation. If the complex parameter to be represented is taken to be the logarithm of the ratios of the distances from the imaginary points at which the fundamental curve cuts the imaginary straight line, then we find by calculation that the above-mentioned conics contain all those points to which we must assign the same real or, respectively, imaginary parts of this parameter.

We should, however, hardly succeed in making our general way of representing complex numbers as fruitful as Gauss's.

The relationship between the two methods of representation corresponds to the relationship between Euclidean geometry and a geometry in which the line at infinity with the two circular points is replaced by a non-degenerate conic.

75

Methods of Calculation based on an Extension of the Concept of Quantity

1 When we consider complex numbers and their geometrical representation, we leave the field of the original concept of quantity, as
contained especially in the quantities of Euclidean geometry: its lines,
surfaces and volumes. According to the old conception, length appears
as something material which fills the straight line between its end
points and at the same time prevents another thing from penetrating
into its space by its rigidity. In adding quantities, we are therefore
forced to place one quantity against another. Something similar holds
for surfaces and solid contents. The introduction of negative quantities
made a dent in this conception, and imaginary quantities made it
completely impossible. Now all that matters is the point of origin and
the end point; whether there is a continuous line between them, and if
so which, appears to make no difference whatsoever; the idea of filling
space has been completely lost. All that has remained is certain general
properties of addition, which now emerge as the essential characteristic
marks of quantity. The concept has thus gradually freed itself from
intuition and made itself independent. This is quite unobjectionable,
especially since its earlier intuitive character was at bottom mere
appearance. Bounded straight lines and planes enclosed by curves can
certainly be intuited, but what is quantitative about them, what is
common to lengths and surfaces, escapes our intuition. This comes out
most clearly in the case of an angle. No beginner will get a correct idea
of an angle if the figure is merely placed before his eyes. This is what
has occasioned numerous attempts to give an explanation of an angle,
even though the situation is at bottom exactly the same in the case of a
length, except that this idea is more familiar to us from our ordinary
lives. If a beginner is shown how to add angles, then he knows what
they are. And it is clear that a concept as comprehensive and abstract
as the concept of quantity cannot be an intuition. There is accordingly
a noteworthy difference between geometry and arithmetic in the way in
which their fundamental principles are grounded. The elements of all

Dissertation for the *Venia docendi* in the Philosophical Faculty of Jena (Friedrich
Frommann, Jena, 1874). (*Tr*. Hans Kaal)

geometrical constructions are intuitions, and geometry refers to intuition as the source of its axioms. Since the object of arithmetic does not have an intuitive character, its fundamental propositions cannot stem from intuition either. And how could intuition guarantee propositions which hold for all such heterogeneous quantities, some species of which may still be unknown to us? Now if these propositions were invalid in some domain, we would not speak of quantities either. From this it follows that we incorporate the propositions that are necessary for the construction of the science in the concept of quantity while excluding everything that does not conform to them. If the concept of quantity can be applied in a different way in the domain of intuition, this is sufficient to assure us | that we are not getting lost in idle speculation. 2 This is the only use we need to make of intuition.

If, as we have shown, we do not find the concept of quantity in intuition but create it ourselves, then we are justified in trying to formulate its definition so as to permit as manifold an application as possible, in order to extend the domain that is subject to arithmetic as far as possible.

Now what is the subject of those fundamental propositions from which the whole of arithmetic grows as from a seed? The answer is, addition; for the other methods of calculation arise from this one. This is why there is such an intimate connection between the concepts of addition and quantity that the latter cannot be grasped at all without the former. In the most general terms, the process of addition is as follows: we replace a group of things by a single one of the same species. This gives us a definition of the concept of quantitative identity. If we can decide in every case when objects agree in a property, we evidently have the correct concept of the property. Thus in specifying under what conditions there is quantitative identity, we *ipso facto* define the concept of quantity. A quantity of a certain kind – e.g. a length – is accordingly a property in which a group of things can agree with a single thing of the same kind independently of the internal constitution of the group. It must always be possible to think of such a property, no matter what group we wish to form out of the things of the species. Of course, this definition of the concept has a real content only if the property we are thinking of allows such scope that it is also possible for things not to agree in it. The multiplicity enclosed within this scope will be called the quantitative domain.

It would take us too far afield to explain in detail how the content of arithmetic is contained in the properties of quantity which we have set out, and how special kinds of quantity, such as a natural number and an angle, can also be defined from this standpoint. The only conclusion

c

we will draw here is that quantity can also be ascribed to operations. If we repeat an operation f by constantly resubmitting its result to it, we can regard the repeated applications of operation f as new operations. Now it is clear that two or more of the operations obtained in this way, ff, fff ..., acting in succession on an object, can always be replaced by a single operation consisting likewise in a repetition of f. It can also be seen that the sequence makes no difference in this case. Let the original operation be,, e.g., the displacement of a point in a certain direction by a certain distance. The repeated displacement by the same distance can then be regarded as a single displacement, and all these displacements form a quantitative domain. This domain can be extended further by asking: what displacement, when repeated n times, would yield the original displacement? and what displacement cancels the original one? And in general we can look for the operation which, when applied n times, can replace the given operation, and for the operation which reverses the given one. It is easy to see that these operations and the ones that can arise from them in the ways indicated together form a quantitative domain. Let us now consider arithmetical operations from this point of view. There are several examples of the repetition of the same operation to be found in arithmetic. Addition for example leads to multiplication, and multiplication to involution. All

3 calculations of approximate values consist in | constantly repeated applications of the same operation. Every recursive formula teaches us how to obtain the result for 2, 3...etc. from the result for 1 by repetition of the same procedure.

This should permit us to recognize those parts of arithmetic that would be covered by a theory of the concept of quantity as it relates to functions. Because such a theory, when developed in its most general and complete form, would range over a wide area and be difficult to grasp, we can indicate here only a few points that result immediately from the concept, and we can consider here only the easiest cases. The applications we intend to make do not have the purpose of tackling hitherto unsolved problems, but are intended partly to call attention to a connection which the concept of the quantity of a function allows us to make between different areas of arithmetic, and partly to bring to notice a class of problems which might be solved with the help of a further developed theory.

I FUNCTIONS OF A SINGLE VARIABLE

1 After what has been said above it will be understood that we assign

to the functions $\varphi(\varphi(x))$, $\varphi(\varphi(\varphi(x)))$ double or triple the quantity of the function $\varphi(x)$. It is no less clear that the function $\psi(x)$ is to be assigned a fourth of the quantity of $\varphi(x)$ when $\varphi(x)$ is identical with $\psi(\psi(\psi(\psi(x))))$, that the quantity $\chi(x)$ is the reciprocal of the quantity of $\varphi(x)$ when $\varphi\chi(x) = x$, and finally, that when x is a function of itself, the quantity of the function must be designated as the null quantity. Accordingly, we distinguish the quantity of a function from the value it assumes for some value of the argument. It should be understood that all possible functions do not make up a single quantitative domain, but divide into infinitely many different domains. We can also get an intuitive understanding of the matter by means of the following geometrical picture. Let $y = f(x)$ represent a curve in a rectangular coordinate system. If the function f is first assigned the quantity 0, $y = x$ will be the curve bisecting the right angle of the coordinates. Let this be called the null line for the sake of brevity. If we let the quantity of $f(x)$ increase gradually, the resulting curve will develop a bulge, which is at first almost unnoticeable, but then becomes more and more pronounced and deviates more and more from the null line. If we then start with 0 and let the quantity of the function run through the reciprocal values in a steady progression, we get a series of images which are congruent with the previous series and symmetrical about the null line. If $f(x_0) = x_0$, then also $ff(x_0) = x_0$, $fff(x_0) = x_0$ etc., i.e., the images of the multiples of a functional quantity cut the null line at the same points as the image of the single functional quantity. The same holds for the negative multiples but not for their parts. For we can conceive of two numbers x_0 and x_1 constituted in such a way that $f(x_0) = x_1$ and $f(x_1) = x_0$. In that case $ff(x_0) = x_0$ and $ff(x_1) = x_1$ without its being the case that $f(x_0) = x_0$ and $f(x_1) = x_1$.

The simplest operation is addition. It is easy to see that the functions of this quantitative domain have the form $X = na + x$, where n shall mean the quantity. An increase in the quantity of this function is represented as a uniform parallel displacement of a straight line out of the position of the null line.

The operation of multiplication $X = a^n x$, as it increases in quantity, gives the image of a non-uniform rotation of a straight line about a point. If $a > 1$, then the X-axis represents the base where $n = +\infty$ and the x-axis the case where $n = -\infty$. Just as the infinite is not a quantity, so the limiting | state which a function approaches with increasing n is 4 no longer a function, for the value of the function becomes independent of the argument.

We can now raise the following questions:

What is the function whose quantity stands in a given relation to the quantity of a given function?

Do the quantities of two given functions belong to the same quantitative domain, and if so, in what relation do they stand?

The answer to these questions presupposes a knowledge of the general form of a function which is n times a given one. In more definite terms, we need a function of n and x which turns into the given function when $n = 1$ and which satisfies the functional equation

$$f(n_0, f(n_1, x)) = f(n_0 + n_1, x). \tag{1}$$

If we call the value of the function X, then we can also say that we need an equation between the quantity n, the value X and the argument x of a function. We will call such equations quantitative equations. If we think of n as being expressed by X and x, so that

$$n = \psi(X, x),$$

then the function ψ must have the property that the elimination of x_0 from

$$n_0 = \psi(X, x_0)$$
$$n_1 = \psi(x_0, x_1)$$

gives rise to the equation

$$n_0 + n_1 = \psi(X, x_1)$$

or

$$\psi(X, x_0) + \psi(x_0, x_1) = \psi(X, x_1). \tag{2}$$

From this follow some propositions about the differential quotients at the points of intersection with the null line. From (1) we can infer by differentiation with respect to x

$$f'(n_0, f(n_1, x))f'(n_1, x) = f'(n_0 + n_1, x)$$

$$f''(n_0, f(n_1, x))f'(n_1, x)^2 + f'(n_0, f(n_1, x))f''(n_1, x) = f''(n_0 + n_1, x).$$

Now if

$$f(n_1, x_0) = x_0, f(n_0, x_0) = x_0,$$

then

$$f'(n_0, x_0)f'(n_1, x_0) = f'(n_0 + n_1, x_0).$$

This shows that the quantities of two functions of the same quantitative domain are related as the logarithms of their differential quotients at a common point of intersection with the null line. Further, if

$$f'(n_1, x_0) = f'(n_0, x_0) = 1,$$

then

$$f''(n_0, x_0) + f''(n_1, x_0) = f''(n_0 + n_1, x_0).$$

This means:

The quantities of two functions which make first-degree contact with each other and the null line at the same point are related as their second differential quotients, or as the curvatures of the curves at that point.

Similar propositions can also be established for higher-degree contacts.

We now turn to methods for solving the problem of quantitative equations. |

Method of Substitution

2   The method to be considered is based on the immediately evident 5 proposition that if formula (2), section 1, i.e.,

$$\psi(X, x_0) + \psi(x_0, x_1) = \psi(X, x_1)$$

holds for arbitrary X, x_0 and x_1, then the following equation is also valid:

$$\psi(\theta(X), \theta(x_0)) + \psi(\theta(x_0), \theta(x)) = \psi(\theta(X), \theta(x)).$$

Hence

$$\psi(\theta(X), \theta(x)) = n$$

is the quantitative equation of a new function. This gives us a means of deriving other quantitative equations from a known one. It can now be shown that every quantitative equation can be found in this way. For if we put $x_1 = X$, then formula (2), section 1, becomes

$$\psi(x_1, x_0) + \psi(x_0, x_1) = 0.$$

If we subtract this equation from (2), we obtain

$$\psi(X, x_0) - \psi(x_1, x_0) = \psi(X, x_1).$$

If we now regard x_0 as constant, we can also write the quantitative equation $n = \psi(X, x)$ as follows:

$$n = \theta(X) - \theta(x),$$

where $\theta(x) = \psi(x, x_0)$. This quantitative equation shows clearly that it arose by substitution from the simplest quantitative equation

$$n = X - x.$$

Let us proceed to some examples.

From the quantitative equation of addition $X - x = n$ it follows, by substitution of the function

$$\theta(X) = \frac{\lg X}{\lg b}, \qquad \theta(x) = \frac{\lg x}{\lg b},$$

that

$$n = \frac{\lg X - \lg x}{\lg b}$$

or

$$X = b^n x,$$

the quantitative equation of multiplication. An exponent can also be defined as the quantity of the multiplicative function, whereupon the meaning of the negative and fractional exponent follows immediately from our general principles.

If we substitute

$$X - a \quad \text{and} \quad x - a$$

in the equation we just found, we obtain

$$X = a(1 - b^n) + b^n x,$$

the quantitative equation of a linear function. For $n = 1$ we get $X = a(1 - b) + bx$. Now if we let $a(1 - b) = c$, then we can also write the quantitative equation as follows:

$$X = c\frac{1 - b^n}{1 - b} + b^n x.$$

The case where $b = -1$ is distinguished by the periodicity according to which the multiples of the quantity of the function $c - x$ are always represented alternately by x and $c - x$. Functions whose quantities are parts of the quantity of the function $c - x$ have the property | that their multiples return periodically into themselves. In this respect they show a similarity to angular quantities. If we also admit complex values of n (and there is no reason for excluding them because the equation $X - x = n$, which was our starting-point, remains valid also for a complex n), then the case where $X = c - x$ is always contained in the general formula

$$X = c\frac{1 - b^n}{1 - b} + b^n x.$$

Functions of this kind form accordingly a quantitative domain of two dimensions, which runs back into itself in one direction like the surface of a cylinder. The same holds for all functions whose quantitative equation is derived from $X - x = n$ by a function θ which is the inverse of a simple periodic one.

The summation of a geometrical series may serve as an example of the application of this. If x is the sum of the first k terms, then we find the sum of the first $(k + 1)$ terms by the formula

$$c + bx,$$

where b is the factor and c the initial term of the series. The n-fold repetition of this operation gives us the sum of the first $(k + n)$ terms:

$$S_{k+n} = c\frac{1 - b^n}{1 - b} + b^n x.$$

Finally, if we let $k = 0$, then we get $x = 0$ and

$$S_n = c\frac{1 - b^n}{1 - b}.$$

Let us now choose

$$\operatorname{arctg}\left(\frac{x + b}{a}\right)$$

as the function θ. We then obtain from $X - x = n$

$$\operatorname{arctg}\left(\frac{X + b}{a}\right) - \operatorname{arctg}\left(\frac{x + b}{a}\right) = n$$

or

$$X = \frac{(a^2 + b^2)\operatorname{tg} n + (a + b\operatorname{tg} n)x}{a - b\operatorname{tg} n - \operatorname{tg} n \cdot x}.$$

This is the quantitative equation of a fractional function with a linear numerator and denominator

$$X = \frac{A + Bx}{C + Dx}.$$

and further

$$b = \frac{C-B}{2D}, \qquad a = \frac{\sqrt{-(C-B)^2 - 4AD}}{2D}$$

$$\operatorname{tg} n = -\frac{\sqrt{-(C-B)^2 - 4AD}}{B+C}.$$

The geometrical projection of such a function is a rectangular hyperbola whose asymptotes run parallel to the axes of the coordinate system. As n increases by real increments, the same functions recur periodically. In these cases the null line is not cut at a real point, so long as all coefficients A, B, C, D are supposed to be real, because for these points of intersection we find that

$$x_0 = -b \pm ia.$$

The case of an imaginary a will be treated below in another way.

The method of substitution affords the unlimited possibility of finding new quantitative equations, but has the drawback that it is often difficult to find the substitution which would allow us to reach a pre-set goal. |

Method of Integration

7   3   A function of the infinitely small quantity δ must have the form

$$X_\delta = x + \delta\varphi(x)$$

if X is to turn into x as δ vanishes. If $X_n = f(n, x)$ is the quantitative equation, then for $n = \delta$

$$X_\delta = f(0, x) + \delta\left(\frac{\partial f(n, x)}{\partial n}\right)_{n=0} = x + \delta\left(\frac{\partial f(n, x)}{\partial n}\right)_{n=0},$$

which brings out the connection between f and φ. We pass over the exceptional case where $f(n, x)$ becomes unsteady for $n = 0$, because this case can hardly be expected to occur. We now assume that the function φ is known, and we are to find the quantitative equation on the basis of it. For this purpose we assign the increment δ to the quantity n by substituting $X_n = f(n, x)$ in $x + \delta\varphi(x)$. This gives us

$$f(n + \delta, x) = f(n, x) + \delta\varphi(f(n, x)).$$

If we now subtract $f(n, x)$ and divide by δ, we get the differential quotient

$$\frac{\partial f(n, x)}{\partial n} \varphi(f(n, x))$$

$$\frac{\partial X}{\partial n} = \varphi(X).$$

By integrating, while regarding x as a constant, we obtain

$$n = \int \frac{dX}{\varphi(X)} + C = \theta(X) + C.$$

The constant is determined by the general rule that if $X = x$, then, necessarily, $n = 0$. Consequently

$$n = \theta(X) - \theta(x).$$

This leads us back to the substitution. But in the process we got to know a new connection between the functions f and θ. We also know now how to find the function θ as soon as φ is known. Everything will therefore turn on our knowledge of this function. If we can recognize the general form of the functions which arise by repetition of the given operation, then we may conjecture that the infinitely small function $x + \delta\varphi(x)$ will have the same form, whereby we will also know the form of φ. But this is what is essential since the undetermined constants can be found subsequently. It may be useful to interpolate another consideration here. The values x_0, $x_1 \ldots$ which correspond to the points of intersection of the curve $y = f(x)$ with the null line divide into two classes, according to whether the equation

$$f(n, x_0) - x_0 = 0$$

holds for all possible n or not. In the former case, which we will consider first, it must also be the case that

$$x_0 + \delta\varphi(x_0) - x_0 = 0, \qquad \varphi(x_0) = 0.$$

Conversely, as $\varphi(x_0)$ vanishes in the first or in a higher degree,

$$\int \frac{dx}{\varphi(x)} = \theta(x)$$

becomes infinite for $x = x_0$, and the equation

$$\underset{X = x = x_0}{\mathrm{Lim}} \{\theta(X) - \theta(x)\} = n \quad |$$

holds for any n; i.e., there is always a way in which X and x approach   8
x_0 simultaneously so as to satisfy the equation, and where x_0 corre-

sponds to one of those points of intersection with the null line that we have been considering. Hence $\varphi(x)$ has the form

$$(x-x_0)^r\psi(x),$$

where r means an integer >0, and where $\psi(x_0)$ does not become infinite or only logarithmically infinite and where it does not vanish either in the first or in a higher degree. Now r must coincide exactly with the degree of multiplicity ρ of the root x_0; for if we assume first that all the roots of $f(x)-x=0$ are different, then $\varphi(x)$ has the form

$$(x-x_0)^{r_0}(x-x_1)^{r_1}(x-x_2)^{r_2}\ldots\psi(x).$$

If we now let ρ roots become equal to one another, then

$$\varphi(x)=(x-x_0)^{r_0+r_1+r_2\cdots r_{\rho}-1}\psi(x),$$

and $\rho\leqq r_0+r_1\ldots r_{\rho-1}=r$. But r must not be greater than ρ either; for if instead of $\varphi(x)$ we first consider the expression

$$(x-x_0)(x-x_0-\delta_1)(x-x_0-\delta_2)\ldots(x-x_0-\delta_{r-1})\psi(x),$$

we find that to each linear factor corresponds a root of $f(x)-x=0$. As $\delta_1,\delta_2\ldots$ are now made to vanish, we get at least an r-fold root. We must therefore conclude that $\rho=r$.

Let x_0 now be of the second kind, so that

$$\theta(x_0)-\theta(x_0)=kn_0$$

holds only when k is an integer and n_0 constant. Then θ is many-valued and in such a way that the inverse function of θ has the period n_0 for the special value x_0. The function φ for the argument x_0 can vanish only in a degree lower than the first.

The following equation serves as a test of whether a given function is the correct φ-function. If $f(x)$ is the given function, then it must be that

$$f(x)+\delta\varphi f(x)=f(x+\delta\varphi(x))$$

i.e.,

$$f(x)+\delta\varphi f(x)=f(x)+\delta\varphi(x)\frac{\mathrm{d}f(x)}{\mathrm{d}x}.$$

$$\varphi f(x)=\varphi(x)\frac{\mathrm{d}f(x)}{\mathrm{d}x}.$$

Take, e.g.,

$$f(x)=\frac{ax+b}{cx+d}.$$

The equation

$$\frac{ax+b}{cx+d} - x = 0$$

means the same as

$$-cx^2 + (a-d)x + b = 0.$$

We therefore conjecture that φ will contain the left-hand side of this equation as a factor. The result of the test is that this is indeed the desired φ-function because

$$-c\left(\frac{ax+b}{cx+d}\right)^2 + (a-d)\left(\frac{ax+b}{cx+d}\right) + b = (-cx^2 + (a-d)x + b)\frac{ad-bc}{(cx+d)^2}.$$

Let us indicate briefly how the $\varphi(x)$ can be found in the form of a series. For when we are dealing with the first kind of intersections with the null line, we can determine all the differential quotients of φ for the special values $x_0, x_1 \ldots$ From $\varphi f(x) = \varphi(x) f'(x)$ we can infer by differentiation |

$$\varphi' f(x) f'(x) = \varphi'(x) f'(x) + \varphi(x) f''(x) \qquad \qquad 9$$

$$\varphi'' f(x) f'(x)^2 + \varphi' f(x) f''(x) = \varphi''(x) f'(x) + 2\varphi'(x) f''(x) + \varphi(x) f'''(x) \quad \text{etc.}$$

If we put $x = x_0 = f(x_0)$, then $\varphi(x_0)$ is equal to 0 and hence single-valued, because only this value of this function can be used in this case. The first of the above equations is now satisfied identically, but the second gives us

$$\varphi''(x_0) = \frac{f''(x_0)}{f'(x_0)^2 - f'(x_0)} \varphi'(x_0).$$

By continuing to differentiate, we can thus express the higher differential quotients of φ for the argument x_0 one after the other by means of the first. We can assume arbitrarily that the first is equal to 1 for example, because a constant factor is inessential to φ. We then know φ by means of Taylor's series. The quantitative equation can also be represented by a series. Thus

$$f(n,x) = x + \frac{\varphi_1(x)}{1} n + \frac{\varphi_2(x)}{1 \cdot 2} n^2 \ldots,$$

where $\varphi_k(x)$ means the same as $(\partial^k f(n,x)/(\partial n^k))_{n=0}$. Now

$$f(n, x + \delta\varphi_1(x)) = f(n+\delta, x)$$

$$x + \delta\varphi_1(x) + \sum_{k=1}^{k=\infty} \left\{ \frac{\varphi_k(x + \delta\varphi_1(x))}{k!} n^k \right\} = x + \sum_{p=1}^{p=\infty} \left\{ \frac{n+\delta)^p}{p!} \varphi_p(x) \right\}$$

or

$$\sum_{j=1}^{k=\infty} \left\{ \frac{\varphi_k(x)}{k!} n^k \right\} + \delta\varphi_1(x) + \delta \sum_{k=1}^{k=\infty} \left\{ \frac{\varphi_1(x)\varphi_k'(x)}{k!} n^k \right\} = \sum_{p=1}^{p=\infty} \left\{ \frac{\varphi_p(x)}{p!} n^p \right\}$$

$$+ \delta \sum_{p=1}^{p=\infty} \left\{ \frac{\varphi_p(x)}{p!} p \cdot n^{p-1} \right\}.$$

By comparing the coefficients of n of the same power in the part multiplied by δ, we get

$$\varphi_{k+1}(x) = \varphi_1(x)\varphi_k'(x).$$

We now know the values of $\varphi_k(x)$ in serial order. By differentiating this equation, we can also determine their differential quotients for the special value x_0 from the differential quotients for $\varphi_1(x)$ which we found earlier. We thus obtain $X = f(n, x)$ developed into a double series which progresses exponentially to the powers of $(x - x_0)$ and n.

II   FUNCTIONS OF SEVERAL VARIABLES

4   Just as we derived from a function $\varphi(x)$ by repeated substitution within itself the functions $\varphi\varphi(x)$ and $\varphi\varphi\varphi(x)$ and ascribed to them double and triple the quantity of the original one, we can also derive from a system of two functions with two variables

$$X = F_1(x, y) \qquad Y = F_2(x, y)$$

the new functional system

$$X = F_1(F_1(x, y), F_2(x, y))$$

$$Y = F_2(F_1(x, y), F_2(x, y))$$

and assign to it double the quantity of the original one. Every variable comes to have a function corresponding to it. From this it can easily be gathered what we understand in general by a functional system whose quantity is some multiple of the quantity of another. Corresponding to our earlier procedure, a functional system must be assigned the reciprocal of the quantity of another when the former arises from the latter by inversion or, what is equivalent in meaning, when arguments and functional values are interchanged. |

10   Our first task is again to specify the connection between the quantity, the values and the arguments of a functional system. Let

$$X_1, X_2 \ldots X_m \text{ be the values,}$$

$x_1, x_2 \ldots x_m$ the arguments

and n the quantity of the functional system; then the connection presents itself at first sight in the following form:

$$X_k = f_k(n, x_1, x_2, \ldots x_m), \qquad (k = 1, 2 \ldots m),$$

which entails that there are $(m-1)$ relations between arguments and functional values independent of n. The following functional system must hold for f_k:

$$f_k(n_0, f_1(n_1), f_2(n_1) \ldots f_m(n_1)) = f_k(n_0 + n_1, x_1, x_2 \ldots x_m), \quad k = 1, 2, 3 \ldots m$$

where $f_i(n_1)$ is short for $f_i(n_1, x_1, x_2 \ldots x_m)$.

Methods of Integration and Substitution

5   In a functional system of quantity 0 the values are successively equal to one. An infinitely small functional system has the form

$$X_1 = x_1 + \delta \varphi_1(x_1, x_2 \ldots x_m)$$

$$X_2 = x_2 + \delta \varphi_2(x_1, x_2 \ldots x_m)$$

$$\ldots\ldots\ldots\ldots\ldots\ldots\ldots\ldots$$

$$X_m = x_m + \delta \varphi_m(x_1, x_2 \ldots x_m),$$

where

$$\varphi_k(x_1, x_2 \ldots x_m) = \left(\frac{\partial f_k(n, x_1, x_2 \ldots x_m)}{\partial n} \right)_{n=0}.$$

Consequently

$$f_k(n + \delta, x_1 \ldots x_m) = f_k(n, x_1 \ldots x_m) + \delta \varphi_k(f_1, f_2 \ldots f_m)$$

and

$$\frac{\partial f_k(n, x_1 \ldots x_m)}{\partial n} = \frac{\partial X_k}{\partial n} = \varphi_k(X_1, X_2 \ldots X_m).$$

Our task is to integrate the system of simultaneous differential equations

$$\frac{\partial X_k}{\partial n} = \varphi_k(X_1, X_2 \ldots X_m), \qquad k = 1, 2, \ldots m \tag{1}$$

while regarding $x_1, x_2 \ldots x_m$ as the integral constants to be introduced. Now if the proposition that quantitative equations can always be found from

$$X_k - x_k = n, \qquad k = 1, 2 \ldots m$$

by suitable substitution is to be proved also in this case, we must think of the integration as being carried out in the following way. We first divide equations (1) by the first equation so as to eliminate n and obtain

$$\frac{\mathrm{d}X_k}{\mathrm{d}X_1} = \frac{\varphi_k}{\varphi_1}, \qquad k = 2, 3 \ldots m.$$

These are the differential equations of the relations which obtain independently of n between the x_k. Let the integrals of these $(m = 1)$ equations be

$$C_k = \lambda_k(X_1, X_2 \ldots X_m), \qquad k = 2, 3, 4 \ldots m. \tag{2}$$

Now since $x_1, x_2 \ldots x_m$ are only special values of X which have been treated as constant during the integration, we also have

$$C_k = \lambda_k(x_1, x_2 \ldots x_m). \,| \tag{3}$$

11   We can now express $X_2 \ldots X_m$ in equations (2) in terms of X_1 and substitute these formulae in

$$\frac{\partial X_1}{\partial n} = \varphi_1(X_1 \ldots X_m).$$

This should give us

$$\frac{\partial X_1}{\partial n} = \rho(X_1, C_2, C_3 \ldots C_m),$$

an equation whose integral has the form

$$n = \sigma(X_1, C \ldots C_m) + D.$$

For the special case where $X_1 = x_1$ we get

$$n = \sigma(X_1, C_2 \ldots C_m) - \sigma(x_1, C_2 \ldots C_m).$$

If in place of the integral constant C we now introduce $X_1, X_2 \ldots X_m$ into the first part according to (2) and $x_1, x_2 \ldots x_m$ into the second part according to (3), our equation assumes the form

$$n = \theta_1(X_1, X_2 \ldots X_m) - \theta_1(x_1, x_2 \ldots x_m),$$

which is what we were seeking. From this we can easily find the remaining integrals by first adding the C and then subtracting them again in succession, while representing them the first time round by X and the second time by x. We thus get

$$n = \theta_k(X_1, X_2 \ldots X_m) - \theta_k(x_1, x_2 \ldots x_m), \tag{4}$$

where $\theta_k = \theta_1 + \lambda_k$. These formulae show that all quantitative equations can be derived by substitution from the simplest system

$$X_k - x_k = n, \qquad k = 1, 2 \ldots m$$

in the same way as in the case of functions of one variable. It can also be shown easily that, conversely, whatever functions we choose for $\theta_1, \theta_2 \ldots \theta_m$, (4) is always a system of quantitative equations; for by eliminating $y_1, y_2 \ldots y_m$ from

$$n_0 = \theta_k(X_1, X_2 \ldots X_m) - \theta_k(y_1, y_2 \ldots y_m)$$

$$n_1 = \theta_k(y_1, y_2 \ldots y_m) - \theta_k(x_1, x_2 \ldots x_m)$$

we obtain

$$n_0 + n_1 = \theta_k(X_1, \ldots X_m) - \theta_k(x_1 \ldots x_m).$$

This brings us to another significant remark. The functional systems

$$\alpha_k = \theta_k(X_1, \ldots X_m) - \theta_k(x_1, \ldots x_m), \qquad k = 1, 2 \ldots m$$

and

$$\beta_k = \theta_k(X_1, \ldots X_m) - \theta_k(x_1 \ldots x_m)$$

belong to the same quantitative domain; for the addition of their quantities leads to the functional system

$$\alpha_k + \beta_k = \theta_k(X_1 \ldots X_m) - \theta_k(x_1 \ldots x_m), \qquad k = 1, 2 \ldots m.$$

Although the quantities of these functional systems can be added, the relations between them can nevertheless be expressed numerically only if the constants β_k are successively proportional to the α_k. There is therefore an m-fold multiplicity of functional systems in this quantitative domain. To the $(m-1)$-fold multiplicity of possible relations between the α_k corresponds the very same multiplicity of quantitative subdomains of functional systems whose quantities can be compared numerically among themselves. We can visualize this by means of a spatial picture. We can regard straight lines in space as belonging to the same quantitative system with respect to their length and direction if we form a sum of them by combining them | in such a way that all   12 directions remain unchanged while the length and direction of the sum is determined by the free points of origin and the free end points of the terms. There is then a threefold multiplicity of quantities and a twofold multiplicity of directions. Every system of relations between the α_k can be compared to a direction in space; for only straight lines with the same direction can be compared numerically. Following this spatial analogy, we can therefore ascribe m dimensions to any quantitative domain of functional systems with m variables, a number which doubles when we also take complex numbers into account. We could now embark on similar considerations as in the case of functions of one variable; but since this would often lead to repetition, we shall instead take a special kind of function, viz. the simplest and most important, as the main object of our investigations.

Linear Homogeneous Functions

6 Since linear homogeneous functions do not change their form when substituted within themselves, we also know the form of the infinitely small functional system and of the functions φ. Let

$$\varphi_1 = c_{11}x_1 + c_{12}x_2 + c_{13}x_3 \ldots c_{1m}x_m$$

$$\varphi_2 = c_{21}x_1 + c_{22}x_2 + c_{23}x_3 \ldots c_{2m}x_m$$

$$\vdots$$

$$\varphi_m = c_{m1}x_1 + c_{m2}x_2 + c_{m3}x_3 \ldots c_{mm}x_m.$$

Our task is then to integrate the differential equations

$$\frac{dX_1}{dn} = c_{11}X_1 + c_{12}X_2 \ldots c_{1m}X_m$$

$$\frac{dX_2}{dn} = c_{21}X_1 + c_{22}X_2 \ldots c_{2m}X_m$$

$$\vdots$$

$$\frac{dX_m}{dn} = c_{m1}X_1 + c_{m2}X_2 \ldots c_{mm}X_m$$

The integrals have the form

$$X_k = A_0 e^{\lambda_0 n} + A_1 e^{\lambda_1 n} \ldots A_{m-1} e^{\lambda_{m-1} n},$$

where $\lambda_0, \lambda_1, \ldots \lambda_{m-1}$ mean the roots of the equation

$$\begin{vmatrix} c_{11} - \lambda & c_{12} & c_{13} \ldots c_{1m} \\ c_{21} & c_{22} - \lambda & c_{23} \ldots c_{2m} \\ \vdots & & \\ c_{m1} & c_{m2} & c_{m3} \ldots c_{mm} - \lambda \end{vmatrix} = 0$$

and all roots are at first assumed to be different from one another. In order to determine the A, we form successively the higher differential quotients of X_k with respect to n for $n = 0$. From the recursive formula

$$\frac{\mathrm{d}^r X_k}{\mathrm{d}n^r} = \sum_{i=1}^{i=m} \left\{ c_{ki} \frac{\mathrm{d}^{r-1} X_i}{\mathrm{d}n^{r-1}} \right\}$$

it appears that the higher differential quotients of X_k with respect to n result from the repeated operation of the functional system |

$$\sum_{k=1}^{k=m} \{c_{1k} X_k\}, \sum_{k=1}^{k=m} \{c_{2k} X_k\}, \dots \sum_{k=1}^{k=m} \{c_{mk} X_k\} \qquad 13$$

upon the X, and hence, that the $\mathrm{d}^r X_k / \mathrm{d}n^r$ are linear homogeneous functions of the X whose quantity is r times the quantity of the above functional system. Let this quantity be designated by

$$\frac{\mathrm{d}^r X_k}{\mathrm{d}n^r} = \sum_{i=1}^{i=m} \{c_{ki}(r) X_i\},$$

where $c_{ki}(1) = c_{ki}$ and

$$c_{ki}(0) = \begin{cases} 1 & \text{for} \quad k = i \\ 0 & \text{for} \quad k \gtrless i \end{cases}, \quad c_{ki}(r+1) = \sum_{s=1}^{s=m} \{c_{ks}(r) c_{si}\}.$$

Then

$$X_k = \sum_{r=0}^{r=m-1} \{A_r e^{\lambda_r n}\}$$

$$x_k = (X_k)_{n=0} = \sum_{r=0}^{r=m-1} \{A_r\} = \sum_{i=1}^{i=m} \{c_{ki}(0) x_i\}$$

$$\left(\frac{\mathrm{d}X_k}{\mathrm{d}n}\right)_{n=0} = \sum_{i=0}^{r=m-1} \{A_r \lambda_r\} = \sum_{i=1}^{i=m} \{c_{ki}(1) x_i\}$$

$$\vdots \qquad \vdots \qquad \vdots$$

$$\left(\frac{\mathrm{d}^{m-1} X_k}{\mathrm{d}n^{m-1}}\right)_{n=0} = \sum_{r=0}^{r=m-1} \{A_r \lambda_r^{m-1}\} = \sum_{i=1}^{i=m} \{c_{ki}(m-1) x_i\}$$

By eliminating the A we get

$$\begin{vmatrix} X_k, & e^{\lambda_0 n}, & e^{\lambda_1 n}, & \dots & e^{\lambda_{m-1} n} \\ \sum_{i=1}^{i=m} \{c_{ki}(0) x_i\}, & \lambda_0^0, & \lambda_1^0, & \dots & \lambda_{m-1}^0 \\ \sum_{i=1}^{i=m} \{c_{ki}(1) x_i\}, & \lambda_0^1, & \lambda_1^1, & \dots & \lambda_{m-1}^1 \\ \vdots & \vdots & \vdots & \vdots & \vdots \\ \sum_{i=1}^{i=m} \{c_{ki}(m-1) x_i\}, & \lambda_0^{m-1}, & \lambda_1^{m-1}, & \dots & \lambda_{m-1}^{m-1} \end{vmatrix} = 0.$$

If we let l_{qr} designate the factor of λ_r^q in

$$L = \begin{vmatrix} \lambda_0^0, & \lambda_1^0 & \cdots & \lambda_{m-1}^0 \\ \lambda_0^1, & \lambda_1^1 & \cdots & \lambda_{m-1}^1 \\ \vdots & \vdots & & \vdots \\ \lambda_0^{m-1}, & \lambda_1^{m-1} & \cdots & \lambda_{m-1}^{m-1} \end{vmatrix},$$

we can also write the equation we have found as follows:

$$LX_k = \sum_{i=1}^{i=m} \left\{ \sum_{r=0}^{r=m-1} \left\{ \sum_{s=0}^{s=m-1} \{ c_{ki}(s) l_{sr} e^{\lambda_r n} x_i \} \right\} \right\}.$$

Now if the way a_{ki} depends on

$$a_{ki} = \sum_{r=0}^{r=m-1} \left\{ \sum_{s=0}^{s=m-1} \{ c_{ki}(s) l_{sr} e^{\lambda_r} \} \right\}$$

is analogous to the way $c_{ki}(n)$ depends on c_{ki}, then |

$$a_{ki}(n) = \sum_{r=0}^{r=m-1} \left\{ \sum_{s=0}^{s=m-1} \left\{ \frac{l_{sr} e^{\lambda_r n}}{L} c_{ki}(s) \right\} \right\}.$$

And the functional system which has n times the quantity of the functional system

$$X_1 = \sum_{i=1}^{i=m} \{ a_{1i} x_i \}, \qquad X_2 = \sum_{i=1}^{i=m} \{ a_{2i} x_i \} \dots X_m = \sum_{i=1}^{i=m} \{ a_{mi} x_i \}$$

is

$$X_1 = \sum_{i=1}^{i=m} \{ a_{1i}(n) x_i \}, \qquad X_2 = \sum_{i=1}^{i=m} \{ a_{2i}(n) x_i \} \dots X_m = \sum_{i=0}^{i=m} \{ a_{mi}(n) x_i \}.$$

It may seem as if this solution of the problem was an illusory one because it contains the expression $c_{ki}(s)$, whose solution already pre-supposes the solution. But $c_{ki}(s)$ is required only for a finite number of integral values of s, whereas the problem is hereby solved for an infinite number of arbitrary values of n. Moreover, the m values of $c_{ki}(s)$ are, in part, known immediately and, in part, easily calculated from the $c_{ki}(l)$. There is another more significant drawback, namely that our formula presupposes a knowledge of the values of $c_{ki}(l)$, which are not given for the most part. If our task were to set up the quantitative equation of the functional system

$$X_1 = \sum_{i=1}^{i=m} \{ a_{1i} x_i \}, \qquad X_2 = \sum_{i=1}^{i=m} \{ a_{2i} x_i \} \dots X_m = \sum_{i=1}^{i=m} \{ a_{mi} x_i \},$$

we would have to eliminate the c_{ki} from the equations

$$La_{ki} = \sum_{r=0}^{r=m-1} \left\{ \sum_{s=0}^{s=m-1} \{c_{ki}(s)l_{sr}e^{\lambda_r}\} \right\} \tag{1}$$

and

$$La_{ki}(n) = \sum_{r=0}^{r=m-1} \left\{ \sum_{s=0}^{s=m-1} \{c_{ki}(s)l_{sr}e^{\lambda_r n}\} \right\} \tag{2}$$

This can be done in the following way.

To begin with, $\zeta_0 = e^{\lambda_0}, \zeta_1 = e^{\lambda_1} \ldots \zeta_{m-1} = e^{\lambda_{m-1}}$ are the roots of the equation

$$\begin{vmatrix} a_{11} - \zeta, & a_{12}, & a_{13}, \ldots a_{1m} \\ a_{21} & a_{22} - \zeta, & a_{23}, \ldots a_{2m} \\ \vdots & \vdots & \vdots \\ a_{m1}, & a_{m2}, & a_{m3}, \ldots a_{mm} - \zeta \end{vmatrix} = 0; \tag{3}$$

for the system of – not entirely vanishing – values $y_1, y_2 \ldots y_m$, which satisfies the equations

$$\sum_{k=1}^{k=m} \{c_{1k}y_k\} = \lambda_v y_1$$

$$\sum_{k=1}^{k=m} \{c_{2k}y_k\} = \lambda_v y_2$$

$$\vdots$$

$$\sum_{k-1}^{k=m} \{c_{mk}y_k\} = \lambda_v y_m \tag{4}$$

also satisfies the equations |

$$\sum_{k=1}^{k=m} \{a_{1k}y_k\} = e^{\lambda_v} y_1 \qquad 15$$

$$\sum_{k=1}^{k=m} \{a_{2k}y_k\} = e^{\lambda_v} y_2$$

$$\vdots$$

$$\sum_{k=1}^{k=m} \{a_{mk}y_k\} = e^{\lambda_v} y_m,$$

and this is possible only if e^{λ_v} is a root of the equation for ζ. Now in order to prove our assertion with respect to the y, we replace a_{pk} by c_{pk}

according to (1). We then have

$$\sum_{k=1}^{k=m}\{a_{pk}y_k\}=\frac{1}{L}\sum_{k=1}^{k=m}\left\{\sum_{r=0}^{r=m-1}\left\{\sum_{s=0}^{s=m-1}\{c_{pk}(s)l_{sr}e^{\lambda_r}y_k\}\right\}\right\}.$$

Now from premise (4) it follows that

$$\sum_{k=1}^{k=m}\{c_{pk}(s)y_k\}=\lambda_v^s y_p.$$

When this is introduced, we get

$$\frac{1}{L}\sum_{r=0}^{r=m-1}\left\{\sum_{s=0}^{s=m-1}\{l_{sr}\lambda_v^s e^{\lambda_r}y_p\}\right\}.$$

Further, because of the meaning of l_{sr},

$$\sum_{s=0}^{s=m-1}\{l_{sr}\lambda_v^s\}=\begin{cases}0, & \text{if } r\gtrless v\\ L, & \text{if } r=v.\end{cases}$$

Our last double sum therefore becomes

$$e^{\lambda_v}y_p,$$

which is what was to be proved. We therefore put $\zeta_v=e^{\lambda_v}$ and write

$$a_{ki}(n)=\sum_{r=0}^{r=m-1}\{\zeta_r^n v_r\},$$

where the v_r are still to be determined. We eliminate the v_r from the equations

$$
\begin{array}{lllllll}
a_{ki}(n) & = & \zeta_0^n v_0 & +\zeta_1^n v_1 & +\zeta_2^n v_2 & \cdots & +\zeta_{m-1}^n v_{m-1}\\
a_{ki}(0) & = & v_0 & + v_1 & + v_2 & \cdots & + v_{m-1}\\
a_{ki}(1) & = & \zeta_0 v_0 & +\zeta_1 v_1 & +\zeta_2 v_2 & \cdots & +\zeta_{m-1} v_{m-1}\\
\vdots & & \vdots & \vdots & \vdots & & \vdots\\
a_{ki}(m-1) & = & \zeta_0^{m-1} v_0 & +\zeta_1^{m-1} v_1 & +\zeta_2^{m-1} v_2 & \cdots & +\zeta_{m-1}^{m-1} v_{m-1}.
\end{array}
$$

This gives us

$$
\begin{vmatrix}
a_{ki}(n), & \zeta_0^n, & \zeta_1^n, & \cdots & \zeta_{m-1}^n\\
a_{ki}(0), & \zeta_0^0, & \zeta_1^0, & \cdots & \zeta_{m-1}^0\\
a_{ki}(1), & \zeta_0^1, & \zeta_1^1, & \cdots & \zeta_{m-1}^1\\
\vdots & \vdots & \vdots & & \vdots\\
a_{ki}(m-1), & \zeta_0^{m-1}, & \zeta_1^{m-1}, & \cdots & \zeta_{m-1}^{m-1}
\end{vmatrix}=0, \qquad (5)
$$

whereby $a_{ki}(n)$ is determined by the m values $a_{ki}(0), a_{ki}(1) \ldots a_{ki}(m-1)$, which can be calculated once and for all from the $a_{ki}(1)$. If by z_{sr} we designate the factor of ζ_r^s in the determinant |

$$
Z = \begin{vmatrix}
\zeta_0^0, & \zeta_1^0, & \cdots & \zeta_{m-1}^0 \\
\zeta_0^1, & \zeta_1^1, & \cdots & \zeta_{m-1}^1 \\
\vdots & \vdots & & \vdots \\
\zeta_0^{m-1}, & \zeta_1^{m-1}, & \cdots & \zeta_{m-1}^{m-1}
\end{vmatrix} ,
$$

16

we can also write the result as follows:

$$
a_{ki}(n) = \frac{1}{Z} \sum_{r=0}^{r=m-1} \left\{ \sum_{s=0}^{s=m-1} \{a_{ki}(s) z_{sr} \zeta_r^n\} \right\} . \tag{6}
$$

This solves the problem for the case where the ζ are different from one another. Where two or more of the roots ζ are equal to one another, (5) vanishes into an identity. In this case, the value of $a_{ki}(n)$ must be determined by differentiation. Suppose, e.g., that $\zeta_1 = \zeta_0$. We first differentiate (5) with respect to ζ_1 and then put $\zeta_1 = \zeta_0$. We thus get the equation

$$
\begin{vmatrix}
a_{ki}(n), & \zeta_0^n, & n\zeta_0^{n-1}, & \zeta_2^n & \cdots & \zeta_{m-1}^n \\
a_{ki}(0), & \zeta_0^0, & 0, & \zeta_2^0 & \cdots & \zeta_{m-1}^0 \\
a_{ki}(1), & \zeta_0^1, & 1, & \zeta_2^1 & \cdots & \zeta_{m-1}^1 \\
\vdots & \vdots & \vdots & \vdots & & \vdots \\
a_{ki}(m-1), & \zeta_0^{m-1}, & (m-1)\zeta_0^{m-2}, & \zeta_2^{m-1} & \cdots & \zeta_{m-1}^{m-1}
\end{vmatrix} = 0 \tag{6b}
$$

for $a_{ki}(n)$. This gives us a general view of how things would turn out in the most general case where the ζ were equal to one another in groups.

Let us add some corollaries to equation (6).

Since

$$
X_k = \sum_{i=1}^{i=m} \{a_{ki}(n)x_i\}
$$

and

$$
\left(\frac{d^q X_k}{dn^q} \right)_{n=0} = \sum_{i=1}^{i=m} \{c_{ki}(q)x_i\},
$$

therefore

$$
\left(\frac{d^q a_{ik}(n)}{dn^q} \right)_{n=0} = c_{ki}(q)
$$

and therefore

$$c_{ki}(q) = \frac{1}{Z} \sum_{r=0}^{r=m-1} \left\{ \sum_{s=0}^{s=m-1} \{a_{ki}(s)z_{sr}(\lg \zeta_r)^q\} \right\},$$

whereby the c_{ki} are expressed by means of the a_{ki}.
Further, by comparing (6) with (2) we get

$$\frac{1}{Z} \sum_{s=0}^{s=m-1} \{a_{ki}(s)z_{sr}\} = \frac{1}{L} \sum_{s=0}^{s=m-1} \{c_{ki}(s)l_{sr}\}.$$

If we put $n = -1$ in (6), we obtain

$$a_{ki}(-1) = \frac{1}{Z} \sum_{r=0}^{r=m-1} \left\{ \sum_{s=0}^{s=m-1} \left\{ \frac{a_{ki}(s)z_{sr}}{\zeta_r} \right\} \right\}. \quad |$$

17   If we now remember that from the equations

$$y_k = \sum_{i=1}^{i=m} \{a_{ki}x_i\}, \qquad k = 1, 2, 3 \ldots m$$

it follows that

$$x_k = \sum_{i=1}^{i=m} \{a_{ki}(-1)y_i\},$$

then we see that

$$a_{ki}(-1) = \frac{A_{ik}}{A},$$

where A means the determinant of the $a_{ki}(1)$, and A_{ik} the factor of $a_{ki}(1)$ in the development of A. We can therefore express the subdeterminant A_{ik} in the following way:

$$A_{ik} = \frac{A}{Z} \sum_{r=0}^{r=m-1} \left\{ \sum_{s=0}^{s=m-1} \left\{ \frac{a_{ki}(s)z_{sr}}{\zeta_r} \right\} \right\}. \tag{7}$$

If we write equation (3) in the form below:

$$\zeta^m = \sum_{q=1}^{q=m} \{\zeta^{m-q}p_q\},$$

then it follows that

$$\sum_{q=1}^{q=m} \{a_{ki}(n-q)p_q\} = \sum_{q=1}^{q=m} \left\{ \sum_{r=0}^{r=m-1} \left\{ \sum_{s=0}^{s=m-1} \{a_{ki}(s)z_{sr}p_q\zeta_r^{n-q}\} \right\} \right\}$$

$$= \sum_{q=1}^{q=m} \left\{ \sum_{r=0}^{r=m-1} \left\{ \sum_{s=0}^{s=m-1} \{a_{ki}(s)z_{sr}\zeta_r^{n-m}\zeta_r^{m-q}p_q\} \right\} \right\}$$

$$= \sum_{r=0}^{r=m-1} \left\{ \sum_{s=0}^{s=m-1} \{a_{ki}(s)z_{sr}\zeta_r^n\} \right\}$$

$$= a_{ki}(n).$$

The equation

$$\sum_{q=1}^{q=m} \{a_{ki}(n-q)p_q\} = a_{ki}(n) \tag{8}$$

gives us a new relation between the subdeterminants A_{ik} and the $a_{ki}(s)$ if we let $n = m - 1$.

Our formulae for $a_{ki}(n)$ contain a general law of inversion of the determinants, since for an arbitrary n

$$\begin{vmatrix} a_{11}, a_{12} \dots a_{1m} \\ a_{21}, a_{22} \dots a_{2m} \\ \vdots \\ a_{m1}, a_{m2} \dots a_{mm} \end{vmatrix}^n = \begin{vmatrix} a_{11}(n), a_{12}(n) \dots a_{1m}(n) \\ a_{21}(n), a_{22}(n) \dots a_{2m}(n) \\ \vdots \\ a_{m1}(n), a_{m2}(n) \dots a_{mm}(n) \end{vmatrix}.$$

The case of non-homogeneous linear functions can be reduced to that of homogeneous ones. If our task is to set up, e.g., the quantitative equation of the functional system

$$X_1 = a_{11}x_1 + a_{12}x_2 + a_{13}$$

$$X_2 = a_{21}x_1 + a_{22}x_2 + a_{23},$$

we consider instead the homogeneous one

$$X_1 = a_{11}x_1 + a_{12}x_2 + a_{13}x_3$$

$$X_2 = a_{21}x_1 + a_{22}x_2 + a_{23}x_3$$

$$X_3 = \qquad\qquad x_3. \quad |$$

III SPECIAL CASES AND APPLICATIONS

7   In the case of two variables we can determine the ζ by means of the   18 equation

$$\zeta^2 - (a_{11} + a_{22})\zeta + a_{11}a_{22} - a_{12}a_{21} = 0.$$

Let its roots be ζ_0 and ζ_1. Then

$$Z = \begin{vmatrix} 1 & 1 \\ \zeta_0 & \zeta_1 \end{vmatrix} = \zeta_1 - \zeta_0.$$

$$z_{00}=\zeta_1, z_{01}=-\zeta_0, z_{10}=-1, z_{11}=1.$$

Consequently

$$a_{11}(n)=\frac{(\zeta_1-a_{11})\zeta_0^n+(-\zeta_0+a_{11})\zeta_1^n}{\zeta_1-\zeta_0},$$

$$a_{12}(n)=\frac{-a_{12}\zeta_0^n+a_{12}\zeta_1^n}{\zeta_1-\zeta_0},$$

$$a_{21}(n)=\frac{-a_{21}\zeta_0^n+a_{21}\zeta_1^n}{\zeta_1-\zeta_0},$$

$$a_{22}(n)=\frac{(\zeta_1-a_{22})\zeta_0^n+(-\zeta_0+a_{22})\zeta_1^n}{\zeta_1-\zeta_0}.$$

(1)

Here

$$\zeta_0=\frac{a_{11}+a_{22}+\sqrt{R}}{2}, \qquad \zeta_1=\frac{a_{11}+a_{22}-\sqrt{R}}{2}, \qquad R=(a_{11}-a_{22})^2+4a_{12}a_{21}.$$

If we can develop ζ_0 and ζ_1 according to the powers of $\sqrt{R}$, then the ittational cancels out and we obtain

$$a_{11}(n)=\frac{(a_{11}-a_{22})V+(a_{11}+a_{22})W}{2^n},$$

$$a_{12}(n)=\frac{a_{12}V}{2^{n-1}}, \qquad a_{21}(n)=\frac{a_{21}V}{2^{n-1}},$$

(2)

$$a_{22}(n)=\frac{(a_{22}-a_{11})V+(a_{22}+a_{11})W}{2^n},$$

where

$$V=\sum_{k=0}^{k=\infty}\left\{\binom{n}{2k+1}(a_{11}+a_{22})^{n-2k-1}R^k\right\}$$

$$W=\sum_{k=0}^{k=\infty}\left\{\binom{n}{2k}(a_{11}+a_{22})^{n-2k-1}R^k\right\}.$$

This allows us to test some formulae we developed earlier. For $n=-1$ we get

$$a_{11}(-1)=\frac{(\zeta_1-a_{11})\zeta_1+(-\zeta_0+a_{11})\zeta_0}{(\zeta_1-\zeta_0)\zeta_0\zeta_1}$$

$$= \frac{\zeta_1 + \zeta_0 - a_{11}}{\zeta_0 \zeta_1}$$

$$= \frac{a_{22}}{a_{11} a_{22} - a_{12} a_{21}}$$

$$= \frac{A_{11}}{A} a_{12}(-1) = \frac{-a_{12}}{a_{11} a_{22} - a_{12} a_{21}}$$

$$= \frac{A_{21}}{A},$$

where

$$A = \begin{vmatrix} a_{11} & a_{12} \\ a_{21} & a_{22} \end{vmatrix}$$

and A_{11}, A_{21} etc. mean the subdeterminants. |

If we are to apply formula (8), section 6, we have to put $p_1 = a_{11} + a_{22}$ 19
and $p_2 = -A$, and we then obtain for $n = 1$

$$a_{ki}(1) = a_{ki}(0)(a_{11} + a_{22}) + a_{ki}(-1)(-A)$$

$$a_{11}(1) = 1 \cdot (a_{11} + a_{22}) + \frac{a_{22}}{A}(-A) = a_{11}$$

$$a_{12}(1) = 0 \cdot (a_{11} + a_{22}) + \frac{-a_{12}}{A}(-A) = a_{12}$$

etc.

A quantitative domain of functions with two variables must, disregarding the imaginary, have two dimensions. To follow this up in our case, we go on to derive the quantitative equation by substitution according to the schema

$$\theta_0(X, Y) - \theta_0(x, y) = n$$
$$\theta_1(X, y) - \theta_1(x, y) = n.$$

Suppose

$$\theta_0(X, Y) = \frac{\lg(X + p_0 Y)}{\lg \zeta_0}$$

$$\theta_1(X, Y) = \frac{\lg(X + p_1 Y)}{\lg \zeta_1}.$$

The solution of the equations

$$\lg(X+p_0Y)-\lg(x+p_0y)=n\lg\zeta_0$$

$$\lg(X+p_1Y)-\lg(x+p_1y)=n\lg\zeta_1$$

for X and Y yields

$$X=\frac{p_1\zeta_0^n-p_0\zeta_1^n}{p_1-p_0}x+\frac{p_0p_1(\zeta_0^n-\zeta_1^n)}{p_1-p_0}y$$

$$Y=\frac{-(\zeta_0^n-\zeta_1^n)}{p_1-p_0}x+\frac{p_1\zeta_1^n-p_0\zeta_0^n}{p_1-p_0}y.$$

Now we know, from what was said earlier, that the quantities of two such functional systems can still be added even when $\lg\zeta_0/\lg\zeta_1$ is changed, but that they can be compared numerically only as long as this relationship has the same value.

All functional systems with the same p_0 and p_1 belong therefore to the same quantitative domain. For $n=1$, we put

$$a_{11}=\frac{p_1\zeta_0-p_0\zeta_1}{p_1-p_0}$$

$$a_{12}=\frac{p_0p_1(\zeta_0-\zeta_1)}{p_1-p_0}$$

$$a_{21}=\frac{-(\zeta_0-\zeta_1)}{p_1-p_0}$$

$$a_{22}=\frac{p_1\zeta_1-p_0\zeta_0}{p_1-p_0},$$

from which it follows that

$$p_0+p_1=-\frac{a_{11}-a_{22}}{a_{21}},\quad p_0p_1=-\frac{a_{12}}{a_{21}}.\quad|$$

20   Thus the quantities of two functional systems

$$X=a_{11}x+a_{12}y,\qquad Y=a_{21}x+a_{22}y$$

and

$$X=b_{11}x+b_{12}y,\qquad Y=b_{21}x+b_{22}y$$

can be added as soon as

$$\frac{a_{11}-a_{22}}{a_{21}}=\frac{b_{11}-b_{22}}{b_{21}},\qquad\frac{a_{12}}{a_{21}}=\frac{b_{12}}{b_{21}};$$

i.e., it makes no difference whether the first is substituted for the second or the other way round, as can easily be verified by an example. But in either case two of the four constants remain arbitrary. There is therefore a twofold multiplicity of functional systems within the same quantitative domain.

Let us now proceed to some applications.

Periodic Continued Fractions

If we are to calculate z, given the approximation formula

$$X = \varphi(x),$$

by means of which we can calculate from an approximate value x, whose margin of error does not exceed a certain quantity, another even more approximate value X, then

$$x, \varphi(x), \varphi\varphi(x), \varphi\varphi\varphi(x) \ldots$$

are the approximate values of z. Thus, given the quantitative equation of $\varphi(x)$, we can calculate any approximate value we like. Similarly, with the help of quantitative equations of a functional system of several variables we can calculate by approximation several quantities at the same time. Let us apply this to periodic continued fractions. Let us represent the irrational u by a periodic continued fraction. Let P_r/Q_r be the approximate fraction which at first precedes the period and P_s/Q_s the approximate fraction which terminates the period. Then

$$u = \frac{(P_s Q_{r-1} - Q_r P_{s-1})u + P_r P_{s-1} - P_s P_{r-1}}{(Q_s Q_{r-1} - Q_r Q_{s-1})u + P_r Q_{s-1} - Q_s P_{r-1}}.$$

If we replace u on the right-hand side by an approximate value, then this expression gives us an even more approximate value on the left-hand side in place of u. We have already considered the above function, which we will write for short as

$$\frac{a_{11}z + a_{12}}{a_{21}z + a_{22}},$$

in considering functions of one variable. However, the quantitative equation assumes a more convenient shape if instead of dealing with the fraction we deal with the two linear homogeneous functions

$$X_1 = a_{11}x_1 + a_{12}x_2$$

$$X_2 = a_{21}x_1 + a_{22}x_2$$

by separating the numerator and the denominator. Our formulae (2), which we established above, then immediately give us the solution of the problem.

Functional Equations

In order to show how functional equations can be solved by setting up quantitative equations, we consider the equation

$$f(n) = \sum_{i=1}^{i=m} \{a_i f(n-i)\}, \quad |$$

21 and seek to determine the function f. We put

$$f(k) = X_1, f(k-i) = X_{i+1} = x_i.$$

This leads to the functional system

$$X_1 = a_1 x_1 + a_2 x_2 + a_3 x_3 \ldots a_m x_m$$

$$X_2 = x_1$$

$$X_3 = x_2$$

$$\vdots$$

$$X_m = x^{m-1}$$

We now need to know m special values, say

$$f(0), f(1), \ldots f(m-1).$$

If we substitute these for $x_m, x_{m-1} \ldots x_1$, we obtain $X_1 = f(m)$. If after finding $X_1, X_2 \ldots X_m$ we substitute them in place of x_1, x_2, x_m, we get $f(m+1)$. This shows that the n-fold operation of the functional system will give us the value of $f(m+n-1)$. Our task is therefore to set up the quantitative equation of our functional system, which calls for the solution of the equation

$$\zeta^m - a_1 \zeta^{m-1} - a_2 \zeta^{m-2} \ldots - a_m = 0.$$

Let Schimper's series

$$0, 1, 1, 2, 3, 5, 8 \ldots$$

serve as an example.

We obtain the general term by solving the functional equation

$$f(n) = f(n-1) + f(n-2).$$

We must therefore set up the quantitative equation of

$$X_1 = x_1 + x_2$$
$$X_2 = x_1.$$

The equation

$$\zeta^2 - \zeta - 1 = 0$$

has the roots

$$\zeta_0 = \frac{1+\sqrt{5}}{2}, \qquad \zeta_1 = \frac{1-\sqrt{5}}{2}.$$

Finally, if we put $x_1 = 1$ and $x_2 = 0$ while counting x_1 as the 0th and x_2 as the (-1)th term, then the general term is $a_{11}(n)$, for which we must put, according to a formula established above,

$$a_{11}(n) = \frac{\left(\dfrac{1+\sqrt{5}}{2}\right)\left(\dfrac{1+\sqrt{5}}{2}\right)^n - \left(\dfrac{1-\sqrt{5}}{2}\right)\left(\dfrac{1-\sqrt{5}}{2}\right)^n}{\sqrt{5}}$$

$$a_{11}(n) = \frac{1}{\sqrt{5}}\left[\left(\frac{1+\sqrt{5}}{2}\right)^{n+1} - \left(\frac{1-\sqrt{5}}{2}\right)^{n+1}\right].$$

Let us use some further examples to illustrate serial development and the summation of a series with the help of quantitative equations.

Development of sin nα

If we call

$$\sin k\alpha = x, \quad \cos k\alpha = y$$
$$\cos \alpha = a_{11}, \quad \sin \alpha = a_{12}$$
$$-\sin \alpha = a_{21}, \quad \cos \alpha = a_{22}, \quad |$$

then

22

$$\sin(k+1)\alpha = a_{11}x + a_{12}y$$
$$\cos(k+1)\alpha = a_{21}x + a_{22}y$$

and consequently

$$\sin(k+n)\alpha = a_{11}(n)x + a_{12}(n)y$$
$$\cos(k+n)\alpha = a_{21}(n)x + a_{22}(n)y.$$

Finally, if we put $k=0$, i.e., $x=0$ and $y=1$, then

$$\sin n\alpha = a_{12}(n) = \frac{a_{12}}{2^{n-1}} V.$$

To calculate V, we require the values $a_{11} + a_{22} = 2\cos\alpha$ and $R = (a_{11} - a_{22})^2 + 4a_{12}a_{21} = -4\sin^2\alpha$. Then

$$V = \sum_{k=0}^{k=\infty} \left\{ \binom{n}{2k+1} (2\cos\alpha)^{n-2k-1} (-4\sin^2\alpha)^k \right\}$$

$$\sin n\alpha = \sum_{k=0}^{k=\infty} \left\{ \binom{n}{2k+1} \cos\alpha^{n-2k-1} \sin\alpha^{2k+1} (-1)^k \right\}.$$

While this derivation comes essentially to the same thing as the ordinary one, it nevertheless appears here to be motivated by general considerations, whereas elsewhere the result presents itself as more of a by-product of an investigation directed at a different goal.

Summation of the Series

$$\sum_{r=0}^{r=n-1} \{\cos(\alpha + r\varepsilon)\}.$$

If we call x_1 the sum of the first k terms and x_2 the $(k+1)$th term, namely

$$x_2 = \cos(\alpha + k\varepsilon)$$

$$x_3 = \sin(\alpha + k\varepsilon),$$

then our task is to set up the quantitative equation of the functional system

$$X_1 = x_1 + x_2$$

$$X_2 = \cos\varepsilon \cdot x_2 - \sin\varepsilon \cdot x_3$$

$$X_3 = \sin\varepsilon \cdot x_2 + \cos\varepsilon \cdot x_3$$

and, finally, to put $k=0$, $x_1 = 0$, $x_2 = \cos\alpha$ and $x_3 = \sin\alpha$. The sum we are looking for is then

$$a_{12}(n)\cos\alpha + a_{13}(n)\sin\alpha.$$

The roots of the cubic equation

$$\zeta^3 - \zeta^2(1 + 2\cos\varepsilon) + \zeta(1 + 2\cos\varepsilon) - 1 = 0$$

are

$$\zeta_0 = \cos \varepsilon + i \sin \varepsilon, \qquad \zeta_1 = \cos \varepsilon - i \sin \varepsilon, \qquad \zeta_2 = 1.$$

$a_{12}(n)$ is determined by the equation

$$0 = \begin{vmatrix} a_{12}(n), & \zeta_0^n, & \zeta_1^n, & 1 \\ 0, & 1, & 1, & 1 \\ 1, & \zeta_0, & \zeta_1, & 1 \\ 1 + \cos \varepsilon, & \zeta_0^2, & \zeta_1^2, & 1 \end{vmatrix}, \qquad \Big|$$

which can be transformed into   23

$$0 = \begin{vmatrix} a_{12}(n), & 2i \sin n\varepsilon, & 2(\cos n\varepsilon - 1), & 1 \\ 0, & 0, & 0, & 1 \\ 1, & 2i \sin \varepsilon, & 2(\cos \varepsilon - 1), & 1 \\ 1 + \cos \varepsilon, & 4i \sin \varepsilon \cos \varepsilon, & 4(\cos \varepsilon - 1)(\cos \varepsilon + 1), & 1 \end{vmatrix},$$

$$0 = \begin{vmatrix} a_{12}(n), & 2i \sin n\varepsilon, & 2(\cos n\varepsilon - 1) \\ 1, & 2i \sin \varepsilon, & 2(\cos \varepsilon - 1) \\ 1 - \cos \varepsilon, & 0, & 4(\cos \varepsilon - 1) \end{vmatrix},$$

from which it follows that

$$a_{12}(n) = \frac{\sin n\varepsilon(\cos \varepsilon + 1) - \sin \varepsilon(\cos n\varepsilon - 1)}{2 \sin \varepsilon},$$

or after the introduction of the half-angles

$$a_{12}(n) = \frac{\cos \dfrac{n-1}{2} \varepsilon \cdot \sin \dfrac{n}{2} \varepsilon}{\sin \dfrac{\varepsilon}{2}}.$$

We likewise find that

$$a_{13}(n) = -\frac{\sin \dfrac{n-1}{2} \varepsilon \cdot \sin \dfrac{n}{2} \varepsilon}{\sin \dfrac{\varepsilon}{2}}.$$

The sum we are looking for is therefore

$$\frac{\cos \left(\alpha + \dfrac{n-1}{2} \varepsilon \right) \sin \dfrac{n}{2} \varepsilon}{\sin \dfrac{\varepsilon}{2}}.$$

In order to show how our concept of the quantity of a function can be brought into connection with the geometrical quantities of lengths and angles, we consider the displacement of a rigid body, as represented analytically by the formulae describing the transformation of a rectangular spatial coordinate system into another one of the same kind.

Displacement of a Rigid Body

If we let the quantity of the system of transformation formulae increase continuously and uniformly, then this is equivalent in meaning to a movement of a solid body. The linear and angular quantities generated by this movement thus enter into relations with the quantity of the functional system.

If we designate the new coordinates by X_1, X_2, X_3 and also introduce the pseudo-variables X_4 and x_4 so as to make the formulae homogeneous, then the transformation formulae are

$$X_1 = a_{11}x_1 + a_{12}x_2 + a_{13}x_3 + a_{14}x_4$$

$$X_2 = a_{21}x_1 + a_{22}x_2 + a_{23}x_3 + a_{24}x_4$$

$$X_3 = a_{31}x_1 + a_{32}x_2 + a_{33}x_3 + a_{34}x_4$$

$$X_4 = \qquad\qquad\qquad\qquad\qquad x_4,$$

where a_{ik} means the cosine of the angle between the axes X_i and x_k in case $i < 4$ and $k < 4$. |

24   In what follows, let the subscripts i, k, l, r be always smaller than 4, and let r always refer to a summation. We then have

$$\Sigma a_{rk}a_{ri} = \begin{cases} 0, & \text{if } i \gtrless k \\ 1, & \text{if } i = k. \end{cases}$$

This system of equations permits many simplifications. To begin with, we also have

$$\Sigma a_{kr}(-1)a_{ri} = \begin{cases} 0, & \text{if } i \gtrless k \\ 1, & \text{if } i = k, \end{cases}$$

from which it follows that

$$a_{ki}(-1) = a_{ik}.$$

Further, the determinant

$$\Delta = \begin{vmatrix} a_{11}, & a_{12}, & a_{13} \\ a_{21}, & a_{22}, & a_{23} \\ a_{31}, & a_{32}, & a_{33} \end{vmatrix}$$

is equal to $+1$ or -1. But only in case it is $+1$ do we get a genuine displacement, whereas in the case where it is -1 the body is transformed at the same time into its symmetrical mirror image. Let $\Delta = 1$. For ζ we then have the equation

$$(\zeta - 1)(\zeta^3 - p\zeta^2 + p\zeta - 1) = 0,$$

where

$$p = a_{11} + a_{22} + a_{33} = a_{11}(-1) + a_{22}(-1) + a_{33}(-1).$$

Two of the roots are equal to each other and to one: $\zeta_0 = \zeta_1 = 1$; the other two are reciprocals of each other:

$$\zeta_2 = \left(\frac{p-1}{2} + \sqrt{\left(\frac{p-1}{2}\right)^2 - 1}\right)$$

$$\zeta_3 = \left(\frac{p-1}{2} - \sqrt{\left(\frac{p-1}{2}\right)^2 - 1}\right).$$

Since the $a_{ki}(n)$ are independent of the a_{14}, we can premise the cubic equation

$$\zeta^3 - p\zeta^2 + p\zeta - 1 = 0$$

in their case, from which it follows, according to a proposition we found earlier (section 6, equation 8), that

$$a_{ki}(2) = pa_{ki}(1) - pa_{ki}(0) + a_{ki}(-1).$$

For $k = i$ this gives us

$$a_{kk}(2) = (p+1)a_{kk} - p.$$

Now since $a_{kk}(2) < 1$, we have

$$\Sigma a_{rr}(2) = (p+1)p - 3p = p^2 - 2p < 3$$

$$\text{or} \quad \left(\frac{p-1}{2}\right)^2 < 1.$$

We therefore write

$$\zeta_2 = \cos \varphi + i \sin \varphi, \qquad \zeta_3 = \cos \varphi - i \sin \varphi,$$

where

$$\frac{p-1}{2} = \cos \varphi.$$

D

For $a_{ki}(n)$ we now have the equation

$$\begin{vmatrix} a_{ki}(n), & 1, & \zeta_2^n, & \zeta_3^n \\ a_{ki}(o), & 1, & 1, & 1 \\ a_{ki}, & 1, & \zeta_2, & \zeta_3 \\ pa_{ki}-pa_{ki}(0)+a_{ik}, & 1, & \zeta_2^2, & \zeta_3^2 \end{vmatrix} = 0, \quad |$$

25   which can also be written as follows:

$$\begin{vmatrix} a_{ki}(n), & 1, & \zeta_2^n-\zeta_3^n, & \zeta_2^n+\zeta_3^n-2 \\ a_{ki}(o), & 1, & 0, & 0 \\ a_{ki}, & 1, & \zeta_2-\zeta_3, & \zeta_2+\zeta_3-2 \\ pa_{ki}-pa_{ki}(o)+a_{ki}, & 1, & (p-1)(\zeta_2-\zeta_3), & (p+1)(\zeta_2+\zeta_3)-2 \end{vmatrix} = 0$$

or:

$$\begin{vmatrix} a_{ki}(n), & 1, & 2i\sin n\varphi, & 2(\cos n\varphi-1) \\ a_{ki}(o), & 1, & 0, & 0 \\ a_{ki}-a_{ik}, & 0, & 4i\sin\varphi, & 0 \\ a_{ki}+a_{ik}, & 2, & 0, & 4(\cos\varphi-1) \end{vmatrix} = 0.$$

From this it follows that

$$a_{ki}(n)=a_{ki}(0)\left(1-\frac{\cos n\varphi-1}{\cos\varphi-1}\right)+\left(\frac{a_{ki}-a_{ik}}{2}\right)\frac{\sin n\varphi}{\sin\varphi}+\frac{a_{ki}+a_{ik}}{2}\frac{\cos n\varphi-1}{\cos\varphi-1}.$$

For $i=k$ this formula becomes

$$a_{kk}(n)=1-\frac{\cos n\varphi-1}{\cos\varphi-1}+a_{kk}\frac{\cos n\varphi-1}{\cos\varphi-1},$$

and for $i \gtrless k$

$$a_{ki}(n)=\frac{a_{ki}-a_{ik}}{2}\frac{\sin n\varphi}{\sin\varphi}+\frac{a_{ki}+a_{ik}}{2}\frac{\cos n\varphi-1}{\cos\varphi-1}.$$

For determining the $a_{k4}(2)$ and $a_{k4}(3)$ we have

$$a_{k4}(2)=\Sigma\{a_{r4}a_{kr}\}+a_{k4}=P_k+a_{k4}$$

$$a_{k4}(3)=\Sigma\{a_{kr}(2)a_{r4}\}+a_{k4}(2) \ =p\Sigma\{a_{kr}a_{r4}\}-pa_{k4}+\Sigma\{a_{rk}a_{r4}\}+P_k+a_{k4}$$

$$=(p+1)P_k+Q_k-(p-1)a_{k4},$$

where

$$P_k=\Sigma\{a_{kr},a_{r4}\}, \qquad Q_k=\Sigma\{a_{rk}a_{r4}\}.$$

Since $\zeta_0 = \zeta_1 = 1$, we have according to section 6, equation 6b, the following equation:

$$\begin{vmatrix} a_{k4}(n), & 1, & n, & \zeta_2^n, & \zeta_3^n \\ 0, & 1, & 0, & 1, & 1 \\ a_{k4}, & 1, & 1, & \zeta_2, & \zeta_3 \\ P_k + a_{k4}, & 1, & 2, & \zeta_2^2, & \zeta_3^2 \\ (p+1)P_k + Q_k - (p-1)a_{k4}, & 1, & 3, & \zeta_2^3, & \zeta_3^3 \end{vmatrix} = 0,$$

which, because of

$$\zeta_2^2 - \zeta_3^2 = (p-1)(\zeta_2 - \zeta_3), \qquad \zeta_2^2 + \zeta_3^2 - 2 = (p+1)(p-3),$$

$$\zeta_2^3 - \zeta_3^3 = p(p-2)(\zeta_2 - \zeta_3), \qquad \zeta_2^3 + \zeta_3^3 - 2 = p^2(p-3),$$

can also be written as follows:

$$\begin{vmatrix} a_{k4}(n), & n, & \zeta_2^n - \zeta_3^n, & \zeta_2^n + \zeta_3^n - 2 \\ a_{k4}, & 1, & \zeta_2 - \zeta_3, & p-3 \\ P_k + a_{k4}, & 2, & (p-1)(\zeta_2 - \zeta_3), & (p+1)(p-3) \\ (p+1)P_k + Q_k - (p-1)a_{k4}, & 3, & p(p-2)(\zeta_2 - \zeta_3), & p^2(p-3) \end{vmatrix} = 0. \ |$$

This entails   26

$$\begin{vmatrix} a_{k4}(n), & n, & \dfrac{\sin n\varphi}{\sin \varphi}, & \dfrac{\cos n\varphi - 1}{\cos \varphi - 1} \\ a_{k4}, & 1, & 1, & 1 \\ P_k, & 1, & p-2, & p \\ Q_k, & 1, & 1, & -1 \end{vmatrix} = 0.$$

Now since $p = 2\cos\varphi + 1$, we have

$$a_{k4}(n) = \frac{2a_{k4}\cos\varphi - P_k - Q_k}{2(\cos\varphi - 1)} n + \frac{-a_{k4}(\cos\varphi + 1) + P_k + Q_k \cos\varphi}{(2\cos\varphi - 1)} \frac{\sin n\varphi}{\sin\varphi}$$

$$+ \frac{a_{k4} - Q_k}{2} \frac{\cos n\varphi - 1}{\cos\varphi - 1}.$$

It is easy to recognize by purely geometrical considerations that, when n is equated with the time, the movement represented by the formulae

$$X_1 = a_{11}(n)x_1 + a_{12}(n)x_2 + a_{13}(n)x_3 + a_{14}(n)$$

$$X_2 = a_{21}(n)x_1 + a_{22}(n)x_2 + a_{23}(n)x_3 + a_{24}(n)$$

$$X_3 = a_{31}(n)x_1 + a_{32}(n)x_2 + a_{33}(n)x_3 + a_{34}(n)$$

is a uniform spiral movement. Our formulae therefore solve the problem of representing analytically the spiral movement by which a solid body is translated from a given initial position to a given terminal position. A discussion of our formulae, which may be passed over here since its connection with our subject is somewhat remote, would show that the axis of the spiral has the cosine of direction

$$\cos\alpha = \sqrt{\frac{a_{11}-\cos\varphi}{1-\cos\varphi}}, \qquad \cos\beta = \sqrt{\frac{a_{22}-\cos\varphi}{1-\cos\varphi}}, \qquad \cos\gamma = \sqrt{\frac{a_{33}-\cos\varphi}{1-\cos\varphi}}$$

and that it is described by the equations

$$(a_{11}-1)x_1 + a_{12}x_2 + a_{12}x_3 + a_{14} - s\cos\alpha = 0$$

$$a_{21}x_1 + (a_{22}-1)x_2 + a_{23}x_3 + a_{24} - s\cos\beta = 0$$

$$a_{31}x_1 + a_{32}x_2 + (a_{33}-1)x_3 + a_{34} - s\cos\gamma = 0,$$

where

$$s = a_{14}\cos\alpha + a_{24}\cos\beta + a_{34}\cos\gamma$$

means the velocity of the translation, while φ is the velocity of the rotation. When $s=0$, the quantity n of the system of transformation formulae can be interpreted geometrically as an angle, but in the case where $\varphi=0$ it can be conceived as a linear quantity and in the most general case as the quantity of a spiral movement composed of an angle and a length. It is known that the order of spiral movements about the same axis makes no difference. This is a special case of our proposition concerning the multiplicity of the dimensions of the quantitative domains of functional systems.

Apart from some general propositions which have been proved to be valid for all functions and functional systems, we have been concerned almost exclusively with linear functions. It would perhaps be of interest to carry out similar investigations of those functional systems that correspond to quadratic and Cremona transformations. |

---

27   *Curriculum vitae.* I, Friedrich Ludwig Gottlob Frege, was born in Wismar on 8 November 1848. My father, Alexander, who had been director of a secondary school for girls in Wismar, suffered an untimely death in the year 1866. My mother, Auguste, born Bialloblotzky, is still alive. I was brought up in the Lutheran faith. After attending the gymnasium of the city of my birth for fifteen years, I graduated with a certificate of maturity around Easter 1869 and pursued mathematical, physical, chemical and philosophical studies, first in Jena for two years, and then in Göttingen for five semesters. I earned the degree of Doctor of Philosophy in Göttingen.

Review of H. Seeger, *Die Elemente der Arithmetik*
[*The Elements of Arithmetic*]

After some explanations of arithmetical operations and their signs, 722
expressed partly in infelicitous ways, we are presented in the second
and third chapters of this text-book, under the names of fundamental
theorems and the most essential transformation formulae, with those
propositions that do indeed form the foundation of the whole of
arithmetic, but which are here all lumped together and unproved,
whereas in later chapters theorems of much narrower scope are
distinguished by special headings and to a large extent proved. There is
also too much emphasis on what is merely conventional and concerns
the sign language of arithmetic, as opposed to the laws themselves and
their foundation. The extended application of concepts, which is of such
great significance for arithmetic and becomes so often a source of great
unclarity to a student, here leaves much to be desired. E.g., in fractional
arithmetic there is no mention at all of the case where the multiplier is
a fraction, even though the definition given in No. 8 fits only integral
multipliers. The author therefore also feels no need to prove the
propositions about multiplication and division for this case. Negative
numbers are defined in No. 35 as differences whose subtrahends are
greater than their minuends. Since he is given no hint about the
possibility of such subtractions, the beginner will not know what to
make of such explanations. It should have been shown that the
possibility of subtraction in this case presupposes an extended application of the concept of subtraction and consequently also of addition.
So it is only natural that Mr. Seeger is also unable either to justify the
geometrical interpretation of the negative or to connect it with the
definition he has given. No more, therefore, is he able to explain the
rules of calculation with negatives or the meaning of a negative number
as a multiplier and exponent. There is only a passing mention in a note
(on p. 12) that the earlier formulae hold in general when the given rules
are observed. Thus wherever proofs and justifications are most needed,
they are found to be wanting. And no attempt has been made, not even
once, gradually to accustom beginners to the sign language of math-

ematics so as to help them overcome the difficulties that stand in the way of their understanding it. The consequence of all these defects will be that the pupil will learn arithmetical laws only by rote and will get used to being satisfied with words he does not understand. The paucity of fundamental considerations is brought out even more clearly by the detailed treatment, superfluous in a text-book, of the divisibility and congruence of numbers. The exercises take up more than half the book and may well be the more valuable part of it. The two appendices: historical notes and a German–French glossary, have no connection with the book itself. It would be difficult to discover a use for them.

Since far better text-books of this kind have long been available, it is hard to see what need it was that prompted the writing of the present one.

Review of A. v. Gall and E. Winter,
Die analytische Geometrie des Punktes und der Geraden und ihre Anwendung auf Aufgaben

[The Analytical Geometry of Point and Line and its Application to Problems]

In several text-books of the newer analytic geometry which have   133
appeared recently I have repeatedly found some false conceptions, and
it may therefore not be superfluous to correct them on the occasion of
the present publication.

The authors show an insufficient insight into the respective positions
of projective and metrical geometry. The true relationship may be
intuited by means of the following picture. Projective geometry may be
likened to a symmetrical figure where every proposition has a proposition corresponding to it according to the principle of duality. If we
cut out some arbitrary portion of this figure, this portion is in general
no longer symmetrical. Metrical geometry may be likened to such a
cut-out, or more precisely, to a cut-out which deserves consideration
for some special reasons. To put it in non-pictorial terms, metrical
geometry arises from projective geometry by specialization, and this is
precisely why the principle of duality loses its validity. Thus if one is
concerned about the principle of duality, the only reasonable thing to
do is not to leave the field of general projective geometry, just as when
one is concerned about symmetry, the only reasonable thing to do is to
consider the figure as a whole. Instead, the authors cut out a portion
which is symmetrical to the first cut-out, even though all the reasons
which called for special consideration in the former case are no longer
present in this case. In this way they arrive at 'parallel points', 'angles
of two points' and similar mysterious concepts to which nothing
corresponds in our intuition. To sum it up in brief, the principle of
duality can never provide a reason for a specialization of general
projective geometry; the consideration of metrical properties can be
justified only by the special significance they have for our intuition.

A second remark concerns trilinear coordinates. A point coordinate
system in a plane is a way of determining unequivocally any point of

Jenaer Literaturzeitung 4 (1877), pp. 133–4. (*Tr.* Hans Kaal) the plane by means of a system of numbers (coordinates). The coordinate system is a trillinear one when these numbers are determined unequivocally, independently of one another and in their relationships to one another, by the corresponding point, and further, when | every straight line within the coordinates is represented by an equation of the first degree. The very general nature of these coordinates is most easily recognized when the concept is defined in this way. But these coordinates can also be defined as three numbers which are related like the distances between a point which is yet to be determined and the three sides of a fixed triangle when each distance is multiplied by a constant. Instead of the sides of the triangle we can also use the three corner points and a fourth point which does not lie on any of the sides. For if we draw rays from each corner point to the two others as well as to the fourth point which is yet to be determined, then the trilinear coordinates are three numbers which are related like the three double relations that arise in this way. Now this coordinate system is most intimately connected with the most general relationship, that of collineation, in virtue of which any point has a point and any straight line a straight line corresponding to it, in that the transformation and substitution formulae which govern collineation are in exact agreement in the case of trilinear coordinates. Just as four fixed points serve to determine the triangular coordinate system, so four pairs of corresponding points determine collineation. Now with respect to this relationship the properties of figures divide into two kinds: they are called projective or metrical depending on whether or not they are preserved under a collinear projection. Because of the relationship we have just brought out between triangular coordinates and collineation, projective properties are expressed in those coordinates in such a way that no determining factors of the coordinate system – e.g., the distance between the four points – enter into the formulae, which is what happens as soon as metrical properties are represented. Thus the significance of trilinear coordinates lies, first, in their great generality and adaptability, for they allow us, subject to a minor restriction, to choose arbitrarily eight constants or four fixed points, and secondly, in that they do not, in spite of this generality, burden the equations in which the projective properties are expressed with constants alien to the properties themselves. Everyone who undertakes to represent the teachings of the newer projective geometry ought to be clear on this point. The authors do not even introduce trilinear coordinates in their most general form, for instead of eight arbitrary constants they assume only six. While, on the one hand, they thus fail to take full advantage of the generality of projective geometry, on the other hand they let the height of generality to which they soar become an obstacle to them in their metrical investigations. They thus arrive at expressions for distances and angles which, because of the intrusion of determining factors into the coordinate system, are well suited to serve as deterrents to others.

Since I am confining myself to the main points, I will only mention in passing that here too the use of signs to distinguish the abscissae on opposite sides of the origin is designated as something purely conventional. When is the fog finally going to lift that has been obscuring this point to so many eyes!

Review of J. Thomae, *Sammlung von Formeln, welche bei Anwendung der elliptischen und Rosenhainschen Funktionen gebraucht werden*

[Collection of Formulae used in the Application of Elliptical and Rosenhain Functions]

472 This collection of formulae is intended to smooth the path for a more varied application of Rosenhain's functions by presenting the formulae in a way in which they can be conveniently applied. On the derivation of the formulae we are given brief hints which closely follow Riemann's considerations. Somewhat more detailed consideration is given to mapping by means of a first-order integral u_1 which, given a suitable choice of diagonals, has the property that the u_1-plane inside a parallelogram is only simply covered over by the image of the surface x, while the limits of the parallelogram are formed not only by its sides, but also by lines inside it which do not, however, cut out a section of it. Appended at the end we find, as examples of the application of elliptic functions, the movement of a centre of gravity in a circle in vertical position and along a parabola with its axis placed either vertically or horizontally, and as an example of the application of Rosenhain's functions, the movement of a centre of gravity in an ellipse with vertical and horizontal axes.

Jenaer Literaturzeitung 4 (1877), p. 472. (*Tr.* Hans Kaal)

Lecture on a Way of Conceiving the Shape of a Triangle as a Complex Quantity

Shape seems at first to be something qualitative since we ask: How is an object shaped? and not: How much is it shaped? In spite of this, the shape of a triangle can also be conceived as a quantity. This is not to be confused with the fact that its shape can be characterized by quantitative determinations. What we are concerned with here is to obtain one and only one metrical number for each triangular shape, so that we can speak of adding two triangular shapes to get a new triangular shape. Let a, b, c be the sides of a triangle conceived as complex quantities such that

$$a + b + c = 0.$$

Each of the quotients

$$\frac{b}{c} = \alpha, \qquad \frac{c}{a} = \beta, \qquad \frac{a}{b} = \gamma$$

characterizes the shape of the triangle. The complex number

$$n = \frac{2i}{3\sqrt{3}}\left(-\alpha - \beta - \gamma - \frac{3}{2}\right) = \frac{i}{3\sqrt{3}}\left(\frac{2 + 3\alpha - 3\alpha^2 - 2\alpha^3}{\alpha^2 + \alpha}\right),$$

which remains unchanged when α, β, γ are interchanged can be taken as the definition of the quantity of the shape of the triangle. The equilateral triangle described by rotating in the direction of rotation from 1 to i will then constitute the unit of shape. Reversing the direction of rotation has the effect of reversing the sign of n, since in that case $1/\alpha$ takes the place of α. A degenerate triangle whose corner points lie in a straight line has a purely imaginary n, since α is then real. An isosceles triangle, for which $\alpha = e^{i\varphi}$, has a purely real n, namely

$$n = \frac{5\sin\varphi + 2\sin 2\varphi}{3\sqrt{3}(1 + \cos\varphi)}.$$

The case where $n = 0$ ($\alpha = 1$) corresponds to a degenerate triangle one of

Sitzungsberichte der Jenaischen Gesellschaft für Medizin und Naturwissenschaft 12
(1878) Supplement, p. XVIII. (*Tr.* Hans Kaal)

whose corner points bisects the distance between the other two. n is ∞ when $\alpha = 0$, that is, when one side vanishes in comparison with another. To conjugate complex values of α correspond triangles similar by virtue of symmetry, and to this value of n, those that differ only by the sign of the real part. The circumstance that triangles similar by virtue of symmetry appear here as different in shape is connected with the fact that only those triangles that lie in parallel planes can be immediately compared with one another, because in any other plane the respective positions of 1 and i must be fixed anew in each case. We cannot therefore, on this conception of a shape, rotate the plane of a triangle without thereby changing its shape. For even though triangles in different planes are expressed by the same n, this is nevertheless done in relation to different units, namely in relation to equilateral triangles in different planes.

Review of Hoppe, *Lehrbuch der analytischen Geometrie* I

[*Textbook of Analytic Geometry* I]

The author divides analytic geometry, not as is customarily done into   210
plane geometry and a geometry of space, but into a theory of curves
and of surfaces. The former is here presented as part I; the latter has
already appeared as part II. There is also something peculiar about the
way the subject is considered in this book. It is possible to distinguish
two lines along which analytic geometry has been developing, one of
which might be called analytic geometry in the narrower sense and the
other algebraic geometry, because the former seeks to exploit the
methods of the higher analysis for the benefit of geometry, while the
latter sets itself the same task for the methods of algebra. The present
work belongs in the former line of development. After demonstrating
how points are determined by means of rectangular parallel coordinates, Hoppe lays the 'Kinematic Foundation of Curve and Surface
Theory' and constructs the theory of curves on this foundation. His
definition of a curve as the path of a point in motion excludes some
things from the concept which would otherwise be counted as part of it,
especially if one attends to the sense in which Hoppe uses the word
motion. It seems to me inappropriate to introduce time as a measured
quantity into a purely geometrical consideration. While this quantity is
again replaced immediately by another quantity, the idea of motion is
surely meant to do more than serve as clothing for the fact that the
coordinates can be thought to depend on a variable parameter: it is
also meant to help prove certain apparent continuities. It might well
have been better if the author had spelled out the assumptions he was
going to make about continuity instead of introducing them all
together under the guise of the name motion, which is itself in need of
explanation.

   Now the transformation of curves plays as important a part in
Hoppe's considerations as collineation does in projective geometry. For
if a curve corresponds point by point to another curve in such a way
that the tangents at the corresponding points are parallel while the

Deutsche Literaturzeitung 1 (1880), columns 210–11. (*Tr.* Hans Kaal)

lengths of the curves can be increased or decreased in various ways, then the properties which the author singles out for special consideration and which he represents by his 'dimensionless determining quantities' characterize both the new curve and the old one, which is analogous to the way in which projective properties are preserved under a collinear transformation. The most noteworthy of those determining quantities is the angle τ described by the tangent, whose use as a variable parameter enables Hoppe to achieve a great simplicity in his formulae. And one of the properties indicated above deserves special emphasis: the one that finds its expression in an equation between τ and the angle θ described by the plane of the curvature. This kind of dependence can serve as a | principle of division for curves. Accordingly the higher curves, together with the spiral line and others, belong to the class of curves for which the equation mentioned above is linear.

211

The theory of curves we have before us is presented from a particular unitary point of view, and for this reason alone it cannot be complete even in an approximate sense. It would also seem to be very far from having exhausted all that could be gained from this standpoint. The way it divides the subject already makes it clear that we are dealing essentially with a geometry of space. But the consideration of it is evidently slanted in favour of spatial curves to the point where plane curves are necessarily given short shrift. One would therefore also look in vain for a theory of conics.

Because of the peculiar delimitation and division of the subject matter, the scantiness of the treatment and the lack of examples, this book is hardly suitable as a first introduction to analytic geometry. It is less a text-book than a scientific monograph, and as such it is worthy of notice.

Lecture on the Geometry of Pairs of Points in the Plane

One of the most far-reaching advances made by analytic geometry in
more recent times is that it regards not only points but also other
forms (e.g., straight lines, planes, spheres) as elements of space and
determines them by means of coordinates. In this way we arrive at
geometries of more than three dimensions without leaving the firm
ground of intuition. The geometry of straight lines in space for example
is a four-dimensional one, and so is the geometry of spheres. But there
is a difference between the two, in that a sphere can always be
determined unequivocally by four numbers, whereas it would seem that
this is not possible in the case of straight lines. We determine a straight
line by an equation between six quantities with a quadratic equation
holding between them. We express this peculiarity of the geometry of
straight lines by calling it a second-order one, whereas the geometry of
spheres is of the first order.

The geometry of pairs of points in the plane, with which we will here
be concerned, is four-dimensional and of the third order. It is therefore
for four dimensions what the geometry of points on a third-order
surface is for two dimensions. We regard a pair of points as a reducible
curve of the second degree

$$s_1 u_1{}^2 + s_2 u_2{}^2 + s_3 u_3{}^2 + 2t_1 u_2 u_3 + 2t_2 u_3 u_1 + 2t_3 u_1 u_2 = 0$$

and we regard the coefficients s and t as its coordinates. For the curve
to reduce, it must be that

$$\begin{vmatrix} s_1 & t_3 & t_2 \\ t_3 & s_2 & t_1 \\ t_2 & t_1 & s_3 \end{vmatrix} = 0 \quad | \qquad (1)$$

This equation is of the third degree, and from this it follows that our
geometry is of the third order.

If x_1, x_2, x_3 and y_1, y_2, y_3 are the homogeneous coordinates of the
two points of a pair, then the following equations hold:

Geometry of Pairs of Points

$$\rho s_i = x_i y_i$$

$$\rho t_1 = \tfrac{1}{2}(x_2 y_3 + x_3 y_2)$$

$$\rho t_2 = \tfrac{1}{2}(x_3 y_1 + x_1 y_3) \tag{2}$$

$$\rho t_3 = \tfrac{1}{2}(x_1 y_2 + x_2 y_1).$$

As one cannot join any two arbitrary points on a third-order surface by a straight line, so here, too, two pairs of points do not always determine a one-dimensional first-order form in our geometry. If s_i, t_i are the coordinates of a pair of points and m_i, n_i those of another, then $s_i + \lambda m_i, t_i + \lambda n_i$ are not in general the coordinates of a third pair of points.

There is nevertheless a third pair of points whose coordinates can be represented in this form, namely the third pair of opposite corner points of a complete quadrilateral whose other two pairs of corner points are s_i, t_i and m_i, n_i. In the geometry of points this corresponds to the circumstance that the connecting line between two points on a third-order surface also meets this plane at a third point. The third pair of points coincides with the first when one and only *one* point of the second pair lies in a straight line with the two points of the first pair.

If $s_i + \lambda m_i, t_i + \lambda n_i$ are to be the coordinates of a third pair of points independently of λ, it is necessary either that the two pairs of points have a point in common or that they lie in the same straight line. In the former case, one of the points of the third pair lies fixed at the common point while the other moves on the connecting line between the two non-common points. In the latter case, all points $s_i + \lambda m_i, t_i + \lambda n_i$ are pairs of points in an involution which is determined by the given pairs of points. We thus have two kinds of one-dimensional first-order forms. A form of the first kind is determined geometrically by a straight line and a point, and a form of the second kind by two points: the double points of the involution. But there are also one-dimensional first-order forms that belong to both kinds. The involution then degenerates, in that the two double points coincide. In this case, the form is determined by a straight line and a point which lies on it. There is a quadruply infinite number of one-dimensional first-order forms of the first kind, and there are just as many of the second kind, while the number of those that belong to both kinds at once is triply infinite. |

We also have here two kinds of two-dimensional first-order forms. A form of the first kind is the totality of pairs of points that have a fixed point in common; it can be represented by the point itself. A form of the second kind is the totality of pairs of points on a straight line; it is determined by the straight line itself. The number of each of these kinds is doubly infinite. There is no two-dimensional first-order form that belongs to both kinds at once. Two two-dimensional first-order forms have an element in common when they are of the same kind; when they are of different kinds, they have nothing in common or else an entire one-dimensional first-order form of the first and second kinds.

There are here no three-dimensional first-order forms.

A linear equation in s and t

$$a_1 s_1 + a_2 s_2 + a_3 s_3 + b_1 t_1 + b_2 t_2 + b_3 t_3 = 0 \qquad (3)$$

represents, together with (1), a three-dimensional third-order form. If we introduce x and y by means of (2), we find that there is a polar relation between x and y with respect to the conic

$$a_1 x_1{}^2 + a_2 x_2{}^2 + a_3 x_3{}^2 + b_1 x_2 x_3 + b_2 x_3 x_1 + b_3 x_1 x_2 = 0. \qquad (4)$$

The form is therefore the totality of pairs of points related by the polarity with respect to a conic, and this form is given by that conic. This form contains a doubly infinite number of one-dimensional first-order forms of the first kind and just as many of the second kind, as well as a singly infinite number of forms belonging to both kinds at once, as long as the conic does not degenerate into a double line. In that case, the number of forms belonging to both kinds is doubly infinite.

Two linear equations in s_i, t_i represent, together with (1), a two-dimensional third-order form. This form is the totality of pairs of points related by simultaneous polarity with respect to two conics. In the general case, we can take the two forms to be reducible and regard the four points of intersection as the geometrical representation of this form. One point in each pair is related with the other by a quadratic transformation. This form contains three one-dimensional first-order forms of the first kind and six one-dimensional first-order forms of the second kind.

If we now add to this a linear equation like (3) which is independent of the first two, we obtain a one-dimensional third-order form consisting of all pairs of points related by simultaneous polarity with respect to three conics. These pairs of points lie on a third-order curve.

Let us ask when a two-dimensional third-order form reduces to a first-order and a second-order one. If a two-dimensional first-order form of the first kind is to be contained in a | three-dimensional third-order form (cf. equation 3), then the corresponding conic (4) must degenerate into a pair of lines. The double point of the pair of lines is then related by polarity with any point of the surface. If this is to happen also with respect to a second conic, it too must reduce, and its double point must coincide with that of the first. These two pairs of lines determine an involution whose double lines have the property that every point on the one is related with every point on the other by the polarity with respect to both conics. The two-dimensional third-order form therefore reduces to a first-order form of the first kind and a second-order one which consists of all pairs of points one of which lies on one straight line while the other lies on another, so that this form can be represented by the two straight lines. It corresponds to a second-order surface of the geometry of points, and as there are two families of generators on such a surface, our form contains two families of one-dimensional first-order forms of the first kind, any one of which is represented by a point of the one straight line together with the other straight line.

If we now subject the pairs of points of this form to the condition that they be polar with respect to a third conic, then we have projective series of points on the two straight lines, and the totality of the pairs of mutually related points is a one-dimensional second-order form corresponding to a conic in the geometry of points. The straight lines which are determined by the pairs of points are tangents of a curve of the second degree, and the straight lines that carry the series of points also belong to it. Our form is therefore determined geometrically by the second-degree curve and two of its tangents, instead of which we can also take their point of intersection. This second-degree curve reduces to a pair of points, and the series of points are in perspective position when the conic we last added passes through the point of intersection of the lines carrying the series of points. The second-degree curve reduces to a pair of points even when the conic we last added degenerates into a pair of lines whose double point lies on one of the two carriers of the series of points. If we then let the fourth line harmonic to this carrier intersect the other carrier, then this point and the double point of the pair of lines gives us the points at which the second-degree curve reduces. Our one-dimensional second-order form, too, reduces therefore to two first-order forms of the first kind, each of them represented by one of the two points and the straight line on which it does not lie.|

102   If a two-dimensional first-order form of the second kind is to be contained in a three-dimensional third-order form (cf. equation 3), then every point on a straight line must be related with every other point by the polarity with respect to a conic. This is possible only if this straight line belongs itself to the conic. Now if the two-dimensional first-order form of the second kind is to belong to a third three-dimensional third-

order form, then the conic corresponding to the latter must also reduce, and in such a way that the same straight line also belongs to it. We then have two pairs of lines with a common line. The pairs of points that lie on the common line form the two-dimensional first-order form of the second kind which belongs to the third-order form. The other form belonging to the third-order form is a second-order one, which consists of the pairs of points whose connecting line passes through the point of intersection Q of the non-common lines and which are separated harmonically by that point and the common line. This two-dimensional second-order form is given by a point Q and a straight line a, and it corresponds to the surface of a cone in the geometry of points. To the family of generators corresponds the family of one-dimensional first-order forms of the second kind, each of which is determined by the point Q and a point of the straight line a. To Q itself, counted as a double point, corresponds the vertex of the cone.

If we now add to this a linear equation like (3), we get a one-dimensional second-order form. This form consists of pairs of points on a conic, all of whose connecting lines pass through a point Q. This one-dimensional second-order form can be represented by a conic and a point.

The pairs of points which consist of two coincident points form a two-dimensional fourth-order form. The totality of the double points on a straight line is a one-dimensional second-order form. An instance of this is the intersection of the conelike two-dimensional second-order form with the two-dimensional first-order form of the second kind to which a third-order form reduces.

Review of H. Cohen, *Das Prinzip der Infinitesimal-Methode und seine Geschichte*

[*The Principle of the Method of Infinitesimals and its History*]

324   Since the subject matter of mathematics recedes into the background and is dominated by thought more than in the other sciences, and since mathematical ideas have been developed into a richer and more subtle structure than elsewhere, this science is especially suited to serve as a basis for epistemological and logical investigations. Here is a quarry which could still be worked to great profit. The reason why so little has been done along this line except by Kant may well be that facility in both mathematical and philosophical thought and an adequate |

325   knowledge of both fields are only rarely combined in one and the same person. The book before us also seems to me to founder on this rock. Now I do not want to wholly exclude the possibility that my defective understanding may perhaps have kept me from a full appreciation of it. If I nevertheless venture to review it, it is with the intention of perhaps provoking an exchange of ideas which might clarify things and might be welcome to the author, as well as in the belief that in the least favourable case I will be excused because of Cohen's style of writing, which is by no means distinguished for its clarity and which is sometimes even illogical. A few passages should convince the reader of this. In section 33, p. 28, the author speaks of the presupposition of intensive reality and goes on to say:

'This presupposition is the sense of reality and the secret of the concept of a differential.' Ergo, the presupposition of intensive reality is the sense of reality; but what is the sense of this proposition?

'Galileo's laws of falling bodies are the prototype of natural forces' (section 48, p. 47).

'The infinitesimal thus comes to be and into being as that value of reality which mathematics as a natural science in search of its foundations has been seeking' (section 58, p. 70).

'An intensive quantity is also to be thought of as a fundamental proposition' (section 68, p. 89).

Zeitschrift für Philosophie und philosophische Kritik 87 (1885), pp. 324–9.
(*Tr.* Hans Kaal)

'To be more precise one would have to say that reality, which already enters effectively into action at the point of geometry, completes and fulfills its activity in the problems of matter, which form the object of physics' (section 94, pp. 137–8).

What I miss here is that striving for precision of expression and logical irreproachability which alone could guarantee clarity of thought in investigations of this kind. And such a guarantee would deserve much more credit than the guarantee Cohen derives from agreement with the historical development of the problem (p. iii). His opinion that historical insight alone can first disclose what has a claim to being a logical presupposition of the science (p. iv) is an erroneous one. | On   326 the contrary, those logical foundations are perhaps always discovered only later on, after a considerable amount of knowledge has been accumulated. From the logical point of view, the historical starting-point appears as something accidental.

I will now try to reproduce in brief the basic idea of the author.

Cohen brings reality into a peculiar connection with the differential by going back, it seems, to the anticipations of perception whose principle according to Kant is this: 'In all appearances, the real that is an object of sensation has intensive magnitude, that is, a degree.' Now the differential is an intensive magnitude. If, e.g., x is a distance on a straight line, then dx, its differential or infinitesimal increment, is not to be thought of as an extensive magnitude or as itself a distance; this would lead to contradictions, and it is precisely because mathematicians wanted to let the differential pass throughout for an extensive magnitude that they got entangled in the well-known difficulties. These difficulties can be removed, not by logic, but by the critique of knowledge, which is the term the author uses for 'theory of knowledge', because it shows that an infinitesimal number is an intensive magnitude which, as such, has a power of realization: 'It does not merely represent the *unit of reality*, but also *realizes as such*; it confers reality upon Being in Quality' (section 45). 'If the *differential* constitutes *reality* as a constitutive condition of thought, then the *integral* designates the *real as object*' (section 99). The dx is therefore to be conceived of as, say, an intensive magnitude concentrated at the end point of x, comparable to an electrical charge, or as a power to increase the distance, like for example the last bud on a bough in which we can recognize a striving for growth. These pictures occurred to me as I was reading the book; they are not to be attributed to the author himself. By way of comparison, let me cite one of his phrases: 'The *unit of reality* which as such fixes an absolute point from which the line emerges, and not just *into* | which the line contracts as its *limit*' (section 68, p. 91), where it   327 should be noted that by the unit of reality is to be understood the differential.

The contrast between extensive and intensive goes back to the contrast between intuition and thought, since the quality which corresponds to the intensive magnitude is a category of thought. The extensive magnitude of intuition is thus opposed to the intensive one of sensation. The two sources of knowledge must always be combined if the knowledge is to be objective (section 21). Reality, as a means of thought, is able to come in where intuition alone fails (section 33), for the latter has the character of ideality. If the infinitesimal is to be fit to do justice to the requirements of reality, it must be withdrawn from intuition, provided that reality is to mean a condition of experience *on the part of thought* (section 22). Accordingly, continuity is also separated from intuition and assigned to thought (section 42 and 58).

Let me now voice my objections to these ideas. What I miss everywhere is proofs. The Kantian transition from the quality of a judgement to qualitative reality and intensive magnitude seems already questionable to me. At any rate the contrast between common and infinitesimal numbers cannot be conceived of as a contrast between the extensive and the intensive. The author does not sufficiently distinguish between arithmetic proper and its applications to geometry and mechanics. The infinitesimal calculus is purely arithmetical in nature, and even though its historical starting-point lay in geometrical and mechanical problems, one must not go back to geometry or mechanics in defining or justifying its fundamental concepts. The arithmetical problem of the differential, which, incidentally, should be nearly settled by now, should be distinguished from the question: what properties must spatial and temporal quantities be assumed to have if the differential calculus is to be applicable to geometry and mechanics? Now the distinction between | intensive and extensive magnitude has no sense in pure arithmetic. Nor does it seem to matter anywhere else in the whole of mathematics. The number 3 for example can serve as the measure of a distance in relation to a unit of length; but it can also serve as the measure of an intensive magnitude, e.g., of the intensity of a light measured in terms of a unit of brightness. The calculation in both cases proceeds according to exactly the same laws. The number 3 is therefore neither an intensive nor an extensive magnitude but rises above this contrast. The same holds also for the infinitesimal. Cohen would perhaps reply to this that intensity of light is not an intensive but an extensive magnitude, even though this would be flying in the face of linguistic usage. I gather this from a passage (section 110, p. 158) where the author contrasts the extensive magnitude of a stimulus with the

328

intensive magnitude of sensation. Elsewhere too he reaches some remarkable conclusions. In section 102, p. 147, he expands on the idea, reminiscent of Pythagoras, that 'the d*x* with its higher orders contains the *ground of the possibility of an unlimited variety of qualities* and things' and that 'differences in quality are to be thought of as differences in reality which are reducible to the different orders of the infinitesimal'. By making sensations correspond to the differential, the author arrives at the pronouncement (section 106, p. 153): 'Sensation, even more than *intuition,* emerges thus as the real *question mark* of mathematics.' On the contrary: pure mathematics has nothing to do with sensation.

The author seems to think of the act of realization performed by the infinitesimal in such a way that a distance for example is generated by the force with which it increases; but does this give it a higher degree of reality than geometrical forms possess elsewhere? It seems that objectification is not always clearly distinguished from realization. While geometrical objects may well be granted objectivity, they cannot very well be granted reality proper, which is also what Cohen says himself; but how can we alter this fact by thinking of the forms as being continuously generated? I do | not find that the infinitesimal has an   329 intimate connection with reality. Nor do I understand how the principle of the anticipations of perception can be so interpreted, or how one could infer from it, that an intensive magnitude or the differential has the power of realization. In section 34 Cohen calls intensive magnitude itself a principle of his, thanks to which the methods of mathematics can enter into reciprocal relations. Does he mean here the Kantian principle of anticipations? If not, how does it read? and how does it do what it is here reputed to do? The author never takes the trouble to formulate in words this principle which he so often mentions.

As far as the foundations of the differential calculus are concerned, we shall, I believe, have to go back for this purpose to the concept of a limit in the sense of algebraic analysis, and though the author belittles this as 'negative', this would seem to be due only to a misunderstanding. In my *Foundations of Arithmetic* (p. 72, note 1) I recently indicated how the differential can preserve a certain independence also on the kind of foundations I have chosen.

I will pass over details which are not very closely connected with the fundamental idea, except for saying that I agree with Cohen that knowledge as a psychic process does not form the object of the theory of knowledge, and hence, that psychology is to be sharply distinguished from the theory of knowledge.

On Formal Theories of Arithmetic

I here want to consider two views, both of which bear the name 'formal theory'. I shall agree with the first; the second I shall attempt to confute. The first has it that all arithmetical propositions can be derived from definitions alone using purely logical means, and consequently that they also must be derived in this way. Herewith arithmetic is placed in direct contrast with geometry, which, as surely no mathematician will doubt, requires certain axioms peculiar to it where the contrary of these axioms – considered from a purely logical point of view – is just as possible, i.e. is without contradiction. Of all the reasons that speak in favour of this view, I here want to adduce only one based on the extensive applicability of mathematical doctrines. As a matter of fact, we can count just about everything that can be an object of thought: the ideal as well as the real, concepts as well as objects, temporal as well as spatial entities, events as well as bodies, methods as well as theorems; even numbers can in their turn be counted. What is required is really no more than a certain sharpness of delimitation, a certain logical completeness. From this we may undoubtedly | gather at least this much, that the basic propositions on which arithmetic is based cannot apply merely to a limited area whose peculiarities they express in the way in which the axioms of geometry express the peculiarities of what is spatial; rather, these basic propositions must extend to everything that can be thought. And surely we are justified in ascribing such extremely general propositions to logic.

I shall now deduce several conclusions from this logical or formal nature of arithmetic.

First, no sharp boundary can be drawn between logic and arithmetic. Considered from a scientific point of view, both together constitute a unified science. If we were to allot the most general basic propositions and perhaps also their most immediate consequences to logic while we assigned their further development to arithmetic, then this would be like separating a distinct science of axioms from that of geometry. Of course, the division of the entire field of knowledge into the various sciences is determined not merely by theoretical but also by pragmatic considerations; and by the preceding I do not mean to say anything against a certain pragmatic division: only it must not become a schism, as is at present the case to the detriment of all sides concerned. If this formal theory is correct, then logic cannot be as barren as it may appear upon superficial examination – an appearance for which logicians themselves must be assigned part of the blame. And the negative attitude of many mathematicians toward anything philosophical is without any objective justification – at least so far as this attitude carries over into logic. This science is capable of no less precision than mathematics itself. On the other hand, we may say to the logicians that they cannot come to know their own discipline thoroughly unless they concern themselves more with mathematics.

My second conclusion is this, that there is no such thing as a peculiarly arithmetical mode of inference that cannot be reduced to the general inference-modes of logic. If such a reduction were not possible for a given mode of inference, the question would immediately arise, what conceptual basis we have for taking it to be correct. In the case of arithmetic, it cannot be spatial intuition, because thereby the discipline would be reduced to geometry – at least so far as some of its propositions are concerned. Nor, likewise, can it be physical observation, because thereby it would also be deprived of its general applicability, which extends far beyond the physical. | We therefore   96 have no choice but to acknowledge the purely logical nature of arithmetical modes of inference. Together with this admission, there arises the task of bringing this nature to light wherever it cannot be recognized immediately, which is quite frequently the case in the writings of mathematicians. I have done this in relation to the inference from n to $(n+1)$.

And as my second conclusion is concerned with modes of inference, so my third conclusion is concerned with definitions. In the case of any definition whatever we must presuppose as known something by means of which we explain what we want understood by this name or sign. We cannot very well define an angle without presupposing knowledge of what constitutes a straight line. To be sure, that on which we base our definitions may itself have been defined previously; however, when we retrace our steps further, we shall always come upon something which, being a simple, is indefinable, and must be admitted to be incapable of further analysis. And the properties belonging to these ultimate building blocks of a discipline contain, as it were in a nutshell, its whole contents. In geometry, these properties are expressed in the axioms in so far as they are independent of one another. Now it is clear that the boundaries of a discipline are determined by the nature of its ultimate building blocks. If, as in the case of geometry, these ultimately are spatial configurations, then the science too will be restricted to what is spatial. Therefore if arithmetic is to be independent of all particular properties of things, this must also hold true of its building blocks: they must be of a purely logical nature. From this there follows the requirement that everything arithmetical be reducible to logic by means of definitions. So, for example, I have replaced the expression 'set', which is frequently used by mathematicians, with the expression customary in logic: 'concept'. Nor is this merely an irrelevant change in terminology, but rather is important so far as an understanding of the true state of affairs is concerned. The word 'set' easily evokes the thought of a heap of things in space, as is evident for example from the expression 'set of dishes'; and thus, like J. S. Mill, one very easily retains the childlike conception of a number itself as a heap or aggregate, or at least as a property of a heap, and in concert with K. Fischer takes calculating to be aggregative thinking. But here one completely forgets that one can also count events, methods, and concepts, though we certainly cannot make a heap of any of these. I characterize as a concept that which has number, and in so doing |

97   indicate that the totality, which is here our primary concern, is held together by characteristics, not spatial proximity, which latter can obtain only in special cases as a by-product of these characteristics, but which generally speaking is unimportant. Thus even the number zero, which otherwise is completely without bearer, becomes intelligible; for where is there a heap in which we could discover this number? But this merely as an example of the way in which what is arithmetical can be reduced to what is logical. Only in this way is it possible to fulfil the first requirement of basing all modes of inference that appear to be peculiar to arithmetic on the general laws of logic.

I now turn to the second of the two views that may be called formal theories; and herewith I come to the central part of my paper. This view has it that the signs of the numbers $\frac{1}{2}$, $\frac{1}{3}$, of the number π, etc. are empty signs. This cannot very well be extended to cover whole numbers, since in arithmetic we cannot do without the content of the signs 1, 2, etc., and because otherwise no equation would have a sense which we could state – in which case we should have neither truths, nor a science, of arithmetic. It is curious that it is precisely the lack of its consequential application that has made the continued existence of this opinion possible. I therefore want to show that no one ever really puts this theory into practice or indeed could put it into practice, since if he did, it would very quickly become useless. Despite the emphatic assertion that the signs are empty and that it is they themselves that are the numbers, in the background there always hovers the thought that they do signify something and that it is these contents of signs that really are the numbers. This is indicated by the use of the word 'sign'; for is something that does not designate anything and does not even have the purpose of designating anything a sign? In such a case I shall use the word 'figure', so as to avoid confusing anyone by means of a wrong expression. By the way, it is unnecessary to lay any stress on the word 'empty'. The essential point of this theory is that a number is called a sign, *ergo* a written sign; and it is really irrelevant if, over and above this, such a figure also serves as sign of a content, as long as it is not this content but the sign itself that is considered the number, i.e. that with which arithmetic is concerned. Let us for once take seriously the contention that $\frac{1}{2}$ does not designate anything. Well, then it is an artefact consisting, perhaps, of printer's ink. The properties of this thing are geometrical, physical, and chemical ones. We now have to distinguish between | halves that are printed, written with ink, or with pencil or 98 chalk, where these differ in most of their properties. Thus, instead of the determinate singular object – the number $\frac{1}{2}$ – we now have a whole species of artefacts that manifest a certain relationship only with respect to their shape. And what great things could possibly be inferred from this shape? Moreover, where is that property upon which everything here depends: that of yielding 1 when added to itself? Nothing can be seen of it. Whence, then, does this property come? It is said that it is established by means of a definition. Now the purpose of a definition is surely to indicate what sense one connects with a word or sign. What is it, then, that is to be defined here? The most obvious answer, and probably also what is most frequently meant, is that it is $\frac{1}{2}$ that is to be explained. But such a definition would not be in agreement with the postulate that the figure $\frac{1}{2}$ is devoid of content. Surely it is impossible to give an explanation of that to which the sign is supposed to refer and at the same time deny that the sign has any content at all. Here we once again see that superficiality, which does not quite put the theory of the emptiness of the sign into practice. But as long as what is taken to be the number is not the content but the sign itself, matters would not be improved even if the sign were in fact granted a content. Since it is arbitrary what reference one wants to give to a sign, it follows that the content of the sign will have these or those properties, depending on the particular choice made. Therefore it in part depends on my will, which properties the content of the sign has. But still, these will always be properties of the content of the sign, not of the sign itself; hence they will not be properties of the number in the sense of this formal theory. Mathematicians – so someone might easily say – are very peculiar people; instead of investigating the properties a thing really has, they don't care about them one iota, but using so-called definitions, ascribe all sorts of properties to a thing that have absolutely no connection with the thing itself, and then investigate these properties. Someone could just as easily hit upon the idea of branding his fellow-citizen a liar by the simple expedient of a definition. It would then be very easy to prove the truth of his charge. He would merely have to say, 'That follows immediately from my definition'. Indeed; it would follow from the definition just as rigorously as it follows from the definition 'this chalk-figure has the property of yielding 1 when added to itself' that when added to itself, the figure yields 1. In this way we could certainly define many things; | a pity, that the things themselves would not care one iota, nor give up their old properties or assume new ones solely for the sake of our definition.

99

This state of affairs, which is really quite obvious, is sometimes obscured by the fact that it is not clearly recognizable precisely what is supposed to be defined: the sign $\frac{1}{2}$, or the plus-sign, or the equality-sign, or perhaps a combination of several of these signs. But surely it is a justifiable demand that only one sign be explained in any one definition, and that it be clearly recognizable which sign it is. This, too, is an error: to pass off as the defintion itself what in fact is merely a rule for constructing definitions or a mere assertion to the effect that one is defining. I should be committing this error if I were to say, for example, 'I define the plus-sign in such a way that $\frac{1}{2}+\frac{1}{2}=1$'. This is just as if I were to say, 'I shall now fly into the air', yet at the same time remained standing on the ground. The important thing is not that one say that one is defining; rather, it is that one actually do so, and in such a way that what is wanted is actually achieved.

Anyone ignorant of the historical development of the subject will scarcely understand how someone can come to represent empty signs as the proper objects of arithmetical investigations. Given what was said above, this may perhaps seem quite nonsensical as long as one is unaware of any motive for this claim which, after all, seems to create quite unnecessary difficulties. Therefore I shall have to delve a little deeper into the matter. Even in pre-scientific times, because of the needs of everyday life, positive whole numbers as well as fractional numbers had come to be recognized. Irrational as well as negative numbers were also accepted, albeit with some reluctance – the Greeks could not quite bring themselves to recognize them – and it was with even greater reluctance that complex numbers were finally introduced. The overcoming of this reluctance was facilitated by geometrical interpretations; but with these, something foreign was introduced into arithmetic. Inevitably there arose the desire of once again extruding these geometrical aspects. It appeared contrary to all reason that purely arithmetical theorems should rest on geometrical axioms; and it was inevitable that proofs which apparently established such a dependence should seem to obscure the true state of affairs. The task of deriving what was arithmetical by purely arithmetical means, i.e. purely logically, could not be put off.

A solution that immediately suggested itself was to define these higher numbers by means of their properties: | for example to say, '$\sqrt{2}$ 100 is something which, when multiplied by itself, yields 2'. Such a definition really presupposes that multiplication has previously been defined in such a way that it does not necessarily apply to whole numbers; else one would easily revert to the previously critized error of defining two things at once – $\sqrt{2}$ and multiplication. But this merely *en passant*. So far, by means of such a definition one has merely obtained a concept, and there arises the question whether this concept is empty or fulfilled. As long as it has not been proved that there exists one and exactly one thing of this kind, it would be a mistake in logic to immediately use the definite article and say, 'the number that when multiplied by itself yields 2', or 'the square root of 2'. Until such a proof has been given, one may only use expressions such as 'a square root of 2', 'all square roots of 2', in which 'square root of 2' is treated like a concept-word and therefore not as a term of an equation. So far, nothing having the desired property has been obtained by means of such a definition; for the concept of a number which when multiplied by itself yields 2 no more has the property of yielding 2 when multiplied by itself than the concept of a right-angled triangle is a triangle or has a right angle. Now it is especially important for the derivation of many theorems that there be such higher numbers. And just as for many proofs in geometry one needs points or lines which do not occur in the theorems themselves, and just as in each of these cases it is then necessary to show that there are such auxiliary points or lines; so too in arithmetic, many theorems are proved with the aid of $\sqrt{-1}$, where this magnitude does not itself occur in the theorems. Now if there were simply no number whose square is -1, these proofs would collapse. It seems that such an existence-proof is now to be rendered superfluous by saying, 'The figure which I am now writing is itself the number, is itself the object of our considerations'. But this clearly makes things a little too easy. If it were correct, it would apparently always lie within our power to prove existence, and consequently we could prove the most wondrous things. It is for this reason that definitions are required to be non-contradictory – about which I shall say something later. At this juncture, it may suffice to point out that the properties indicated by a definition do not belong to the sign; and that if a sign is not supposed to have any reference, | a definition of it will also be impossible. Thus the situation may surely be stated like this: Either a number is a written figure, in which case, of course, one cannot very well doubt its existence, although at the same time it also does not have the properties required of it; or a number is the content of a sign, in which case one will have to give a proof to the effect that the sign does indeed designate something and is not perhaps empty, contrary to all intentions. In the latter case, existence can no longer be established merely by pointing to the sign which lessens in significance to that of an inessential expedient which need not be mentioned at all in the initial justification of numbers.

101

Now one might perhaps attempt to avoid this difficulty by defining not numbers, but rather methods of computation. The following example will show why this does not work. The addition of fractions, for example, must be explained generally, perhaps like this: The sum of a/b and c/d is

$$\frac{a \times d + b \times c}{b \times d}.$$

It is quite impossible to prove in this way that the sum of $\frac{1}{2}$ and $\frac{1}{2}$ is 1. For what we obtain is

$$\frac{1 \times 2 + 1 \times 2}{2 \times 2}.$$

This is an empty figure and not the number 1. According to the above, one also could not say that $\frac{1}{2}$ is equal to $\frac{3}{6}$, for both are merely figures. The situation changes radically when one takes these figures to be signs of contents; in that case, the equation states that both signs have the very same content. But if no content is present, the equation has no sense.

However, one can give the matter another turn that seems to favour this formal theory. One could say something like this: 'We don't define at all, but merely stipulate rules in accordance with which one can move from given equations to new ones, just as one can give rules for moving chess pieces. Unless an equation contains only positive numbers, it no more has a sense than the position of chess pieces express a truth. Now in virtue of these rules it may happen that an equation of positive whole numbers finally does occur. And if the rules are of such a kind that if one has started with true equations they can never lead to false conclusions, then only two cases are possible: either the final equation is senseless, or it has a | content about which we can pass 102 judgement. This last will always be the case if it contains only positive whole numbers; and then it must be true, for it cannot be false.' The only question is, how the rules are to be arranged so that nothing false ever results. One might say something like this: 'If these rules contain no contradictions among themselves and do not contradict the laws of positive whole numbers, then no matter how often they are applied, no contradiction can ever enter in. Consequently, if the final equation has any sense at all, it must also be non-contradictory, and hence be true.' Now already this last is a mistake; for a proposition may very well be non-contradictory without for all that being true. Non-contradictoriness, therefore, does not suffice. And even if it did, still, it would first have to be proved. It seems that this is frequently deemed unnecessary; but surely the example of indirect proofs shows that contradictions are not always evident but instead are often brought to light only by a series of inferences. It is impossible to say at the outset, how many inferences will be needed for this. Therefore if after a series of inferences no contradiction has been discovered, one still cannot know whether upon further continuation of the inference-chain a contradiction might not come to light after all. A proof of non-contradictoriness, then, cannot be given by saying that these rules have been proved as laws for the positive whole numbers and therefore must be without contradiction; for after all, they might conflict with the peculiar properties of the higher numbers, e.g. that of yielding -1 when squared. And in fact, not all rules can be retained in the case of complex higher numbers in a three-dimensional domain. At least the theorem that a product can be zero only if one of the factors is zero – a theorem fundamental to algebra – must be dropped. It is therefore evident that in virtue of the peculiar nature of the complex higher numbers, there may arise a contradiction where so far as the positive whole numbers are concerned, no contradiction obtains.

Therefore so far as this formal theory is concerned, the confidence that no contradiction is contained in the computation-rules stipulated for ordinary complex numbers no doubt rests on the fact that so far, none has been found. If one then proves the formula

$$\cos^n \alpha = \cos^n \alpha - \frac{n(n-1)}{1 \cdot 2} \cos^{n-2} \alpha \sin^2 \alpha + \ldots$$

with the aid of the complex numbers by raising $(\cos \alpha + i \sin \alpha)$ | to the 103 nth power, one is really moving in a circle. Despite this proof, the formula might still be false; and if by some other means one were to arrive at an equation that is incompatible with the former, one would have to say that it here becomes obvious that the postulated rules for complex numbers contain a contradiction. The proof of the above formula is based on the non-contradictoriness of the rules for complex numbers, and the latter in turn is established by the fact that no contradiction has ever been found. In any other descipline we should rest content with such a great probability; mathematics, however, wants to prove all of its theorems, and the preceding is not a proof – at least not so far as this formal theory is concerned.

One is doubtless moving in a similar circle when one says that numbers exist if one can compute with them. In the first place, one would be quite justified in asking what inner connection there obtains between existence and computing. Then, for the answer to be of any use at all, one would have to have a definition of computing, so as to know whether what one is doing with a sign is to be called computing. Can one not also compute with diverging series? Judging by appearances, yes; only sometimes what results is false. This suggests the following definition: What is to be called computing is an operation that never yields false results. And with this we have once more landed in a circle. What means are there for proving non-contradictoriness? I see no other principle that could serve here except the following: that properties which are found in one and the same object can never stand in contradiction to one another. But if one had such an object, this formal theory would be superfluous. It therefore seems to me that it is unlikely that a strict proof of the non-contradictoriness of the computation-rules can succeed without going beyond the limits of this formal theory. But even if it should succeed, it would still not suffice; for not everything that is non-contradictory is true.

Clearly we are here faced with a difficulty consisting in the fact that we are defining objects, whereas otherwise we are merely concerned with defining concepts; $\frac{1}{2}$, for example, must be considered an object, albeit one that is neither sensibly perceptible nor spatial. Despite this non-spatiality and non-reality, $\frac{1}{2}$ is not a concept in the sense that objects | can fall under it. One cannot say 'this is a $\frac{1}{2}$', as one can say 'this is a right angle'; expressions like 'all $\frac{1}{2}$' or 'some $\frac{1}{2}$' are equally inadmissible. Rather, $\frac{1}{2}$ is treated as a single determinate object, as is evident from the expression 'the number $\frac{1}{2}$', and from the fact that it stands on one side of the equality-sign. It would here be going too far to indicate how I conceive of the solution of this difficulty. Let me merely say this, that the case of fractions, negative numbers, etc. is not essentially different from that of positive whole numbers; and that

104

therefore a reduction of all propositions or equations to those that deal with positive whole numbers merely pushes the difficulty back one step further and does not solve it. The only reason why this is not noticed quite so easily is the fact that usually one does not feel the need to justify the most primitive of all numbers.

Reply to Cantor's Review of
Grundlagen der Arithmetik
[Foundations of Arithmetic]

1030   In his critical notice of my *Foundations of Arithmetic* in no. 20 of this
journal Mr. Cantor remarks that the extension of a concept is
quantitatively determined only in certain cases, that it does indeed
come to have a number in case it is finite, but that for such a
determination the concept 'number' must already be given in come
other way. These remarks would be very fitting, and I should acknowledge them to be quite justified, if it followed from my definition that,
e.g., the number of Jupiter's moons was the extension of the concept
'Jupiter's moon'. But they do not fit the definition I have given,
according to which the number of Jupiter's moons is the extension of
the concept 'equinumerous to the concept "Jupiter's moon"'; for there is
no question here of a quantitative determination of the extension of
this concept. I therefore suspect that there has been a misunderstanding, which should now have been removed. This invalidates at the same
time the unfavourable verdict in the third paragraph of that notice. It
would be just as correct or rather incorrect to say, in reference to the
explanation Mr. Cantor gives in the fifth paragraph, that, in general, a
general concept is quantitatively completely undetermined, that it does
indeed come to have a number under certain circumstances, but that
for such a quantitative determination the concept 'number' must
already be given in some other way. Incidentally, the difference that
Mr. Cantor speaks of a 'general concept' where I speak of the extension
of a concept appears to be an incidental one, in view of what I say in
the note on p. 80 of my work.

Deutsche Literaturzeitung 6 (1885), column 1030. (*Tr.* Hans Kaal)

On the Law of Inertia

Many readers will, no doubt, find it strange that a law recognized
long ago as being beyond doubt, such as the law of inertia, should once
again be subjected to a searching examination and that a new
formulation should be sought for it.[1] 'Without the action of an external
force, a body at rest remains at rest, and a body in motion maintains
its motion in respect of magnitude and direction': this has been
corroborated in countless instances; and what it means for a body to
'be in motion' or to 'be at rest' seems to be so clear that there seems
nothing left to be explained. The work cited below is nevertheless worth
reading and well-suited to shake that false sense of security and to
stimulate further thought. It is well known, and the author shows it in
detail, that the ancient philosophers had already discovered difficulties
in the answer to the question whether a given body was in motion. As
reminders I will mention only the ship anchored in a current and the
man on board a sailingship who walks backwards as he sails away
from shore so that his distance from the objects on the shore remains
unchanged. In such cases it is easy to get different answers to our
question, as one person attaches more importance to one relative
position and another to another, and as there is no generally recognized criterion. All these disputes can of course be settled quite
easily | by recognizing that an expression of the form 'a is in motion' is   146
incomplete, and by substituting for it an expression of the form 'a is in
motion relative to b'. The propositions 'a is in motion relative to b' and
'a is in motion relative to c' need not then contradict each other. Our
physicists too will admit that we can never experience the motion of a
body as such, but always only its motion relative to another body. But
this is to recognize that the law of inertia, as cited above, is defective in
the way it is expressed, for it talks about motion and rest as such. And
the worst part of it is that this defect cannot be repaired at all by
adding a reference to a body; for which body are we supposed to take

---

[1]This is a discussion of Dr. Ludwig Lange, *Die geschichtliche Entwicklung des
Bewegungsbegriffs und ihr voraussichtliches Endergebnis* [*The Historical Development of the
Concept of Motion and its Prospective End Result*] (Leipzig, 1886).

Zeitschrift für Philosophie und philosophische Kritik 98 (1891), pp. 145–61.
(*Tr.* Hans Kaal)

as a referent? Depending on which body we chose, a given body would appear to be either at rest or in motion, and if in motion, then either in a straight line or along a curve, and either at a uniform or at a non-uniform rate. The sense of the law of inertia prohibits a reference to a body because there is none that would merit this distinction, and yet motion as such remains unknowable. That is the difficulty. But how is it that physicists in general pay so little attention to it? The incomplete expression '*a* is in motion' is so convenient and so well sanctioned by linguistic usage that it is applied also, and only too frequently, in physics. Its theoretical unsuitability is all the more readily overlooked as it helps one to sidestep many a difficulty without being noticed. If one cannot answer a question, one can at least make it disappear behind the cloud of an imprecise turn of expression, which is especially welcome in the present case; for if one were to treat this as an open question, the whole of physics would seem to rest on a shaky foundation. This would explain why physicists have unconsciously been wary of using the complete form '*a* is in motion relative to *b*' throughout. Besides, the law of inertia has become a piece of common property so unquestionable that we do not notice it so easily when we tacitly presuppose it in trying to prove it. For when we try to prove it, we readily make use of laws of motion and expressions like 'mass' and 'force', even though all laws of motion are founded on the law of inertia

147 | and even though those expressions are first given a sense and made usable by it. But how is it that physics makes such steady progress in spite of this defect in its foundation? Well, astronomy introduces us to a coordinate system which is sufficient for all practical purposes and which will do to go on with. If we refer motions to this system and express the law of inertia with respect to them, we find that all of its consequences are sufficiently in accord with experience. There is of course nothing to be gained from this from a theoretical point of view; for there is no doubt that the fixed stars, which we need to fix our coordinate system, are only apparently at rest relative to one another, and that this appearance is due to the lack of precision in our observations. Besides, by its very nature, a law of nature requires universality, and reference to particular objects conflicts with this requirement. On the other hand, there is of course no doubt that, as far as explanations of natural phenomena are concerned, our coordinate system perfectly satisfies our needs, and that this perfection points to a lawfulness without which that satisfaction would be inexplicable.

It would seem that Newton's point of view is still generally accepted and that motion is still referred to absolute time and absolute space, even though Newton's theological justification may have lost its appeal to our tastes, and even though there is no way of recognizing again a place in absolute space, so that it is impossible to state what velocity a body has with reference to absolute space and absolute time. It makes no difference if we avoid the expressions 'absolute space' and 'absolute time' and speak instead of real and apparent motion. The author asks: 'What justifies Newton in asserting that the paths of bodies left to themselves are rectilinear with reference to absolute space when by his own admission its parts cannot be perceived ... Newton could not refute us in the least if we were to counter his assertion by asserting that the absolute paths of bodies left to themselves had a spiral curvature.' And again: 'How does Newton know that the oscillations of the pendulum of a clock are isochronous as measured in absolute time?' In trying to justify the law of inertia, Newton | is obviously moving in a   148 circle, and even now there are many who follow his lead. In order to demonstrate the existence of real motion and its difference from an apparent one, they make use of laws of motion, which include the law of inertia, and they then establish the law of inertia with respect to this real motion, which is the only way it can be done. Lange does not even value Newton's absolute space and absolute time as necessary evils, but calls them superfluous products of the metaphysical spirit. Here he does seem to me to be overshooting the target. This is because he considers in separation from one another hypotheses that have a meaning only as a whole. If we consider the hypothesis of absolute space by itself, then it appears to us as something that transcends all possible experience; motion in relation to absolute space is unknowable, and no laws about it can therefore be derived from experience. The matter is different if we combine the hypotheses of absolute space and absolute time with the law of inertia into a single hypothesis. This brings absolute space into connection with perceptible phenomena, and under this presupposition it is possible to do what Newton did: to make statements about absolute space that can be compared with experience. It may well be true that Newton himself was never fully aware of the situation. The defects of his presentation are to be explained by his unwillingness to set up anything explicitly as an hypothesis; he was determined to derive each step immediately either from experience or from first principles whose truth seemed to him beyond doubt; and he was therefore forced to divide into separate parts what admits of being compared with experience only as a whole. The difference between Newton's theory and the author's does not seem to me as great as it does to the author. But this is not to deny that, thanks to his efforts, the problem is now a good deal closer to being solved. Lange relates motion to 'inertial systems'. Thus he imagines three material points, left to themselves and

not lying in a straight line, starting out simultaneously from a single
149   point in space, | and he gives the name 'inertial system' to any
coordinate system with reference to which the paths of those points are
straight lines. A coordinate system of this kind can always be given: its
position at any moment is, of course, necessarily determined by the
locations of the three points. The proposition that the paths of those
points in such a coordinate system are rectilinear is not an experiential
one, but follows from the definition of an inertial system; but the
proposition that a fourth point left to itself in that inertial system
moves likewise in a straight line no longer follows from the definition;
and if it is none the less true, and if it is also true of any material point
left to itself, then this proposition is a law of nature. Following C.
Neumann's procedure, Lange introduces an 'inertial time scale' for the
temporal part of the law, that is, a way of measuring the time in which
a material point left to itself progresses at a uniform rate in an inertial
system. The proposition that any other material point not acted on by
an external force progresses likewise at a uniform rate in the inertial
system no longer follows from the definition, but is a law of nature. But
what do we gain by this? The author calls his system of reference an
ideal one, whereas Newton's absolute space is supposed to be trans-
cendently real. It may seem so if we go by what Newton says. But if
Newton's absolute space were really transcendent, it could not have
served to explain natural phenomena as in fact it did over a long
period of time. It is, moreover, linked with experience by the law of
inertia, though admittedly in a hidden way. The author deserves much
credit for having replaced this hidden link by a clearly expressed one.
Newton's assumption of a single absolute space contains more than is
needed for explaining natural phenomena. Among the infinite number
of possible inertial systems that move relative to one another at a
uniform rate without rotation, there is none that distinguishes itself
from the others, so as to enable us to regard it – in preference to any
other – as being at rest in absolute space. Newton cannot therefore tell
150   rest and uniform motion apart in relation to absolute space, | for
experience provides no basis for this distinction. Lange has happily
avoided distinguishing one inertial system from the others, a distinction
which goes beyond experience and is useless for explanatory purposes,
and to this extent he is right in blaming Newton for admitting
something transcendent.

However, I cannot consider the question to be settled once and for
all. The same or almost the same reproach that the author levels
against Newton can also be levelled against the author himself. For the
question whether a material point is 'left to itself' transcends experience,

just like the question whether it is absolutely at rest. In Newton's case the question was: how do we distinguish real from apparent motion? In the present case the question is: how do we distinguish a motion influenced by an external force from the motion of a material point left to itself? To be able to answer the question in Newton's case, we needed a knowledge of absolute space which we did not have; in the present case we need a knowledge of an inertial system which we likewise lack. For to know whether a given coordinate system was an inertial system, we would already have to have answered our question. In the same way, in order to know in Newton's case whether a given coordinate system belonged to absolute space, we would already have to have answered the question whether the point of origin of the coordinates was at rest in absolute space. This defect is due in both cases to dividing hypotheses into separate parts. Only the whole of the fundamental laws of dynamics – considered as a single hypothesis – can be compared with experience and be confirmed by it. My revered teacher K. Snell used to express the law of inertia in something like this way: 'A material point has an acceleration only as a result of its interaction with other material points.' What is to be understood by interaction is then to be determined more precisely by the other fundamental laws of dynamics. This brings the law of inertia at once into connection with those laws.

Lange's presentation needs to be supplemented also in another respect. While it may at first seem strange, it will be found to be true upon reflection that we have no means of observing whether lengths, for example, change in the course of time, and if so by how much. In judging a length, we always |•presuppose that our standard of measure-   151
ment is unchangeable. What we observe is therefore not the change of a length in itself, but merely the change of the relationship to another length.[2] If all distances were to decrease simultaneously by one half, we would have no means at all of noticing it; for the visual angles at which objects appeared to us would remain the same, and so would the parallaxes with respect to our eyes and all relationships to the parts of

[2]It is therefore completely false to say that a stable standard of measurement belongs‍ to the foundations of geometry. Whether or not a given length changes in the course of time is a matter of indifference to geometry, and from a purely geometrical point of view, this question does not even have a sense. The problem of comparing lengths not given at the same time falls outside the domain of geometry. Geometry has nothing to do with time, nor consequently with stability which can only be spoken of in relation to the course of time. Stability belongs to physics. Would one not also have to say that the phosphorus content of the brain and the extreme temperature of the sun belonged to the foundations of geometry?

our bodies, since our bodies would have shrunk along with everything else. It might be said: the accommodation of our eyes has to be changed; but we cannot say anything at all about this, for this already brings in something belonging to dynamics, namely the elastic forces of the ether. We ought here to adopt a point of view from which we do not yet know anything about forces. What force is, will be explained later on. We ought to ask: what can we observe without bringing in some hypothesis about the motion of matter? What is purely experiential? And if we do ask this, then we cannot deny that we have no means of observing the constancy of a distance, just as we have no means of recognizing again a point in space after a certain lapse of time, and just as we have no means of deciding whether there is an inertial system in relation to which a material point is at rest. Let it be clearly understood: we have no means – unless we bring in hypotheses. This is not to say that there is no difference between the uniform and the accelerated motion of a point, or between the constancy and the

52   change of a distance; but these differences | can be recognized only after a whole system of hypotheses has been recognized. As the assumption that the earth is at rest forces itself upon us with a certain degree of compulsion because the earth displays an overwhelming wealth of phenomena that are at rest relative to one another, and as from a loftier point of view the sky with its fixed stars is regarded as being at rest because the fixed stars in it appear to be at rest relative to one another, so we can hardly help assuming that a length is unchanged when it belongs to the overwhelming number of lengths whose relationships do not appear to change. In all these cases, we are led by the perception of an extensive comparative constancy to the assumption of absolute constancy, even though from a purely geometrical point of view, non-relative rest makes, properly speaking, as little sense as non-relative rigidity. Leibniz says in a passage cited by Lange: 'This is why motion is relative by its very nature. But this is true only if we speak with mathematical strictness. In practice we ascribe motion to bodies in conformity to those hypotheses that give us the most adequate explanation of the phenomena, and there is no difference at all between a true hypothesis and a suitable one.'[3] Lange rightly objects here to the expression 'hypothesis' and prefers 'convention' instead. One could also speak of 'definition'. Conventions are, properly speaking, neither true nor false, but appropriate or inappropriate. We always prefer that way of speaking in which the laws of nature can be expressed in the simplest way. So also in this case: we shall not be able to assert that a length

[3]G. W. Leibniz, *Mathematische Schriften*, ed. Gerhardt, vol. VI, p. 507.

remains unchanged until we have said how distances not given at the same time are to be compared with one another; and according to the method we stipulate, we shall then be able to say of a distance that it did or did not change. But not all possible stipulations are appropriate, if we want to express the laws of nature succinctly. Thus if we want to introduce a coordinate system into our considerations on motion, we must also determine the unit of length at each moment. |

To elucidate this point, I will add the following considerations. 153
Suppose we are given a system of parallel coordinates and a way of measuring time and length, such that three material points left to themselves progress at a uniform rate in three straight lines all of which pass through the point of origin, and suppose that the points progress as if they had been simultaneously at the point of origin of the coordinates. Let the moment corresponding to their being together be taken as point zero of time. Their coordinates are then proportional to time, and the triangle formed by them remains similar to itself. We now refer everything to a new coordinate system which differs from the first only in that the unit of length in it is proportional to time, as measured by the unit of length in the first system. Let the old and the new units of length coincide at time 1. If we now call a coordinate in the old system x and the corresponding coordinate in the new system ξ, then

$$\xi = \frac{x}{t}$$

at time t. Our three points are now at rest in relation to this new coordinate system. The old coordinates of any point moving at a uniform rate in a straight line in relation to the old system are integral first-degree functions of time and hence of the form

$$x = a + b \times t.$$

From this it follows that the coordinates in the new system are of the form

$$\xi = a \times \frac{1}{t} + b;$$

i.e., in the new system, the coordinates are integral first-degree functions of $1/t$. In the new system, the point would therefore no longer be moving at a uniform rate, given the previous way of measuring time. But we can introduce a new way of measuring time according to which the point will continue to move at a uniform rate. We only need to put |

$$\frac{1}{t} = \tau,$$

154

where τ is the number that designates the same time according to the new way of measuring time as t did according to the old way of measuring time. The points that were in uniform rectilinear motion in the old system according to the old way of measuring time are then again either in uniform rectilinear motion or at rest in the new system according to the new way of measuring time. Both systems are by definition inertial systems, since we assumed that the three points we considered in the beginning were left to themselves; and it is true of both systems that any fourth material point left to itself will progress at a uniform rate in a straight line. True, these lines are generally different, and the former point of origin of time has receded into an infinite temporal distance, and conversely, what was formerly an infinite temporal distance has become point $\tau = 0$ of time. To speak metaphorically, what formerly hovered before us only as an ideal goal never to be fully attained, has actually been attained, though once having been attained, it has also been left behind immediately. Now we have the equation

$$\zeta = x \times \tau,$$

from which it follows that ζ can become infinite only when either x or τ becomes infinite. The latter alternative would agree with what can happen, given our familiar ways of determining place and time, namely, that a body can move in the course of time farther and farther away beyond any limit. But that a material point could get lost in the infinity of space within a finite stretch of time, only to reappear at once at a finite distance – this strikes us as an absurdity, and it might seem at first as if this was possible, given our new ways of measuring space and time, since it would seem that ζ could become infinite even when τ was finite provided only that x became infinite. Let us suppose that the old way of measuring is in fact our familiar way of measuring: then x could become infinite only if t was infinite; and on the basis of our knowledge of nature we may also suppose that if x does not remain finite, then it becomes infinite only in the same degree as t. Accordingly, x/t or ζ would remain finite even if | x was infinite; and it would remain true, even given our new way of measuring space and time, that a material point could not vanish into infinite space as long as the point of time remained finite, but only as time itself became infinite.

155

Acceleration according to the new way of measuring must become 0 simultaneously with acceleration according to the old way of measuring; for we saw that a non-accelerated and hence uniform motion in the old system was again represented as such in the new system. We shall not therefore be surprised if our calculations yield the following relationship between the acceleration in the two systems:

$$\frac{d^2\xi}{d\tau^2}=t^3\frac{d^2x}{dt^2} \quad \text{or} \quad \frac{d^2x}{dt^2}=\tau^3\frac{d^2\xi}{d\tau^2}.$$

From this it follows that, for the same point of time, all accelerations in the new system have the same relations to one another as the corresponding accelerations in the old system. Now all universal laws of motion refer only to the relations between accelerations occurring at the same time. Therefore all these laws remain valid also for the new way of measuring time and space. As examples of such laws I cite the proposition concerning the parallelogram of accelerations; further, the proposition that the accelerations resulting from the interaction of two material points are contained in opposite directions in the connecting line between the two points, and that the relations in which they stand are always the same for the same two points; and furthermore, the proposition that the relations between the accelerations of material points *A* and *B* are simply composed of the relations between the accelerations of points *A* and *C* on the one hand and points *B* and *C* on the other. All these laws continue to hold when all component accelerations occurring at the same time are increased or decreased in the same proportion; and once again, there is nothing to be gathered from any of these laws that would allow us to decide for one, and against the other, of those ways of measuring space and time. The matter is different if we focus on the dependence of acceleration on the distance between the points involved in an interaction. According to Newton's law, the acceleration of a | material point arising from its 156 interaction with another is inversely proportional to the square of the distance:

$$p=\frac{a}{r^2},$$

where *p* is such an acceleration, *r* the distance between the two points, and *a* a constant independent of time – all this according to our familiar way of measuring space and time. In the new system, let π correspond to *p*, and ρ to *r*. We then have

$$p=\tau^3\pi \quad \text{and} \quad r=\frac{\rho}{\tau},$$

and we obtain

$$\pi=\frac{a}{\tau\times\rho^2}.$$

The acceleration would then be directly dependent on time or else indirectly: if we went on to replace the constant a by a number a/τ which is dependent on time. Our familiar way of measuring space and time is therefore distinguished by the fact that according to it Newton's law assumes a form that contains no reference to time. And this is what we demand of a law of nature. When the same circumstances recur, we expect them to be followed also by the same consequences, irrespective of the time of the recurrence. If we nevertheless see different consequences occurring, we conclude from this that we did not attend to all the relevant circumstances; we do not shift the blame onto the point of time as such.

It seems to me that for the present we have no choice but to say:

It is possible to set up a coordinate system and a way of measuring lengths and time in such a way that all the material points in the world will move as follows in relation to it: the acceleration of any one of them can be resolved, according to the law of the parallelogram of accelerations, into components each of which corresponds to an interaction with another material point; further, these interactions are governed by the laws stated above, and the magnitude of each separate interaction conforms to a law | that contains no reference either to time or to the position of the material points relative to the coordinate system; consequently, one can displace the point of origin of time and introduce another coordinate system to replace the original one, which will be congruent with the former and which will be closely linked to it, without changing the analytic expressions of those laws in any way, except for the replacement of the old letters by the corresponding new ones.

It is thus a mathematical theorem that there is an infinite number of such coordinate systems moving relative to one another at a uniform rate, without rotation and without change of scale.

The question of the reality of motion now threatens to degenerate into a verbal dispute – or so it seems to me. The only substantive issue is whether or not the distinction between accelerated and non-accelerated motion – or, as Lange puts it, between inertial rotation and inertial rest (cf. p. 56) – and the distinctions between the different kinds of accelerated motion are real distinctions. The best way to settle the matter would be the following. Those distinctions between different kinds of motion are real in the same sense in which the constancy of a length (e.g., of a standard metre rod at the same temperature) is called real. In both cases we are dealing with arbitrary stipulations, but with stipulations which are so closely linked to the lawfulness of nature that they are specially distinguished by this from all other stipulations which are logically and mathematically equally possible. If we want to express this close link to the lawfulness of nature by using the word 'real', we must do it in both cases. But the word 'objective' is perhaps more suitable.

Let me make room for some remarks concerning the expressions 'concept' and 'idea'. The former, it seems to me, is best assigned to logic; for logic would seem to have the oldest claim to it, and logic needs such an expression to be able to express its laws; and what is required of a concept for this purpose is a sharp boundary – not freedom from contradiction, which is in no way required. If something fails to display a sharp | boundary, it cannot be recognized in logic as a   158 concept, just as something that is not extensionless cannot be recognized in geometry as a point, because otherwise it would be impossible to set up geometrical axioms. The technical language of any science must conform to a single standard and must be judged with that standard in mind: does it enable the lawfulness of nature to be expressed as simply as possible and at the same time with perfect precision? And with this in mind I find it regrettable that the word 'concept' is now frequently used in phrases which are incompatible with its logical sense. A logical concept does not develop and it does not have a history, at least not in the currently fashionable sense. Unlike the author, I see no great need for being able to talk about the history of the development of a concept, and I find that there is good reason to avoid this phrase. If we said instead 'history of attempts to grasp a concept' or 'history of the grasp of the concept', this would seem to me much more to the point; for a concept is something objective: we do not form it, nor does it form itself in us, but we seek to grasp it, and in the end we hope to have grasped it, though we may mistakenly have been looking for something where there was nothing. 'The number three falls under the concept of a prime number' is an objective truth; in uttering it I do not mean: I find in my mind an idea which I call 'three' and another which I call 'prime number', and these ideas stand in a peculiar relation to each other; whether similar ideas occur in other minds, and whether they stand in a similar relation to each other – this remains to be discovered; and whether the idea which I call 'prime number' will not undergo a very gradual change till it ceases to stand in that peculiar relation to that other idea – this I have no way of knowing now: only future experience can teach me whether it will have been so. |

If one were to say this, one would obviously be missing the proper   159 sense of the proposition entirely; but one would also be missing it if one were to say 'I form these concepts in my mind' instead of 'I find these ideas in my mind', for one would still be reporting on a process within oneself. What we want to assert in using that proposition is something that always was and always will be objectively true, quite independently of our waking or sleeping, life or death, and irrespective of whether there were or will be other beings who recognize or fail to recognize this truth.

Lange is of the opinion 'that by its very nature a concept that is still developing is not free from internal contradictions: if it were, one would lack any motive for its further development'. This seems to me quite false in general, and it does not fit the particular case before us. A contradiction in a concept is no reason whatsoever for developing it. The concept of not being identical with itself contains a contradiction and remains none the less what it is and always was, and still does not look as if it was about to develop further. It has a good claim to being recognized in logic as a concept, for its boundary is as sharp as it can possibly be; and one can make good use of it in defining the number 0, as I have shown in my book, *The Foundations of Arithmetic*. In our case too, it is not contradictions in the concept of motion that are the driving force behind its development. Contradictions have indeed appeared; but it is not as if they had been created by combining mutually contradictory characteristic marks in the definition; they have, rather, been created by treating as a concept something that was not a concept in the logical sense because it lacked a sharp boundary. In the search for a boundary line, the contradictions, as they emerged, brought to the attention of the searchers that the assumed boundary was still uncertain or blurred, or that it was not the one they had been searching for. So contradictions were indeed a driving force behind the search, but not contradictions in the concept; for these always carry with them a sharp boundary: it is known that nothing falls under a
160 contradictory concept; it is therefore impossible to doubt | whether or not a given object falls under the concept, once the contradiction in it has been recognized. The real driving force is the perception of the blurred boundary. In our case too, all efforts have been directed at finding a sharp boundary. We are now perhaps in a position to say that the reason why these efforts were unsuccessful was that there was no boundary to be found at the place where it was being looked for. A different boundary line has been found instead: not the one between motion and non-motion, but the one between inertial rest and non-inertial rest; and the honour of having been the first to see it clearly and distinctly belongs to the present author. This should console him if it should turn out that he has been unsuccessful in 'speeding up the development of the concept of motion towards its ultimate goal'.

I cannot accept the current use of the word 'idea' any more than I can accept the current use of the word 'concept'. As the latter is to be assigned to logic, the former is to be assigned, most appropriately, to psychology. In assigning it to psychology, we remain in close touch, not only with everyday linguistic usage, but also with psychological tradition. We say 'I imagine [or ideate] something' and mean by this an inner mental process, while by 'idea' [or 'image'] we understand an inner mental picture. Accordingly, the word 'idea' ought never to be used in physics, mathematics or logic, or used only in order to dismiss it as inappropriate. Physics for instance is concerned with bodies and also, like any science, with concepts, but not with ideas: these may be reserved for psychology. In scientific discourse, one ought never to speak of an idea without at least indicating its relation to the person who has it, to its owner. For one person's idea is his and no one else's, just as his nose is his and no one else's even if it is congruent with some one else's nose. The non-relative use of the word 'idea' is just as unacceptable in science as the non-relative use of the word 'motion'.

Lange says, e.g.: 'We overlook the fact that the idea of the earth enters into our judgements about "real" motion', | and elsewhere: 'the idea of the position of a system of points is the idea of the locations of all of its points'. Can the author imagine the locations of all the atoms of a piece of paper? But that is a different matter altogether; if the position of a system of points includes the locations of its points, then we have everything we need. Who cares what ideas some person has of it? When will scientists stop intermingling what is psychological and what is logical: ideas and concepts? It is true that the author could, as I have done, appeal to linguistic usage, but use it instead to back his case: he could cite hundreds of books and articles to the purpose. He could unfortunately do this; and these remarks are therefore not directed especially against him and the present book. I deduce the need to make a distinction and to assign one expression to logic and another to psychology from the nature of the thing and from the needs of science, and I appeal to linguistic usage only to justify my choice between the expressions. But linguistic usage can never be used to justify covering up existing differences.

I should not, however, like to take leave of this stimulating book by emphasizing a divergence of opinion, but I should like, in parting, to endorse the author's destructive criticism of the so-called 'absolute translation of the sun', which is contained in the first appendix, and I should like to subscribe to his statement 'that elementary concepts are not the original data of a science', or as I should like to express it, that they must first be discovered by logical analysis. Similarly, the chemical elements are not the original data of chemistry, but their discovery indicates an advanced stage of the development of the science. What comes first in the logical and objective order is not what comes first in the psychological and historical order.

Function and Concept

PREFACE

I publish this lecture separately, hoping thereby to reach a number of i
readers who would never come across it in the proceedings of the Jena
Medical and Scientific Society. In the near future, as I have indicated
elsewhere, it is my intention to give an exposition of how I express in
my conceptual notation the fundamerftal definitions of arithmetic and
of how, starting from these, I construct proofs that make exclusive use
of my own signs. For that purpose I shall find it useful to be able to
refer to this lecture rather than be drawn, in the course of my
exposition, into discussions which some might regard as necessary but
others as reprehensibly irrelevant to the main point. In keeping with its
occasion, my lecture was not addressed solely to mathematicians, and I
sought to express myself in terms that would be as widely understood
as the time available and the matter in hand permitted. May it
therefore awaken interest in its subject in wider scholarly circles,
particularly among logicians.

*　　*　　*

Rather a long time ago[1] I had the honour of addressing this Society 1
about the symbolic system that I entitled *Begriffsschrift*. Today I should
like to throw light upon the subject from another side, and tell you
about some supplementations and new conceptions, whose necessity
has occurred to me since then. There can here be no question of setting
forth my conceptual notation [*Begriffsschrift*] in its entirety, but only of
elucidating some fundamental ideas.

My starting-point is what is called a function in mathematics. The
original meaning of this word was not so wide as that which it has
since obtained; it will be well to begin by dealing with this first usage,
and only then consider the later widenings of it. I shall for the moment
be speaking only of functions of a single argument. The first place

---

[1] On 10 and 27 January 1879.

Hermann Pohle, Jena, 1891. (*Tr.* (text) Peter Geach; (preface) ed.)

where a scientific expression appears with a clear-cut meaning is where
it is required for the statement of a law. This case arose as regards |
2 functions upon the discovery of higher Analysis. Here for the first time
it was a matter of setting forth laws holding for functions in general. So
we must go back to the time when higher Analysis was discovered, if
we want to know what the word 'function' was originally taken to
mean. The answer that we are likely to get to this question is: 'A
function of x was taken to be a mathematical expression containing x,
a formula containing the letter x.'

Thus, e.g., the expression

$$2x^3 + x$$

would be a function of x, and

$$2.2^3 + 2$$

would be a function of 2. This answer cannot satisfy us, for here no
distinction is made between form and content, sign and thing signified;
a mistake, admittedly, that is very often met with in mathematical
works, even those of celebrated authors. I have already pointed out on
a previous occasion[2] the defects of the current formal theories in
arithmetic. We there have talk about signs that neither have nor are
meant to have any content, but nevertheless properties are ascribed to
them which are unintelligible except as belonging to the content of a
3 sign. So also here; | a mere expression, the form for a content, cannot
be the heart of the matter; only the content itself can be that. Now
what is the content of '$2.2^3 + 2$'? What does it mean? The same thing as
'18' or '3.6'. What is expressed in the equation '$2.2^3 + 2 = 18$' is that the
right-hand complex of signs has the same meaning as the left-hand one.
I must here combat the view that, e.g., $2 + 5$ and $3 + 4$ are equal but not
the same. This view is grounded in the same confusion of form and
content, sign and thing signified. It is as though one wanted to regard
the sweet-smelling violet as differing from *Viola odorata* because the
names sound different. Difference of sign cannot by itself be a sufficient
ground for difference of the thing signified. The only reason why in our
case the matter is less obvious is that what the numeral 7 means is not
anything perceptible to the senses. There is at present a very widespread tendency not to recognize as an object anything that cannot be
perceived by means of the senses; this leads here to numerals' being

[2]*Die Grundlagen der Arithmetik* [*The Foundations of Arithmetic*] (Wilhelm Köbner,
Breslau, 1884) [English translation, tr. J. L. Austin, 2nd edn, Oxford, 1953] and 'On
Formal Theories of Arithmetic' (1885) [this volume p. 112].

taken to be numbers, the proper objects of our discussion;[3] and then, I admit, 7 and $2 + 5$ would indeed be different. But such a conception is untenable, for we | cannot speak of any arithmetical properties of 4 numbers whatsoever without going back to what the signs mean. For example, the property belonging to 1, of being the result of multiplying itself by itself, would be a mere myth; for no microscopical or chemical investigation, however far it was carried, could ever detect this property in the possession of the innocent character that we call a figure one. Perhaps there is talk of a definition; but no definition is creative in the sense of being able to endow a thing with properties that it has not already got – apart from the one property of expressing and signifying something in virtue of the definition.[4] The characters we call numerals have, on the other hand, physical and chemical properties depending on the writing material. One could imagine the introduction some day of quite new numerals, just as, e.g., the Arabic numerals superseded the Roman. Nobody is seriously going to suppose that in this way we should get quite new numbers, quite new arithmetical objects, with properties still to be investigated. Thus we must distinguish between numerals and what they mean; and if so, we shall have to recognize that the expressions '2,' '1 + 1,' '3 − 1,' '6:3' all | mean the same thing, for 5 it is quite inconceivable where the difference between them could lie. Perhaps you say: $1 + 1$ is a sum, but 6:3 is a quotient. But what is 6:3? The number that when multiplied by 3 gives the result 6. We say '*the* number', not 'a number'; by using the definite article, we indicate that there is only a single number. Now we have:

$$(1 + 1) + (1 + 1) + (1 + 1) = 6$$

and thus $(1 + 1)$ is the very number that was designated as (6:3). The different expressions correspond to different conceptions and aspects, but nevertheless always to the same thing. Otherwise the equation $x^2 = 4$ would not just have the roots 2 and -2, but also the root $(1 + 1)$ and countless others, all of them different, even if they resembled one another in a certain respect. By recognizing only two real roots, we are rejecting the view that the sign of equality does not mean a complete

---

[3]Cf. the essays: H. von Helmholtz, 'Zählen und Messen erkenntnistheoretisch betrachtet' [English translation, 'Numbering and Measuring from an Epistemological Viewpoint' in H. von Helmholtz, *Epistemological Writings* (Dordrecht and Boston, 1977), p. 72], and Leopold Kronecker, 'Über den Zahlbegriff', in *Philosophische Aufsätze: Eduard Zeller zu seinem fünfzigjährigen Doctorjubiläum gewidmet* (Leipzig, 1887).

[4]In definition it is always a matter of associating with a sign a sense or a meaning. Where sense and meaning are missing, we cannot properly speak either of a sign or of a definition.

coincidence but only a partial agreement. If we adhere to this truth, we see that what the expressions:

$$\text{'}2.1^3 + 1\text{'},$$

$$\text{'}2.2^3 + 2\text{'},$$

$$\text{'}2.4^3 + 4\text{'},$$

mean are numbers, viz. 3, 18, 132. So if a function were really the meaning of a mathematical expression, it would just be a number; and nothing new would have been gained for arithmetic by speaking of functions. Admittedly, people who use the word 'function' ordinarily

6 have in mind expressions | in which a number is just indicated indefinitely by the letter x, e.g.

$$\text{'}2.x^3 + x\text{'};$$

but that makes no difference; for this expression likewise just indefinitely indicates a *number*, and it makes no essential difference whether I write it down or just write down 'x'.

All the same, it is precisely by the notation that uses 'x' to indicate a number indefinitely that we are led to the right conception. People call x the argument, and recognize the same function again in

$$\text{'}2.1^3 + 1\text{'}.$$

$$\text{'}2.4^3 + 4\text{'},$$

$$\text{'}2.5 + 5\text{'},$$

only with different arguments, viz. 1, 4, and 5. From this we may discern that it is the common element of these expressions that contains the essential peculiarity of a function; i.e. what is present in

$$\text{'}2.x^3 + x\text{'}$$

over and above the letter 'x'. We could write this somewhat as follows:

$$\text{'}2.(\ \ )^3 + (\ \ )\text{'}.$$

I am concerned to show that the argument does not belong with a function, but goes together with the function to make up a complete whole; for a function by itself must be called incomplete, in need of supplementation, or 'unsaturated.' And in this respect functions differ fundamentally from numbers. Since such is the essence of functions, we can explain | why, on the one hand, we recognize the same function in '$2.1^3 + 1$' and '$2.2^3 + 2$', even though the numbers these expressions mean are different, whereas, on the other hand, we do not find one and the same function in '$2.1^3 + 1$' and '$4 - 1$' in spite of their equal numerical values. Moreover, we now see how people are easily led to regard the form of an expression as what is essential to a function. We recognize the function in the expression by imagining the latter as split up, and the possibility of thus splitting it up is suggested by its structure.

The two parts into which a mathematical expression is thus split up, the sign of the argument and the expression of the function, are dissimilar; for the argument is a number, a whole complete in itself, as the function is not. (We may compare this with the division of a line by a point. One is inclined in that case to count the dividing-point along with both segments; but if we want to make a clean division, i.e. so as not to count anything twice over or leave anything out, then we may only count the dividing-point along with one segment. This segment thus becomes fully complete in itself, and may be compared to the argument; whereas the other is lacking in something – viz. the dividing-point, which one may call its endpoint, does not belong to it. Only by completing it with this endpoint, or with a line that has two endpoints, do we get from it something entire.) For instance, if I say 'the function $2.x^3 + x$', x must not be considered as | belonging to the function; this 8 letter only serves to indicate the kind of supplementation that is needed; it enables one to recognize the places where the sign for the argument must go in.

We give the name 'the value of a function for an argument' to the result of completing the function with the argument. Thus, e.g., 3 is the value of the function $2.x^3 + x$ for the argument 1, since we have: $2.1^3 + 1 = 3$.

There are functions, such as $2 + x - x$ or $2 + 0.x$, whose value is always the same, whatever the argument; we have $2 = 2 + x - x$ and $2 = 2 + 0.x$. Now if we counted the argument as belonging with the function, we should hold that the number 2 is this function. But this is wrong. Even though here the value of the function is always 2, the function itself must nevertheless be distinguished from 2; for the expression for a function must always show one or more places that are intended to be filled up with the sign of the argument.

The method of analytic geometry supplies us with a means of intuitively representing the values of a function for different arguments. If we regard the argument as the numerical value of an abscissa, and the corresponding value of the function as the numerical value of the ordinate of a point, we obtain a set of points that presents itself to intuition (in ordinary cases) as a curve. Any point on the curve corresponds to an argument together with the associated value of the function. |

9   Thus, e.g.,

$$y = x^2 - 4x$$

yields a parabola; here '*y*' indicates the value of the function and the numerical value of the ordinate, and '*x*' similarly indicates the argument and the numerical value of the abscissa. If we compare with this the function

$$x(x - 4),$$

we find that they have always the same value for the same argument. We have generally:

$$x^3 - 4x = x(x - 4),$$

whatever number we take for *x*. Thus the curve we get from

$$y = x^3 - 4x$$

is the same as the one that arises out of

$$y = x(x - 4).$$

I express this as follows: the function $x(x - 4)$ has the same range of values as the function $x^2 - 4x$.

If we write

$$x^3 - 4x = x(x - 4),$$

we have not put one function equal to the other, but only the values of one equal to those of the other. And if we so understand this equation that it is to hold whatever argument may be substituted for *x*, then we have thus expressed that an equality holds generally. But we can also say: 'the value-range of the function $x(x - 4)$ is equal to that of | the

10   function $x^2 - 4x$', and here we have an equality between value-ranges. The possibility of regarding the equality holding generally between values of functions as a particular equality, viz. an equality between value-ranges is, I think, indemonstrable; it must be taken to be a fundamental law of logic.[5]

We may further introduce a brief notation for the value-range of a function. To this end I replace the sign of the argument in the expression for the function by a Greek vowel, enclose the whole in

[5] In many phrases of ordinary mathematical terminology, the word 'function' certainly corresponds to what I have here called the value-range of a function. But function, in the sense of the word employed here, is the logically prior notion.

brackets, and prefix to it the same Greek letter with a smooth breathing. Accordingly, e.g.,

$$\grave{\varepsilon}(\varepsilon^2 - 4\varepsilon)$$

is the value-range of the function $x^2 - 4x$ and

$$\grave{\alpha}(\alpha.(\alpha - 4))$$

is the value-range of the function $x(x-4)$, so that in

$$`\grave{\varepsilon}(\varepsilon^2 - 4\varepsilon) = \grave{\alpha}(\alpha.(\alpha - 4))`$$

we have the expression for: the first range of values is the same as the second. A different choice of Greek letters is made on purpose, in order to indicate that there is nothing that obliges us to take the same one. |

If we understand   11

$$`x^2 - 4x = x(x - 4)`$$

in the same sense as before, this expresses the same sense, but in a different way. It presents the sense as an equality holding generally; whereas the newly-introduced expression is simply an equation, and its right side, and equally its left side, will mean something complete in itself. In

$$`x^2 - 4x = x(x - 4)`$$

the left side considered in isolation indicates a number only indefinitely, and the same is true of the right side. If we just had '$x^2 - 4x$' we could write instead '$y^2 - 4y$' without altering the sense; for 'y' like 'x' indicates a number only indefinitely. But if we combine the two sides to form an equation, we must choose the same letter for both sides, and we thus express something that is not contained in the left side by itself, nor in the right side, nor in the 'equals' sign; viz. generality. Admittedly what we express is the generality of an equality; but primarily it is a generality.

Just as we indicate a number indefinitely by a letter, in order to express generality, we also need letters to indicate a function indefinitely. To this end people ordinarily use the letters f and F, thus: '$f(x)$', '$F(x)$', where 'x' replaces the argument. Here the need of a function for supplementation is expressed by the fact that the letter f or F | carries along with it a pair of brackets; the space between these   12 is meant to receive the sign for the argument. Thus

$$\grave{\varepsilon}f(\varepsilon)$$

indicates the value-range of a function that is left undetermined.

Now how has the meaning of the word 'function' been extended by the progress of science? We can distinguish two directions in which this has happened.

In the first place, the field of mathematical operations that serve for constructing functions has been extended. Besides addition, multiplication, exponentiation, and their converses, the various means of transition to the limit have been introduced – to be sure, people have not always been clearly aware that they were thus adopting something essentially new. People have gone further still, and have actually been obliged to resort to ordinary language, because the symbolic language of Analysis failed; e.g. when they were speaking of a function whose value is 1 for rational and 0 for irrational arguments.

Secondly, the field of possible arguments and values for functions has been extended by the admission of complex numbers. In conjunction with this, the sense of the expressions 'sum', 'product', etc., had to be defined more widely.

In both directions I go still further. I begin by adding to the signs $+$,
13    $-$, etc., which serve for constructing a functional expression, $|$ also signs such as $=$, $>$, $<$, so that I can speak, e.g., of the function $x^2 = 1$, where x takes the place of the argument as before. The first question that arises here is what the values of this function are for different arguments. Now if we replace x successively by $-1, 0, 1, 2$, we get:

$$(1)^2 = 1,$$

$$0^2 = 1,$$

$$1^2 = 1,$$

$$2^2 = 1.$$

Of these equations the first and third are true, the others false. I now say: 'the value of our function is a truth-value', and distinguish between the truth-values of what is true and what is false. I call the first, for short, the True; and the second, the False. Consequently, e.g., what '$2^2 = 4$' means is the True just as, say, '2^2' means 4. And '$2^2 = 1$' means the False. Accordingly

$$\text{`}2^2 = 4\text{'}, \quad \text{`}2 > 1\text{'}, \quad \text{`}2^4 = 4^2\text{'},$$

all mean the same thing, viz. the True, so that in

$$(2^2 = 4) = (2 > 1)$$

we have a correct equation.

The objection here suggests itself that '$2^2 = 4$' and '$2 > 1$' nevertheless tells us quite different things, express quite different thoughts; but likewise '$2^4 = 4^2$' and '$4.4 = 4^2$' express different thoughts; and yet we can replace '2^4' by '4.4', since both signs have the same meaning. Consequently, '$2^4 = 4^2$' and '$4.4 = 4^2$' likewise have the same meaning. We see | from this that from sameness of meaning there does not follow   14 sameness of the thought expressed. If we say 'the Evening Star is a planet with a shorter period of revolution than the Earth', the thought we express is other than in the sentence 'the Morning Star is a planet with a shorter period of revolution than the Earth'; for somebody who does not know that the Morning Star is the Evening Star might regard one as true and the other as false. And yet both sentences must mean the same thing; for it is just a matter of interchange of the words 'Evening Star' and 'Morning Star', which mean the same thing, i.e. are proper names of the same heavenly body. We must distinguish between sense and meaning. '2^4' and '$4^2 2$' certainly have the same meaning, i.e. are proper names of the same number; but they have not the same sense; consequently, '$2^4 = 4^2$' and '$4.4 = 4^2$' mean the same thing, but have not the same sense (i.e., in this case: they do not contain the same thought).[6]

Thus, just as we write:

$$`2^4 = 4.4\text'$$

we may also write with equal justification

$$`(2^4 = 4^2) = (4.4 = 4^2)\text'$$

and $\qquad\qquad$ '$(2^2 = 4) = (2 > 1)$'. |

It might further be asked: What, then, is the point of admitting the   15 signs $=$, $>$, $<$, into the field of those that help to build up a functional expression? Nowadays, it seems, more and more supporters are being won by the view that arithmetic is a further development of logic; that a more rigorous establishment of arithmetical laws reduces them to purely logical laws and to such laws alone. I too am of this opinion, and I base upon it the requirement that the symbolic language of arithmetic must be expanded into a logical symbolism. I shall now have to indicate how this is done in our present case.

We saw that the value of our function $x^2 = 1$ is always one of the two truth-values. Now if for a definite argument, e.g. -1, the value of the

---

[6]I do not fail to see that this way of putting it may at first seem arbitrary and artificial, and that it would be desirable to establish my view by going further into the matter. Cf. my forthcoming essay 'Über Sinn und Bedeutung' ['On Sense and Meaning'] in the *Zeitschrift für Philosophie und philosophische Kritik* [this volume pp. 157–77].

function is the True, we can express this as follows: 'the number -1 has the property that its square is 1'; or, more briefly, '-1 is a square root of 1'; or '-1 falls under the concept: square root of 1'. If the value of the function $x^2 = 1$ for an argument, e.g. for 2, is the False, we can express this as follows: '2 is not a square root of 1' or '2 does not fall under the concept: square root of 1'. We thus see how closely that which is called a concept in logic is connected with what we call a function. Indeed, we may say at once: a concept is a function whose value is always a truth-value. Again, the value of the function

$$(x+1)^2 = 2(x+1) \quad |$$

16 is always a truth-value. We get the True as its value, e.g., for the argument -1, and this can also be expressed thus: -1 is a number less by 1 than a number whose square is equal to its double. This expresses the fact that -1 falls under a concept. Now the functions

$$x^2 = 1 \qquad \text{and} \qquad (x+1)^2 = 2(x+1)$$

always have the same value for the same argument, viz. the True for the arguments -1 and $+1$, and the False for all other arguments. According to our previous conventions we shall also say that these functions have the same range of values, and express this in symbols as follows:

$$\grave{\varepsilon}(\varepsilon^2 = 1) = \grave{\alpha}((\alpha+1)^2 = 2(\alpha+1)).$$

In logic this is called identity of the extension of concepts. Hence we can designate as an extension the value-range of a function whose value for every argument is a truth-value.

We shall not stop at equations and inequalities. The linguistic form of equations is a statement. A statement contains (or at least purports to contain) a thought as its sense; and this thought is in general true or false; i.e. it has in general a truth-value, which must be regarded as what the sentence means, just as (say) the number 4 is what the expression '$2+2$' means or London what the expression 'the capital of England' means. |

17 Statements in general, just like equations or inequalities or expressions in Analysis, can be imagined to be split up into two parts; one complete in itself, and the other in need of supplementation, or 'unsaturated.' Thus, e.g., we split up the sentence

'Caesar conquered Gaul'

into 'Caesar' and 'conquered Gaul'. The second part is 'unsaturated' – it contains an empty place; only when this place is filled up with a proper name, or with an expression that replaces a proper name, does a complete sense appear. Here too I give the name 'function' to what is meant by this 'unsaturated' part. In this case the argument is Caesar.

We see that here we have undertaken to extend the application of the term in the other direction, viz. as regards what can occur as an argument. Not merely numbers, but objects in general, are now admissible; and here persons must assuredly be counted as objects. The two truth-values have already been introduced as possible values of a function; we must go further and admit objects without restriction as values of functions. To get an example of this, let us start, e.g., with the expression

'the capital of the German Empire'.

This obviously takes the place of a proper name, and stands for an object. If we now split it up into parts |

'the capital of' and 'the German Empire'   18

where I count the German genitive form as going with the first part, then this part is 'unsaturated,' whereas the other is complete in itself. So in accordance with what I said before, I call

'the capital of x'

the expression of a function. If we take the German Empire as the argument, we get Berlin as the value of the function.

When we have thus admitted objects without restriction as arguments and values of functions, the question arises what it is that we are here calling an object. I regard a regular definition as impossible, since we have here something too simple to admit of logical analysis. It is only possible to indicate what is meant. Here I can only say briefly: An object is anything that is not a function, so that an expression for it does not contain any empty place.

A statement contains no empty place, and therefore we must take what it means to be an object. But what a statement means is a truth-value. Thus the two truth-values are objects.

Earler on we presented equations between value-ranges, e.g.:

$$\text{`}\acute\varepsilon(\varepsilon^2 - 4\varepsilon) = \acute\alpha(\alpha(\alpha - 4))\text{'}.$$

We can split this up into '$\acute\varepsilon(\varepsilon^2 - 4\varepsilon)$' and '$(\ ) = \acute\alpha(\alpha(\alpha - 4))$'. This latter part needs supplementation, since on the left of the 'equals' sign it contains an empty | place. The first part, '$\acute\varepsilon(\varepsilon^2 - 4\varepsilon)$', is fully complete in   19 itself and thus stands for an object. Value-ranges of functions are objects, whereas functions themselves are not. We gave the name 'value-range' also to $\grave{\varepsilon}(\varepsilon^2 = 1)$, but we could also have termed it the extension of the concept: square root of 1. Extensions of concepts likewise are objects, although concepts themselves are not.

After thus extending the field of things that may be taken as arguments, we must get more exact specifications as to what is meant by the signs already in use. So long as the only objects dealt with in arithmetic are the integers, the letters a and b in '$a+b$' indicate only integers; the plus-sign need be defined only between integers. Every widening of the field to which the objects indicated by a and b belong obliges us to give a new definition of the plus-sign. It seems to be demanded by scientific rigour that we should have provisos against an expression's possibly coming to have no meaning; we must see to it that we never perform calculations with empty signs in the belief that we are dealing with objects. People have in the past carried out invalid procedures with divergent infinite series. It is thus necessary to lay down rules from which it follows, e.g., what

$$\text{'}\odot + 1\text{'}$$

is to mean, if '$\odot$' means the Sun. What rules we lay down is a matter
20 of comparative | indifference; but it is essential that we should do so –
that '$a+b$' should always have meaning, whatever signs for definite objects may be inserted in place of 'a' and 'b'. This involves the requirement as regards concepts, that, for any argument, they shall have a truth-value as their value; that it shall be determinate, for any object, whether it falls under the concept or not. In other words: as regards concepts we have a requirement of sharp delimitation; if this were not satisfied it would be impossible to set forth logical laws about them. For any argument x for which '$x+1$' were devoid of meaning, the function $x+1 = 10$ would likewise have no value, and thus no truth-value either, so that the concept:

'what gives the result 10 when increased by 1'

would have no sharp boundaries. The requirement of the sharp delimitation of concepts thus carries along with it this requirement for functions in general that they must have a value for every argument.

We have so far considered truth-values only as values of functions, not as arguments. By what I have just said, we must get a value of a function when we take a truth-value as the argument; but as regards the signs already in common use, the only point, in most cases, of a rule to this effect is that there should *be* a rule; it does not much matter what is determined upon. But now we must deal with certain functions that are of importance to us precisely when their argument is a truth-value. |

I introduce the following as such a function:

$$\qquad x \qquad\qquad 21$$

I lay down the rule that the value of this function shall be the True if the True is taken as argument, and the contrariwise, in all other cases the value of this function is the False – i.e. both when the argument is the False and when it is not a truth-value at all. Accordingly, e.g.

$$\qquad 1+3=4$$

is the True, whereas both

$$\qquad 1+3=5$$

and also

$$\qquad 4$$

are the False. Thus this function has as its value the argument itself, when that is a truth-value. I used to call this horizontal stroke the content-stroke (*Inhaltsstrich*) – a name that no longer seems to me appropriate. I now wish to call it simply the horizontal.

If we write down an equation or inequality, e.g. $5>4$, we ordinarily wish at the same time to express a judgement; in our example, we want to assert that 5 is greater than 4. According to the view I am here presenting, '$5>4$' and '$1+3=5$' just give us expressions for truth-values, without making any assertion. This separation of the act from the subject matter of judgement seems to be indispensable; for otherwise we could not express a mere supposition | – the putting of a case without a   22 simultaneous judgement as to its arising or not. We thus need a special sign in order to be able to assert something. To this end I make use of a vertical stroke at the left end of the horizontal, so that, e.g., by writing

$$\vdash 2+3=5$$

we assert that $2+3$ equals 5. Thus here we are not just writing down a truth-value, as in

$$2+3=5,$$

but also at the same time saying that it is the True.[7]

---

[7]The assertion sign (*Urtheilsstrich*) cannot be used to construct a functional expression; for it does not serve, in conjunction with other signs, to designate an object. '$\vdash 2+3=5$' does not designate anything; it asserts something.

The next simplest function, we may say, is the one whose value is the False for just those arguments for which the value of ——x is the True, and, conversely, is the True for the arguments for which the value of ——x is the False. I symbolize it thus:

$$\top x,$$

and here I call the little vertical stroke the stroke of negation. I conceive of this as a function with the argument ——x:

$$(\top x) = (\top(\text{——}x))$$

where I imagine the two horizontal strokes to be fused together. But we also have:

$$(\text{——}(\top x)) = (\top x), \quad |$$

23   since the value of $\top x$ is always a truth-value. I thus regard the bits of the stroke in '$\top x$' to the right and to the left of the stroke of negation as horizontals, in the sense of the word that I defined previously. Accordingly, e.g.:

$$\top 2^2 = 5$$

stands for the True, and we may add the assertion sign:

$$\vdash \top 2^2 = 5;$$

and in this we assert that $2^2 = 5$ is not the True, or that 2^2 is not 5. But moreover

$$\top 2$$

is the True, since ——2 is the False:

$$\vdash \top 2$$

i.e. 2 is not the True.

My way of presenting generality can best be seen in an example. Suppose what we have to express is that every object is equal to itself. In

$$x = x$$

we have a function, whose argument is indicated by 'x'. We now have to say that the value of this function is always the True, whatever we take as argument. I now take the sign

$$-\underset{\cup}{\overset{\mathfrak{a}}{}}- f(\mathfrak{a})$$

to mean the True when the function $f(x)$ always has the True as its value, whatever the argument may be; in all other cases |

$$—\underset{\smile}{\overset{\mathfrak{a}}{}}— f(\mathfrak{a})$$

is to mean the False. For our function $x = x$ we get the first case. Thus

$$—\underset{\smile}{\overset{\mathfrak{a}}{}}— f(\mathfrak{a})$$

is the True; and we write this as follows:

$$\vert—\underset{\smile}{\overset{\mathfrak{a}}{}}— \mathfrak{a} = \mathfrak{a}$$

The horizontal stroke to the right and to the left of the concavity are to be regarded as horizontals in our sense. Instead of '$\mathfrak{a}$', any other Gothic letter could be chosen; except those which are to serve as letters for a function, like $\mathfrak{f}$ and $\mathfrak{F}$.

This notation affords the possibility of negating generality, as in

$$—\underset{\overset{\vert}{}}{}—\underset{\smile}{\overset{\mathfrak{a}}{}}— \mathfrak{a}^2 = 1.$$

That is to say,

$$—\underset{\smile}{\overset{\mathfrak{a}}{}}— \mathfrak{a}^2 = 1$$

is the False, since not every argument makes the value of the function $x^2 = 1$ to be the True. (Thus, e.g., we get $2^2 = 1$ for the argument 2, and this is the False.) Now if

$$—\underset{\smile}{\overset{\mathfrak{a}}{}}— \mathfrak{a}^2 = 1$$

is the False, then

$$—\underset{\overset{\vert}{}}{}—\underset{\smile}{\overset{\mathfrak{a}}{}}— \mathfrak{a}^2 = 1$$

is the True, according to the rule that we laid down previously for the stroke of negation. Thus we have

$$\vert—\underset{\overset{\vert}{}}{}—\underset{\smile}{\overset{\mathfrak{a}}{}}— \mathfrak{a}^2 = 1;$$

i.e. 'not every object is a square root of 1', or 'there are objects that are not square roots of 1'. |

25   Can we also express: there are square roots of 1? Certainly: we need only take, instead of the function $x^2 = 1$, the function

$$\rule[0.5ex]{1.2em}{0.4pt}\!\!\top\, x^2 = 1.$$

By fusing together the horizontals in

$$\rule[0.5ex]{1em}{0.4pt}\overset{\mathfrak{a}}{\underset{\smile}{}}\rule[0.5ex]{1em}{0.4pt}\!\!\top\, \mathfrak{a}^2 = 1$$

we get

$$\rule[0.5ex]{1em}{0.4pt}\overset{\mathfrak{a}}{\underset{\smile}{}}\rule[0.5ex]{1em}{0.4pt}\!\!\top\, \mathfrak{a}^2 = 1.$$

What this means is the False, since not every argument makes the value of the function

$$\rule[0.5ex]{1.2em}{0.4pt}\!\!\top\, x^2 = 1$$

to be the True. E.g.:

$$\rule[0.5ex]{1.2em}{0.4pt}\!\!\top\, 1^2 = 1$$

is the False, for $1^2 = 1$ is the True. Now since

$$\rule[0.5ex]{1em}{0.4pt}\overset{\mathfrak{a}}{\underset{\smile}{}}\rule[0.5ex]{1em}{0.4pt}\!\!\top\, \mathfrak{a}^2 = 1$$

is thus the False,

$$\rule[0.5ex]{1.2em}{0.4pt}\!\!\top\rule[0.5ex]{0.6em}{0.4pt}\overset{\mathfrak{a}}{\underset{\smile}{}}\rule[0.5ex]{1em}{0.4pt}\!\!\top\, \mathfrak{a}^2 = 1$$

is the True:

$$\rule[0.5ex]{1em}{0.4pt}\vert\!\vert\rule[0.5ex]{0.2em}{0.4pt}\top\rule[0.5ex]{0.6em}{0.4pt}\overset{\mathfrak{a}}{\underset{\smile}{}}\rule[0.5ex]{1em}{0.4pt}\!\!\top\, \mathfrak{a}^2 = 1;$$

i.e. 'not every argument makes the value of the function $x^2 = 1$ to be the False', or: 'there is at least one square root of 1'.

At this point there may follow a few examples in symbols and words.

$$\rule[0.5ex]{1em}{0.4pt}\vert\!\vert\rule[0.5ex]{0.2em}{0.4pt}\top\rule[0.5ex]{0.6em}{0.4pt}\overset{\mathfrak{a}}{\underset{\smile}{}}\rule[0.5ex]{1em}{0.4pt}\!\!\top\, \mathfrak{a} \geqq 0,$$

26   there is at least one positive number; |

$$\rule[0.5ex]{1em}{0.4pt}\vert\!\vert\rule[0.5ex]{0.2em}{0.4pt}\top\rule[0.5ex]{0.6em}{0.4pt}\overset{\mathfrak{a}}{\underset{\smile}{}}\rule[0.5ex]{1em}{0.4pt}\!\!\top\, \mathfrak{a} < 0,$$

there is at least one negative number;

$$\vdash\!\!-\!\!\underset{\alpha}{\smile}\!\!-\!\!-\ \alpha^3 - 3\alpha^2 + 2\alpha = 0,$$

there is at least one root of the equation

$$x^3 - 3x^2 + 2x = 0.$$

From this we may see how to express existential sentences, which are so important. If we use the functional letter f as an indefinite indication of a concept, then

$$-\!\!-\!\!\underset{\alpha}{\smile}\!\!-\!\!-\ f(\alpha)$$

gives us the form that includes the last examples (if we abstract from the assertion-sign). The expressions

$$-\!\!-\!\!\underset{\alpha}{\smile}\!\!-\!\!-\ \alpha^2 = 1, \qquad -\!\!-\!\!\underset{\alpha}{\smile}\!\!-\!\!-\ \alpha \geqq 0,$$

$$-\!\!-\!\!\underset{\alpha}{\smile}\!\!-\!\!-\ \alpha < 0, \qquad -\!\!-\!\!\underset{\alpha}{\smile}\!\!-\!\!-\ \alpha^2 - 3\alpha^2 + 2\alpha = 0$$

arise from this form in a manner analogous to that in which x^2 gives rise to '1^2', (2^2', '3^2'. Now just as in x^2 we have a function whose argument is indicated by 'x', I also conceive of

$$-\!\!-\!\!\underset{\alpha}{\smile}\!\!-\!\!-\ f(\alpha)$$

as the expression of a function whose argument is indicated by 'f'. Such a function is obviously a fundamentally different one from those we have dealt with so far; for only a function can occur as its argument. Now just as functions are fundamentally different from objects, so also functions whose arguments are and must be functions are fundamentally different from functions whose arguments are objects and cannot be | anything else. I call the latter first-level, the former 　27 second-level, functions. In the same way, I distinguish between first-level and second-level concepts.[8] Second-level functions have actually long been used in Analysis; e.g. definite integrals (if we regard the function to be integrated as the argument).

I will now add something about functions with two arguments. We

---

[8]Cf. my *Foundations of Arithmetic*. I there used the term 'second-order' instead of 'second-level'. The ontological proof of God's existence suffers from the fallacy of treating existence as a first-level concept.

F

get the expression for a function by splitting up the complex sign for an object into a 'saturated' and an 'unsaturated' part. Thus, we split up this sign for the True,

$$3 > 2,$$

into '3' and '$x > 2$'. We can further split up the 'unsaturated' part '$x > 2$' in the same way, into '2' and

$$x > y,$$

where 'y' enables us to recognize the empty place previously filled up by '2'. In

$$x > y$$

we have a function with two arguments, one indicated by 'x' and the other by 'y'; and in

$$3 > 2$$

28   we have the value of this function for the | arguments 3 and 2. We have here a function whose value is always a truth-value. We called such functions of one argument concepts; we call such functions of two arguments relations. Thus we have relations also, e.g., in

$$x^2 + y^2 = 9$$

and in

$$x^2 + y^2 > 9,$$

whereas the function

$$x^2 + y^2$$

has numbers as values. We shall therefore not call this a relation.

At this point I may introduce a function not peculiar to arithmetic. The value of the function

$$\begin{array}{l} \rule{0.7cm}{0.4pt}\, x \\ \rule{0.7cm}{0.4pt}\, y \end{array}$$

is to be the False if we take the True as the y-argument and at the same time take some object that is not the True as the x-argument; in all other cases the value of this function is to be the True. The lower horizontal stroke, and the two bits that the upper one is split into by the vertical, are to be regarded as horizontals in our sense. Consequently, we can always regard as the arguments of our function ——x and ——y, i.e. truth-values.

Among functions of one argument we distinguished first-level and second-level ones. Here, a greater multiplicity is possible. A function of two arguments may be | of the same level in relation to them, or of 29 different levels; there are equal-levelled and unequal-levelled functions. Those we have dealt with up to now were equal-levelled. An example of an unequal-levelled function is the differential quotient, if we take the arguments to be the function that is to be differentiated and the argument for which it is differentiated; or the definite integral, so long as we take as arguments the function to be integrated and the upper limit. Equal-levelled functions can again be divided into first-level and second-level ones. An example of a second-level one is

$$F(f(1)),$$

where 'F' and 'f' indicate the arguments.

In regard to second-level functions with one argument, we must make a distinction, according as the role of this argument can be played by a function of one or of two arguments; for a function of one argument is essentially so different from one with two arguments that the one function cannot occur as an argument in the same place as the other. Some second-level functions of one argument require that this should be a function with one argument; others, that it should be a function with two arguments; and these two classes are sharply divided.

$$\underset{\smile\ \smile\ \smile}{\mathfrak{e}\quad\mathfrak{d}\quad\mathfrak{a}}\!\!-\!\!\mathfrak{d}=\mathfrak{a}$$

$$f(\mathfrak{e},\mathfrak{a})$$

$$f(\mathfrak{e},\mathfrak{d})$$

is an example of a second-level function with | one argument, which 30 requires that this should be a function of two arguments. The letter f here indicates the argument, and the two places, separated by a comma, within the brackets that follow 'f' bring it to our notice that f represents a function with two arguments.

For functions of two arguments there arises a still greater multiplicity.

If we look back from here over the development of arithmetic we discern an advance from level to level. At first people did calculations with individual numbers, 1, 3, etc.

$$2+3=5, \qquad 2.3=6$$

are theorems of this sort. Then they went on to more general laws that hold good for all numbers. What corresponds to this in symbolism is the transition to the literal notation. A theorem of this sort is

$$(a+b)c = a.c + b.c.$$

At this stage they had got to the point of dealing with individual functions; but were not yet using the word, in its mathematical sense, and had not yet formed the conception of what it now means. The next higher level was the recognition of general laws about functions, accompanied by the coinage of the technical term 'function'. What corresponds to this in symbolism is the introduction of letters like f, F, to indicate functions indefinitely. A theorem of this sort is

$$\frac{df(x) \cdot F(x)}{dx} = F(x) \cdot \frac{df(x)}{dx} + f(x) \cdot \frac{dF(x)}{dx}.$$

31   Now at this point people had | particular second-level functions, but lacked the conception of what we have called second-level functions. By forming that, we make the next step forward. One might think that this would go on. But probably this last step is already not so rich in consequences as the earlier ones; for instead of second-level functions one can deal, in further advances, with first-level functions – as shall be shown elsewhere. But this does not banish from the world the difference between first-level and second-level functions; for it is not made arbitrarily, but founded deep in the nature of things.

   Again, instead of functions of two arguments we can deal with functions of a single but complex argument; but the distinction between functions of one and of two arguments still holds in all its sharpness.

On Sense and Meaning

Equality[1] gives rise to challenging questions which are not altogether   25
easy to answer. Is it a relation? A relation between objects, or between
names or signs of objects? In my *Begriffsschrift*[2] I assumed the latter.
The reasons which seem to favour this are the following: $a = a$ and $a = b$
are obviously statements of differing cognitive value; $a = a$ holds *a priori*
and, according to Kant, is to be labelled analytic, while statements of
the form $a = b$ often contain very valuable extensions of our knowledge
and cannot always be established *a priori*. The discovery that the rising
sun is not new every morning, but always the same, was one of the
most fertile astronomical discoveries. Even today the re-identification of
a small planet or a comet is not always a | matter of course. Now if we   26
were to regard equality as a relation between that which the names 'a'
and 'b' designate, it would seem that $a = b$ could not differ from $a = a$
(i.e. provided $a = b$ is true). A relation would thereby be expressed of a
thing to itself, and indeed one in which each thing stands to itself but
to no other thing. What we apparently want to state by $a = b$ is that the
signs or names 'a' and 'b' designate the same thing, so that those signs
themselves would be under discussion; a relation between them would
be asserted. But this relation would hold between the names or signs
only in so far as they named or designated something. It would be
mediated by the connection of each of the two signs with the same
designated thing. But this is arbitrary. Nobody can be forbidden to use
any arbitrarily producible event or object as a sign for something. In
that case the sentence $a = b$ would no longer refer to the subject matter,
but only to its mode of designation; we would express no proper
knowledge by its means. But in many cases this is just what we want to
do. If the sign 'a' is distinguished from the sign 'b' only as an object
(here, by means of its shape), not as a sign (i.e. not by the manner in

---

[1] I use this word in the sense of identity and understand '$a = b$' to have the sense of 'a is
the same as b' or 'a and b coincide'.

[2] [The reference is to Frege's *Begriffsschrift, eine der arithmetischen nachgebildete
Formelsprache des reinen Denkens* (Halle, 1879); English translation, *Conceptual Notation*
(London, 1972).]

Zeitschrift für Philosophie und philosophische Kritik 100 (1892), pp. 25–50.
(*Tr*. Max Black)

which it designates something), the cognitive value of $a=a$ becomes essentially equal to that of $a=b$, provided $a=b$ is true. A difference can arise only if the difference between the signs corresponds to a difference in the mode of presentation of the thing designated. Let a, b, c be the lines connecting the vertices of a triangle with the midpoints of the opposite sides. The point of intersection of a and b is then the same as the point of intersection of b and c. So we have different designations for the same point, and these names ('point of intersection of a and b', 'point of intersection of b and c') likewise indicate the mode of presentation; and hence the statement contains actual knowledge.

It is natural, now, to think of there being connected with a sign (name, combination of words, written mark), besides that which the sign designates, which may be called the meaning of the sign, also what I should like to call the *sense* of the sign, wherein the mode of presentation is contained. In our example, accordingly, the | meaning of the expressions 'the point of intersection of a and b' and 'the point of intersection of b and c' would be the same, but not their sense. The meaning of 'evening star' would be the same as that of 'morning star,' but not the sense.

It is clear from the context that by sign and name I have here understood any designation figuring as a proper name, which thus has as its meaning a definite object (this word taken in the widest range), but not a concept or a relation, which shall be discussed further in another article.[3] The designation of a single object can also consist of several words or other signs. For brevity, let every such designation be called a proper name.

The sense of a proper name is grasped by everybody who is sufficiently familiar with the language or totality of designations to which it belongs;[4] but this serves to illuminate only a single aspect of the thing meant, supposing it to have one. Comprehensive knowledge of the thing meant would require us to be able to say immediately whether any given sense attaches to it. To such knowledge we never attain.

[3]['On Concept and Object', this volume pp. 182–93.]

[4]In the case of an actual proper name such as 'Aristotle' opinions as to the sense may differ. It might, for instance, be taken to be the following: the pupil of Plato and teacher of Alexander the Great. Anybody who does this will attach another sense to the sentence 'Aristotle was born in Stagira' than will a man who takes as the sense of the name: the teacher of Alexander the Great who was born in Stagira. So long as the thing meant remains the same, such variations of sense may be tolerated, although they are to be avoided in the theoretical structure of a demonstrative science and ought not to occur in a perfect language.

The regular connection between a sign, its sense, and what it means is of such a kind that to the sign there corresponds a definite sense and to that in turn a definite thing meant, while to a given thing meant (an object) there does not belong only a single sign. The same sense has different expressions in different languages or even in the same language. To be sure, exceptions to this regular behaviour occur. To every expression belonging to a complete totality of signs, there should certainly correspond a definite sense; but natural languages | often do 28 not satisfy this condition, and one must be content if the same word has the same sense in the same context. It may perhaps be granted that every grammatically well-formed expression figuring as a proper name always has a sense. But this is not to say that to the sense there also corresponds a thing meant. The words 'the celestial body most distant from the Earth' have a sense, but it is very doubtful if there is also a thing they mean. The expression 'the least rapidly convergent series' has a sense but demonstrably there is nothing it means, since for every given convergent series, another convergent, but less rapidly convergent, series can be found. In grasping a sense, one is not certainly assured of meaning anything.

If words are used in the ordinary way, what one intends to speak of is what they mean. It can also happen, however, that one wishes to talk about the words themselves or their sense. This happens, for instance, when the words of another are quoted. One's own words then first designate words of the other speaker, and only the latter have their usual meaning. We then have signs of signs. In writing, the words are in this case enclosed in quotation marks. Accordingly, a word standing between quotation marks must not be taken as having its ordinary meaning.

In order to speak of the sense of an expression 'A' one may simply use the phrase 'the sense of the expression "A"'. In indirect speech one talks about the sense, e.g., of another person's remarks. It is quite clear that in this way of speaking words do not have their customary meaning but designate what is usually their sense. In order to have a short expression, we will say: In indirect speech, words are used *indirectly* or have their *indirect* meaning. We distinguish accordingly the *customary* from the *indirect* meaning of a word; and its *customary* sense from its *indirect* sense. The indirect meaning of a word is accordingly its customary sense. Such exceptions must always be borne in mind if the mode of connection between sign, sense, and meaning in particular cases is to be correctly understood. |

The meaning and sense of a sign are to be distinguished from the 29 associated idea. If what a sign means is an object perceivable by the senses, my idea of it is an internal image,[5] arising from memories of sense impressions which I have had and acts, both internal and external, which I have performed. Such an idea is often imbued with feeling; the clarity of its separate parts varies and oscillates. The same sense is not always connected, even in the same man, with the same idea. The idea is subjective: one man's idea is not that of another. There result, as a matter of course, a variety of differences in the ideas associated with the same sense. A painter, a horseman, and a zoologist will probably connect different ideas with the name 'Bucephalus'. This constitutes an essential distinction between the idea and sign's sense, which may be the common property of many people, and so is not a part or a mode of the individual mind. For one can hardly deny that mankind has a common store of thoughts which is transmitted from one generation to another.[6]

In the light of this, one need have no scruples in speaking simply of *the* sense, whereas in the case of an idea one must, strictly speaking, add whom it belongs to and at what time. It might perhaps be said: Just as one man connects this idea, and another that idea, with the same word, so also one man can associate this sense and another that sense. But there still remains a difference in the mode of connection. They are not prevented from grasping the same sense; | but they cannot have the same idea. *Si duo idem faciunt, non est idem.* If two persons picture the same thing, each still has his own idea. It is indeed sometimes possible to establish differences in the ideas, or even in the sensations, of different men; but an exact comparison is not possible, because we cannot have both ideas together in the same consciousness.

The meaning of a proper name is the object itself which we designate by using it; the idea which we have in that case is wholly subjective; in between lies the sense, which is indeed no longer subjective like the idea, but is yet not the object itself. The following analogy will perhaps clarify these relationships. Somebody observes the Moon through a telescope. I compare the Moon itself to the meaning; it is the object of the observation, mediated by the real image projected by the object glass in the interior of the telescope, and by the retinal image of the

30

---

[5]We may include with ideas direct experiences: here, sense-impressions and acts themselves take the place of the traces which they have left in the mind. The distinction is unimportant for our purpose, especially since memories of sense-impressions and acts always go along with such impressions and acts themselves to complete the perpetual image. One may on the other hand understand direct experience as including any object in so far as it is sensibly perceptible or spatial.

[6]Hence it is inadvisable to use the word 'idea' to designate something so basically different.

observer. The former I compare to the sense, the latter is like the idea or experience. The optical image in the telescope is indeed one-sided and dependent upon the standpoint of observation; but it is still objective, inasmuch as it can be used by several observers. At any rate it could be arranged for several to use it simultaneously. But each one would have his own retinal image. On account of the diverse shapes of the observers' eyes, even a geometrical congruence could hardly be achieved, and an actual coincidence would be out of the question. This analogy might be developed still further, by assuming A's retinal image made visible to B; or A might also see his own retinal image in a mirror. In this way we might perhaps show how an idea can itself be taken as an object, but as such is not for the observer what it directly is for the person having the idea. But to pursue this would take us too far afield.

We can now recognize three levels of difference between words, expressions, or whole sentences. The difference may concern at most the ideas, or the sense but not the meaning, or, finally, the meaning as well. With respect to | the first level, it is to be noted that, on account of the   31 uncertain connection of ideas with words, a difference may hold for one person, which another does not find. The difference between a translation and the original text should properly not overstep the first level. To the possible differences here belong also the colouring and shading which poetic eloquence seeks to give to the sense. Such colouring and shading are not objective, and must be evoked by each hearer or reader according to the hints of the poet or the speaker. Without some affinity in human ideas art would certainly be impossible; but it can never be exactly determined how far the intentions of the poet are realized.

In what follows there will be no further discussion of ideas and experiences; they have been mentioned here only to ensure that the idea aroused in the hearer by a word shall not be confused with its sense or its meaning.

To make short and exact expressions possible, let the following phraseology be established:

> A proper name (word, sign, sign combination, expression) *expresses* its sense, *means* or *designates* its meaning. By employing a sign we express its sense and designate its meaning.

Idealists or sceptics will perhaps long since have objected: 'You talk, without further ado, of the Moon as an object; but how do you know that the name "the Moon" has any meaning? How do you know that anything whatsoever has a meaning?' I reply that when we say 'the Moon', we do not intend to speak of our idea of the Moon, nor are we satisfied with the sense alone, but we presuppose a meaning. To assume that in the sentence 'The Moon is smaller than the Earth' the idea of the Moon is in question, would be flatly to misunderstand the sense. If this is what the speaker wanted, he would use the phrase 'my idea of the Moon'. Now we can of course be mistaken in the presupposition, and such mistakes have indeed occurred. But the question whether the presupposition is perhaps always mistaken need | not be answered here; in order to justify mention of that which a sign means it is enough, at first, to point our intention in speaking or thinking. (We must then add the reservation: provided such a meaning exists.)

So far we have considered the sense and meaning only of such expressions, words, or signs as we have called proper names. We now inquire concerning the sense and meaning of an entire assertoric sentence. Such a sentence contains a thought.[7] Is this thought, now, to be regarded as its sense or its meaning? Let us assume for the time being that the sentence does mean something. If we now replace one word of the sentence by another having the same meaning, but a different sense, this can have no effect upon the meaning of the sentence. Yet we can see that in such a case the thought changes; since, e.g., the thought in the sentence 'The morning star is a body illuminated by the Sun' differs from that in the sentence 'The evening star is a body illuminated by the Sun'. Anybody who did not know that the evening star is the morning star might hold the one thought to be true, the other false. The thought, accordingly, cannot be what is meant by the sentence, but must rather be considered as its sense. What is the position now with regard to the meaning? Have we a right even to inquire about it? Is it possible that a sentence as a whole has only a sense, but no meaning? At any rate, one might expect that such sentences occur, just as there are parts of sentences having sense but no meaning. And sentences which contain proper names without meaning will be of this kind. The sentence 'Odysseus was set ashore at Ithaca while sound asleep' obviously has a sense. But since it is doubtful whether the name 'Odysseus', occurring therein, means anything, it is also doubtful whether the whole sentence does. Yet it is certain, nevertheless, that anyone who seriously took the sentence to be true or false would ascribe to the name 'Odysseus' a meaning, not merely a sense; for it is of what | the name means that the predicate is affirmed or denied. Whoever does not admit the name has meaning can neither apply nor withhold the predicate. But in that case it would be

---

[7]By a thought I understand not the subjective performance of thinking but its objective content, which is capable of being the common property of several thinkers.

superfluous to advance to what the name means; one could be satisfied with the sense, if one wanted to go no further than the thought. If it were a question only of the sense of the sentence, the thought, it would be needless to bother with what is meant by a part of the sentence; only the sense, not the meaning, of the part is relevant to the sense of the whole sentence. The thought remains the same whether 'Odysseus' means something or not. The fact that we concern ourselves at all about what is meant by a part of the sentence indicates that we generally recognize and expect a meaning for the sentence itself. The thought loses value for us as soon as we recognize that the meaning of one of its parts is missing. We are therefore justified in not being satisfied with the sense of a sentence, and in inquiring also as to its meaning. But now why do we want every proper name to have not only a sense, but also a meaning? Why is the thought not enough for us? Because, and to the extent that, we are concerned with its truth-value. This is not always the case. In hearing an epic poem, for instance, apart from the euphony of the language we are interested only in the sense of the sentences and the images and feelings thereby aroused. The question of truth would cause us to abandon aesthetic delight for an attitude of scientific investigation. Hence it is a matter of no concern to us whether the name 'Odysseus', for instance, has meaning, so long as we accept the poem as a work of art.[8] It is the striving for truth that drives us always to advance from the sense to the thing meant.

We have seen that the meaning of a sentence may always be sought, whenever the meaning of its components is involved; and that this is the case when and only when we are inquiring after the truth-value. |

We are therefore driven into accepting the *truth-value* of a sentence   34 as constituting what it means. By the truth-value of a sentence I understand the circumstance that it is true or false. There are no further truth-values. For brevity I call the one the True, the other the False. Every assertoric sentence concerned with what its words mean is therefore to be regarded as a proper name, and its meaning, if it has one, is either the True or the False. These two objects are recognized, if only implicitly, by everybody who judges something to be true – and so even by a sceptic. The designation of the truth-values as objects may appear to be an arbitrary fancy or perhaps a mere play upon words, from which no profound consequences could be drawn. What I am

---

[8]It would be desirable to have a special term for signs intended to have only sense. If we name them say, representations, the words of the actors on the stage would be representations; indeed the actor himself would be a representation.

calling an object can be more exactly discussed only in connection with concept and relation. I will reserve this for another article.[9] But so much should already be clear, that in every judgement,[10] no matter how trivial, the step from the level of thoughts to the level of meaning (the objective) has already been taken.

One might be tempted to regard the relation of the thought to the True not as that of sense to meaning, but rather as that of subject to predicate. One can, indeed, say: 'The thought that 5 is a prime number is true'. But closer examination shows that nothing more has been said than in the simple sentence '5 is a prime number'. The truth claim arises in each case from the form of the assertoric sentence, and when the latter lacks its usual force, e.g., in the mouth of an actor upon the stage, even the sentence 'The thought that 5 is a prime number is true' contains only a thought, and indeed the same thought as the simple '5 is a prime number'. It follows that the relation of the thought to the True may not be compared with that of subject to predicate. |

35   Subject and predicate (understood in the logical sense) are just elements of thought; they stand on the same level for knowledge. By combining subject and predicate, one reaches only a thought, never passes from sense to meaning, never from a thought to its truth-value. One moves at the same level but never advances from one level to the next. A truth-value cannot be a part of a thought, any more than, say, the Sun can, for it is not a sense but an object.

If our supposition that the meaning of a sentence is its truth-value is correct, the latter must remain unchanged when a part of the sentence is replaced by an expression with the same meaning. And this is in fact the case. Leibniz gives the definition: '*Eadem sunt, quae sibi mutuo substitui possunt, salva veritate*'. If we are dealing with sentences for which the meaning of their component parts is at all relevant, then what feature except the truth-value can be found that belongs to such sentences quite generally and remains unchanged by substitutions of the kind just mentioned?

If now the truth-value of a sentence is its meaning, then on the one hand all true sentences have the same meaning and so, on the other hand, do all false sentences. From this we see that in the meaning of the sentence all that is specific is obliterated. We can never be concerned only with the meaning of a sentence; but again the mere thought alone yields no knowledge, but only the thought together with its meaning, i.e. its truth-value. Judgements can be regarded as ad-

---

[9] ['On Concept and Object', this volume pp. 182–94.]

[10] A judgement, for me is not the mere grasping of a thought, but the admission of its truth.

vances from a thought to a truth-value. Naturally this cannot be a definition. Judgement is something quite peculiar and incomparable. One might also say that judgements are distinctions of parts within truth-values. Such distinction occurs by a return to the thought. To every sense attaching to a truth-value would correspond its own manner of analysis. However, I have here used the word 'part' in a special sense. I have in fact transferred the relation between the parts and the whole of the sentence to its meaning, by calling the meaning of a word part of the meaning of the sentence, if the word itself | is a part   36 of the sentence. This way of speaking can certainly be attacked, because the total meaning and one part of it do not suffice to determine the remainder, and because the word 'part' is already used of bodies in another sense. A special term would need to be invented.

The supposition that the truth value of a sentence is what it means shall now be put to further test. We have found that the truth-value of a sentence remains unchanged when an expression is replaced by another with the same meaning: but we have not yet considered the case in which the expression to be replaced is itself a sentence. Now if our view is correct, the truth-value of a sentence containing another as part must remain unchanged when the part is replaced by another sentence having the same truth-value. Exceptions are to be expected when the whole sentence or its part is direct or indirect quotation; for in such cases as we have seen, the words do not have their customary meaning. In direct quotation, a sentence designates another sentence, and in indirect speech a thought.

We are thus led to consider subordinate sentences or clauses. These occur as parts of a sentence complex, which is, from the logical standpoint, likewise a sentence – a main sentence. But here we meet the question whether it is also true of the subordinate sentence that its meaning is a truth-value. Of indirect speech we already know the opposite. Grammarians view subordinate clauses as representatives of parts of sentences and divide them accordingly into noun clauses, adjective clauses, adverbial clauses. This might generate the supposition that the meaning of a subordinate clause was not a truth-value but rather of the same kind as the meaning of a noun or adjective or adverb – in short, of a part of a sentence, whose sense was not a thought but only a part of a thought. Only a more thorough investigation can clarify the issue. In so doing, we shall not follow the grammatical categories strictly, but rather group together what is logically of the same kind. Let us first search for cases in which the sense of the subordinate clause, as we have just supposed, is not an independent thought. |

37   The case of an abstract[11] noun clause, introduced by 'that,' includes
the case of indirect quotation, in which we have seen the words to have
their indirect meaning, coincident with what is customarily their sense.
So here, the subordinate clause has for its meaning a thought, not a
truth-value and for its sense not a thought, but the sense of the words
'the thought that (etc.)', which is only a part of the thought in the entire
complex sentence. This happens after 'say', 'hear', 'be of the opinion',
'be convinced', 'conclude', and similar words.[12] There is a different, and
indeed somewhat complicated, situation after words like 'perceive',
'know', 'fancy', which are to be considered later.

That in the cases of the first kind the meaning of the subordinate
clause is in fact the thought can also be recognized by seeing that it is
indifferent to the truth of the whole whether the subordinate clause is
true or false. Let us compare, for instance, the two sentences 'Copernicus believed that the planetary orbits are circles' and 'Copernicus
believed that the apparent motion of the Sun is produced by the real
motion of the Earth'. One subordinate clause can be substituted for the
other without harm to the truth. The main clause and the subordinate
clause together have as their sense only a single thought, and the truth
of the whole includes neither the truth nor the untruth of the
subordinate clause. In such cases it is not permissible to replace one
expression in the subordinate clause by another having the same
customary meaning, but only by one having the same indirect meaning,
i.e. the same customary sense. Somebody might conclude: The meaning
of a sentence is not its truth-value, for in that case it could always be
replaced by another sentence of the same truth-value. But this proves
too much; one might just as well claim that the meaning of 'morning
star' is not Venus, since one may not always say 'Venus' in place of
'morning star'. One has the right to conclude only that the meaning of
a sentence is not *always* its truth-value, and that 'morning star' does
38   not | always mean the planet Venus, viz. when the word has its indirect
meaning. An exception of such a kind occurs in the subordinate clause
just considered, which has a thought as its meaning.

If one says 'It seems that ...' one means 'It seems to me that ...' or 'I
think that ...' We therefore have the same case again. The situation is
similar in the case of expressions such as 'to be pleased', 'to regret', 'to

[11][Frege probably means clauses grammatically replaceable by an abstract noun-
phrase; e.g. 'Smith denies *that dragons exist*' = 'Smith denies *the existence of dragons*'; or
again, in this context after 'denies', 'that Brown is wise' is replaceable by 'the wisdom of
Brown'. (*Tr.*)]
[12]In 'A lied in saying he had seen B', the subordinate clause designates a thought
which is said (1) to have been asserted by A (2) while A was convinced of its falsity.

approve', 'to blame', 'to hope', 'to fear'. If, toward the end of the battle of Waterloo, Wellington was glad that the Prussians were coming, the basis for his joy was a conviction. Had he been deceived, he would have been no less pleased so long as his illusion lasted; and before he became so convinced he could not have been pleased that the Prussians were coming – even though in fact they might have been already approaching.

Just as a conviction or a belief is the ground of a feeling, it can, as in inference, also be the ground of a conviction. In the sentence: 'Columbus inferred from the roundness of the Earth that he could reach India by travelling towards the west', we have as the meanings of the parts two thoughts, that the Earth is round, and that Columbus by travelling to the west could reach India. All that is relevant here is that Columbus was convinced of both, and that the one conviction was a ground for the other. Whether the Earth is really round and Columbus could really reach India by travelling west, as he thought, is immaterial to the truth of our sentence; but it is not immaterial whether we replace 'the Earth' by 'the planet which is accompanied by a moon whose diameter is greater than the fourth part of its own'. Here also we have the indirect meaning of the words.

Adverbial final clauses beginning 'in order that' also belong here; for obviously the purpose is a thought; therefore: indirect meaning for the words, subjunctive mood.

A subordinate clause with 'that' after 'command', 'ask', 'forbid', would appear in direct speech as an imperative. Such a sentence has no meaning but only a sense. A command, a request, are indeed not thoughts, but they stand on the same level as thoughts. Hence in subordinate clauses depending upon 'command,' | 'ask,' etc., words have their indirect meaning. The meaning of such a clause is therefore not a truth-value but a command, a request, and so forth. 39

The case is similar for the dependent question in phrases such as 'doubt whether', 'not to know what'. It is easy to see that here also the words are to be taken to have their indirect meaning. Dependent clauses expression questions and beginning with 'who', 'what', 'where', 'when', 'how', 'by what means', etc., seem at time to approximate very closely to adverbial clauses in which words have their customary meanings. These cases are distinguished linguistically in German by the mood of the verb. With the subjunctive, we have a dependent question and indirect meanings of the words, so that a proper name cannot in general be replaced by another name of the same object.

In the cases so far considered the words of the subordinate clauses had their indirect meaning, and this made it clear that the meaning of the subordinate clause itself was indirect, i.e. not a truth-value but a thought, a command, a request, a question. The subordinate clause could be regarded as a noun, indeed one could say: as a proper name of that thought, that command, etc., which it represented in the context of the sentence structure.

We now come to other subordinate clauses, in which the words do have their customary meaning without however a thought occurring as sense and a truth-value as meaning. How this is possible is best made clear by examples.

> Whoever discovered the elliptic form of the planetary orbits died in misery.

If the sense of the subordinate clause were here a thought, it would have to be possible to express it also in a separate sentence. But it does not work, because the grammatical subject 'whoever' has no independent sense and only mediates the relation with the consequent clause 'died in misery.' For this reason the sense of the subordinate clause is not a complete thought, and what it means is Kepler, not a truth-value. One might object that the sense of the whole does contain a thought as part, viz. that there was somebody who first discovered the elliptic form of the planetary orbits; for whoever takes the whole to be true | cannot deny this part. This is undoubtedly so; but only because otherwise the dependent clause 'whoever discovered the elliptic form of the planetary orbits' would have nothing to mean. If anything is asserted there is always an obvious presupposition that the simple or compound proper names used have meaning. If therefore one asserts 'Kepler died in misery,' there is a presupposition that the name 'Kepler' designates something; but it does not follow that the sense of the sentence 'Kepler died in misery' contains the thought that the name 'Kepler' designates something. If this were the case the negation would have to run not

> Kepler did not die in misery

but

> Kepler did not die in misery, or the name 'Kepler' has no reference.

That the name 'Kepler' designates something is just as much a presupposition for the assertion

> Kepler died in misery

as for the contrary assertion. Now languages have the fault of containing expressions which fail to designate an object (although their grammatical form seems to qualify them for that purpose) because the truth of some sentence is a prerequisite. Thus it depends on the truth of the sentence:

There was someone who discovered the elliptic form of the planetary orbits

whether the subordinate clause

Whoever discovered the elliptic form of the planetary orbits

really designates an object, or only seems to do so while in fact there is nothing for it to mean. And thus it may appear as if our subordinate clause contained as a part of its sense the thought that there was somebody who discovered the elliptic form of the planetary orbits. If this were right the negation would run:

Either whoever discovered the elliptic form of the planetary orbits did not die in misery or there was nobody who discovered the elliptic form of the planetary orbits. |

This arises from an imperfection of language, from which even the symbolic language of mathematical analysis is not altogether free; even there combinations of symbols can occur that seem to mean something but (at least so far) do not mean anything, e.g. divergent infinite series. This can be avoided, e.g., by means of the special stipulation that divergent infinite series shall mean the number 0. A logically perfect language (*Begriffsschrift*) should satisfy the conditions, that every expression grammatically well constructed as a proper name out of signs already introduced shall in fact designate an object, and that no new sign shall be introduced as a proper name without being secured a meaning. The logic books contain warnings against logical mistakes arising from the ambiguity of expressions. I regard as no less pertinent a warning against apparent proper names without any meaning. The history of mathematics supplies errors which have arisen in this way. This lends itself to demagogic abuse as easily as ambiguity – perhaps more easily. 'The will of the people' can serve as an example; for it is easy to establish that there is at any rate no generally accepted meaning for this expression. It is therefore by no means unimportant to eliminate the source of these mistakes, at least in science, once and for all. Then such objections as the one discussed above would become impossible, because it could never depend upon the truth of a thought whether a proper name had meaning.

With the consideration of these noun clauses may be coupled that of types of adjective and adverbial clauses which are logically in close relation to them.

Adjective clauses also serve to construct compound proper names, though, unlike noun clauses, they are not sufficient by themselves for this purpose. These adjective clauses are to be regarded as equivalent to adjectives. Instead of 'the square root of 4 which is smaller than 0', one can also say 'the negative square root of 4'. We have here the case of a compound proper name constructed from the expression for a concept with the help of the singular definite article. This is at any rate permissible if the concept applies to one | and only one single object.[13] Expressions for concepts can be so constructed that marks of a concept are given by adjective clauses as, in our example, by the clause 'which is smaller than 0'. It is evident that such an adjective clause cannot have a thought as sense or a truth-value as meaning, any more than the noun clause could. Its sense, which can also in many cases be expressed by a single adjective, is only a part of a thought. Here, as in the case of the noun clause, there is no independent subject and therefore no possibility of reproducing the sense of the subordinate clause in an independent sentence.

Places, instants, stretches of time, logically considered, are objects; hence the linguistic designation of a definite place, a definite instant, or a stretch of time is to be regarded as a proper name. Now adverbial clauses of place and time can be used to construct such a proper name in much the same way as we have seen noun and adjective clauses can. In the same way, expressions for concepts that apply to places, etc., can be constructed. It is to be noted here also that the sense of these subordinate clauses cannot be reproduced in an independent sentence, since an essential component, viz. the determination of place or time, is missing and is just indicated by a relative pronoun or a conjunction.[14]

---

[13]In accordance with what was said above, an expression of the kind in question must actually always be assured of meaning, by means of a special stipulation, e.g. by the convention that it shall count as meaning 0 when the concept applies to no object or to more than one.

[14]In the case of these sentences, various interpretations are easily possible. The sense of the sentence, 'After Schleswig–Holstein was separated from Denmark, Prussia and Austria quarrelled' can also be rendered in the form 'After the separation of Schleswig–Holstein from Denmark, Prussia and Austria quarrelled.' In the version, it is surely sufficiently clear that the sense is not to be taken as having as a part the thought that Schleswig–Holstein was once separated from Denmark, but that this is the necessary presupposition in order for the expression 'after the separation of Schleswig–Holstein from Denmark' to have any meaning at all. To be sure, our sentence can also be interpreted as saying that Schleswig–Holstein was once separated from Denmark. We then have a case which is to be considered later. In order to understand the difference more clearly, let us project

In conditional clauses, also, there most often | recognizably occurs an 43
indefinite indicator, with a correlative indicator in the dependent clause.
(We have already seen this occur in noun, adjective, and adverbial
clauses.) In so far as each indicator relates to the other, both clauses
together form a connected whole, which as a rule expresses only a
single thought. In the sentence

> If a number is less than 1 and greater than 0, its square is less
> than 1 and greater than 0

the component in question is 'a number' in the antecedent clause and
'its' in the consequent clause. It is by means of this very indefiniteness
that the sense acquires the generality expected of a law. It is this which
is responsible for the fact that the antecedent clause alone has no
complete thought as its sense and in combination with the consequent
clause expresses one and only one thought, whose parts are no longer
thoughts. It is, in general, incorrect to say that in the hypothetical
judgement two judgements are put in reciprocal relationship. If this or
something similar is said, the word 'judgement' is used in the same
sense as I have connected with the word 'thought,' so that I would use
the formulation: 'A hypothetical thought establishes a reciprocal relationship between two thoughts.' This could be true only if no
indefinite indicator were present;[15] but in such a case there would also
be no generality.

If an instant of time is to be indefinitely indicated in both the
antecedent and the consequent clause, this is often achieved merely by
using the present tense of the verb, which in such a case however does
not indicate the temporal present. This grammatical form is then the
indefinite indicator in the main and subordinate clauses. An example of
this is: 'When | the Sun is in the tropic of Cancer, the longest day in the 44
northern hemisphere occurs'. Here, also, it is impossible to express the
sense of the subordinate clause in a full sentence, because this sense is
not a complete thought. If we say: 'The Sun is in the tropic of Cancer',
this would refer to our present time and thereby change the sense.

---

ourselves into the mind of a Chinese who, having little knowledge of European history,
believes it to be false that Schleswig–Holstein was ever separated from Denmark. He will
take our sentence, in the first version, to be neither true nor false but will deny it to have
any meaning, on the ground that its subordinate clause lacks a meaning. This clause
would only apparently determine a time. If he interpreted our sentence in the second way,
however, he would find a thought expressed in it which he would take to be false, beside
a part which would be without meaning for him.

[15] At times there is no linguistically explicit indicator and one must be read off from the
entire context.

Neither is the sense of the main clause a thought; only the whole, composed of main and subordinate clauses, has such a sense. It may be added that several common components may be indefinitely indicated in the antecedent and consequent clauses.

It is clear that noun clauses with 'who' or 'what' and adverbial clauses with 'where', 'when', 'wherever', 'whenever' are often to be interpreted as having the sense of antecedent clauses, e.g. 'who touches pitch, defiles himself'.

Adjective clauses can also take the place of conditional clauses. Thus the sense of the sentence previously used can be given in the form 'The square of a number which is less than 1 and greater than 0 is less than 1 and greater than 0'.

The situation is quite different if the common component of the two clauses is designated by a proper name. In the sentence:

Napoleon, who recognized the danger to his right flank, himself led his guards against the enemy position

two thoughts are expressed:

1. Napoleon recognized the danger to his right flank
2. Napoleon himself led his guards against the enemy position.

When and where this happened is to be fixed only by the context, but is nevertheless to be taken as definitely determined thereby. If the entire sentence is uttered as an assertion, we thereby simultaneously assert both component sentences. If one of the parts is false, the whole is false. Here we have the case that the subordinate clause by itself has a complete thought as sense (if we complete it by indication of place and time). The meaning of the subordinate clause is accordingly a truth-value. We can therefore expect that it may be replaced, without harm to the truth-value of the whole, by a sentence having the | same truth-value. This is indeed the case; but it is to be noted that for purely grammatical reasons, its subject must be 'Napoleon', for only then can it be brought into the form of an adjective clause attaching to 'Napoleon'. But if the demand that it be expressed in this form is waived, and the connection shown by 'and', this restriction disappears.

Subsidiary clauses beginning with 'although' also express complete thoughts. This conjunction actually has no sense and does not change the sense of the clause but only illuminates it in a peculiar fashion.[16] We could indeed replace the concessive clause without harm to the truth of the whole by another of the same truth-value; but the light in

[16]Similarly in the case of 'but', 'yet'.

which the clause is placed by the conjunction might then easily appear unsuitable, as if a song with a sad subject were to be sung in a lively fashion.

In the last cases the truth of the whole included the truth of the component clauses. The case is different if an antecedent clause expresses a complete thought by containing, in place of an indefinite indicator, a proper name or something which is to be regarded as equivalent. In the sentence

If the Sun has already risen, the sky is very cloudy

the time is the present, that is to say, definite. And the place is also to be thought of as definite. Here it can be said that a relation between the truth-values of antecedent and consequent clauses has been as-serted, viz. that the case does not occur in which the antecedent means the True and the consequent the False. Accordingly, our sentence is true if the Sun has not yet risen, whether the sky is very cloudy or not, and also if the Sun has risen and the sky is very cloudy. Since only truth-values are here in question, each component clause can be replaced by another of the same truth-value without changing the truth-value of the whole. To be sure, the light in which the subject then appears would usually be unsuitable; the thought might easily seem | inane; but this has nothing to do with its truth-value. One must always 46 observe that there are overtones of subsidiary thoughts, which are however not explicitly expressed and therefore should not be reckoned in the sense. Hence, also, no account need be taken of their truth-values.[17]

The simplest cases have now been discussed. Let us review what we have learned.

The subordinate clause usually has for its sense not a thought, but only a part of one, and consequently no truth-value is being meant. The reason for this is either that the words in the subordinate clause have indirect meaning, so that the meaning, not the sense, of the subordinate clause is a thought; or else that, on account of the presence of an indefinite indicator, the subordinate clause is incomplete and expresses a thought only when combined with the main clause. It may happen, however, that the sense of the subsidiary clause is a complete thought, in which case it can be replaced by another of the same truth value without harm to the truth of the whole – provided there are no grammatical obstacles.

[17]The thought of our sentence might also be expressed thus: 'Either the Sun has not risen yet or the sky is very cloudy' – which shows how this kind of sentence connection is to be understood.

An examination of all the subordinate clauses which one may encounter will soon provide some which do not fit well into these categories. The reason, so far as I can see, is that these subordinate clauses have no such simple sense. Almost always, it seems, we connect with the main thoughts expressed by us subsidiary thoughts which, although not expressed, are associated with our words, in accordance with psychological laws, by the hearer. And since the subsidiary thought appears to be connected with our words on its own account, almost like the main thought itself, we want it also to be expressed. The sense of the sentence is thereby enriched, and it may well happen that we have more simple thoughts than clauses. In many cases the sentence must be understood in this way, in others it may be doubtful whether 47 the subsidiary thought belongs to the sense of the sentence or | only accompanies it.[18] One might perhaps find that the sentence

> Napoleon, who recognized the danger to his right flank, himself led his guards against the enemy position

expresses not only the two thoughts shown above, but also the thought that the knowledge of the danger was the reason why he led the guards against the enemy position. One may in fact doubt whether this thought is just slightly suggested or really expressed. Let the question be considered whether our sentence is false if Napoleon's decision had already been made before he recognized the danger. If our sentence could be true in spite of this, the subsidiary thought should not be understood as part of the sense. One would probably decide in favour of this. The alternative would make for a quite complicated situation: We should have more simple thoughts than clauses. If the sentence

> Napoleon recognized the danger to his right flank

were now to be replaced by another having the same truth-value, e.g.

> Napoleon was already more than 45 years old

not only would our first thought be changed, but also our third one. Hence the truth-value of the latter might change – viz. if his age was not the reason for the decision to lead the guards against the enemy. This shows why clauses of equal truth-value cannot always be substituted for one another in such cases. The clause expresses more through its connection with another than it does in isolation.

Let us now consider cases where this regularly happens. In the

---

[18]This may be important for the question whether an assertion is a lie, or an oath a perjury.

sentence:

> Bebel fancies that the return of Alsace-Lorraine would appease
> France's desire for revenge

two thoughts are expressed, which are not however shown by means of
antecedent and consequent clauses, viz:

> (1) Bebel believes that the return of Alsace-Lorraine would
>   appease France's desire for revenge |
> (2) the return of Alsace-Lorraine would not appease France's   48
>   desire for revenge.

In the expression of the first thought, the words of the subordinate
clause have their indirect meaning, while the same words have their
customary meaning in the expression of the second thought. This shows
that the subordinate clause in our original complex sentence is to be
taken twice over, with different meanings: once for a thought, once for
a truth-value. Since the truth-value is not the total meaning of the
subordinate clause, we cannot simply replace the latter by another of
equal truth-value. Similar considerations apply to expressions such as
'know', 'discover', 'it is known that'.

By means of a subordinate causal clause and the associated main
clause we express several thoughts, which however do not correspond
separately to the original clauses. In the sentence: 'Because ice is less
dense than water, it floats on water' we have

> (1) Ice is less dense than water;
> (2) If anything is less dense than water, it floats on water;
> (3) Ice floats on water.

The third thought, however, need not be explicitly introduced, since it
is contained in the remaining two. On the other hand, neither the first
and third nor the second and third combined would furnish the sense
of our sentence. It can now be seen that our subordinate clause

> because ice is less dense than water

expresses our first thought, as well as a part of our second. This is how
it comes to pass that our subsidiary clause cannot be simply replaced
by another of equal truth-value; for this would alter our second
thought and thereby might well alter its truth-value.

The situation is similar in the sentence

> If iron were less dense than water, it would float on water. |

Here we have the two thoughts that iron is not less dense than water,   49 and that something floats on water if it is less dense than water. The subsidiary clause again expresses one thought and a part of the other.

If we interpret the sentence already considered

> After Schleswig–Holstein was separated from Denmark, Prussia and Austria quarrelled

in such a way that it expresses the thought that Schleswig–Holstein was once separated from Denmark, we have first this thought, and secondly the thought that, at a time more closely determined by the subordinate clause, Prussia and Austria quarrelled. Here also the subordinate clause expresses not only one thought but also a part of another. Therefore it may not in general be replaced by another of the same truth-value.

It is hard to exhaust all the possibilities given by language; but I hope to have brought to light at least the essential reasons why a subordinate clause may not always be replaced by another of equal truth-value without harm to the truth of the whole sentence structure. These reasons arise:

(1) when the subordinate clause does not, have a truth-value as its meaning, inasmuch as it expresses only a part of a thought;

(2) when the subordinate clause does have a truth-value as its meaning but is not restricted to so doing, inasmuch as its sense includes one thought and part of another.

The first cases arises:

(a) for words having indirect meaning

(b) if a part of the sentence is only an indefinite indicator instead of a proper name.

In the second case, the subsidiary clause may have to be taken twice over, viz. once in its customary meaning, and the other time in indirect meaning; or the sense of a part of the subordinate clause may likewise be a component of another thought, which, taken together with the thought directly expressed by the subordinate clause, makes up the sense of the whole sentence.

It follows with sufficient probability from the foregoing that the cases where a subordinate clause is not replaceable by another of the same

50   value cannot be brought in disproof of our view | that a truth-value is the meaning of a sentence that has a thought as its sense.

Let us return to our starting point.

If we found '$a = a$' and '$a = b$' to have different cognitive values, the explanation is that for the purpose of acquiring knowledge, the sense of the sentence, viz., the thought expressed by it, is no less relevant than its meaning, i.e. its truth-value. If now $a = b$, then indeed what is meant by 'b' is the same as what is meant by 'a', and hence the truth-value of '$a = b$' is the same as that of '$a = a$'. In spite of this, the sense of 'b' may differ from that of 'a', and thereby the thought expressed in '$a = b$' differs from that of '$a = a$'. In that case the two sentences do not have the same cognitive value. If we understand by 'judgement' the advance from the thought to its truth-value, as in the present paper, we can also say that the judgements are different.

Review of Georg Cantor, *Zur Lehre vom Transfiniten: Gesammelte Abhandlungen aus der Zeitschrift für Philosophie und philosophische Kritik*

[*Contributions to the Theory of the Transfinite: Collected Articles from* ZPhphK]

269 Since the papers in this collection originally appeared in this journal, I may assume familiarity with their contents and confine myself to an evaluation of them. Their aim is to get mathematicians to acknowledge the proper infinite, and this aim is pursued partly negatively, by refuting would-be counter-arguments, and partly positively, by demonstrating its existence. The considerations involved belong partly to theology and the philosophy of religion and partly to mathematics and logic. Let me be permitted here to examine only the latter, which by themselves provide sufficient material for discussion. The refutation of the objection to the infinite seems to me on the whole well-done and to the point. The objections arise when the infinite is assigned properties it does not have, either because the properties of the finite are carried over to the infinite as a matter of course (p. 3) or because a property belonging only to the absolute infinite is carried over to all of the infinite. To point emphatically to the differences within the infinite is one of the merits of this work. All of this relates only to the proper or 'actual' infinite. Part of the reluctance shown by mathematicians to acknowledge the actual infinite is to be traced back to a confusion of it with the potential infinite, a reluctance which is justified only when it is directed against the conception of the potential infinite as if it were the actual infinite. Some scholars thus acknowledge only the potential infinite. Mr. Cantor now shows with felicity that this infinite presupposes the proper or actual infinite: that there must be an infinite path if the 'travelling limit' is to travel further and further (cf. p. 30 n.).

Mr. Cantor shows less felicity in defining his terms. He does not even quite succeed in grasping the meaning of the potential infinite. He calls it the variable finite (pp. 7 and 28). But the word 'variable' (like the word 'increase') can be used properly only in relation to a second

Zeitschrift für Philosophie und philosophische Kritik 100 (1892), pp. 269–72.
(*Tr.* Hans Kaal)

something which varies simultaneously with the first. When it seems to occur in a non-relative sense, it is usually to be related to the time with which | something varies. But to admix time is hardly part of the   270
author's intention, and it would be wrong if it was, and the use of our word in a genuinely non-relative sense is nonsensical. The potential infinite is also called an indeterminate quantity (p. 53); but there are no indeterminate quantities any more than there are indeterminate men.

If Mr. Cantor had not only reviewed my *Foundations of Arithmetic* but also read them thoughtfully, he would have avoided many mistakes. I believe I have done there already a long time ago what he is here trying in vain to do. Mr. Cantor repeats (p. 13) a definition he had given in his review of my book as his own intellectual property. It seemed to me at the time that it differed from my own, not in its essentials, but only in its wording, which is also what I said in a reply, and I was then able to think that he had arrived by his own labours at essentially the same results as I myself. I now see that the truths I enunciated in my book were not, after all, like coins dropped in the street which anybody could make his own simply by bending down. For Mr. Cantor goes on to give some other definitions (pp. 23 and 56) which show that he is still firmly ensconced in an antiquated position. He is asking for impossible abstractions, and it is unclear to him what is to be understood by a 'set', even though he has an inkling of the correct answer, which comes out faintly when he says (p. 67 n.): 'A set is already completely delimited by the fact that everything that belongs to it is determined in itself and well distinguished from everything that does not belong to it.' This delimitation is, of course, achieved by characteristic marks and is nothing other than the definition of a concept. On this point compare my proposition (*Foundations,* §46): '...the content of a statement of number is an assertion about a concept'. It cannot be my task here to repeat what I set forth at length in my book. But in order not to leave my statement without any support at all, I cite the fact that, inevitably, we once again encounter those unfortunate Ones which are different even though there is nothing to distinguish them from one another. The author evidently did not have the slightest inkling of the presence of this difficulty, which I dealt with at length in §§34 to 54 of my *Foundations.* His definition of a finite set (p. 61 n.) is similar | in its fundamental idea to my definition   271
of a natural number (*Foundations,* §83); only it is carried out faultily; for what does it mean to say 'that the original element can also be got backwards out of *M* by *successive* removal of the elements in reverse order'? The 'can' would have to be defined more precisely by stating what obstacles would not count as reasons for not getting it; for even

in the case of a finite set we might be confronted with obstacles we could not overcome, e.g., the shortness of our lives. What proves to be harmful here is the psychological and hence empirical turn which Mr. Cantor gives to the matter, really against his will; for this removal of the elements is presumably meant to be a psychic process. What the author means by the word 'successive' is defined precisely in my *Conceptual Notation* and again in my *Foundations* (§97) without the admixture of time, and the connection with complete induction is also clearly recognizable in my works. Mr. Dedekind has done something similar with his chains in his paper 'What is the Nature and Function of Numbers?'. In section 5, proposition 64, p. 17, Mr. Dedekind gives as the characteristic mark of the infinite that it is similar to a proper part of itself (or, as Mr. Cantor would say, equivalent to one of its constituent parts), after which the finite is to be defined as the non-infinite, whereas Mr. Cantor tries to do what I have done: first to define the finite, after which the infinite appears as the non-finite. Either plan can be carried through correctly, and it can be proved that the infinite systems of Mr. Dedekind are not finite in my sense. This proposition is convertible; but the proof of it is rather difficult, and it is hardly executed with sufficient rigour in Mr. Dedekind's paper.

In chapter VI Mr. Cantor deals with the question whether there are actually infinitely small numerical quantities and gives a negative answer to the question for those infinitesimals that can be mapped as limited rectilinear continuous distances. The main part of the proof, which is not carried out, I accept as valid. But when the author expresses the opinion that he can transform the axiom of Archimedes into a theorem, I must nevertheless contradict him, at least in so far as this is supposed to save one axiom. It only substitutes one axiom for another. The new axiom would read for example: there is always a finite | or transfinite ordinal number which, when multiplied by a finite distance limited by two different points, yields a distance which is greater than a given distance. The word 'multiplied' would have to be understood here in Cantor's sense. I do not find that this axiom is more evident than the axiom of Archimedes, where πολλαπλασιαζόμενα has the ordinary sense of 'multiplied'. While the new axiom would indeed say less, it would, on the other hand, include more difficult concepts.

Now as far as ordinal numbers and ordinal types are concerned, I cannot accept the claim that the foundation Mr. Cantor gives them is adequate, any more than in the case of cardinal numbers. He indicates how we must abstract in order to obtain them. But such an indication cannot pass for a definition; for it either presupposes that we are

272

already acquainted with what is to be defined, or it does not determine it unequivocally, in case the abstraction can be carried out at all which it cannot even in this case. Besides, the verb 'abstract' is a psychological expression and, as such, to be avoided in mathematics. But this is not to deny that what Mr. Cantor is after could be given an unobjectionable definition. However, we do not yet have a general view of the significance which ordinal types would then acquire for mathematics. They would perhaps enter into an intimate connection with the rest of mathematics and exert a fertilizing influence on it. I would not want to exclude this possibility.

I do not want to conclude this discussion without repeating a sentence (p. 19) with which I am in full agreement: 'As we can see, that mighty academic positivistic scepticism which now prevails in Germany ... has finally reached arithmetic, where it seems to draw the ultimate consequences still open to it with the utmost and most fateful rigour, fatal perhaps for itself.' Indeed, here is the rock on which it will founder. For surely the infinite cannot ultimately be denied in arithmetic, and on the other hand it is incompatible with that epistemological outlook. Here, it seems, is the field where a decisive battle will be fought.

On Concept and Object

192 In a series of articles in this Quarterly on intuition and its psychical elaboration, Benno Kerry has several times referred to my *Foundations of Arithmetic* and other works of mine, sometimes agreeing and sometimes disagreeing with me. I cannot but be pleased at this, and I think the best way I can show my appreciation is to take up the discussion of the points he contests. This seems to me all the more necessary, because his opposition is at least partly based on a misunderstanding, which might be shared by others, of what I say about concepts; and because, even apart from this special occasion, the matter is important and difficult enough for a more thorough treatment than seemed to me suitable in my *Foundations*.

The word 'concept' is used in various ways; its sense is sometimes psychological, sometimes logical, and sometimes perhaps a confused mixture of both. Since this licence exists, it is natural to restrict it by requiring that when once a usage is adopted it shall be maintained. What I decided was to keep strictly to a purely logical use; the question whether this or that use is more appropriate is one that I should like to leave on one side, as of minor importance. Agreement about the mode of expression will easily be reached when once it is recognized that there is something that deserves a special term.

It seems to me that Kerry's misunderstanding results from his unintentionally confusing his own usage of the word 'concept' with mine. This readily gives rise to contradictions, for which my usage is not to blame. |

193 Kerry contests what he calls my definition of 'concept'. I would remark, in the first place, that my explanation is not meant as a proper definition. One cannot require that everything shall be defined, any more than one can require that a chemist shall decompose every substance. What is simple cannot be decomposed, and what is logically simple cannot have a proper definition. Now something logically simple is no more given us at the outset than most of the chemical elements are; it is reached only by means of scientific work. If something has been discovered that is simple, or at least must count as simple for the

Vierteljahrsschrift für wissenschaftliche Philosophie 16 (1892), pp. 192–205.
(*Tr.* Peter Geach)

time being, we shall have to coin a term for it, since language will not originally contain an expression that exactly answers. On the introduction of a name for something logically simple, a definition is not possible; there is nothing for it but to lead the reader or hearer, by means of hints, to understand the word as is intended.

Kerry wants to make out that the distinction between concept and object is not absolute. 'In a previous passage', he says, 'I have myself expressed the opinion that the relation between the content of the concept and the concept-object is, in a certain respect, a peculiar and irreducible one; but this was in no way bound up with the view that the properties of being a concept and of being an object are mutually exclusive. The latter view no more follows from the former than it would follow, if, e.g., the relation of father and son were one that could not be further reduced, that a man could not be at once a father and a son (though of course not, e.g., father of the man whose son he was)'.

Let us fasten on this simile. If there were, or had been, beings that were fathers but could not be sons, such beings would obviously be quite different in kind from all men who are sons. Now it is something like this that happens here. A concept (as I understand the word) is predicative.[1] On the other hand, a name of an object, a proper name, is quite incapable of being used as a grammatical predicate. This admittedly needs elucidation, otherwise it might appear false. Surely one can just as well assert of a thing that it is Alexander the Great, or is the number four, or is the planet Venus, as that it is green or is a mammal? | If anybody thinks this, he is not distinguishing the uses of the word 194 'is'. In the last two examples it serves as a copula, as a mere verbal sign of predication. (In this sense the German word *ist* can sometimes be replaced by the mere personal suffix: cf. *dies Blatt ist grün* and *dies Blatt grünt*.) We are here saying that something falls under a concept, and the grammatical predicate means this concept. In the first three examples, on the other hand, 'is' is used like the 'equals' sign in arithmetic, to express an equation.[2] In the sentence 'The morning star is Venus', we have two proper names, 'morning star' and 'Venus', for the same object. In the sentence 'the morning star is a planet' we have a proper name, 'the morning star', and a concept-word, 'planet'. So far

[1] It is, in fact, the meaning of a grammatical predicate.
[2] I use the word 'equal' and the symbol '=' in the sense 'the same as', 'no other than', 'identical with'. Cf. E. Schröder, *Vorlesungen über die Algebra der Logik* (Leipzig, 1890), Vol. 1, §1. Schröder must however be criticized for not distinguishing two fundamentally different relations; the relation of an object to a concept it falls under, and the subordination of one concept to another. His remarks on the *Vollwurzel* are likewise open to objection. Schröder's symbol does not simply take the place of the copula.

as language goes, no more has happened than that 'Venus' has been replaced by 'a planet'; but really the relation has become wholly different. An equation is reversible; an object's falling under a concept is an irreversible relation. In the sentence 'the morning star is Venus', 'is' is obviously not the mere copula; its content is an essential part of the predicate, so that the word 'Venus' does not constitute the whole of the predicate.[3] One might say instead: 'the morning star is no other than Venus'; what was previously implicit in the single word 'is' is here set forth in four separate words, and in 'is no other than' the word 'is' now really is the mere copula. What is predicated here is thus not *Venus* but *no other than Venus*. These words stand for a concept; admittedly only one object falls under this, but such a concept must still always be distinguished from the object.[4] We have here a word 'Venus' that can

195   never be a proper predicate, although it can | form part of a predicate. The meaning[5] of this word is thus something that can never occur as a concept, but only as an object. Kerry, too, would probably not wish to dispute that there is something of this kind. But this involves admitting a distinction, which it is very important to recognize, between what can occur only as an object, and everything else. And this distinction would not be effaced even if it were true, as Kerry thinks it is, that there are concepts that can also be objects.

There are, indeed, cases that seem to support his view. I myself have indicated (in *Foundations* §53, *ad fin.*) that a concept may fall under a higher concept – which, however, must not be confused with one concept's being subordinate to another. Kerry does not appeal to this; instead, he gives the following example: 'the concept "horse" is a concept easily attained', and thinks that the concept 'horse' is an object, in fact one of the objects that fall under the concept 'concept easily attained'. Quite so; the three words 'the concept "horse"' do designate an object, but on that very account they do not designate a concept, as I am using the word. This is in full accord with the criterion I gave – that the singular definite article always indicates an object, whereas the indefinite article accompanies a concept-word.[6]

Kerry holds that no logical rules can be based on linguistic distinctions; but my own way of doing this is something that nobody can avoid who lays down such rules at all; for we cannot come to an

---

[3]Cf. my *Grundlagen der Arithmetik* [*The Foundations of Arithmetic*], §66, footnote.

[4]Cf. *Foundations*, §51.

[5]Cf. my paper, 'Über Sinn und Bedeutung' ['On Sense and Meaning'], shortly to appear in the *Zeitschrift für Philosophie und philosophische Kritik* [this volume pp. 157–77].

[6]*Foundations*, §51; §66, footnote; §68, footnote on p. 80.

understanding with one another apart from language, and so in the end we must always rely on other people's understanding words, inflexions, and sentence-construction in essentially the same way as ourselves. As I said before, I was not trying to give a definition, but only hints; and to this end I appealed to the general feeling for the German language. It is here very much to my advantage that there is such good accord between the linguistic distinction and the real one. As regards the indefinite article there are probably no exceptions to our rule at all for us to remark, apart from obsolete formulas like *Ein edler Rath* ['Councillor']. The matter is not so simple for the definite article, especially in the plural; but | then my criterion does not relate to this 196 case. In the singular, so far as I can see, the matter is doubtful only when a singular takes the place of a plural, as in the sentence 'the Turk besieged Vienna', 'the horse is a four-legged animal'. These cases are so easily recognizable as special ones that the value of our rule is hardly impaired by their occurrence. It is clear that in the first sentence 'the Turk' is the proper name of a people. The second sentence is probably best regarded as expressing a universal judgement, say 'all horses are four-legged animals' or 'all properly constituted horses are four-legged animals'; these will be discussed later.[7] Kerry calls my criterion unsuitable; for surely, he says, in the sentence 'the concept I am now talking about is an individual concept,' what the name composed of the first eight words means is a concept; but he is not taking the word 'concept' in my sense, and it is not in what I have laid down that the contradiction lies. But nobody can require that my mode of expression shall agree with Kerry's.

It must indeed by recognized that here we are confronted by an awkwardness of language, which I admit cannot be avoided, if we say

[7]Nowadays people seem inclined to exaggerate the scope of the statement that different linguistic expressions are never completely equivalent, that a word can never be exactly translated into another language. One might perhaps go even further, and say that the same word is never taken in quite the same way even by men who share a language. I will not enquire as to the measure of truth in these statements; I would only emphasize that nevertheless different expressions quite often have something in common, which I call the sense, or, in the special case of sentences, the thought. In other words, we must not fail to recognize that the same sense, the same thought, may be variously expressed; thus the difference does not here concern the sense, but only the apprehension, shading, or colouring of the thought, and is irrelevant for logic. It is possible for one sentence to give no more and no less information than another; and, for all the multiplicity of languages, mankind has a common stock of thoughts. If all transformation of the expression were forbidden on the plea that this would alter the content as well, logic would simply be crippled; for the task of logic can hardly be performed without trying to recognize the thought in its manifold guises. Moreover, all definitions would then have to be rejected as false.

G

197   that the concept *horse* is not a concept,[8] whereas, e.g., the city | of
Berlin is a city, and the volcano Vesuvius is a volcano. Language is
here in a predicament that justifies the departure from custom. The
peculiarity of our case is indicated by Kerry himself, by means of the
quotation-marks around 'horse'; I use italics to the same end. There
was no reason to mark out the words 'Berlin' and 'Vesuvius' in a
similar way. In logical discussions one quite often needs to say
something about a concept, and to express this in the form usual for
such predications – viz. to make what is said about the concept into
the content of the grammatical predicate. Consequently, one would
expect that what is meant by the grammatical subject would be the
concept; but the concept as such cannot play this part, in view of its
predicative nature; it must first be converted into an object,[9] or, more
precisely, an object must go proxy for it. We designate this object by
prefixing the words 'the concept'; e.g.:

   'The concept *man* is not empty'.

Here the first three words are to be regarded as a proper name,[10]
which can no more be used predicatively than 'Berlin' or 'Vesuvius.'
When we say 'Jesus falls under the concept *man*,' then, setting aside the
copula, the predicate is:

   'someone falling under the concept *man*'

and this means the same as:

   'a man'.

But the phrase

   'the concept *man*'

is only part of this predicate.

   Somebody might urge, as against the predicative nature of concepts,
that nevertheless we speak of a subject-concept. But even in such cases,
e.g. in the sentence

   'all mammals have red blood'

---

[8]A similar thing happens when we say as regards the sentence ' this rose is red': The
grammatical predicate 'is red' belongs to the subject 'this rose'. Here the words, 'The
grammatical predicate "is red"' are not a grammatical predicate but a subject. By the
very act of explicitly calling it a predicate, we deprive it of this property.

[9]Cf. my *Foundations*, p. x.

[10]I call anything a proper name if it is a sign for an object.

we cannot fail to recognize the predicative nature[11] of the concept; for we could say instead: |

'whatever is a mammal has red blood'

or:

'if anything is a mammal, then it has red blood'

When I wrote my *Foundations of Arithmetic*, I had not yet made the distinction between sense and meaning;[12] and so, under the expression 'a content of possible judgement', I was combining what I now designate by the distinctive words 'thought' and 'truth-value'. Consequently, I no longer entirely approve of the explanation I then gave (*Foundations*, p. 77), as regards its wording; my view is, however, still essentially the same. We may say in brief, taking 'subject' and 'predicate' in the linguistic sense: A concept is what is meant by a predicate; an object is something that can never be the total meaning of a predicate, but can be what a subject means. It must here be remarked that the words 'all', 'any', 'no', 'some', are prefixed to concept-words. In universal and particular affirmative and negative sentences, we are expressing relations between concepts; we use these words to indicate the special kind of relation. They are thus, logically speaking, not to be more closely associated with the concept-words that follow them, but are to be related to the sentence as a whole. It is easy to see this in the case of negation. If in the sentence

'all mammals are land-dwellers'

the phrase 'all mammals' expressed the logical subject of the predicate *are land-dwellers*, then in order to negate the whole sentence we should have to negate the predicate: 'are not land-dwellers'. Instead, we must put the 'not' in front of 'all'; from which it follows that 'all' logically belongs with the predicate. On the other hand, we do negate the sentence 'The concept *mammal* is subordinate to the concept *land-dweller*' by negating the predicate: 'is not subordinate to the concept *land-dweller*'.

If we keep it in mind that in my way of speaking expressions like 'the

---

[11]What I call here the predicative nature of concepts is just a special case of the need of supplementation, the 'unsaturatedness', that I gave as the essential feature of a function in my work *Funktion und Begriff* [*Function and Concept*] (Jena, 1891) [this volume pp. 137–56]. It was there scarcely possible to avoid the expression 'the function $f(x)$', although there too the difficulty arose that what this expression means is not a function.

[12]Cf. my essay, 'On Sense and Meaning'.

concept *F*' designate not concepts but objects, most of Kerry's objec-
199 tions already | collapse. If he thinks (cf. p. 281) that I have identified
concept and extension of concept, he is mistaken; I merely expressed
my view that in the expression 'the number that applies to the concept
F is the extension of the concept *like-numbered to the concept F*' the
words 'extension of the concept' could be replaced by 'concept'. Notice
carefully that here the word 'concept' is combined with the definite
article. Besides, this was only an incidental remark; I did not base
anything upon it.

Thus Kerry does not succeed in filling the gap between concept and
object. Someone might attempt, however, to make use of my own
statements in this sense. I have said that to assign a number involves
saying something about the concept;[13] I speak of properties ascribed to
a concept, and I allow that a concept may fall under a higher one.[14] I
have called existence a property of a concept. How I mean this to be
taken is best made clear by an example. In the sentence 'there is at
least one square root of 4', we are saying something, not about (say)
the definite number 2, nor about -2, but about a concept, *square root
of 4*; viz. that it is not empty. But if I express the same thought thus:
'The concept *square root of 4* is realized', then the first six words form
the proper name of an object, and it is about this object that something
is being said. But notice carefully that what is being said here is not the
same thing as was being said about the concept. This will be surprising
only to somebody who fails to see that a thought can be split up in
many ways, so that now one thing, now another, appears as subject or
predicate. The thought itself does not yet determine what is to be
regarded as the subject. If we say 'the subject of this judgement', we do
not designate anything definite unless at the same time we indicate a
definite kind of analysis; as a rule, we do this in connection with a
definite wording. But we must never forget that different sentences may
express the same thought. For example, the thought we are considering
could also be taken as saying something about the number 4:

> 'The number 4 has the property that there is something of
> which it is the square'.

Language has means of presenting now one, now another, part of the
200 | thought as the subject; one of the most familiar is the distinction of
active and passive forms. It is thus not impossible that one way of
analysing a given thought should make it appear as a singular

---

[13]*Foundations*, § 46.
[14]*Foundations*, § 53.

judgement; another, as a particular judgement; and a third, as a universal judgement. It need not then surprise us that the same sentence may be conceived as saying something about a concept and also as saying something about an object; only we must observe that *what* is being said is different. In the sentence 'there is at least one square root of 4' it is impossible to replace the words 'square root of 4' by 'the concept *square root of 4*'; i.e. what is suitably said of the concept does not suit the object. Although our sentence does not present the concept as a subject, it says something about it; it can be regarded as expressing that a concept falls under a higher one.[15] But this does not in any way efface the distinction between object and concept. We see to begin with that in the sentence 'there is at least one square root of 4' the predicative nature of the concept is not belied; we could say 'there is something that has the property of giving the result 4 when multiplied by itself'. Hence what is here said concerning a concept can never be said concerning an object; for a proper name can never be a predicative expression, though it can be part of one. I do not want to say it is false to say concerning an object what is said here concerning a concept; I want to say it is impossible, senseless, to do so. The sentence 'there is Julius Caesar' is neither true nor false but senseless; the sentence 'there is a man whose name is Julius Caesar' has a sense, but here again we have a concept, as the indefinite article shows. We get the same thing in the sentence 'there is only one Vienna'. We must not let ourselves be deceived because language often uses the same word now as a proper name, now as a concept-word; in our example, the numeral indicates that we have the latter; 'Vienna' is here a concept-word, like 'metropolis'. Using it in this sense, we may say: 'Trieste is no Vienna'. If, on the other hand, we | substitute 'Julius 201 Caesar' for the proper name formed by the first six words of the sentence 'the concept *square root of 4* is realized', we get a sentence that has a sense but is false; for that so-and-so is realized (as the word is being taken here) is something that can be truly said only concerning a quite special kind of objects, viz. such as can be designated by proper names of the form 'the concept *F*'. Thus the words 'the concept *square root of 4*' have an essentially different behaviour, as regards possible substitutions, from the words 'square root of 4' in our original sentence; i.e. the meaning of the two phrases is essentially different.

What has been shown here in one example holds good generally; the behaviour of the concept is essentially predicative, even where some-

---

[15]In my *Foundations* I called such a concept a second-order concept; in *Function and Concept* I called it a seond-level concept, as I shall do here.

thing is being said about it; consequently it can be replaced there only by another concept, never by an object. Thus what is being said concerning a concept does not suit an object. Second-level concepts, which concepts fall under, are essentially different from first-level concepts, which objects fall under. The relation of an object to a first-level concept that it falls under is different from the (admittedly similar) relation of a first-level to a second-level concept. (To do justice at once to the distinction and to the similarity, we might perhaps say: An object falls *under* a first-level concept; a concept falls *within* a second-level concept.) The distinction of concept and object thus still holds, with all its sharpness.

With this there hangs together what I have said (*Foundations* §53) about my usage of the words 'property' and 'mark'; Kerry's discussion gives me occasion to revert once more to this. The words serve to signify relations, in sentences like 'Φ is a property of Γ' and 'Φ is a mark of Ω'. In my way of speaking, a thing can be at once a property and a mark, but not of the same thing. I call the concepts under which an object falls its properties; thus

'to be Φ is a property of Γ'

is just another way of saying:

'Γ falls under the concept of a Φ'.

If the object Γ has the properties Φ, X, and Ψ, I may combine them into Ω; so that it is the same thing if I say that Γ has the property Ω, or, that Γ | has the properties Φ, X, and Ψ. I then call Φ, X, and Ψ marks of the concept Ω, and, at the same time, properties of Γ. It is clear that the relations of Φ to Γ and to Ω are quite different, and that consequently different terms are required. Γ falls under the concept Φ; but Ω, which is itself a concept, cannot fall under the first-level concept Φ; only to a second-level concept could it stand in a similar relation. Ω is, on the other hand, subordinate to Φ.

Let us consider an example. Instead of saying:

'2 is a positive number' and
'2 is a whole number' and
'2 is less than 10'

we may also say

'2 is a positive whole number less than 10'.

Here

to be a positive number,
to be a whole number,
to be less than 10,

appear as properties of the object 2, and also as marks of the concept

positive whole number less than 10.

This is neither positive, nor a whole number, nor less than 10. It is indeed subordinate to the concept *whole number*, but does not fall under it.

Let us now compare with this what Kerry says in his second article (p. 224). 'By the number 4 we understand the result of additively combining 3 and 1. The concept–object here occurring is the numerical individual 4; a quite definite number in the natural number-series. This object obviously bears just the marks that are named in its concept, and no others besides – provided we refrain, as we surely must, from counting as *propria* of the object its infinitely numerous relations to all other individual numbers; "the" number 4 is likewise the result of additively combining 3 and 1'.

We see at once that my distinction between property and mark is here quite slurred over. Kerry distinguishes here between the number 4 and 'the' number 4. I must confess that this distinction is incomprehensible to me. The number 4 is to be a concept; 'the' number 4 is to be a concept-object, and none other than the numerical individual 4. It needs no proof that what we have here is not my distinction between concept and | object. It almost looks as though what was floating 203 (though very obscurely) before Kerry's mind were my distinction between the sense and the meaning of the words 'the number 4'.[16] But it is only of that which the words mean that we can say: this is the result of additively combining 3 and 1.

Again, how are we to take the word 'is' in the sentences 'the number 4 is the result of additively combining 3 and 1' and '"the" number 4 is the result of additively combining 3 and 1'? Is it a mere copula, or does it help to express a logical equation? In the first case, 'the' would have to be left out before 'result', and the sentences would go like this:

'The number 4 is a result of additively combining 3 and 1';

'"The" number 4 is a result of additively combining 3 and 1'.

---

[16]Cf. my essay, 'On Sense and Meaning'.

In that case, the objects that Kerry designates by

'the number 4' and '"the" number 4'

would both fall under the concept

result of additively combining 3 and 1.

And then the only question would be what difference there was between these objects. (I am here using the words 'object' and 'concept' in my accustomed way.) I should express as follows what Kerry is apparently trying to say:

'The number 4 has those properties, and those alone, which are marks of the concept: *result of additively combining 3 and 1*'.

I should then express as follows the sense of the first of our two sentences:

'To be a number 4 is the same as being a result of additive combination of 3 and 1'.

In that case, what I conjectured just now to have been Kerry's intention could also be put thus:

'The number 4 has those properties, and those alone, which are marks of the concept *a number 4*'.

204   (We need not here decide whether this is true.) The | inverted commas around the definite article in the words '"the" number 4' could in that case be omitted.

But in these attempted interpretations we have assumed that in at least one of the two sentences the definite articles in front of 'result' and 'number 4' were inserted only by an oversight. If we take the words as they stand, we can only regard them as having the sense of a logical equation, like:

'The number 4 is none other than the result of additively combining 3 and 1'.

The definite article in front of 'result' is here logically justified only if it is known (i) that there is such a result; (ii) that there is not more than one. In that case, the phrase designates an object, and is to be regarded as a proper name. If both of our sentences were to be regarded as logical equations, then, since their right sides are identical, it would follow from them that the number 4 is 'the' number 4, or, if you prefer, that the number 4 is no other than 'the' number 4; and so Kerry's distinction would have been proved untenable. However, it is not my present task to point out contradictions in his exposition; his way of taking the words 'object' and 'concept' is not properly my concern here. I am only trying to set my own usage of these words in a clearer light, and incidentally show that in any case it differs from his, whether that is consistent or not.

I do not at all dispute Kerry's right to use the words 'concept' and 'object' in his own way, if only he would respect my equal right, and admit that with my use of terms I have got hold of a distinction of the highest importance. I admit that there is a quite peculiar obstacle in the way of an understanding with the reader. By a kind of necessity of language, my expressions, taken literally, sometimes miss my thought; I mention an object, when what I intend is a concept. I fully realize that in such cases I was relying upon a reader who would be ready to meet me half-way – who does not begrudge a pinch of salt.

Somebody may think that this is an artificially created difficulty; that there is no need at all to take account of such an unmanageable thing as what I call a concept; that one might, like Kerry, regard an object's falling under a concept as a relation, in which the same thing could occur now as object, now as concept. | The words 'object' and 'concept' 205 would then serve only to indicate the different positions in the relation. This may be done; but anybody who thinks the difficulty is avoided this way is very much mistaken; it is only shifted. For not all the parts of a thought can be complete; at least one must be 'unsaturated', or predicative; otherwise they would not hold together. For example, the sense of the phrase 'the number 2' does not hold together with that of the expression 'the concept *prime number*' without a link. We apply such a link in the sentence 'the number 2 falls under the concept *prime number*'; it is contained in the words 'falls under', which need to be completed in two ways – by a subject and an accusative; and only because their sense is thus 'unsaturated' are they capable of serving as a link. Only when they have been supplemented in this twofold respect do we get a complete sense, a thought. I say that what such words or phrases mean is a relation. We now get the same difficulty for the relation that we were trying to avoid for the concept. For the words 'the relation of an object to the concept it falls under' designate not a relation but an object; and the three proper names 'the number 2', 'the concept *prime number*', 'the relation of an object to a concept it falls under', hold aloof from one another just as much as the first two do by themselves; however we put them together, we get no sentence. It is thus easy for us to see that the difficulty arising from the 'unsaturated-ness' of one part of the thought can indeed be shifted, but not avoided.

'Complete' and 'unsaturated' are of course only figures of speech; but all that I wish or am able to do here is to give hints.

It may make it easier to come to an understanding if the reader compares my work *Function and Concept*. For over the question what it is that is called a function in Analysis, we come up against the same obstacle; and on thorough investigation it will be found that the obstacle is essential, and founded on the nature of our language; that we cannot avoid a certain inappropriateness of linguistic expression; and that there is nothing for it but to realize this and always take it into account.

Review of E. G. Husserl,
Philosophie der Arithmetik I
[*Philosophy of Arithmetic* I]

In the introduction, the author decides to take a preliminary look at   313
numbers (in the sense of cardinal numbers) and then begins a discussion of multiplicity, plurality, collectivity, aggregate, assemblage, set.
He uses these words to mean essentially the same thing; the concept of
number on the other hand is supposed to differ from this. However, the
logical relation of multiplicity and number (p. 9) does not become
entirely clear. The words 'The concept of number comprises the same
concrete phenomena as the concept of multiplicity, though only via the
extensions of its specific concepts, those of the numbers two, three, four
...' might lead one to infer that they are co-extensive. On the other
hand, multiplicity is supposed to be more indefinite and more general
than number. The matter would probably be clearer if falling under a
concept had been more clearly distinguished from being subordinated
to one. The author first strives for an analysis of the concept of
multiplicity. From it are supposed to spring, by determination, the
specific numbers and the generic concept of number that presupposes
them. We are thus led first downwards from the general to the
particular and then again upwards.

Collectivities are wholes whose parts are combined collectively. The
parts must be noticed individually and we must be conscious of them
as such. The collective connection consists neither in the fact that | the   314
contents are simultaneously present in consciousness nor in the fact
that they enter consciousness in succession. Nor is the reason for the
union to be found in space as an all-encompassing form. The connection consists in the unifying act itself (p. 43). 'But alongside the act
there does not exist as its creative result a relational content different
from it.' Collective connection is a relation *sui generis*. Following J. S.
Mill, the author goes on to explain what is to be understood by a
'relation', namely, the state of consciousness or the phenomenon (the
meanings of these expressions are supposed to coincide) in which the

Zeitschrift für Philosophie und philosophische Kritik 103 (1894), pp. 313–32.
(*Tr.* Hans Kaal)

related contents, the terms of the relation, are contained (p. 70). The author goes on to distinguish between primary and mental relations. Only the latter are of direct concern to us here. 'If a unitary mental act is directed at several contents, then they are connected or related to one another with respect to it. If we perform such an act, then we would naturally look in vain for a relation or connection among the ideas ... contained in the act (unless there is a primary relation *over and above it*). The contents are here united only by the act, and this union can therefore be noticed only by a special reflection on the act' (p. 73). Among the mental relations belongs the relation of difference, in whose case two contents are brought into relation by a self-evident negative judgement (p. 74). Equality or identity on the other hand is a primary relation (p. 77). (Accordingly, perfect coincidence would also, presumably, be a primary relation, while its negation, that is, difference, would be a mental one. I miss here a statement of the distinction between the relation of difference and collective connection which in the author's opinion is likewise a mental relation because there is no union to be noticed by intuition in the ideas contained in the act.) When one speaks of 'unrelated' contents, one thinks of the contents as being merely 'together', i.e., as a collectivity. 'But in reality they are not at all unconnected, unrelated. On the contrary, they are connected by the mental act that holds them together. What is missing is only any |

315   noticeable union in the contents of the mental act' (p. 78). The conjunction 'and' fixes in a perfectly appropriate manner the fact that the given contents are collectively connected (p. 81). 'An idea ... falls under the concept of multiplicity in so far as it collectively connects what was noticed individually' (p. 82). (By 'idea' here seems to be understood an act.) 'Multiplicity in general ... is nothing other than: some thing and some thing and some thing, etc.; or some one and some one and some one, etc.; or more briefly: one and one and one, etc.' (p. 83). If we remove the indeterminacy that lies in the 'etc.', we arrive at the numbers one and one; one, one, and one; one, one, one, and one; etc. These concepts can also be reached directly by starting out from arbitrary concrete multiplicities, for each one falls under one, and a determinate one, of these concepts (p. 87). For this purpose we abstract from the peculiar constitution of the individual contents that make up the multiplicity and retain each one only in so far as it is a something or a one, thus obtaining with respect to their collective connection the general form of multiplicity that corresponds to the present multiplicity, i.e., the corresponding number (p. 88). This process of abstracting the number goes hand in hand with a process of emptying of all content (p. 100). There is no other way of explaining the general concept of

number than by pointing to the similarity that all number concepts bear to one another (p. 88).

After this brief presentation of the fundamental idea of part one, I proceed to a general characterization of this way of thinking. We are dealing here with an attempt to justify a naive conception of number in a scientific way. I call 'naive' any view on which a statement of number is *not* a statement about a concept or about the extension of a concept, for when one first reflects on number, one is led by a certain necessity to such a conception. Now a view is, properly speaking, naive only as long as it ignores the difficulties that stand in its way, which is not quite true of the author's view. The most naive view is the one on which a number | is something like a heap or swarm in which things   316 are contained with all their peculiarities. Then comes the conception of a number as a property of a heap, aggregate, or whatever else it may be called. Here one feels the need to cleanse things of their peculiarities. The present attempt belongs to those that carry out the cleansing operation in the wash-tub of the mind. The advantage this offers is that the things in it assume a quite peculiar pliancy; they no longer knock so hard against each other in space and shed many of their bothersome peculiarities and differences. The mixture of psychology and logic, which is so popular nowadays, yields a strong lye for this purpose. First everything is turned into ideas. The meanings of words are ideas. Thus the thing to do with, e.g., the word 'number' is to point to the corresponding idea and to describe its origin and composition. Objects are ideas. Thus J. S. Mill, to the author's applause, allows objects ('whether physical or mental') to enter into a state of consciousness and to form part of this state of consciousness (p. 70). But would not, e.g., the moon sit a bit heavy on the stomach of one's state of consciousness? Now since all things are ideas, we can easily change objects by directing our attention towards them or away from them. The latter is especially effective. We attend less to a property, and it disappears. By thus making one characteristic mark after another disappear, we obtain more and more abstract concepts. Concepts too are therefore ideas, only less complete ones than objects: they have only the properties of those objects from which we have not yet abstracted. Inattention is a most effective logical power; this is presumably why professors are absent-minded. Suppose, e.g., that there are a black and a white cat sitting side by side before us. We do not attend to their colour, and they become colourless – but they still sit side by side. We do not attend to their posture, and they cease to sit without, however, assuming a different posture – but each of them is still in its place. We no longer attend to the place, and they cease to occupy one – but they continue presumably to be separate. We have thus perhaps obtained from each of them a general concept of a cat. By continued application of this procedure, each object is transformed into a more and more bloodless phantom. As the end result, we obtain from each object a something emptied of all content; but the something obtained from one object differs nevertheless from the something obtained from another object, even though it is not easy to say how. But wait a minute! This last transition to the something seems to be more difficult; at least the author speaks of reflection on the mental act of imagining (p. 86). But however this may be, the result at least is exactly as I have described it. While, on my view, to bring an object under a concept is merely to recognize a relation that already existed beforehand, on the present view, objects are essentially changed by being brought under concepts, in that objects brought under the same concept become more alike. The matter is perhaps also to be conceived in such a way that each object gives rise to a new idea lacking all those determinations that do not occur in the concept. Here we have a blurring of the difference between idea and concept, between imagining and thinking. Everything is transposed into the subjective mode. But by the very fact that the boundary between the subjective and the objective is obliterated, the subjective acquires in its turn the appearance of the objective. One speaks, e.g., of this or that idea as if it could be detached from the imagining mind and exposed to public view. And yet no one has another's idea, only his own, and no one even knows how far his idea – e.g., of red – coincides with another's; for I cannot express what is peculiar to the idea I associate with the word 'red'. To be able to compare one person's idea with another's, one would have to unite them in the same consciousness, and one would have to be certain that they had not changed in being transferred. It is quite otherwise with thoughts: one and the same thought | can be grasped by many men. The parts of thought and even more so the things themselves are to be distinguished from the ideas which in some mind accompany the grasping of a thought and which some person forms of things. Now by subsuming the subjective and the objective under the word 'idea', one blurs the boundary between the two in such a way that an idea in the proper sense of the word is sometimes treated as something objective, while something objective is sometimes treated as an idea. Thus in the case of our author, a collectivity (set, multiplicity) appears sometimes as an idea (pp. 15, 17, 24, 82) and sometimes as something objective (pp. 10–11, 235). But is it not at bottom a rather innocent pastime to call, e.g., the moon an idea? Yes; as long as one does not fancy that one can transform or generate the moon by psychological means! But this is what happens only too easily as a result.

Given the partly psychological, partly logical way of thinking we have just characterized, it is easy to understand the author's verdict on definition. An example from elementary geometry may illustrate this. The usual definition given there is: 'A right angle is an angle equal to its adjacent angle'. The author's comment on this would probably be: 'The idea of rectangularity is a simple one; so it is a wholly misguided undertaking to want to give a definition of it. Our idea of rectangularity contains nothing of its relation to another, adjacent angle. It is indeed correct to say that the concepts "right angle" and "angle equal to its adjacent angle" have the same extension, but it is not correct to say that they have the same content. So what is being defined is not the content, but the extension of the concept. If this definition were correct, then any assertion of rectangularity, instead of being as such about the concrete pair of sides before us, would always be about its relation to another pair. All I can admit (cf. p. 114) is that equality with an adjacent angle gives us a necessary and sufficient criterion of rectangularity.' It is in a similar way that the author judges the definition of numerical equality by means of the concept of a one–one | correlation.   319 'The simplest criterion of equality of number is just that the *same* number results in counting the sets to be compared' (p. 115). Naturally; the simplest way of testing rectangularity is by applying a protractor! The author forgets that this counting rests itself on a one–one correlation, namely of the numerals 1 to *n* and the objects of the set. Each of the two sets needs to be counted. This makes the matter less simple than it is if we consider a relation that correlates the objects of the two sets without numerals as intermediaries.

If words and combinations of words mean ideas, then for any two of them there are only two possibilities: either they designate the same idea or they designate different ideas. In the former case it is pointless to equate them by means of a definition: this is 'an obvious circle'; in the latter case it is wrong. These are also the objections the author raises, one of them regularly. A definition is also incapable of analysing the sense, for the analysed sense just is not the original one. In using the word to be explained, I either think clearly everything I think when I use the defining expression: we then have the 'obvious circle'; or the defining expression has a more richly articulated sense, in which case I do not think the same thing in using it as I do in using the word to be explained: the definition is then wrong. One would think that a definition was unobjectionable in the case where the word to be explained had as yet no sense at all, or where we were asked explicitly to regard its sense as non-existent so that it was first given a sense by the definition. But in the last case too, the author refutes the definition by reminding us of the difference between the ideas (p. 107). To evade all objections, one would accordingly have to create a new verbal root and form a word out of it. This reveals a split between psychological logicians and mathematicians. What matters to the former is the sense of the words, as well as the ideas which they fail to distinguish from the sense; whereas what matters to the latter is the thing itself: the |

320   meaning of the words.[1] The reproach that what is defined is not the concept but its extension actually affects all mathematical definitions. For the mathematician, it is no more right and no more wrong to define a conic as the line of intersection of a plane with the surface of a circular cone than to define it as a plane curve with an equation of the second degree in parallel coordinates. His choice of one or the other of these expressions or of some other one is guided solely by reasons of convenience and is made irrespective of the fact that the expressions have neither the same sense nor evoke the same ideas. I do not mean by this that a concept and its extension are one and the same, but that coincidence in extension is a necessary and sufficient criterion for the occurrence between concepts of the relation that corresponds to identity between objects.[2] It should be noted in this connection that I am using the word 'equal' or 'identical' without further addition in the sense of 'not different', 'coinciding', 'same'. As psychological logicians lack any understanding of definition, they also lack any understanding of identity. This relation cannot but remain perfectly mysterious to them; for if words designated ideas throughout, one could never say '*a* is the same as *b*'; for to be able to say this, one would first have to distinguish *a* from *b*, and they would then just be different ideas. All the same, I agree with the author that Leibniz's explanation that 'two things are the same when one can be substituted for the other without loss of truth' does not deserve to be called a definition, even if my reasons are different from his. Since any definition is an identification, identity itself cannot be defined. Leibniz's explanation could be called a principle that brings out the nature of the relation of identity, and as such it is of fundamental importance. The author's explanation, 'We

321   simply say of any two contents that they are identical | if there is an

---

[1]On this point the reader is asked to compare my essay on sense and meaning in the present journal [this volume pp. 157–77].

[2]For identity in the proper sense of the word does not occur between concepts. Cf. my essay on concept and object in the *Vierteljahrsschrift für wissenschaftliche Philosophie* [this volume pp. 182–94].

identity between ... the characteristic marks which happen to be at the centre of our interest' (p. 108) is not at all to my taste.

Let us now enter into the details. According to the author, a statement of number refers to the collectivity (set, multiplicity). Such a collectivity finds its perfectly adequate expression in the conjunction 'and'. This would lead one to expect that statements of number are all of the form '*a* and *b* and *c* and ... *q* is *n*', or at least that they can be reduced to this form. But what do we actually learn from the proposition 'Berlin and Munich and Dresden are three' or, what is supposed to be the same proposition, 'Berlin and Dresden and Munich are something and something and something'? Who would take the trouble to ask a question in order to get such an answer? The proposition is not even meant to say that Berlin is different from Dresden, Dresden from Munich, and Munich from Berlin; and indeed, the second form at least contains neither the difference between Berlin and Dresden nor their identity. It is surely strange that a number statement of this form hardly ever occurs in everyday life, and that when it does, it is not meant as a statement of number. I find that it is actually used in only two cases: first, with the numeral 'two', in order to express difference ('Rape-seed and rape are two') and secondly, with the numeral 'one', in order to express identity ('I and the Father are one'). The latter example is especially devastating; for according to the author it would have to read 'are something and something' or 'are two'. In real life we do not ask 'How many is Caesar and Pompey and London and Edinburgh?' or 'How many is Great Britain and Ireland?', and I would be curious to know what the author's answer would be. On the other hand, we ask, e.g., 'How many moons has Mars?' or 'What is the number of Martian moons?', and from the answer 'The number of Martian moons is two' we learn something worth asking about. We thus see that both the question and the answer contain a word or a complex designation for a concept | instead of the 'and' demanded by the author. How does he extricate himself from this difficulty? By saying that the number belongs to the extension of the concept, i.e., to the collectivity. 'We can at best say only indirectly that the concept has the property that the number ... belongs to its extension' (p. 189). This actually concedes all that I am maintaining: a statement of number states something about a concept. I will not quibble over whether the statement is directly about the concept and indirectly about its extension, or indirectly about the concept and directly about the extension, for one goes with the other. This much is certain: what is designated directly is neither the extension of a concept nor a collectivity, but only a concept. If the author had used the word 'extension of a concept' in the same sense as I, we should hardly differ in opinion about the sense of a number statement. This is not the case, though; for the extension of a concept is not a collectivity in the author's sense. A concept under which only one object falls has a determinate extension, as does a concept under which no object falls, or a concept under which infinitely many objects fall, but in these cases there is no collectivity at all according to Mr. Husserl. The sense of the words 'extension of the concept Martian moon' is different from the sense of the words 'Deimos and Phobos', and the proposition 'The number of Deimos and Phobos is two', if it contains a thought at all, contains at least a different thought from the proposition 'The number of Martian moons is two'. Now since a proposition of the former form is never used to state a number, the author misses the sense of a statement of number.

Let us now look a little more closely at the alleged origin of a collectivity (pp. 77ff.). I must confess that I have not succeeded in forming a collectivity according to the author's instructions. In the case of a collective connection, we are to think or imagine the contents as being merely together, without imagining any relation or connection between them (p. 79). I find this impossible. I cannot imagine redness, the moon and Napoleon at the same time without imagining a connection between them; | e.g., the figure of Napoleon standing out against the redness of a burning village and illuminated by the moon on the right. What is present to me at the same time I imagine as a whole; and I cannot disregard the connection without losing the whole. I suspect that there is no such thing in my mind as what the author calls 'collectivity' ('set', 'multiplicity'), i.e., an idea of parts whose union, though present, is not part of the idea. It is therefore no wonder that Mr. Husserl himself says later on of a set that it possesses an element of configuration, an articulation, which distinguishes it as a whole (p. 242). He speaks of a row, swarm, chain and heap as special kinds of sets (p. 235). And is there no union to be noticed in the idea of a swarm? Or is this union present side by side with the collective connection? In that case it would have nothing to do with the collectivity, and the 'element of configuration' could not serve to distinguish kinds of sets. How does the author arrive at his opinion? Probably because he is trying to find definite ideas to correspond to words and combinations of words as their meanings. There would therefore have to be a complex of ideas corresponding to the combination of words 'redness and the moon and Napoleon'; but since 'and' all by itself does not express an imaginable relation or union, one must not try to imagine one either. To this may be added the following. If the union of the parts was imagined along

323

with the parts, nearly all of our ideas would be collectivities, e.g., the idea of a house as well as the idea of a swarm or heap; but in that case it would be too easy to notice the absurdity of thinking of a number as the property of a house or of the idea of a house.

The author himself finds some difficulty in the process of abstraction that provides the general concept of a collectivity (p. 84): 'One must abstract completely ... from the peculiarities of the individual contents of the collection while at the same time holding on to their connection. This seems to involve a difficulty, if not a psychological impossibility. If we take that process of abstraction seriously, then the collective connection vanishes naturally along with the individual contents instead of remaining behind as a | conceptual extract. The solution lies at hand. To abstract from something simply means: not to attend to it especially.'   324

The kernel of this explanation is obviously to be found in the word 'especially'. Inattention is a very strong lye: it must not be applied in too great a concentration if it is not to dissolve everything; but neither must it be applied too diluted if it is to produce an adequate change. It all depends on the right degree of dilution, a mark difficult to hit; I at any rate have not succeeded in hitting it.

Since the author finally concedes that I am at bottom right in saying that a statement of number contains a statement about a concept, I need not go in detail into his reason to the contrary. I will remark only that he has obviously failed to grasp my distinction between a characteristic mark and a property. This is no wonder, though, given his partly logical, partly psychological way of thinking. He thus comes to attribute to me the view that a statement of number amounts to a determination or definition of a concept (p. 185). Nothing could have been further from my mind.

Naive views of the nature of number and especially psychological views are in danger of being wrecked on three rocks. The first is connected with the question how to reconcile the identity of the units with their distinguishability. The second consists of the numbers zero and one, and the third of the large numbers. Let us ask how the author seeks to circumnavigate these rocks. In dealing with the first, he cites (p. 156) my words:

If we try to produce the number by putting together different distinct objects, the result is an agglomeration in which the objects contained remain still in possession of precisely those properties which serve to distinguish them from one another; and that is not the number. But if we try to do it in the other way, but putting together identicals [or equals], the result runs perpetually together into one and we never reach a plurality.[3]

It is clear that I am here using the word 'identical' [or 'equal'] in the sense of 'not different'. The author's reproach that I am confusing equality with identity does not therefore touch me. Using his blurred concept of identity, Mr. Husserl | seeks to blunt the contrast I am making: 'In a certain respect there is an identity and in another respect a difference ... This would present us with a difficulty or, better, an impossibility only if the expression "putting together identicals", which is supposed to describe the origin of the number, required absolute identity, as Frege falsely supposes' (pp. 164–5). But if the identity is not absolute, then the objects differ in some of their properties and carry them with them into the union. Now compare this with the following remark: 'The identity of the units that results from our psychological theory is evidently an absolute one. Even the mere thought of an approximation is already absurd. For we are dealing with the identity of contents in relation to the fact *that* they are contents' (p. 168). According to the author, a number consists of units (p. 149). By 'unit' in this connection he understands a 'member of a concrete multiplicity in so far as it is subjected to numerical abstraction' or as a 'numbered object as such'. If we put all this together, we find it rather difficult to get clear about what the author had in mind. At first the objects are obviously different; then they become absolutely identical by abstraction; but their identity is supposed to be absolute only in relation to the fact that they are contents. I should have thought that such an identity was very far from being an absolute one. But however this may be, a number consists of such absolutely identical units, and here we run into the impossibility which the author himself brings out. It must surely be assumed that the process of abstraction, the bringing of objects under the concept of a something, effects some change: that the objects thought by means of this concept, i.e., those absolutely identical units, are different from the original objects; otherwise they would be no more alike than the original objects were, and the process of abstraction would have been of no use. It must therefore be assumed that those absolutely identical units come into being only as a result of the process of bringing under the concept of a something, whether as | transformations of those different distinct objects or as new creations by their side. This would lead one to think that alongside the other objects there were also units, and alongside sets of apples sets of units.

325

326

[3] *Die Grundlagen der Arithmetik* [*The Foundations of Arithmetic*], §39. [As translated by J. L. Austin. (*Tr.*)]

But the author disputes this in the most vehement terms (p. 139). Numerical abstraction just has the marvellous and very useful property of making things absolutely identical without changing them. This is possible only in the wash-tub of the mind. If the author really succeeded in avoiding the first rock, it was because he took the road of magic rather than of science.

Mr. Husserl goes on (p. 156) to quote my words: 'If we use 1 to stand for each of the objects to be numbered, we make the mistake of assigning the same symbol to different things. But if we provide the 1 with differentiating strokes, it becomes unusable for arithmetic.'[4] His comment on this is (p. 165): 'We none the less commit this mistake every time we apply general names. When we call Hans, Kunz, etc. each one a man, we have the same case and the same "mistaken notation" as when in numbering we write 1 for each object to be numbered.' If we did designate Hans by 'man' and likewise Kunz, we should indeed be committing this mistake. Fortunately this is not what we do. In calling Hans a man, we are saying that Hans falls under the concept *man*; we are not writing or saying 'man' instead of 'Hans'. What would correspond to the proposition 'Hans is a man' would be 'Hans is a 1'. Naturally, when we call A B in the sense of assigning the proper name 'B' to A, we can always say 'B' instead of 'A'; but then we must not give the same name 'B' also to another object. This confusion is surely due to the unfortunate expression 'common name'. A so-called common name – or, better, concept-word – does not immediately have anything to do with objects, but means a concept; and while there may perhaps be objects falling under this concept, the concept may also be empty, and in this case the concept-word may mean just as much as in the other case. I | have explained this at sufficient length in §47 of my   327 *Foundations of Arithmetic.* It should be clear that someone who utters the proposition 'All men are mortal' does not want to state something about a certain chief Akpanya whom he may never have heard of.

According to the author, $5 + 5 = 10$ says as much as: 'a (some, any) set falling under the concept five and some other set' – why 'other'? – 'falling under the same concept yield, when united, a set falling under the concept 10' (p. 202). As an illustration take, e.g., the fingers of your right hand as your first set and, as your second set, a pen plus the fingers of your right hand minus your thumb. Could the author have learned this from Mr. O. Biermann?[5]

[4][Ibid. (*Tr.*)]

[5][Frege's criticisms of O. Biermann's account of number can be read in *Posthumous Writings* (Oxford, 1979), pp. 72ff. (*Ed.*)]

We now go on to the second rock, consisting of the numbers zero and one. The easy way out is to say: 'These are not numbers at all'. But this raises the question: What then are they? The author says that they are negative answers to the question 'How many?' (p. 144). They are like the answer 'Never' to the question 'When?' 'Not many or "no multiplicity" is not a special case of many.' Somebody might even get the idea that two is not yet a multiplicity but merely a twosome (or a duality as opposed to a plurality), so that 'None', 'One' and 'Two' would be the three negative answers to the question 'How many?' By way of confirmation he might adduce the fact that two is the only even prime number. It is really asking too much to ask us to regard the answer 'One' to the question 'How many moons has the earth?' as a negative answer. In the case of zero, the matter is inherently more plausible. What then is the proper way to conceive such answers as 'Never', 'Nowhere', 'Nothing' to the questions 'When?', 'Where?', 'What?' Obviously not as proper answers, but as refusals to answer in the form of an answer. One says: 'I cannot specify a time, a place, an object of the desired kind because there is none'. The corresponding reply to the question 'How many?' would be: 'I cannot name such a
328   number | because there is none'. On my conception of the sense of a statement of number, that is how I would reply to such a question as 'How many is Great Britain and Ireland?' I cannot regard either the answer 'One' or the answer 'Zero' to the question 'How many?' as equivalent in meaning to 'There is no such number'. How is it that we have two negative replies in this case? In replying 'Nobody' to the question 'Who was the predecessor of Romulus on the throne of Rome?', one is denying that somebody preceded Romulus. The negation belongs therefore to the predicate and is fused – incorrectly from a logical point of view – with the grammatical subject, which gives rise to the illusion that 'Nobody' just like 'Romulus' designates a man. This is notoriously the ground of the possibility of certain fallacies. One would think that such dangers lurked also in zero and one; but these are used just like all other numbers without special precautions. Why the difference? The answer 'Zero' to the question 'What is the number of predecessors of Romulus on the throne of Rome?' is no more negative than 'Two' would be. In answering 'Zero', we are not denying that there is such a number: we are naming it. The author says: 'The number one belongs to each unit' (p. 170) (presumably as its negative property!) and he calls zero and one concepts (p. 145). This leads one to suppose that 'unit' and 'one' are coextensive concepts. Or are there ones that are not units? What is the difference between the thoughts expressed by the two propositions 'Hans is one' and 'Hans is a unit'?

And whom does the number zero belong to? Following the author, we have unwittingly slipped back into speaking of 'the number one'! There remain so many riddles which the author has failed to solve that I cannot admit that he has successfully circumnavigated this rock.

This brings us to the third rock: the large numbers. If numbers are ideas, then the limits on our imaginative powers must also entail a limitation of the number domain. Thus the author says: 'It is only in exceptionally favourable circumstances that we can | imagine concrete 329 multiplicities of as many as about a dozen elements' (p. 214). As a way out of this difficulty, he now introduces improper or symbolic ideas, with which the whole of his second volume will be concerned. The author is nevertheless forced to admit: 'Even now, in following the path of mere signs, we are not of course entirely unrestricted; but we are no longer sensible of these restrictions ...' (p. 274). This is to concede that the domain of numbers is a finite one. There cannot be infinitely many numbers if numbers are ideas which I or some other human being must form, and no symbolism can free us of this restriction. According to the author, a symbolic idea is an idea by means of signs that characterize unequivocally what is to be imagined. 'We have, e.g., a proper idea of the outward appearance of a house when we are actually looking at it, and a symbolic idea when someone gives us the indirect characterization: the house at the corner of such and such streets and on such and such a side.' Since this explanation applies to the case where there is something objective of which I am to form an idea, it does not fit our case very well. It is clear enough that according to the author numbers are supposed to be ideas, the results of mental processes or activities (pp. 24, 46); but where is the objective something of which a number is an idea? What in this case corresponds to the corner house in the example above? And yet it is precisely this object which makes the connection between a proper and a symbolic idea: this is what justifies one in saying that the symbolic idea belongs to the proper one, and this is what is characterized unequivocally by signs when we have a symbolic idea. The mingling of the subjective and the objective, the circumstance that expressions like 'moon' and 'idea of the moon' are never clearly distinguished, spreads such an impenetrable fog that the attempt to get clear on this point is doomed to failure. I can only say that I got the following impression of what the author had in mind. If I want to have a symbolic idea | where I lack a proper one, I *idealize* my 330 imaginative capacity (cf. p. 251); i.e., I fancy or imagine having an idea which I do not in fact have and which I cannot have; and this fancy would be my symbolic idea. I can thus form a symbolic idea, e.g., by means of the sign '15', by imagining that I imagine a set consisting of the elements of a set to which the number 10 belongs and of the elements of a set to which the number 5 belongs, and that I now imagine applying to this imagined set the procedure which according to the author produces the corresponding number. The ideas of signs enter into the symbolic ideas. 'The sensible signs do not merely accompany the concepts in the manner of linguistic signs. They play a pre-eminent part in the formation of our symbols ... to the point where they take over almost the entire field' (p. 273; cf. also p. 264). This brings the author close to Helmholtz's and Kronecker's views. The number would be changed if the signs were changed. Our numbers would be quite different from those of the ancient Greeks and Romans. But would symbolic ideas also have the properties that the proper ones are supposed to have? I believe not, just as little as my idea of a green meadow is green. The author does indeed note (on p. 217) that a proper idea and a corresponding symbolic one stand in the relation of logical equivalence. 'Two concepts are logically equivalent if any object belonging to the one is also an object belonging to the other and vice versa.' This is supposed to explain how a symbolic idea can act as a 'surrogate' for a corresponding proper one. But the mingling of ideas and concepts interferes with our understanding of this. If we go by the example of the corner house, we are led to suppose that this 'equivalence' is to consist in the fact that my proper idea and the symbolic one are made to refer to the same object (namely the corner house). Now when can the latter act as a 'surrogate' for the former? Presumably when I speak of the corner house itself, | not of my idea of it. Reading this book has enabled me to fully appreciate how difficult it is for the light of truth to penetrate the fog that rises from the mixture of psychology and logic. I am glad to report that we catch at least a glimpse of the sun. Overcoming all obstacles in its course, the truth will out that our ideas matter little in this connection: that it is rather the thing itself of which we seek to form an idea that we are concerned with and that our statements are about. And such pronouncements occur repeatedly in the second part of this book, which is the more remarkable, the less they really fit the author's whole way of thinking. We read (at the bottom of p. 214): 'Even though we have not given the concepts in a *proper* way, we have at least given them in a *symbolic* way.' Here concepts appear as something objective, and the distinction between the proper and the symbolic refers only to the way they are given. There is talk of species of the concept of number which are inaccessible to us in the proper sense of the word (p. 265) and of *real* numbers, of numbers *in themselves,* which are in general inaccessible to us (p. 295). We read (on p. 234) of the formation of symbolic numbers which belong to one and the same *real* number. On the author's view,

331

one would have expected the word 'non-existent' instead of the word 'real'; for if a number were a proper idea, there would be no number in this case. What are those numbers 'in themselves' (cf. p. 294), those 'real' numbers, if not objective numbers which are completely independent of our thought and which exist even if they are 'inaccessible to us' (cf. p. 296)? The author says (p. 295): 'Any number ... can be characterized unequivocally ... by manifold relations to other numbers, and each such characterization provides a new symbolic idea of that very number. Here the objective number 'in itself' is obviously what the corner house was in the example of the corner house. It is not my idea which is the number, but I form, or at least try to form, one or more ideas *of* one and the same number. The pity is that the author did not clearly separate the expressions '*A*' and 'idea of *A*'. | But if my idea of a   332 number is not the number itself, then the psychological approach has the rug pulled out from under it, in so far as it is out to investigate the nature of number. If I want to examine an idea, I must keep it as much as possible from changing, which is admittedly difficult; whereas if I investigate something objective, then my ideas must conform, as best they can, to the thing, to the result of my investigation, and must therefore, in general, be changed. It makes a great difference to the method of investigation whether an idea of a number is to be examined in itself or whether it is merely an idea *of* the proper object under investigation. The author's procedure fits only the former alternative, whereas the passages last cited can only be interpreted on the latter. If a geographer was given an oceanographic treatise to read which gave a psychological explanation of the origin of the oceans, he would undoubtedly get the impression that the author had missed the mark and shot past the thing itself in a most peculiar way. The present work has left me with exactly the same impression. An ocean is of course something real and a number is not; but this does not prevent a number from being something objective, and this is what is important.

Reading this work has enabled me to gauge the extent of the devastation caused by the irruption of psychology into logic, and I have taken it to be my task to exhibit that damage in the proper light. The errors which I believe I was compelled to point out are to be laid to the charge, not so much of the author, as of a widespread philosophical disease. Since my point of view is so radically different from the author's, I have found it difficult to do justice to his merits which, I suspect, lie in the field of psychology, and I should like to call the attention of psychologists especially to chapter XI, where the author discusses the possibility of conceiving a set at a single moment. However, I do not take myself to be expert enough in this field to give a verdict on this.

A Critical Elucidation of some Points
in E. Schröder, *Vorlesungen über die*
Algebra der Logik
[*Lectures on the Algebra of Logic*]

433 Mr. Schröder rejects Boole's *universe of discourse* in virtue of a peculiar consideration, which I should like to subject here to a more exact inquiry; for in this way there is made apparent the necessity of a distinction that seems to be unknown to many logicians.

For the sake of intelligibility, it will be desirable to begin by presenting the main lines of Mr. Schröder's domain-calculus. As the author expounds it, the calculus is always intertwined with logic proper; and this makes if difficult to see into the heart of the matter. So, to begin with, I here leave logic quite out of consideration, in order that the peculiarity of this calculus may be better brought out.

Following Mr. Schröder, we imagine given to us a manifold of elements. The nature of this manifold and its elements is not in question, and so any manifold can represent any other. To make the
434 matter intuitively | clear it is best to consider the manifold of points on a plane surface, or the manifold of areas into which such a surface is divided by two sets of parallel straight lines, so that no two areas have a point in common. 'Any aggregation of elements of the manifold we call a *domain* of the latter (p. 157).[1] The most important relation that can hold between domains is represented to be inclusion; this is taken to mean that the first domain is contained in the second, and to cover the case where the two domains coincide. About this relation of inclusion we now get two axioms laid down:

1. Every domain is included in itself.
2. If one domain is included in a second, and this in a third, then the first is likewise included in the third.

Instead of 'domains' we may here always also say 'classes', if we take classes to be collective wholes, such as a wood, for example, and do not

---

[1] In what follows page references are to the first volume.

Archiv für systematische Philosophie 1 (1895), pp. 433–56. (*Tr.* Peter Geach)

bring them into connection with concepts. Of course usage is always likely to mislead us here, since it suggests expressions like 'classes of men, of trees', etc., in which a concept is mentioned every time. What Mr. Schröder calls 'inclusion' or 'subsumption' is here, properly speaking, nothing but the part–whole relation, extended in such a way that every whole is to be treated as a part of itself. From the point of view we are now adopting, we do not need the words 'individual' and 'single thing'. Divisibility can be imagined as going on *ad infinitum*. Thus, moreover, the expression 'element' has as yet no importance here, properly speaking; for it is all one whether in the example mentioned above we choose to regard as elements the square areas of which the surface consists or (say) the triangles into which these are divided by their diagonals. If we take the German Army as our manifold and an infantry regiment as a domain within it, it is all one whether we choose to regard as elements the battalions, the companies, or the single soldiers. Thus it is all one so far which parts of the whole shall be called elements, so long as any domain we consider can be | com-   435
pounded out of them; and we have no need at all to assume that there are parts insusceptible of further division; so perhaps it is better at this stage not to talk about elements at all. Like the word 'class', the word 'manifold' also may produce obscurity; for it is often used in conjunction with a concept-word, e.g. 'manifold of points', 'manifold of trees', etc.; and in this way something logical gets mixed up with our discussion, whereas for the time being we still have to keep that out. So in order to develop the domain-calculus in its full purity we do best to avoid the words 'manifold', 'class', 'element', 'subsumption', and use instead of 'manifold' something like 'principal domain'.

I give some passages from Mr. Schröder's book that support this view of the domain-calculus. 'And *one* individual may likewise be termed a class – one that contains only this individual itself.... But also any class that itself contains many individuals can again be represented as an object of thought and accordingly as an individual (in a broader sense, e.g. as a "relative" individual in regard to higher classes)' (p. 148). Here there is indeed talk of individuals; but we also see straightaway that the distinction between individual and class is treated as a fluctuating one. It is apparent from several passages that a class is to be viewed as a totality of objects, a collective unity. Thus, on p. 67 there is talk about individual things making up a class. The class is called a collection (p. 83). 'We are able to take any objects of thought whatsoever as "individuals" and unite, "combine" them into a "class"' (p. 148). We saw above that a class may coincide with a single individual, and so, in that case, consists of it. So also we read on p. 150

'If we say "some men are shrewd", the subject is a class consisting of an indefinite number of men, "some" men.' Let us observe that on this showing a class consists of objects. Admittedly we have here already an admixture of logic. On p. 161 we have: 'We are led on to this field of application (*β*), to which we now go on from (*α*), through noticing, having it pointed out, that the "elements" of our manifold can also be 436 so-called "*individuals*", | and then the "domains" of this manifold will have to be termed "systems", "*classes*" if you like, of such individuals'. Here it is to be observed that in Mr. Schröder's use of language 'system' stands for a collective unity (pp. 71–2).

Up to this point everything is consistent; and moreover the definition of the 'identical' sum (p. 196) may be admitted, in spite of its not being logically unexceptionable, if we throw in the interpretation on p. 217; according to this, 'identical' addition results in an aggregation or collection of the two classes; the individuals of the two classes are thereby collected or 'gathered together' into a single class. Here too the so-called individuals may be themselves assumed to be further divisible *ad libitum* without our meeting with any difficulties. This, 'identical' addition, like everything that has gone before, admits of an excellent intuitive representation in Euler's diagrams.

But now we are approaching the point where the pure domain-calculus is no longer adequate and the analogy of the Euler diagrams becomes a lame one. In fact, the pure domain-calculus is quite unfruitful; and its apparent fruitfulness in this book arises just because it is not pure; something logical is always intruding, a thing that happens almost imperceptibly by way of the words 'manifold', 'individual', 'class', 'subsumption'.

We pass on to 'identical' multiplication; by the interpretation on p. 217, this results from isolation or selection; we 'gather out' from one class those individuals that belong to another. Even here, the basis of the way of thinking we have adopted so far need not always be abandoned; and Euler's diagrams can still be used, so long as the areas of the plane answering to the two classes have a part in common. In that case, this part is precisely a representation of the 'identical' product. But what if the areas have no part in common? For classes too there arises the case where two of them have no part in common. A class, in the sense in which we have so far used the word, consists of objects; it is an aggregate, a collective unity, of them; if so, it must 437 vanish when these | objects vanish. If we burn down all the trees of a wood, we thereby burn down the wood. Thus there can be no empty class. Now if we said that there is not always an 'identical' product, and inquired each time whether there were one before we made use of it, all would be in order, but the calculus would be grievously crippled. Mr. Schröder pays no heed to this; he speaks of an empty class (p. 147) and uses the 'identical' product in his calculations without more ado; he thus departs from the basis of the pure domain-calculus. He relies here on the *identical* zero, of which he says (p. 197) that its mission is to earn us the right of always being able to speak of the 'identical' product. One may ask: What then earns us the right to speak of the 'identical' zero? But let us leave this question on one side for the moment.

We must next bring into our discussion the logical aspect that has so far been kept out. According to the author, the transition would be made somewhat as follows. The 'identical' calculus, which is originally a pure domain-calculus, nevertheless admits of various sorts of application (p. 160). We obtain logic in this way: the letters that we have so far interpreted as domains we now interpret as classes – as concepts taken in extension. Of course if we kept to the use of the word 'class' that we have adopted so far, then we should not have anything new. Classes in this sense are not to be distinguished from domains. But if we take classes to be extensions of concepts; and if the relation of inclusion, also called subsumption, which was nothing over and above the relation of part to whole, is now replaced by the relation that holds between the extensions when one concept is subordinate to the other; we are then entering on quite a new field. Mr. Schröder admittedly does not seem to take proper notice of this. He does indeed count this way of applying the calculus under the heading (β) (p. 160), and so places it side by side with the 'domain' interpretation mentioned under (α), as something different; but when he says (p. 161) that the elements of our manifold may also be *'individuals'* and that in this case the 'domains' of the manifold are to be termed 'systems', | or, if you like,   438
'classes' of such individuals, then he is thinking of this as just a particular case. On this showing classes are also domains, and it needs bo proof that the laws of domain-calculus are still valid here. But because of the connection established between classes and concepts, viz. that classes are to be the extensions of concepts, the matter nevertheless assumes a new aspect; this is shown externally, in the first instance, in the new translations given for the formulae. What has so far been properly translatable as '*A* is part of *B*' is now to be rendered as 'all *A*s are *B*s'. I should first like to point out a small inaccuracy. If we take *A* and *B* to be classes or extensions of concepts, then we cannot say 'all *A*s are *B*s', for here *A* and *B* are used in a different sense. If, e.g., *A* is the extension of the concept *square*, and *B* the extension of the concept *rectangle*, we cannot say 'all extension of the concept *square* is

extension of the concept *rectangle*', or 'all extensions of the concept *square* are extensions of the concept *rectangle*', or 'the extension of the concept *square* is the extension of the concept *rectangle*'. Mr. Schröder, who elsewhere laudably practises accuracy of language, has unfortunately here been untrue to his habit, and has thus obscured the matter. We now also have *A* called the subject and *B* the predicate (pp. 132–3), or again they are called the subject-concept and the predicate-concept. This too is inexact, unless the expressions 'concept' and 'extension of a concept' are being used as equivalents. Again, the sign of inclusion, which previously expressed *A*'s being a part of *B*, now has to correspond to the copula '*is*' or '*are*' (pp. 132–3). But if instead of 'all mammals are vertebrates' we say 'the class of mammals is included in the class of vertebrates', the predicate is not *the class of vertebrates* but *included in the class of vertebrates*; and *is included* is not the copula alone but the copula *plus* a bit of the predicate.

All sorts of things have got out of order here; and the bad consequences of this will be immediately apparent now that we are proceeding to Mr. Schröder's rejection of Boole's *universe of discourse*. |
439   The author has always spoken of a manifold, containing the classes or domains within which the movement of thought occurs in a given case. This manifold is named 1; and Mr. Schröder now tries to show that it is not all-embracing like Boole's *universe of discourse*. On p. 245 we have:

> As we have laid down, 0 would have to be contained in *every* class that can be got out of the manifold 1; ... 0 would have to be a subject to *every* predicate.
>
> Now suppose we took *a* to be *the class of those classes of the manifold that are equal to* 1 (which would certainly be permissible if we could bring everything thinkable into the manifold 1), then this class of its very nature contains just one class, viz. the symbol 1 itself, or alternatively the whole of the manifold, which constitutes the reference of the symbol; *but therefore besides this it would contain 'nothing'*, i.e. 0. Hence 1 and 0 would make up the class of the objects that are to be equal to 1; and so we should have to admit not only: $1 = 1$ but *also*: $0 = 1$. For a predicate that applies to a class – in our case, the predicate: to be identically equal to 1 – must also apply to every individual in the class, by Principle II.

On p. 246 the author shows that we can apply these considerations to any class *b* of the manifold, instead of 1, and thus reaches the conclusion $0 = b$. This contradiction comes like a thunderbolt from a clear sky. How could we be prepared for anything like this in exact logic! Who can go surety for it that we shall not again suddenly encounter a contradiction as we go on? The possibility of such a thing points to a mistake in the original design. Mr. Schröder derives from this the conclusion that the original manifold 1 must be so made up that, among the elements given as individuals within it, there are found no classes that, for their part, contain within themselves as individuals any elements of the same manifold. This expedient, as it were, belatedly gets the ship off the sandbank; but if she had been properly steered, she could have kept off it altogether. It now becomes clear why at the very outset, in shrewd prevision of the imminent danger, | a certain manifold   440 was introduced as the theatre of operation, although there was no reason for this in the pure domain-calculus. The subsequent restriction of this field for our logical activities is by no means elegant. Whereas elsewhere logic may claim to have laws of unrestricted validity, we are here required to begin by delimiting a manifold with careful tests, and it is only then that we can move around inside it. A consequence of this is that the 'identical' zero likewise depends on the delimitation of the manifold. Thus it may come about that what is something in one manifold is zero or nothing in the other. Now negation is defined in terms of 0 and 1 (p. 302), and therefore this also depends on the manifold chosen, so that a class *a* may perhaps be the negation of *b* in one manifold, but not in another. Hence in a rigorously scientific statement one would always have to give an exact specification of the manifold within which the inquiry is being carried out. Now this suggests the question whether these inconveniences cannot be avoided, and what is the advantage anyhow in this restriction of the theatre of operations.

When Mr. Schröder stipulates (p. 248), as regards the original manifold, that among the elements given as 'individuals' there shall be found no classes that, for their part, comprise within them as individuals any elements of the same manifold, he is obviously distinguishing the case where something is given as an individual belonging to a manifold or class, where something is comprised within a class as an individual, from the case where something is contained as a class within a manifold or class. Mr. Husserl makes a similar distinction, in his review[2] of Mr. Schröder's work, between the expressions 'a class contains something as an element' and 'a class contains something as a sub-class', and by this he tries to remove the difficulty. The important thing here is that our attention is drawn to the essential difference

[2]*Göttingische gelehrte Anzeigen* (1891), p. 272.

between two relations, for which the author uses the same sign (the sign
441 of '*eventuelle Subordination*' or inclusion). | We see again from this that
we are no longer standing on the basis of the domain-calculus; for there
we had only the part–whole relation, and there was no ground for this
distinction between the cases where a class contains something as an
individual and where it contains it as a class. The Euler diagrams are a
lame analogy for logical relations, since they do not bring out this
important distinction.[3]

In order to bring clarity into the matter, it will be necessary to
correct Mr. Schröder's mistake, and, when things are different, to use
different signs for them. So we lay it down that

'*A sub B*'

is to assert that *A* is a class subordinate to the class *B*. On the other
hand

'*A subter B*'

is to express *A*'s being comprised as an individual under the class *B*. In
doing this we have of course done no more than just to recognize that
there is a difference; we still do not know exactly what it consists in.
Anyhow, we can now express Schröder's stipulation as follows: The
manifold *A* must be so made up that for no *A* and *B* are the
propositions: |

442   *B subter M*

A subter B

A subter M

[3]To be sure, not all of those who inveigh against Euler's diagrams show any better
understanding of the matter. When, in the judgement 'some numbers are primes', they
regard 'some numbers' as the subject; or when, in the judgement 'all bodies are heavy',
they represent 'all bodies', or the concept *bodies* in its full extension, as the subject; what
lies at the bottom of this is just the superficial view about concepts (one might call it a
mechanical or quantitative view) that comes out also in Euler's diagrams. If we negate
such sentences, the sign of negation must come before 'some' or 'all', and this makes it
clear that so far as their sense goes these words must be counted in with the predicative
part of the sentence. The word 'some' states a relation that holds (in our example)
between the concepts 'number' and 'prime'. Similarly 'all' in the second example states a
relation between the concepts *bodies* and *heavy*. An expression answering better to the
logical structure is: 'bodies are universally heavy'. Mr Schröder gives an example (p. 180)
of *quaternio terminorum* that arises because the expression 'some gentlemen' does not
always designate the same part of the class of gentlemen. Accordingly such an expression
would have to be rejected as ambiguous; and it must, in fact, be rejected if one regards it
(like our author, p. 150) as designating a class that consists of 'some' gentlemen. Of
course what I am here rejecting is not the particular judgement, but only a wrong
conception of it.

true simultaneously. Now how does this avoid the absurdity that apparently we can prove $0 = b$? That conclusion was possible only because of the interpretation that Mr. Schröder gives to his formulae by bringing classes into connection with concepts; in the pure domain-calculus there is no occasion for the absurdity to arise. It becomes necessary, and possible, to distinguish between the *sub*-relation and the *subter*-relation only when we leave the pure domain-calculus – as soon as we adopt the mode of interpretation mentioned above, and thus bring concepts into the discussion, and pass over into the domain of logic. So if we want to make clear to ourselves the distinction between the two relations, we must regard classes as extensions of concepts and make this the basis of our interpretation.

Accordingly, let us make trial of the following rules:

If v is a single thing and A is the class of things that *are a*, then we interpret

$$\text{'}v \text{ subter } A\text{'}$$

to mean 'v is an a'; and if B is the class of objects that *are b*, we translate

$$\text{'}B \text{ sub } A\text{'}$$

by 'all bs are as'.[4]

It must here be further noticed that *is* or *are* in italics is to be regarded as the mere copula, with no particular content at all, and that thus no identity is meant.

Let us now discuss more precisely the possibility of our sophism. To this end, we need to decide whether in Mr. Schröder's definition of the 'identical' zero the relation of being included is to be taken as the *sub* or the *subter* relation. It runs, in fact, as follows: '0 is our name for a domain that stands to every domain a in the relation of being included' (p. 188). Thus the question is whether zero is subordinate, as a class, to every class of the | manifold, or whether zero is comprised as an individual within every class of the manifold. Let us first try the latter assumption. In that case   44?

$$0 \text{ subter } a$$

will hold when

$$a \text{ sub } M$$

---

[4]Mr. G. Peano uses instead of '*sub*' and '*subter*' the signs 'Ⅽ' and 'ϵ'. See G. Peano, *Notations de logique mathématique* (Turin, 1894), §6.

H

does, where *M* is to be our manifold. Now let *Q* be the class of objects that coincide with *P*. Then *P* is the only individual comprised within *Q*, and we have

P subter Q.

Now if *Q sub M* holds, then we have also, in accordance with our supposition about zero,

0 *subter Q*

i.e. 0 coincides with *P*. This possibility is of course removed by the author's stipulation. For from

P subter Q

and   *Q sub M*

there follows   *P subter M.*

Now, on the other hand, *P* is the same as *Q*; the class *Q*, in fact, contracts into *P*. Thus *Q subter M* also holds, and we have:

Q subter M,

P subter Q,

P subter M,

contrary to Mr. Schröder's stimulation. A doubt might arise over the question whether *Q* coincides with *P*. At any rate this answers perfectly to the view of the class as consisting of single things. In line with this we read on p. 247: 'And in particular the individuals (of the manifold) themselves belong among the classes; in this case, since they contract to just one individual, we may use the term "monadic" or "*singular*" classes.' And we thus get on p. 148: 'And *one* individual may likewise be termed a class – one that contains only this individual itself.' In the light of this it can scarcely be doubted that on Mr. Schröder's principles *Q* in our case coincides with *P*.

At this point, however, we encounter a peculiar difficulty. If a class 444 that consists of just one object | coincides with that object, then Mr. Schröder's stipulation cannot be satisfied for any manifold that contains individuals at all. Let *a* be such an individual, so that we have:

a subter M.

Then *a* itself belongs among the classes, and is in fact a singular class, so that we have:

a subter a.

Thus the stimulation that for no *A* and *B* shall we have simultaneously

B subter M,

A subter B,

and: *A subter M,*

cannot be satisfied; for if we take both *A* and *B* to be *a*, we get our present case. Now Mr. Schröder writes: 'Even if we constructed only one singular (class) in this (manifold), and admitted it as a new individual, the identical zero would at once intrude into the class; would slip in, so to speak, through the door of Def. (2 ×)' (p. 248). This is not in accord with the principles elsewhere expressed by the author. For, by these, there is no need at all for a singular class to be constructed first; if *a* is an individual in the manifold, then *a* already is also a class; and it is unnecessary to go on and admit *a* into the manifold as a new individual, for *a* is there already. Moreover, what is required in order that the 'identical' zero should slip into a class is *not* that the class should be given as an individual in a manifold, but that it should be included in the manifold as a (sub-)class. It is not the *subter* but the *sub* relation that is in question.

The doubt whether each individual may be regarded as the class that consists of it alone is made stronger by the following consideration. In the discussion set forth above we may take *P* to be itself likewise a class comprising a number of individuals; for, as the author says (p. 148), such a class can be presented as an object of thought and consequently as an individual. Now if *Q*, as before, is the class of objects that coincide with *P*, then *Q* is a singular | class containing only   445 *P* as an individual. Now if it were right to hold that a singular class coincides with the only individual it contains, then *Q* would coincide with *P*. Let is now suppose that *a* and *b* are different objects, contained within *P* as individuals; then they would also be contained within *Q*; i.e. both *a* and *b* would coincide with *P*. Consequently *a* would also coincide with *b*, contrary to our permissible supposition that they are different. The author would perhaps object to our bringing *a* and *b* into the matter at all, because by his stipulation they could not be counted among the elements of the manifold. But as we have seen already, this stipulation cannot be satisfied anyhow, on our present supposition; so it must be abandoned.

Now our supposition that singular classes coincide with individuals is a necessary inference from the conception that classes consist of individuals – a view that accords with, and arises out of, the domain–calculus. As we see here, this conception is not suitable for logical use;

and the domain–calculus, far from being profitable for logic, here shows itself merely misleading. It is worth our notice that this last discussion need make no reference at all to the 'identical' zero; and thus the force of the proof does not depend in any way on whether the definition of this zero can be upheld.

We have seen that the conception of the class as consisting of individuals, so that the single thing coincides with the singular class, cannot be upheld in any case – whether we retain or abandon Mr. Schröder's stipulation. In the latter case, the conception leads to contradictions; in the former, we must abandon it if we are to make Mr. Schröder's stipulation at all realizable. Moreover, it follows that our sophism cannot be avoided by the stipulation.

Let us, for example, take as our manifold the manifold of integers. The class of numbers coincident with 3 contains no individual but the number 3 itself. Let us first suppose that the number 3 is this singular class; then this class is given as | an individual in the manifold, and contains the number 3 as an individual within itself – which is in its turn an element in the manifold, contrary to Mr. Schröder's stipulation. Let us secondly suppose that the singular class just mentioned does not coincide with 2 or with any other integer. In that case the class would not be given as an individual in our manifold, and Mr. Schröder's stipulation would be fulfilled; but on the other hand our sophism would be possible. For this singular class would comprise 3 as an individual within it; but it would likewise contain the 'identical' zero; i.e. the 'identical' zero would coincide with the number 3, and likewise with every integer; so all integers would coincide.

At this point, however, there arises the doubt whether on the author's view there can be singular classes at all containing any individual other than 0. For if a class contracts to an individual a, then we have:

$$a \; subter \; a$$

and also: $$0 \; subter \; a.$$

So if a is different from 0, the class a contains within it the individuals a and 0, and is thus *not* a singular class. The 'identical' zero always slips in as well. Cf., however, the following passage (p. 241): 'We have seen that 0 means "nothing"; the sign "*subter*"[5] answers to the copula and must be translated "is" in ordinary language; finally, a may be any

---

[5]Here I replace Mr. Schröder's sign by *subter*, in accordance with what we are assuming to be the sense of the definition of the identical zero.

arbitrary predicate[6] – let us say for instance "black". The subsumption
0 *subter a* is undoubtedly correct, since the class of all of all the things
we should call black contains nothing besides these, and so, as I may
put it, over and above these it contains "nothing"'.

Let us now take *a* to be the class consisting of the Moon and the
'identical' zero: then '0 *subter a*' would have to be understood,
according to Mr. Schröder, as: the class *a* contains nothing besides the
Moon: or as: the class *a* contains the Moon and over and above that it
also contains 'nothing'. The first expression would lead one to think
that this | class was a singular one and contained only the Moon; but   447
by the second expression it looks as though it contained the identical
zero as well as the Moon, and were thus not a singular class. Cf. what
the author says on p. 197: 'There is at least one domain *c* that satisfies
the hypotheses of Def. (3), for by Def. (2x) ... at any rate 0 is such a *c*.'
The visual field of our mind's eye is now in the same state as that of
our bodily eyes when one of them is looking through a blue, and the
other through a yellow, glass; one moment there is nothing, next
moment there is something. Are we not here befooled by language,
because negation, which really belongs with the predicate, is amalgamated with another constituent of the sentence to form a spurious
proper name? If we say that the class *a* contains nothing besides the
Moon, then we are denying the proposition that the class contains
something besides the Moon; but we are not thereby asserting that the
class contains, besides the Moon, an object with the name 'nothing'.
Thus language produces for us a mirage of an object; and Mr. Schröder
seems to be doing the same, when he speaks of his 'identical' zero. And
yet he himself surely recognizes that a name must be a name for
something. For after calling a name many-sensed when it does not
satisfy the requirement of univocality, he goes on (p. 50): 'so long, that
is, as it ... has a sense at all, really is a name *for something*, i.e. so long
as we are leaving out of account ... only senseless or "*nonsense*" names,
like "round square" ...' Isn't 'the identical zero' such a senseless or
nonsense name? The affirmative answer is implied by the author's
calling the name 'nothing' senseless and meaningless (p. 69); for
'nothing', as we have seen, is his rendering for his zero (p. 189).

This is the place for discussing more precisely the definition of the
'identical' zero. It runs thus (p. 188):

'We must now go on to introduce two special domains into the
algebra of logic; the numerals 0 and 1 recommend themselves ... as
names for these. We want to define these also by means of the

---

[6]The author is here referring to the requirement he imposes on the manifold.

relational sign for inclusion; and in fact the definition $(2\times)$ of the "*identical zero*" is to follow from our presenting the subsumption |

448                                $0 \text{ } subter \text{ } a^7$

as a *generally valid* one, i.e. one that must be recognized as holding for *every* domain of our manifold. This means to say: 0 *is our name for a domain that* stands to every domain *a* in the relation of being included – *is contained in every domain of the manifold.*'

By its phraseology this definition belongs entirely to the domain-calculus, but it is irreconcilable with it as regards its sense. An objection that we previously postponed must now be more precisely examined. After the definitions of his 0 and 1 Mr. Schröder goes on as follows:

'The symbols 0 and 1 to which we ascribe these properties are in any case henceforth counted among the "domains" of our manifold. Eventually they will perhaps turn out to be "improper" domains; i.e. they are still empty names, if it should prove impossible to point them out among the actual or proper domains that have been regarded as such so far, that appear to be virtually or potentially given to us at the same time as the manifold.'

Here we are first struck by the confusion between sign and thing signified. In the definition itself the author says: '0 is our name for a domain...' and from this it clearly follows that the zero-sign is to be a name for something that is a domain. In the explanation just quoted, the signs themselves suddenly appear as domains. This confusion is so dear to the author that he cannot abandon it, in spite of my admonitions.[8]

Now for zero the circumstance foreseen in this explanation does actually arise. There is in fact, e.g., no domain contained in all the domains of the States of the German Empire. Mr. Schröder does not let this worry him. For him, definition guarantees the existence of the thing defined, inasmuch as it itself, after a fashion, generates or creatively introduces it (p. 212); very much after a fashion, of course! |

449   By definition, the symbol 0 has had assigned to it the property of being included in every domain of the manifold; and thus, by means of this creative definition, we have now got a domain that is contained in every domain of our manifold. Of course this is only an empty sign; but since it has the desired property, we have all that we need. At least, so

---

[7] Here I write '*subter*' in place of Schröder's inclusion-sign.
[8] Cf. my *Grundlagen der Arithmetik* [*Foundations of Arithmetic*] (Breslau, 1884), p. 54 and p. 95 footnote. On p. 200 the author uses the phrase 'an *a* that means zero'; does *a* here mean the zero-sign, or the meaning that this hasn't got?

Mr. Schröder thinks. The mistake he commits here is a favourite one with mathematicians, and I have repeatedly called attention to it without making any impression; I suppose one must infer from this that mathematicians have a well-established prescriptive right to their procedure. For logicians it is otherwise. On the other hand, it is to be desired that no such right should come into being in their case; as a bar to this, I hope the present statement still does not come too late. If the zero-sign is an empty sign, then it designates nothing; and thus as a sign it misses its end, at least so far as science is concerned (and in fiction, for that matter, there will hardly be any use for it). The author himself says (p. 128) that when we put one thing equal to another, or express or assert identity, the question is not about the sound of names, or about how expressions may look, but entirely and solely about what they *mean*.[9] But what if there is nothing they do mean? The zero-sign is an oval figure made, e.g., on paper with printer's ink. Now what more does the definition do? Can it endow this figure with any new property whatsoever? On the contrary, the very most that the figure can get is the property of serving as a sign for the thing we fix upon for it to mean. Or does this figure become a domain contained in every domain of some manifold or other, simply in virtue of my saying it is such a domain? If that were possible, it might also not be hard to make diamonds. Now Mr. Schröder himself in the definition does not in fact say that this figure is such a domain, but only that it is to be a sign or name for such a domain. He thus attempts an act of naming, and it could be foreseen that the attempt must fail; for an act of naming involves above all | something that is named, and here this is lacking.   450 Now how can such an abortive attempt make any difference at all to that which was chosen to be a name or sign? Thus in the domain-calculus the definition must be rejected. But just the same holds true of the logical calculus; for there is not a thing that is contained as an individual within every class of a manifold, at any rate not if more than one class is contained in the manifold; and this is always the case if empty classes are admitted and the manifold is not empty. If, however, it is empty, there is nothing at all to be contained in a class of the manifold.

No wonder that such a faulty definition leads to contradictions! We can certainly count as another of these what the author says on p. 238: '"*Nothing*" *is thus a subject to every predicate*: Nothing is black, at the same time Nothing is also not black.' Assertions of the form '*a* is *b*' and

---

[9]On p. 199, to be sure, he requires that Principle I (the principle of Identity) shall be admitted also for names – regardless of whether they have a sense or not.

'*a* is not *b*' assuredly constitute a contradiction. Mr. Schröder would perhaps add: if they are not devoid of content; but if they are, they are properly speaking not assertions at all, but nonsense; and all that logic can do with nonsense is to recognize it as such – it cannot make use of it.

Let us now consider the other way of taking our definition. We may replace Mr. Schröder's sign of inclusion by '*sub*.' In that case, therefore,

$$0 \; sub \; a$$

is to hold good generally, for any class[10] *a* within the manifold. Here, too, we must regard 0 and *a* as extensions of concepts in order to get a sense for '0 *sub* *a*.' Accordingly 0 will have to be regarded as a class of objects that have a certain property. Let us say for short that 0 is the class of objects that are *b*,[11] postponing the decision what '*b*' must be taken to mean. Further, let *a* be the class of objects that are *c*.[11] Then

$$0 \; sub \; a \quad |$$

451   must be taken to mean: 'all *b*s are *c*'; and this is to hold for any arbitrary class *a*, so long as it is contained in our manifold. Now if there were a single thing *v* that was *a b*,

$$v \; subter \; 0,[12]$$

then we should also have

$$v \; subter \; a;$$

and this would have to hold good for any class *a* in our manifold, which, as I have said, is impossible. The only possibility remaining is that there is no single object that is a *b* – in short, that there is no *b*. In that case 0 is an empty class. But there cannot be an empty class if we take a class to be a collection or totality of individuals, so that, as the author says (p. 67),[13] the class consists of individuals or individuals make up the class. In the course of this discussion we have once more had it shown to us that this way of talking is logically useless; that the extension of a concept is constituted in being, not by the individuals,

---

[10]I here write 'class' instead of 'domain', because in the calculus neither the *sub* nor the *subter* relation occurs, but only the part–whole relation.

[11]This 'are' must be regarded as a mere copula. Cf. p. 442 *supra* [of the original].

[12][In the original text, *v subter b*; '*b*' is certainly a misprint for '0'. (*Tr.*)]

[13]We can, however, also find assertions opposed to this. On p. 147 he says that the concept of class must not be taken too narrowly, and thus empty classes also are admitted. To be sure, the way this is to be reconciled with the other assertions remains obscure.

but by the concept itself; i.e. by what is said of an object when it is brought under a concept. There is then no objection to our talking about the class of objects that are *b*s even when there are no *b*s. Moreover, all empty concepts now have the same extension.[14] We can, e.g., take *b* to be *object that is not the same as itself.* If we now call the extension of this concept 0, then the question is how in that case we are to take the proposition '0 *sub a*' or 'all *b*s are *c*'. Mr. Schröder (p. 239) reads it in this case as meaning 'all *b*s, in so far as there are any, are *c*', or: '*either* there are no *b*s,[15] *or*, if there are any, then all of them are *c*'. I can agree to this way of taking it, for it is a suitable way and the only way that is of any use in logic, even though it does some violence to usage. Accordingly

$$0 \ sub \ a \quad |$$

must be rendered: 'either there are no objects that are not the same as   452 themselves; or, if there are any, then all of them are *c*'. There is nothing to be said against this; and so we have a class such that it is *sub a* whatever class *a* may be. And the zero-sign now really does mean something that has the property required by our definition.

Let us now inquire whether the sophism that provoked this whole discussion is possible. Let *Q* be once more the class of objects that coincide with *P*. We have now

$$0 \ sub \ Q;$$

i.e. 'either there are no objects that are not the same as themselves; or, if there are any, they all coincide with *P*.' This proposition is unexceptionable, and there can be no question of a sophism. So in this case we simply do not need to confine our thought to a manifold that satisfies certain requirements; when once we avoid a mistake in definition, everything falls into proper order.

In support of many of the assertions that I have here been expounding, passages could be quoted from Mr. Schröder also; but so could passages contradicting them. What can be the source of this inconsistency? Mr. Schröder, as he says in his Introduction, found great difficulties in the theory of the construction of concepts, and in explaining their nature. He observed the battle over these questions wavering endlessly this way and that without being decided. He wanted to escape this uncertainty by founding logic not on the content of

---

[14]Cf. also my *Grundgesetze der Arithmetik* I (Herman Pohle, Jena, 1893) [partial English translation, *The Basic Laws of Arithmetic* (Berkeley, Ca., 1964)], §§3 and 10.

[15]['*a*' misprinted for '*b*' in the original. (*Tr.*)]

concepts but on the extension, and he thought he could here leave it undecided how the delimitation of classes comes about. This led him to the domain-calculus, to the view that classes consist of single things, are collections of individuals; for in fact what else is there to constitute a class, if we ignore the concepts, the common properties! The single thing is then likewise a class. The natural result is that the fundamental relation is that of part to whole. All this is intuitively very clear, and indubitable; only unfortunately it is barren, and it is not logic. Only because classes are determined by the properties that individuals in

453   them | are to have, and because we use phrases like this: 'the class of objects that are *b*': only so does it become possible to express thoughts in general by stating relations between classes; only so do we get a logic. The complete difference, and indeed incompatibility, between this conception of classes and the one first mentioned is, of course, concealed at first. Thus there arises a cruder conception of classes and extensions, side by side with a subtler one, the only one that can be used in logic; and the incompatibility of the two becomes noticeable only incidentally, by means of contradictions. It is understandable that this happens most obviously where there is no class in the 'domain-calculus' sense – when we have empty concepts. Somebody might have the idea of rejecting such concepts as illegitimate; but this would involve excluding from logic wide and particularly fruitful domains. Mr Schröder is quite right in not wanting to do this and in stressing the importance of introducing the 'identical' zero (p. 189) – though the recognition of empty concepts need not be made exactly in this form. If we admit a sentence 'there is a ——', we may not exclude a sentence 'there is no ——'; for unless the negation of a sentence has a sense, the sentence itself is without sense.

We must here keep well apart two wholly different cases that are easily confused, because we speak of existence in both cases. In one case the question is whether a proper name designates, names, something; in the other, whether a concept takes objects under itself. If we use the words 'there is a ——' we have the latter case. Now a proper name that designates nothing has no logical justification, since in logic we are concerned with truth in the strictest sense of the word; it may on the other hand still be used in fiction and fable.[16] For concepts that do not comprehend anything under them it is quite different; they are entirely legitimate. The author confuses these two cases when he calls

454   'Nothing' and 'round square' alike senseless, nonsensical, or | meaningless names (pp. 50, 69). His 'Nothing' is in many cases, e.g. in the

---

[16]Cf. my paper 'Über Sinn und Bedeutung' ['On Sense and Meaning'], *Zeitschrift für Philosophie und philosophische Kritik* 100 [this volume pp. 157–77]

sentences 'Nothing is black' and 'Nothing is not black' (p. 238), a proper name without any meaning, and hence logically illegitimate. 'Round square' on the other hand is not an empty name, but a name of an empty concept, and thus one not devoid of meaning, in sentences like 'there is no round square' or 'the Moon is not a round square'. The word 'common name' is confusing here, for it makes it look as though the common name stood in the same, or much the same, relation to the objects that fall under the concept as the proper name does to a single object. Nothing could be more false! In this case it must, of course, appear as though a common name that belongs to an empty concept were as illegitimate as a proper name that designates nothing. The word 'planet' has no direct relation at all to the Earth, but only to a concept that the Earth, among other things, falls under; thus its relation to the Earth is only an indirect one, by way of the concept; and the recognition of this relation of *falling under* requires a judgement that is not in the least already given along with our knowledge of what the word 'planet' means. If I utter a sentence with the grammatical subject 'all men', I do *not* wish to say something about some Central African chief wholly unknown to me. It is thus utterly false that I am in any way designating this chief when I use the word 'man', or that this chief belongs in any way whatsoever to what the word 'man' means. It is likewise equally false that in such a sentence many judgements are put together by means of the common name, as Mr. Schröder thinks (p. 69). In order that a word like 'man' or 'planet' should have logical justification, it is necessary only that there should answer to it a sharply delimited concept; whether the concept comprehends something under itself is not here relevant.

It is easily seen how the use of the word 'common name' hangs together with the conception that the class or extension consists or is compounded of single things. In both cases the emphasis is laid on the things and the concept is overlooked. Now we do admittedly also get in Mr. Schröder's work passages like this: 'In this way we show | that   455 for us what characterizes a concept ... is just that a definite group of traits, distinguishable from all others ... are associated and invariably correlated with its name' (pp. 89–90). But this is only another sign of the pervasive inconsistency that the author has not noticed and has thus not been able to escape.[17]

---

[17]It would take us too far here to explain more precisely the nature of the concept. I therefore refer to my address *Funktion und Begriff* [*Function and Concept*] (Pohle, Jena, 1891) [this volume pp. 137–56]; to my paper 'Über Begriff und Gegenstand' ['On Concept and Object'], *Vierteljahrsschrift für wissenschaftliche Philosophie* 16 (1982) [this volume pp. 182–94]; and to what I have said in my *Basic Laws of Arithmetic*, Introduction and §3.

Someone may get the impression from my procedure that in the battle between extensionalist and intensionalist logicians I take the side of the latter. I do, in fact, maintain that the concept is logically prior to its extension; and I regard as futile the attempt to take the extension of a concept as a class, and make it rest, not on the concept, but on single things. That way we get a domain-calculus, not a logic. All the same, in many respects my position may be closer to the author than to those who could in contrast to him be termed intensionalist logicians.

In conclusion, we may sum up the results of this discussion:

1. The domain-calculus, in which the fundamental relation is that of part to whole, must be wholly separated from logic. For logic Euler's diagrams are only a lame analogy.

2. The extension of a concept does not consist of objects falling under the concept, in the way, e.g., that a wood consists of trees; it attaches to the concept and to this alone. The concept thus takes logical precedence of its extension.

3. We must keep separate from one another:

456   (*a*) the relation of an object (an individual) to | the extension of a concept when it falls under the concept (the *subter* relation);

(*b*) the relation between the extension of one concept and that of another when the first concept is subordinate to the second (the *sub* relation).

4. By means of a definition we can neither create an object with any properties we like, nor magically confer any properties we like on an empty name or symbol.

5. The questions whether a proper name means something, and whether a concept comprehends something under itself, must be kept separate. Proper names without any meaning are illegitimate in science; empty concepts cannot be banished.

Whole Numbers

I have noticed that this Journal is trying to reconcile mathematics and 73
philosophy, and to me this seems very valuable. Indeed, these sciences
cannot but profit by exchanging ideas. It is this that prompts me to
enter the discussion. The views put forward by M. Ballue in the May
number[1] are doubtless shared by most mathematicians. But they
embody logical difficulties which to me seem serious enough to be
worth exposing – all the more because they might obscure the issues,
and make philosophers stop bothering about the principles of arithmetic. To begin with, it seems worth pointing out that a frequent fault of
mathematicians is their mistaking symbols for the objects of their
investigations. In fact, symbols are only the means – albeit very useful:
indispensable, even – of investigation, not its objects. These latter are
represented by the symbols. The *shapes* of the signs, and their physical
and chemical properties, can be more or less appropriate, but they are
not essential. There is no symbol that cannot be replaced by another of
different shape and qualities, the connection between things and
symbols being purely conventional. This goes for any system of signs
and for any language. Language is a powerful instrument of the human
intelligence, no doubt: | 'but one language can be as useful as another. 74
So it is necessary not to overrate words and symbols, either by
ascribing to them quasi-magical powers over things, or by mistaking
them for the actual things of which they are at most the (more or less
accurate) representations. It hardly seems worth insisting on the point,
but M. Ballue's article is perhaps not immune from the error in
question. His topic is whole numbers. What are they? M. Ballue says:
'Pluralities are represented by symbols called whole numbers.' According to him, then, whole numbers are symbols, and it is of these symbols
that he wants to speak. But symbols are not, and cannot be the
foundation of mathematical analysis. When I write down $1+2=3$ I am
putting forward a proposition about the numbers 1, 2 and 3, but it is
not these symbols that I am talking about. I could substitute A, B and
Γ for them; I could write p instead of $+$ and $é$ instead of $=$. By writing

[1]'Le Nombre entier considéré comme fondement de l'analyse mathématique.'

Revue de Métaphysique et de Morale 3 (1895), pp. 73–8 (in French.)
(*Tr.* V. H. Dudman)

Α*p*Βέ́Γ I should then express the same thought as before – but by means of different symbols. The theorems of arithmetic are never about symbols, but about the things they represent. True, these objects are neither palpable, visible, nor even real, if what is called real is what can exert or suffer an influence. Numbers do not undergo change, for the theorems of arithmetic embody eternal truths. We can say, therefore, that these objects are outside time; and from this it follows that they are not subjective percepts or ideas, because those are continually changing in conformity with psychological laws. Arithmetical laws form no part of psychology. It is not as if every man had a number of his own, called *one*, forming part of his mind or his consciousness: there is just one number of that name, the same for everybody, and objective. Numbers are therefore very curious objects, uniting in themselves the apparently contrary qualities of being objective and of being unreal. But it emerges from a more serious consideration that there is no contradiction here. Negative numbers, fractions, etc. are of the same nature; and perhaps that is why in arithmetic too much store is often set by the symbols. Because of the difficulty of identifying objects which are neither discernible to the sense nor psychological, visible objects have been substituted for them. But this is to forget that these symbols are not what we want to study. And so numbers have a double nature

75   conferred | upon them: they are called symbols; and yet they are themselves represented – they are given names. M. Ballue writes: 'Like all symbols, a whole number admits of a double representation: the sound which it produces upon the ear, the impression which its written name produces upon the sight … Besides this, a whole number possesses its own particular written representation, requiring the use of special characters called *figures*. The aim of *numeration* is to study the means of representing all whole numbers with a small number of words and figures.' What is it then that the figure 2 designates? A number; which is to say, a symbol, according to M. Ballue. Is it the word *deux*? If that were the case, we Germans should have numbers which were different from those of Frenchmen, and our arithmetic would be a different science from theirs, having different objects of investigation. Perhaps M. Ballue's opinion is that the word *deux* represents the same number as the figure 2. But whatever this number might be, it represents a plurality, and is itself represented by the figure 2. What then do we want with this somewhat mysterious intermediary? Why will it not do to designate the plurality directly by the figure?

It might be thought that this is only a verbal slip on M. Ballue's part, which could easily be corrected by substituting *plurality* for *whole number* in the title of his article. For it is pluralities of which whole numbers are the symbolic representatives, according to M. Ballue. But this will not save us from all the difficulties. What is a plurality? M. Ballue replies: 'The assemblage of several distinct objects, considered as distinct, without attention to the nature or shape of these objects, is called a *plurality*. It will be seen that a plurality is an assemblage of units.'

This definition is not as clear as the author seems to think. The sense of the word *plurality* could be found contained in the word *several* and the plural form, but M. Ballue adds some restrictions, saying 'distinct objects, considered as distinct, without attention to the nature or shape of these objects'. What he is calling *distinct* here he has previously called *isolated*, saying: 'An isolated object, considered as isolated, in abstraction from its nature or shape, is given the name of unit.' It will perhaps be objected that if the objects were absolutely isolated there would be no assemblage. And besides, it is to be doubted whether an absolutely isolated object exists, every material particle being related to every other by gravitation. | So the precise degree of isolation required 76 would have to be specified. I shall not labour this point, but I do want to inquire more closely into what M. Ballue intends by the words 'considered as distinct, without attention to the nature or shape of these objects', and by the words 'considered as isolated, in abstraction from its nature or shape', What strikes me here . is that the way of considering an object, and the abstractions performed in the mind of a subject, seem to be being taken for qualities of the object. I ask: after the object has been considered as isolated, is it the same object as before? – or has one created a new object by considering it? In the former case, nothing essential would be changed. And surely, if I consider the planet Jupiter as distinct or isolated, its gravitational ties to the other heavenly bodies do not become any the weaker; and if I abstract from its mass and its spheroidal shape, Jupiter loses neither its mass nor its shape. So what is the point of performing this abstraction? There would by a psychological difficulty over this as well. While I am considering an object, I can be sure that it is being considered. But in conducting a proof I have to fix my attention upon other objects successively, for I am incapable of considering each of even a hundred objects at the same time. It is all the more difficult in that, without getting the objects mixed up, I am not to attend to their nature or shape. I should thus lose the assurance that these objects were all in fact units. Certainly they would not be units with respect to me: perhaps with respect to other people they would but I should probably know nothing of this. And even if I did know, it would be useless from the point of view of my proof, for I could infer nothing thence.

Orion is an assemblage of stars. If it is possible in general to consider objects as distinct, without attention to the nature or shape of these objects, then it will be possible in this case. After performing this consideration we shall say, if we take M. Ballue at his word, that the constellation is a plurality. And since the name *Orion* is a symbol for that plurality, we shall regard this word as a number. Admittedly he does not actually say that the stars are considered as distinct, etc. But that is neither here nor there: granted that constellation is a plurality, the name of the constellation is a symbol for a plurality.

Let us examine the alternative conception, that the considered object is different from the original object. The sun for instance, as a material, 77 | luminous body, having a shape and occupying a position, would be different from the sun considered as distinct, in abstraction from its nature or shape. It might be said that the latter is created by the act of considering it and that, since an external object cannot be created in this way, it would have to be a subjective idea or something of the sort in the mind of the person performing that consideration and that abstraction. By thus considering the sun, everyone would form such an idea of his own, distinct from anyone else's. Pluralities would then be subjective too. And that would be at variance with the fact that naturalists are giving objective information when they specify the precise number of pistils in a flower.

What could be the effect of abstracting from the nature or shape of an object? Does it lose its nature and shape? This is apparently the effect M. Ballue is after. But it is obvious that an external object cannot be changed in this way. As for the idea of an object that someone forms for himself, there is no need for abstraction in order that *it* lack the qualities of the object itself. An idea of the sun is not a material, luminous body. But still, such an idea is in general qualitatively different from the same person's idea of the moon. M. Ballue's abstraction can efface the difference between these ideas. – But then what remains of the plurality?

Closely bound up with this is another difficulty. M. Ballue says: 'The simplest plurality is formed by adding one unit to another unit.' But if there exist more than two units there will be several pluralities formed by adding one unit to another unit, and the definite article in the singular that M. Ballue uses is therefore inaccurate. It should be: The simplest pluralities are formed, etc. But the number *two* is neither a particular plurality of that sort nor the symbol for such a plurality. It is perhaps nearer the truth to say that it is the species or class of pluralities formed by adding one unit to another unit. But then, to meet the demands of precision, we want good definitions of *unit* and *plurality.* Readers of this Journal will easily verify that the first of these terms is not used with any uniformity by authors. Comparing M. Ballue's thesis ('The simplest plurality is formed by adding one unit to another unit') with what MM. Le Roy and Vincent say (in their article, published in the September number, p. 519: 'The possibility of the mind's forming whole numbers indefinitely by adding unity to itself') we see that the latter use this term [*unité*] as a proper name, | whereas 78 M. Ballue uses it as a general term by assuming the existence of several units. At the same time we see that the words *assemblage* and *adding*, used by M. Ballue, require explanation. MM. Le Roy and Vincent employ the verb *to add*: apparently this is an action that takes place in people's minds. But it is difficult to conceive how a thing could be added to itself. What sort of relations are they that yield these assemblages? Are they physical, historical, geometrical or psychological? – or are they purely logical?

Readers will perhaps be dissatisfied, because I have done no more than enter protests and pose questions. But since positive solutions to the problems are set forth in my works cited below,[2] I can confine myself at present to showing that some pretty thorny issues are involved, and that the matter is more complicated than it appears at first sight.

---

[2] *Die Grundlagen der Arithmetik* [*The Foundations of Arithmetic*] (Breslau, 1884); *Grundgesetze der Arithmetik* I (Jena, 1893) [partial English translation, *The Basic Laws of Arithmetic* (Berkeley, Ca., 1964)].

On Mr. Peano's Conceptual Notation and My Own

362   I read a paper about Mr. Peano's conceptual notation and my own to the Mathematics Section of the Natural Science Congress at Lübeck. But I was prevented from doing the matter justice in the short time at my disposal, and so decided to forgo publication of the paper in the form in which it was delivered. However, I have been keeping in mind a somewhat more thorough treatment of the subject, and shall try to present such a treatment in what follows. In view of the large number of problems which arise here, I still of course have to disclaim an exhaustive account of the subject.

Since I am myself an interested party, it is difficult for me to do complete justice to Mr. Peano's conceptual notation: perhaps it will seem that I am over-harsh in my assessment. If I do in fact fall into this error, I plead as my excuse the fact that this is difficult to avoid. For it is natural that I should understand my own conceptual notation better than an unfamiliar one, and that its advantages should impress me more than its shortcomings. Mr. Peano found himself in a similar position when he reviewed my *Foundations of Arithmetic*.[1] In fact my impression is that he was not altogether fair to my conceptual notation. And there were some obvious misunderstandings as well. Still, that does not prevent my welcoming this review with thanks, as a starting-point for further discussion in which the misunderstandings can be cleared up and the solutions of contentious questions brought closer. But what I am presenting here is not to be regarded as a reply to that review, for that is something I propose making in *Rivista di Matematica*.

If in what follows reproach perhaps seems too heavily to outweigh approbation, then the difference between the respective aims we have pursued should be taken into account. For the same notation or stipulation can seem appropriate or inappropriate depending upon one's purposes. To begin with, therefore, intentions and motives should be examined more closely.

---

[1] *Rivista di Matematica* 5, pp. 122ff.

Verhandlungen der Königlich Sächsischen Gesellschaft der Wissenschaften zu Leipzig (Mathematisch-Physische Klasse) 48 (1897), pp. 362–8. (*Tr.* V. H. Dudman)

I became aware of the need for a conceptual notation when I was looking for the fundamental principles or axioms upon which the whole of mathematics rests. Only after this question is answered can it be hoped to trace successfully the springs of knowledge upon which this science thrives. Even if this question belongs largely to philosophy, it must still be regarded as mathematical. The question is an old one: apparently it was already being asked by Euclid. If is has nevertheless not yet been answered satisfactorily, the reason is to be sought in the logical imperfection of our languages. In order to test whether a list of axioms is complete, we have to try and derive from them all the proofs of the branch of learning to which they relate. And in doing this it is imperative that we draw conclusions only in accordance with purely logical laws, for otherwise something might intrude unobserved which should have been laid down as an axiom. The reason why verbal languages are ill suited to this purpose lies not just in the occasional ambiguity of expressions, but above all in the absence of fixed forms for inferring. Words like 'thus', 'consequently' and 'because' do indeed intimate | that an inference has been made, but they say nothing about 363 the law in accordance with which it has been made, and can be used with linguistic propriety where there is no logically justified inference. For an investigation such as I have in mind here it is not sufficient for us just to convince ourselves of the truth of a conclusion, as we are usually content to do in mathematics; on the contrary, we must also be made aware of what it is that justifies our conviction, and upon what primitive laws it is based. For this are required fixed guiding-lines, along which the deductions are to run; and in verbal languages these are not provided. If we try to list all the laws governing the inference which occur when arguments are conducted in the usual way, we find an almost unsurveyable multitude which apparently has no precise limits. The reason for this, obviously, is that these inferences are composed of simpler ones. And hence it is easy for something to intrude which is not of a logical nature and which consequently ought to be specified as an axiom. This is where the difficulty of discerning the axioms lies: for this the inferences have to be resolved into their simple components. By so doing we shall arrive at just a few modes of inference, with which we must then attempt to make do at all times. And if at some point this attempt fails, then we shall have to ask whether we have hit upon a truth issuing from a non-logical source of cognition, whether a new mode of inference has to be acknowledged, or whether perhaps the intended step ought not to be taken at all. But such a resolution of composite modes of influence into their simple components has as a necessary consequence the lengthening of proofs;

and because of this, the prolixity of verbal languages (quite apart from their logical imperfection) constitutes an almost insurmountable obstacle – unless we decide to use an entirely new expedient for the expression of thoughts, which combines logical perfection with the utmost brevity. We should thus limit to the bare minimum the number of modes of inference, and set these up as rules of this new language. This is the fundamental idea of my conceptual notation. As the name indicates, its primitive constituents are neither sounds not syllables, but written symbols; it is, to use a Leibnizian expression, a *lingua charac-*

364   *terica.* | This difference from spoken language is not without its consequences, and manifests itself in two main ways: written signs endure while sounds perish; written signs appear upon a two-dimensional surface while sounds occur in unidimensional time. Because of their persistence written signs are more like concepts, and thus better adapted to logical use than sounds. They are also more precise, and hence induce a greater precision in our thinking. A group of written symbols can be reiterated, and can be surveyed visually in different ways; thus its sense, with all the ingredient relations of the parts to one another, can be presented to the mind more than once, and it is easier to grasp the whole and to keep it present. Because of the two-dimensional expanse of the writing surface, a multitude of dispositions of the written signs with respect to one another is possible, and this can be exploited for the purpose of expressing thoughts. In an ordinary written or printed text it is of course quite incidental which written sign happens to appear underneath another: in tabular lists, on the other hand, the two-dimensional expanse is utilised to achieve perspicuity. In much the same way I am trying to do this in my conceptual notation. I attain a clear articulation of the sentence by writing the individual clauses – e.g. consequent and antecedents – one beneath the other, and to the left of these, by means of combination of strokes, I exhibit the logical relation which binds the whole together. I mention this because efforts are now being made to squeeze each formula on to one line. In the Peano conceptual notation the presentation of formulas upon a single line has apparently been accomplished in principle. To me this seems a gratuitous renunciation of one of the main advantages of the written over the spoken. After all, the convenience of the typesetter is certainly not the *summum bonum*. For physiological reasons it is more difficult with a long line to take it in at a glance and apprehend its articulation, than it is with shorter lines (disposed one beneath the other) obtained by fragmenting the longer one – provided that this partition corresponds to the articulation of the sense. It seems to me that even more serious drawbacks have resulted

from this unilinear feature of the Peano conceptual notation. But of this anon. In my conceptual notation inference is conducted | like a   365 calculation. I do not mean this in the narrow sense, as if it were subject to an algorithm the same as or similar to that of ordinary addition and multiplication, but only in the sense that there is an algorithm there at all, i.e. a totality of rules which govern the transition from one sentence or from two sentences to a new one in such a way that nothing happens except in conformity with these rules.

What I am aiming for, then, is uninterrupted rigour of demonstration and maximal logical precision, together with perspicuity and brevity.

I cannot so definitely specify what aim it is that Peano is pursuing with his conceptual notation or mathematical logic: I have to rely largely upon conjecture. He has written a short paper, 'Notations de Logique Mathématique: Introduction au Formulaire de mathématiques' published by *Rivista di Matematica*, in which he sets forth his notational system, and it is chiefly from this that I derive my information. I shall refer to it in what follows as '*Introduction*'. This much I think I can gather from it, that an examination of the foundation of mathematics is not what initiated it – nor has it been a determinant for its mode of execution. For straightaway, in §2 of this *Introduction*, brief tags are introduced for the classes of the real numbers, the rational numbers, the prime numbers, etc., which means that all these concepts are assumed as already familiar. The same thing happens with the meanings of the operation-signs '$+$', '$-$', '$\times$', '$\sqrt{}$', etc., from which it is to be gathered that an analysis of these logical structures into their simple components was not the intention. And since, without such an analysis, an investigation like the one I projected is impossible, such an investigation could not have been among Mr. Peano's intentions. As the above mentioned title indicates, this paper is the introduction to a larger work, *Formulaire de Mathématiques*,[2] in which several scholars have collaborated, and which is to include the totality of mathematical knowledge, written out in Mr. Peano's conceptual notation. Hence the intention seems orientated towards the storage of knowledge rather than towards proof, | towards brevity and   366 international intelligibility rather than towards logical perfection. However, in the Preface to *Formulaire*, p. VI, Mr. Peano says:[3]

> 20. Having written a formula in symbols, it is appropriate to apply some logical transformations to the formula. In this way

---

[2]Turin, 1895.
[3][In Frege's version all the excerpts from *Formulaire* and *Notations* are quoted in Peano's original French. (*Tr.*)]

it will be seen whether it is possible to reduce it to a simpler form: and it is easily recognised if the formula is not well written.

21. For the notations of logic are not just a tachygraphy for representing the propositions of mathematics in an abridged form; they are a powerful instrument for analysing propositions and theories.

On this showing the author obviously had in mind a logical treatment as well; but by the words 'analysing propositions and theories' he seems just to have meant the work that has to be done in order to write out a sentence as simply as possible in symbols. For this, to be sure, a more concise form of expression, and a reduction into simpler components, is often necessary or desirable, but this reduction need not be continued right down to the simplest elements. In any case, less emphasis is placed upon strictness in conducting a proof, and upon logical perfection, here than in my conceptual notation. In the Preface to *Formulaire* it says on p. VII:

25. The demonstrations of propositions, or at any rate the links that connect the propositions of a sequence, can also be published. But the transformation of a demonstration into symbols is in general more difficult than the enunciation of a theorem.

That the conduct of proofs is thrust into the background here is due also to the absence of rules of inference, for the the formulae in Part I of *Formulaire* can offer no substitute for them. The question here is simply how, from one of those formulae, or from two of them, a new one is obtained.

The manner of defining, especially, I find wanting in logical perfection. That the same symbol is explained more than once is almost the rule. Conditional definitions are also very numerous. As against this, I require that each sign be defined just once, and completely, not several times over and in piecemeal fashion; I require that the meaning of the defining expression coincide unconditionally with the meaning of the defined one; I do not allow the legitimacy of a definition to depend upon a proposition which requires to be proved – something which 367 always happens when the same symbol | is explained more than once, because it is then necessary that these explanations be proved consistent. I can find no trace of this in Mr. Peano's work.

Even if the striving for logical precision is less marked here than in my conceptual notation, it is nevertheless present, and has more than

once led to the corroboration of my own dicta – and this, when nearly all logicians seem to be of a different opinion, is especially valuable to me. Particular affirmative propositions are a case in point. Here the Peano notation rests upon the same conception as that which underlies my own, the conception namely that what we have here is the negation of the generality of a negation (*Introduction*, §9, at the end), whereas most logicians, misled by language, take the words 'some numbers' in the sentence 'some numbers are prime numbers' together, and treat their meaning as a logical subject of which the property of being a prime number is predicated, just as it is predicated of say the number 2 in the sentence 'two is a prime number'. And if we now ask for the meaning of the word-combination 'some numbers', the answer we get is something like 'a part of the total collection of all numbers' or 'a part of all numbers' – whereupon it may justly be inquired: which part? And to this there is no single answer possible which would cover all the sentences in which these words occur as grammatical subject. Such being the case, they would be ambiguous without limit and hence, logically, to be rejected out of hand. In fact, these words cannot be taken together at all, and we must not ask for the meaning of this combination. We have here a grammatical pseudo-subject, similar to 'all men', 'no man', and 'nothing' – constructions in which language seems to have indulged in order to mislead logicians. Mr. E. Schröder too has fallen into this trap in his *Algebra der Logik*, and even Mr. Peano himself has not avoided it entirely, for at *Introduction* §33 he introduces notations which are constructed exactly on the model of these verbal expressions and are hence logically wrong. Fortunately, however, he appears to make no use of them. Existential sentences, beginning 'there is', are closely related to particular ones: compare the sentences 'there are numbers which are prime' and 'some numbers are prime'. This existence is still often confused with reality and objectivity. Here again | Mr. Peano's notation points toward the correct concep-   368
tion: compare *Introduction* p. 13, at the bottom.[4]

For my tenet that a statement of number contains a declaration about a concept, I find corroboration in the Peano symbolism

'num u'

(*Introduction* §19) in which 'u' is to indicate a class. Of course everything depends on how the word 'class' is to be understood. If, following Mr. E. Schröder, we were to conceive a class as a collective unity, so that the relation of the class to an object belonging to it was

---

[4]The question of existence plays a positive role in mathematics. It is by no means all the same, therefore, how it is construed.

that of whole to part, then that symbolism would certainly not be in agreement with my doctrine. Which interpretation Mr. Peano advocates is a moot point. At first it seems as if on his view (as on Boole's) a class is something primitive which is not further reducible. But in *Introduction* §17 I find a designation '$\overline{x}\varepsilon p_x$' of a class of objects which satisfy a certain specific condition or have certain specific properties. As against a concept, a class thus appears here as something derived: it appears as the extension of a concept. And with this I can declare myself in complete agreement – although the notation '$\overline{x}\varepsilon p_x$' does not greatly appeal to me.

In another case my agreement with Mr. Peano is less evident, requiring that an inference first be drawn to throw it into bold relief. This concerns my doctrine of truth and falsity, according to which all true sentences mean the same thing, namely the True, and likewise all false sentences mean the same thing, the False. Since at first sight this doctrine has something strange about it, and is in danger of being dismissed out of hand without closer examination, the corroboration in Peano is of particular value to me, even though in fact only the premises thereunto are to be found in his work. Specifically, he introduces the sign 'Λ', saying (*Introduction* §9): 'Λ represents the absurd'. I say 'the False' for this. By its means the proposition that 2 is not greater than 3 is written thus:

$$'(2>3)=\Lambda'. \mid$$

369   From this we see that for Mr. Peano all false sentences must mean the same thing, at least in so far as the sign of equality here denotes complete coincidence or identity. Now in fact, in *Introduction* §40 it says:

> The equation $a=b$ always has the same meaning: a and b are identical, or a and b are two names given to the same thing.

According to this, '$2>3$', '$7^2=0$' and 'Λ' are signs for the same thing, i.e., the meanings of these signs coincide. Now since Mr. Peano also allows the sign of equality to occur between any two true sentences, he apparently subscribes completely to my above-stated doctrine. If he nevertheless nowhere (so far as I can see) expressly states it, then that is probably because he has been deterred by the strangeness of my tenet. Nay, I am not even sure whether he grants this inference from his premises. The agreement with my doctrine is on this account no less remarkable, since it happens to hold in spite of this repugnance. The natural objection to this would be that true sentences can express different thoughts. According to Mr. Peano the sentences '$2.2=4$' and

'3 > 2' can be connected by the sign of equality: '$(2.2 = 4) = (3 > 2)$'; and yet anyone would agree that they by no means signify the same thing. Without my distinction between sense and meaning this difficulty would be insuperable. Hence this distinction gains indirect confirmation from what is maintained by my doctrine of the True and the False. The following might serve as an elucidation. We sometimes label the same object with different names without being aware of it. E.g. we speak of astronomer X's comet and astronomer Y's comet, only subsequently discovering that we have been tagging the same celestial body with these two labels. In such a case I say that both designations have the same meaning – that they denote or stand for or name the same thing – but that they have different senses, because it requires a special act of cognition to apprehend the coincidence. Thus I also say of the designations

$$'3 + 1', '1 + 3', '2 + 2', '2.2',$$

that they *mean* the same thing, but have different *senses*, or *express* different things. Now if, in a | combination of signs '$\Phi(A)$' which has a 370 meaning, a sign 'A' is replaced by another sign 'Δ' with the same meaning, then obviously the new combination of signs '$\Phi(\Delta)$' will mean the same thing as the original '$\Phi(A)$'. But if the sense of 'Δ' deviates from the sense of 'A', then in general the sense of '$\Phi(\Delta)$' will also deviate from the sense of '$\Phi(A)$'. Let us apply this to the sentence '$3 + 1 = 2.2$' by substituting for '$3 + 1$' the sequence of equi-referential signs '$1 + 3$', '$2 + 2$' and '2.2'. We thus obtain the sentences

$$'1 + 3 = 2.2'$$

$$'2 + 2 = 2.2'$$

$$'2.2 = 2.2'$$

all of which must have the same *meaning* – and this I call *the True* – while expressing different things. The sense of a sentence I call a thought. These sentences thus express different thoughts. If a sentence has a meaning at all, then this is either the True or the False. In poetry and legend, however, there occur sentences which, although they have a sense, have no meaning – like, e.g., 'Scylla has six heads'. This sentence in neither true nor false since, for it to be one or the other, it would have to have a meaning; but no such meaning is available, because the proper name 'Scylla' designates nothing. In poetry we are satisfied with the sense merely, whereas science demands the meaning as well.[5]

[5] In this connection compare my paper 'Über Sinn und Bedeutung' ['On Sense and Meaning'], *Zeitschrift für Philosophie und philosophische Kritik* 100 (this volume pp. 157–77].

I shall now inquire more closely into the essential nature of the Peano conceptual notation. It is presented as a descendant of Boole's logical calculus but, it may be said, as one different from the others. I do not mean that in a condemnatory sense: on the contrary, I regard the divergences from Boole as improvements, by and large. But the fundamental idea has been altered entirely. Boole's logic is logic and nothing more. It deals solely with logical form, and not at all with the injecting of a content into this form – while this is exactly the intention of Mr. Peano. In this regard his enterprise more closely resembles my conceptual notation than it does Boole's logic. From another point of 371 view, however, we can recognise a closer affinity | between Boolean logic and my conceptual notation, in as much as the main emphasis is on inference, which is not stressed so much in the Peano logical calculus. In Leibnizian terminology we can say: Boole's logic is a *calculus ratiocinator* but not a *lingua characterica*; Peano's mathematical logic is in the main a *lingua characterica*, and at the same time also a *calculus ratiocinator*; whereas my conceptual notation is both, with equal emphasis. Mr. Peano could not have left the Boolean system of notation entirely unmodified, for it was ill-suited to receive a content, particularly a mathematical one. Not least disturbing, it seems to me, is its falling apart into the calculus of classes and the calculus of judgements,[6] as it is customary to put it. And this separation is already less marked in Mr. Peano's work. E.g. the sign 'ε', which in '*A* ε *B*' assigns an object *A* to a class *B*, and which I regard as a substantial enrichment of Boole's notation, does not share the characteristic feature of the other primitive symbols, that namely of being used in a double manner (I had almost said, of being used with a double meaning) depending upon whether it occurs in the calculus of classes or in the calculus of judgements. Concerning this, compare *Introduction* §9: 'The signs already explained between classes are adopted between propositions, with the following meanings.' This twofold use holds little appeal for me, of course. The very reason which deterred Mr. Peano from using the plus-sign (not just as an arithmetical symbol but also, like Boole), as a logical symbol argues against it.[7] Even if perhaps no mistake results from it, still the comprehensibility of the formulae suffers because of it, when one always has first to call to mind how a sign is to be understood. It is especially disturbing when the same sign occurs more than once in the same formula with different uses.

---

[6]Mr. Peano says '*proposition*'; I should say 'truth-value', since I use the word '*Satz*' in the sense of a combination of symbols whose sense is a thought and whose reference a truth-value – either the True or the False.
[7]Compare *Introduction* p. 28, at the top.

This same twofold mode of employment is also encountered in the case of the sign '⊃', which, when it occurs in the calculus of judgements, may be called the sign of deduction. Only as such can we | give it a closer consideration here. What then does the combination of   372 signs '$a \supset b$' stand for when a and b represent sentences? To this Mr. Peano responds with three distinct explanations.[8] This triad strikes me as a superfluity, and this superfluity strikes me as a deficiency. For questions arise at once about the relations of these explanations to one another: are they mutually consistent? does one follow from another? Let us consider these explanations in order. In *Introduction* §9 it says: '$a \supset b$ means "from a, b is deduced" ["de la a on deduit la b"] or "b is a consequence of a".' This explanation is scarcely satisfactory, for straight away, in few examples, it leaves us in the lurch. Consider say

$$'(2^2 = 4) \supset (3 + 7 = 10)'.$$

Can it be said that the sentence '$3 + 7 = 10$' is deduced from the sentence '$2^2 = 4$'? Hardly. Is '$3 + 7 = 10$' a consequence of '$2^2 = 4$'? Apparently not: and yet according to Mr. Peano the deduction sign is correctly placed here, as we shall see. Let us consider the further example

$$'(2 > 3) \supset (7^2 = 0)'.$$

It will not do to say that the sentence '$7^2 = 0$' is deduced from '$2 > 3$': it is not deduced at all, for it is false. Neither can we call '$7^2 = 0$' a consequence of '$2 > 3$'. According to our explanation we should imagine, therefore, that it is impermissible to use the deduction sign here; but the third of Mr. Peano's explanations will set us right.

Let us turn next to the second explanation. In *Introduction* §14 it says:

> If a and b are propositions containing indeterminate letters x, $y, \ldots$, that is to say, are conditions between these letters, then the deduction $a \supset b$ signifies: 'whatever values of x and y satisfy the condition a also satisfy the condition b'.

This explanation relates only to the case in which so-called undetermined letters occur. In §15 Mr. Peano attempts to reduce the other case to this one | by mentioning that in Analysis even expressions devoid of   373 x, or from which x is eliminable, may be regarded as function of x. Accordingly he says:

---

[8]If we count the explanation for the application of the sign in the class calculus, we have four explanations.

If a and b are propositions containing no indeterminate letters, the deduction $a \supset b$ always signifies 'if a is true, b is also true'.

According to that, '$(2 > 3) \supset (7^2 = 0)$' would be rendered 'if it is true that 2 is greater than 3, then it is also true that the square of 7 is 0' – of which, however, one is hard put to make any sense. It is therefore just as well that Mr. Peano continues:

> that is to say, either a is true and b is true, or a is false and b is true, or a is false and b is false; and the one case 'a is true and b is false' is alone excluded.

This is the third explanation. It coincides with that which I gave in 1879 for the corresponding sign in my conceptual notation. From it, we see that in point of fact the deduction sign is correctly employed in our examples '$(2^2 = 4) \supset (3 + 7 = 10)$' and '$(2 > 3) \supset (7^2 = 0)$'.

But how are we to interpret the case in which undetermined letters are present (as Mr. Peano puts it) or (as I should prefer to say) in which indefinite indicating occurs? Take as an example the sentence

$$'(x > 2) \supset (x^2 > 2)',$$

which we may translate 'if something is greater than 2 then its square is also greater than 2'. Here we have what is known in the terminology of logic as an hypothetical judgement, and in this two very different things have to be distinguished: the meaning of the sign '$\supset$', and the generality which is marked by means of the indefinitely indicating letter 'x'. These two are run together in the second of Mr. Peano's above-quoted explanations, and this is a methodological fault. The correct procedure would be to establish the meaning of the deduction sign first, and then, quite independently, to explain how generality is signified by means of indefinitely indicating letters. From both of these taken together it must then follow without further ado what is meant by a deduction when indeterminately indicating letters appear on its left-hand and right-hand sides. Let us test this in the following way. Suppose a sentence '$\Phi(x)$' is put forward in | which 'x' occurs. We then stipulate that the presence of 'x' is to signify that the sentence is true no matter what meaning we assign to 'x'. In the present instance, '$\Phi(x)$' would correspond to

$$'(x > 2) \supset (x^2 > 2)'.$$

Suppose we in fact give 'x' the meanings 1, 2 and 3, one after the other. First we obtain

$$(1 > 2) \supset (1^2 > 2)$$

which is true because both sides of the deduction are false. Secondly we obtain

$$(2>2) \supset (2^2>2)$$

which is true because the left hand side is false while the right hand side is true. Thirdly we obtain

$$(3>2) \supset (3^2>2)$$

which is true because both sides are true. Whatever we put for 'x' we never get a case where the left hand side of the deduction is true and the right hand side false, and it is this that we are intending to say. It can still be asked what happens if something which is not a numeral at all – say the sign '$\odot$', for the sun – is inserted. Surely this case has to be taken into account as well. The sentence '$\odot > 2$' is false, because the sun is not a number, and only numbers can be greater than 2. Accordingly the sentence

$$'(\odot > 2) \supset (\odot^2 > 2)'$$

would be true, regardless of whether its right hand side were true or false – and it ought to be one or the other. However, according to the usual explanation of the combination of signs 'x^2', this right hand side has no meaning. Thus there must be presupposed here an explanation of 'x^2' such that a meaning is always forthcoming no matter what sign is inserted for 'x', provided only that this sign itself has a meaning – i.e., provided only that it designates an object. This makes evident the necessity of my claim that functions should be explained in such a way that they receive a value for every argument. In the present case it might, e.g., be laid down that the reference of 'x^2' is to coincide with that of 'x' when 'x' means an object other than a number. What is stipulated is a matter of comparative indifference, | but it is essential 375 that 'x^2' be assured a meaning for every meaning assigned to 'x'. Mr. Peano seems not to recognize the necessity of this claim.

Another consideration needs closer investigation too. We have interpreted the whole deduction

$$'(x>2) \supset (x^2>2)'$$

as corresponding to '$\Phi(x)$'; but its left hand side taken on its own is already a sentence containing 'x', as also is its right hand side. Now if we apply our account of the marking of generality to '$x>2$' it will say 'every object is greater than 2', which is obviously false. We get the same sort of thing on the right hand side. On this account the whole deduction would of course again be true, but it would require quite a different sense: if every object is greater than 2, then the square of every object is greater than 2.[9] From this we see that yet another stipulation, one about limiting the scope of generality, has to be decided upon. Mr. Peano has perceived this as well. I shall try to explain by means of an example how he satisfies this requirement. In

$$'(\Phi(x) \supset \Psi(x, y)) \supset X(y)'$$

let '$\Phi(x)$', '$\Psi(x, y)$' and '$X(y)$' represent sentences in which the bracketed letters 'x' and 'y' occur. We then have a deduction whose left hand sign contains a further deduction sign. Now if Mr. Peano wants to restrict the central 'x' to signifying generality on the left hand side of the main deduction sign, he appends 'x' to the subordinate deduction sign as an index, as follows:

$$'(\Phi(x) \supset_x \Psi(x, y)) \supset X(y)'.$$

To advertise that the generality with respect to 'y' is to extend over the content of the whole formula, he attaches 'y' as an index to the main deduction sign:

$$'(\Phi(x) \supset_x \Psi(x, y)) \supset_y X(y)'.$$

However, if this is an independent formula, not part of another, he even
376   omits the index 'y'. | Besides appearing with the deduction sign, these indices also occur with other relational signs, e.g. with the sign of equality. I do not find this procedure particularly felicitous, because it gets the designation of the generality mixed up with the designation of a relation, which has nothing to do with it. Moreover, new signs, additional to the simple relation signs, are obtained in this way – namely those relation signs having one or more indices – and these must receive separate explanation. In *Introduction* §18 Mr. Peano says:

> The indices to the sign $\supset$ satisfy laws which have not yet been sufficiently studied. This theory, already abstruse in itself, becomes even more so unless the rules are accompanied by examples. The best thing would be to examine the roles of these signs, and their transformations, in the formulae and demonstrations of mathematics.

In point of fact, only examples are given. Hence we see that the indices get transferred from one relation sign to another without the laws in accordance with which this is done having been specified. In this respect my conceptual notation of 1879 is superior to the Peano one.

---

[9]Here again it has to be presupposed that the words 'the square of x' or the combination of signs 'x^2' have a reference no matter what object is understood by 'x'.

Already, at that time, I specified all the laws necessary for my designation of generality, so that nothing fundamental remains to be examined. These laws are few in number, and I do not know why they should be said to be abstruse. If it is otherwise with the Peano conceptual notation, then this is due to the unsuitable notation. And this, no doubt, has as its main cause the above-mentioned unidimensional arrangement. This arrangement makes it more difficult to ensure that the force of a sign extends over a whole sentence. The brackets would get much too crowded. Nor does this difficulty seem to be overcome completely by the ingenious method of punctuation which Mr. Peano uses instead of brackets for articulating sentences. The fact that the sign of negation is often amalgamated with the relation sign, thus also increasing the number of necessary stipulations, is doubtless attributable to the same cause. Nevertheless it is to be regarded as a great improvement upon Boole that there is a notation for generality here at all, | and that this notation makes it possible to restrict the 377 generality to a definite part of the whole.

I append a few remarks about my own notation for generality. In the formula

$$(2 > 3) \supset (7^2 = 0)$$

considered above, a sense of strangeness is felt at first, due to the unusual employment of the signs '=' and '>'. For usually such a sign serves two distinct purposes: on the one hand it is meant to designate a relation, while on the other it is meant to assert the holding of this relation between certain objects. Accordingly, it appears as if something false $(2 > 3, 7^2 = 0)$ is being asserted in that formula – which is not the case at all. That is to say, we must deprive the relation sign of the assertoric force with which it has been unintentionally invested. And this holds just as much for my conceptual notation as for Mr. Peano's. However, we do still sometimes want to assert something, and for this reason I have introduced a special sign with assertoric force, the judgement-stroke. This is a manifestation of my endeavour to have every objective distinction reflected in symbolism. With this judgement-stroke I close off a sentence, so that each condition necessary for its holding is also effectively to be found within it; and by means of the self-same sign I assert the content of the sentence thus closed off as true. Mr. Peano has no such sign: he, on the contrary, uses his relation signs now with and now without assertoric force, and in fact the principal relation sign invariably carries assertoric force. From this it follows that for Mr. Peano it is impossible to write down a sentence which does not occur as part of another sentence without putting it forward as true. Also because of this his sentences lack compactness, and it not infrequently happens that conditions get separated from the main formula. Thus you cannot tell just by looking at it whether one of Mr. Peano's sentences is complete.

Now when the scope of the generality is to extend over the whole of a sentence closed off by the judgement stroke, then as a rule I employ Latin letters, proceeding in essentially the same way as Mr. Peano does in those cases where he attaches no indices – except that I distinguish function-letters from object-letters, using the former to indicate only functions | and the latter to indicate only objects, in conformity with my sharp differentiation between functions and objects, with which Mr. Peano is unacquainted. But if the generality is to extend over only part of the sentence then I adopt gothic letters, by whose means I also delimit the scope of this generality, in a way my most recent account of which is to be found in §8 of my *Foundations of Arithmetic*. This corresponds to Mr. Peano's notational device of applying an index to a relation sign. Instead of the German letters I could have chosen Latin ones here, just as Mr. Peano does. But from the point of view of inference, generality which extends over the content of the entire sentence is vitally different significance from that whose scope constitutes only a part of the sentence. Hence it contributes substantially to perspicuity that the eye discerns these different roles in the different sorts of letters, Latin and German. There is a similar distinction in the way the letters 'α' and 'x' are used in the formula

$$\int_0^\infty \frac{\sin \alpha x}{\alpha}\, d\alpha,$$

in which α really serves as a calculation sign. Mr. Peano too appreciates this distinction without, however, marking it by the choice of different sorts of letters. In this connection, compare *Introduction* §13 and *Formulaire, preface*, p. V under 16 and p. VI under 17, where *lettres apparentes* and *variables apparentes* are dealt with.

While reserving for a later occasion a comparison of our conceptual notations in respect of some other points, I observe merely that the Peano notation is unquestionably more convenient for the typesetter, and in many cases takes up less room than mine, but that these advantages seem to me, due to the inferior perspicuity and logical defectiveness, to have been paid for too dearly – at any rate for the purposes I want to pursue.

378

On Mr. H. Schubert's Numbers

PREFACE

It is really a scandal that science is still in the dark about the nature III
of number. It would not be so bad if there were no generally
recognized definition of number, provided that there were at least
agreement in substance. But science has not even decided whether a
number is a group of things or a figure drawn with chalk on a
blackboard by a human hand, whether it is something mental so that it
is up to psychology to inform us of its origin or whether it is a logical
construction, whether it is created and may eventually perish or
whether it is eternal. Is this not a scandal? Arithmetic does not know
whether its theorems deal with those configurations consisting of
carbonate of lime or with insensible objects. Nor is there any agreement
about the meaning in arithmetic of the word 'identical' and the sign of
identity. Science, therefore, does not know what thought content is
associated with its theorems or what subject matter it deals with: it is
completely in the dark about its own nature. Is this not a scandal? And
is it not a scandal that a string of thoughtless utterances can succeed in
making the claim to be representing the latest state of the science? |

This is what I have thought and felt on more than one occasion IV
when, with a view to continuing my *Foundations of Arithmetic*, I have
been dealing with the writings of other mathematicians on this matter.
To these writings belongs also Mr. H. Schubert's account of the foundations of arithmetic in the *Encyclopedia of the Mathematical Sciences*.
My first impression of it was an unfavourable one; but gradually my
spirits began to lift. What I had regarded as a defect, as an infirmity,
even as a fatal disease, I learned to appreciate as a peculiar virtue. For
initially I was still too enslaved by the former custom of overestimating
thought. Only slowly was I able to work my way through towards a
more liberated point of view. Indeed, is not thought perhaps more often
an impediment to science than a force that impels it forward? How
many bothersome incidental questions and cross-questions, how many
doubts are raised by thought which simply would not exist without it!
How many efforts are misdirected by such questions away from the

Hermann Pohle, Jena, 1899. (*Tr*. Hans Kaal)

main points and are therefore lost to the advancement of science! How much shorter, how much more convenient, and even how much clearer everything would be if we could leave aside the stones cast in our path by thought! In absence of thought, a state so closely related to the state of oblivion induced by drinking of the river Lethe, I have also found the balm which, I hope, will still the pains I mentioned in the beginning.

The more I occupy myself with the body of teachings that have ripened this insight in my mind, the more I am convinced that their completion will redound to the glory of the end of the nineteenth century in the eyes of posterity. Mr. Schubert's classical account will then be cited as among the first and foremost. But the task is so enormous that the honour of having accomplished it can hardly be bestowed on a single author. The muse of history will find herself compelled to divide the full crown of honour into smaller ones, | and this opens up the prospect of gaining perhaps a small part of it, if only a single laurel leaf. This temptation I have been unable to resist.

How would it be, I said to myself, if I were to do my bit to propagate these teachings, if I presented their more difficult parts in greater detail to a larger audience and elucidated them by various examples? This would perhaps also give me an opportunity to add something of my own and in so doing to make a minor contribution to the enlargement of the whole. One would also have to go into possible objections in order to secure the acquired knowledge against any attack. And I have some confidence in my qualifications, especially when it comes to defending it, because I myself have been among its enemies and know their weapons. There may well be someone from an older school who rises up in anger at the thought that teachings of such shallowness should have the temerity to pass themselves off in an encyclopedia of mathematics as the flower of the science. Especially in our time, where one is in constant danger of running shallow and of conjuring up the illusion of knowledge by mere words, especially in our time – he may well think – there is an urgent need to destroy such an illusion over and over again and to tear up the web of words. I myself used to think so, and I am all the more confident that I can meet his challenge and vindicate the subtlety and power of our teachings.

Although I confine myself essentially to reproducing what others have created, I have nevertheless striven here and there for a deeper justification; but as my special merit I should like to claim that I have given a precise verbal expression to principles and methods which up to now have been used only tacitly, thus making a wider application of them possible. Above all, I should like to point to two of them: the method of making undesirable properties disappear by disregarding them and the principle of the non-differentiation of the different, as I have allowed myself to call it. As I said before, this is not a matter of saying something new, but of making accessible to pedestrians, as it were, what could be attained up to now only on the wings of genius and in a flash of insight.

In doing my best to accomplish this and to bring out the scope of these methods, I hope to have paved the way for further, unforeseeable advances.

As for the tone of this account, it will, I think, be found to be in keeping with the worthiness of the subject matter.

Jena, October 1899

*   *   *

In the *Encyclopedia of the Mathematical Sciences* (I, A I) Mr. H.   1
Schubert explains a number as a result of counting. Indeed, is not the weight of a body also the result of weighing? And, as is well known, to weigh a body means to put it on one scale of a balance while putting certain other bodies on the other scale until the tongue balances out, to conceive those other bodies all together, to disregard their colour, hardness, etc. etc. Likewise the chemical composition of a body is the result of chemical analysis, and in order to explain the latter, one will first have to specify what it means to make a chemical analysis. Now what does it mean to count things? According to Mr. Schubert, counting things consists of four actions:

(1)   regarding the things to be counted as being of the same kind,

(2)   conceiving them together,

(3)   correlating other things with them one by one,

(4)   regarding these other things also as being of the same kind.

According to our author, each of the things with which other things are correlated in counting is called a unit, and each of the things which are correlated with other things in counting is called a one.

Now at least we know what goes on when a census is taken. But at the same time we also see the enormous difficulty of the task. It will not be easy to conceive the inhabitants of the German Empire all together, as can easily be verified by just | trying to conceive the   2 spectators in a theatre together. However, there remain some doubts: must these four actions all be performed by the same person, or can several persons share the burden and divide the labour among themselves? The task would be easier if, e.g., one person could regard the inhabitants of the German Empire as being of the same kind, while another person conceived them all together, etc. Of what kind are the units employed in taking a census, and how are they correlated? It would be very nice if, e.g., nickels were chosen as ones and if the correlation consisted in pressing a nickel into the palm of each inhabitant. It would be even nicer if ten-mark coins were substituted for nickels. The result of the counting – the number – would naturally turn out to be different according to the chemical and physical difference between the metals nickel and gold. Since horn buttons, badges, burrs and other things can also be used as ones, it will be recognized that there is a great multiplicity of numbers to be gained in this way.

Armed with our explanation, let us now try to get a bit clearer on the nature of number. The four components of counting seem to be mental activities. This leads us naturally to the assumption that the result will also be something mental. The following example seems to confirm this hypothesis. A pupil has kicked a fellow pupil, he has been inattentive, and he has failed to learn his lesson. The teacher reprimands him for his faults, which causes the boy to conceive them together and to regard them as being of the same kind, namely faults. The teacher thereupon boxes his ears while indicating at each box for which fault it is intended as a punishment. And so it happens that the pupil correlates the boxes on his ears one by one with his faults. It goes almost without saying that he regards them also as being of the same

3   kind, given the unmistakable resemblance between them. | With this all conditions are satisfied: the boy is counting! And what is the result of this counting? Well, let us hope, remorse and reform. This is therefore the number, and the faults are the únits, while the boxes on the ears are the ones. It is easy to recognize how the ones influence the number; for if one of them turns out to be too weak, the outcome is perhaps a very different number: increased boisterousness instead of remorse. Let us not therefore underestimate the importance of the ones!

We should be mistaken, however, if we were to regard this as a complete account of the formation of the concept of number. We have to distinguish between named and unnamed numbers. On p. 3 we read:

> If we add a collective concept to a number to remind us to what extent we regarded the units as being of the same kind, then we express a *named* number. By completely disregarding the nature of the things we counted, we get from the concept of a named number to the concept of an *unnamed* number. By a number as such is to be understood always an unnamed number.

Unfortunately, the author has nothing to say about the case where we neither add a collective concept to remind us to what extent we regard the units we counted as being of the same kind nor completely disregard the nature of the things we counted. Nor are there any indication on how the collective concept (in our example, presumably, *fault*) is to be applied. Armed with our example, we can nevertheless get some idea of the origin of an unnamed number or of a number as such. While it may still be an open question whether remorse is a named number, it is certain that it is not yet a number as such. To obtain the latter, the pupil will have to induce in himself a state of dizziness in which he still remembers having his ears boxed and still has a faint inkling that it was for something, but in which he no longer knows whether | it was for his faults or perhaps even for some praiseworthy 4 actions. Hypnotism and suggestion will serve him here in good stead. The more stupid he is, the better he will succeed. We are still much too inclined to overestimate thought. Absence of thought or forgetfulness is a much greater force, and it is marvellous what can be achieved by merely disregarding something or by not thinking of it. Absence of thought is obviously closely related to stupidity; we thus realize that stupidity is a world power and understand at last Talbot's exclamation: 'Even the gods struggle in vain against stupidity.' Let us now observe how we can make use of this force. If we are, e.g., bothered by the fact that the leaves of a tree are green, let us disregard their colour, and they will at once be colourless. If in disregarding the colour of the leaves we are careful not to disregard the shape of the tree, the colour of its bark, the distances of its branches from neighbouring trees etc., we shall obtain a tree which stands in exactly the same place as the one we first looked at, has exactly the same shape and, indeed, looks exactly the same in all other respects, the only difference being that its leaves are colourless. We have thus obtained a new botanical specimen. If we run into difficulties in a scientific investigation, let us disregard them, and they will be overcome. This is the easiest and least risky way of doing scientific work. It is especially to be recommended for investigating the foundations of arithmetic. With it the greatest difficulties melt away like snow under the spring sun. In short:

> *Given objects whose properties are partly conducive to a purpose and partly obstructive to it, disregard the undesirable properties, but take care not to disregard the desired ones as well.* | *The* 5 *objects so obtained will have only the conducive properties and will lack the obstructive ones.*

This principle is very far from having been sufficiently exploited. It might therefore be desirable to give some hints on further uses of it. It can be applied in metallurgy (dephosphorizing iron), education (bringing up model boys), medicine (avoiding undesirable side effects of drugs), politics (disarming opposition parties and hostile powers) and certainly in many other fields as well.[1] Given the importance of the matter, it may not be inadmissible to attempt a deeper epistemological justification of it. It is well known that we have only our own ideas. What are called blue, soft, big, far-away things are actually blue, soft, big, far-away ideas. Thus if I succeed in changing my ideas, I shall thereby have succeeded in changing the things; for things are ideas. Now I can make certain properties of ideas, such as their colour, disappear by disregarding them, while I can retain others by attending to them. And this gives us all we need.

We also make use here of not thinking. We have seen that counting alone does not yet generate a number as such; we must add to it an act of forgetting. This process of completely disregarding the nature of things is not to be confused with the general abstraction of the logicians by which we are supposed to acquire concepts. We are dealing here with something far more significant. Suppose for example that we are counting peas. By abstraction the logician acquires the concept *pea*, and to him it does not usually matter whether he has | a handful more or less. The individual peas remain completely unchanged in the process and are not for example transformed into the concept *pea* or replaced by it, but continue to exist beside it. The present process is much more marvellous: each individual pea divests itself entirely of its nature as a pea, but – and this is the most marvellous part – continues nevertheless to have a shadowy being separate from its fellow peas and without fusing with them. Originally we had a group, and we naturally took great heed not to disregard either its being a group or the separate being of each individual pea. This therefore remains. We are left with a group of separate things; but these things are no longer peas, for by forgetting their nature as peas, we have entirely stripped them of it; nor have they assumed some other nature instead; rather, they have become entirely natureless. So they are no longer things at all in the ordinary sense of the word, which always presupposes some properties or other; we must, rather, recognize a special class, that of natureless things, whose nature consists precisely in not having a nature. Such natureless things therefore form groups and are the units of a number as such.

---

[1] This idea, however, has little claim to novelty: the ostrich is said to have had a similar idea already.

We are not told to disregard the nature of the ones, and that is a good thing. Otherwise everything might easily get blurred before our mind's eye, and we should be in danger of confusing the ones with the units. So the nature of the ones does make a difference. Whether the ones are made, e.g., of nickel or of gold makes an essential difference to a number, even to a number as such.

To make certain that we have formed the right conception of the process of forming a number, it would be desirable if we could observe it in the example of a number named by Mr. Schubert himself. On p. 14 | the number 1 appears before us without having been introduced to us, and acts at once in perfectly familiar ways like an old acquaintance. Τίς, πόθεν εἶς: To which blessed soul do you owe your being? What objects did this soul regard as being of the same kind? What objects did it conceive together? Were the ones made of gold? And did this soul likewise regard them as being of the same kind? And did it correlate them one by one with the former? Unfortunately we do not know, but we must assume that a named number – the larva, as it were, of the number 1 – arose in this way in former times and that the number 1 itself emerged from it like a butterfly by metamorphosis – by a process of disregarding the nature of the objects counted. How interesting it would be if we could observe all this! But this may well have happened long, long ago, and nature may well have produced such a creature only once.

Definitions must prove themselves in their application, and we may therefore ask: does Mr. Schubert's definition of a number have a use? Certainly! 'Since the units are of the same kind with respect to one another, and the ones with respect to one another, the number is independent of the order in which the ones are correlated with the units.' Order? This is the first time we hear of it. What this seems to mean is that it makes no difference to the result which ones are correlated with which units. Earlier we were told only that things should be regarded as being of the same kind; now it is simply presupposed that they are of the same kind. What is of the same kind? Are, e.g., pens from different factories of the same kind? Are unbruised Borsdorf apples of the same kind as windfallen ones? The answer has to be: after they have been regarded as being of the same kind, they will also be of the same kind. I only need to regard Julius Caesar as being of the same kind as Sirius, and the two will be of the same kind; and it will then be all the same whether I correlate the name 'Sirius' with the first and the name 'Julius Caesar' with the second or vice versa. Suppose we give a master mason | a plan and tell him: build a house according to this plan; but before you start, regard the air-dried

7

8

bricks, the fired bricks and the quarry-stones as being of the same kind. Since they will all be of the same kind, it will make no difference, after the building is completed, where the air-dried bricks have been employed, where the fired bricks, and where the quarry-stones. Some fool will perhaps insist that he did not notice any change when the mason regarded then as being of the same kind. Oh, you of little faith! Don't you know that all things are nothing but ideas?

Suppose we are to distribute quarterly report-cards to a class of pupils. Let us now regard the pupils as being of the same kind: they then are of the same kind. And since they are of the same kind, it is all the same whether the good pupils get good report-cards and the bad ones bad report-cards, or whether the report-cards are simply issued by lottery. After having regarded the pupils as being of the same kind, we must perhaps stop talking altogether of good and bad pupils, as well as of tall and short, broad- and narrow-shouldered pupils. All of them would now also have the same hair colour and the same facial expression. As long as there remain differences between them, it does not matter whether they are big or small. The units must not differ at all; for if there is even the slightest difference, a change in the correlation will effect a change in the result. Now it never happens that we are given objects that do not differ at all. For if a thing a does not differ at all from a thing b, not even in the place it occupies, then a coincides with b. In regarding things as being of the same kind, we manipulate them in such a way as to make them lose their differences. And it is easy to see | how this is possible if we remember that things are ideas.

9

While this manipulation may be useful in one respect, in another it creates new difficulties. We must obviously see to it that one and no more than one of the ones is correlated with each unit, and likewise one and only one unit with each of the ones. This is possible only if we distinguish the units and likewise the ones from one another. The more we succeed in cleansing the ones of their distinguishing properties, the more difficult it becomes to tell them clearly apart and to correlate the ones with them in the right way. And it becomes impossible – what am I saying: 'impossible'? – it becomes extremely difficult if we succeed in cleansing them completely. It cannot be impossible; for otherwise there would be no numbers, and what would then become of arithmetic? But it is at any rate no easy matter, and counting things belongs, no doubt, among the most difficult scientific labours. There must be exceptionally powerful minds who are capable of cleansing things of all their properties and who nevertheless succeed, provided that they make a real effort, in distinguishing things that are no longer different, and in such a way that they can correlate other things with them one by one with certainty, even though these other things are likewise no longer different. If things differed ever so slightly, a change in the correlation would influence the result, and this must not be allowed to happen. On the other hand, the correlation must still be possible; for otherwise no number will arise. The numbers produced by those exceptionally powerful minds must then be transferred into ordinary human minds. And the superior minds would do well to provide for quite a large supply of numbers, so as to enable every human being to have an exemplar of at least the most useful kinds. But with all due respect to those minds, I do not believe that they can manage to produce infinitely many numbers. | And when Euclid believed he has proved that there were 10 infinitely many prime numbers, he must have been mistaken. He took a prescription for preparing a number for the number itself, as if the recipe for a pancake were already a pancake. He seems to have been too sanguine.

On p. 5 we learn when two numbers *a* and *b* are called equal to one another, namely when the units of *a* and those of *b* can be correlated in such a way that all units of *a* and *b* take part in the correlation. It should be emphasized, first, that equality as here explained is not complete coincidence or identity. 'The numbers *a* and *b* are equal to one another' is not supposed to mean as much as 'The number *a* is the same as the number *b*' or 'the number *a* coincides with the number *b*'. The numbers whose units can be correlated in the way indicated need not have the same units and may in addition differ by their ones. Since the word 'number' is here used without further addition, what is meant here is obviously a number as such. The propositions 'Three kings is equal to two boys' and 'Two pairs of gloves is equal to three dozen shirts' will not do as examples because the numbers here seem to be named. But do we still have units at all? The things were first regarded as being of the same kind, and as being so much of the same kind that they could no longer be distinguished; i.e., presumably, all properties by which they differed were made to disappear. Finally, to produce the unnamed number, the nature of the units had to be completely disregarded; i.e., the properties they had in common had to be obliterated as well. Does anything at all remain after this? Certainly; there remain the natureless things! Are there things which do not coincide and yet do not differ in any way? Certainly: those natureless things! | What things are the units of the number 1? We also speak of a 11 number 9 and say of it, e.g., that it is a square number. Since I know of no statement of his to the contrary, I assume that Mr. Schubert too would recognize the number 9. Well, what things are the units of the

number 9? We may suppose that not all natureless things are such units, but that there is a strictly delimited class of things which are called units of the number 9. But how is this delimitation effected? How do the units of the number 9 differ from other natureless things, e.g., from the units of the number 1? For it seems that there are no longer any properties or any nature to be found in either case. Given the meaning of the word 'equals' as just defined, we are naturally led to ask: are there one or more numbers equal to the number 1, and are there numbers equal to the number 9? If the answer is in the affirmative, we are led to ask further about the units of these other numbers and about their ones. Let no one be misled by such questions into doubting the existence of the units of unnamed numbers! By completely disregarding the nature of the things we counted, we have of course obliterated the tracks that would have led us back from an unnamed number to the named number and its units. But every number as such must have had a named number for its mother; otherwise it would not exist. And this maternal number must have had units (counted things). By having their nature completely disregarded, these units must have given rise to the units of a number as such, and these too must therefore exist. So any number as such has units, and these are natureless things. Against this it might still be objected that while the units of a named number must indeed have existed at one time, they may perhaps have been annihilated later on. Suppose we had originally counted logs, thus obtaining at first a named number, and
12 then completely disregarded the nature of the logs | – that is, their being logs – thus producing a number as such. Somebody might now get the idea of burning the logs and then asking sarcastically: Where is your number now? Did it burn up with the logs? And if not, where are its units now? Come, come, my dear sir! Some named numbers may indeed be combustible. But combustibility belongs obviously to the nature of the logs; this has been completely disregarded, and the logs have therefore become incombustible. You cannot burn them even if you stand on your head! There does remain the difficulty of picking out the completely natureless logs or rather non-logs from the set of equally natureless things. But with good will we can overcome the greatest difficulties. And the best way of doing so is always the same: to disregard them completely.

We are now sufficiently prepared to be able to go on to addition. On p. 6 we read:

> If we have two groups of units which are not only such that all units of each group are of the same kind, but also such that

each unit of the one group is of the same kind as each unit of the other group, then we can do either of two things: we can either count each group individually and conceive each of the two results of counting as a number,[2] or we can extend the counting over both groups and conceive this result of counting as a number. In the former case we obtain two numbers, in the latter case only one number. The number obtained in the latter case is then said to be the *sum* of the two numbers obtained in the former case, and these two numbers are called | the *addends*   13 of the sum. The passage from two numbers to a single one as just described is called *addition*.

The pity is that this is not at all a passage from two numbers to a single one! For we are supposed to have been given, not two numbers, but two groups of units, and from these we pass, first, to two numbers and, secondly, to a single number. To pass from the two numbers to the single one, we would first have to regress to the two groups of units and then progress from there to the single number. Of course that regression is not always easy to carry out. But as we have just seen, this difficulty can always be overcome.[3]

Given the two groups of things, we may ask further whether they satisfy the conditions laid down for addition. The fact that the units within each of the two groups are of the same kind follows from the fact that they were regarded as being of the same kind when they were counted. But the units of the first group may not be of the same kind as the units of the second group. This obstacle is easy to remove: regard the things of the first group as being of the same kind as those of the second, and they will at once be of the same kind. The following objection may appear to carry more weight. It might turn out that some units belonged to the first as well as to the second group. This case may arise, not only when the numbers are named so that their units are ordinary things, but also when the numbers are unnamed so that their units are natureless. I do not know what sort of obstacle this would be, for we are nowhere told | how to exclude this case. At any   14 rate, the second group must not consist of exactly the same units as the first; for in that case it would coincide with it, and we would have only

---

[2]Since according to Mr. Schubert's explanation the result of counting is a number, it may naturally be conceived as a number; otherwise this would hardly be permissible without further ado.

[3]It is of course doubtful whether it is possible to add 9^{9^9} and 1, because in all probability 9^{9^9} did not arise by counting and is therefore not a number. Where there is no group of units, there is no possibility of addition either.

a single group, whereas we would need two groups for addition. From this it follows that a number cannot be added to itself; for the second group, just like the first, would then consist of the units of that number and only of those units, and we would have only a single group.

Mr. Schubert goes on to write about addition:

> From the concept of counting it follows that there can always be only one number which is the sum of two arbitrary numbers, and conversely, that there can be only one number which, when combined with a given number by addition, yields a *greater* given number as the sum.

However, both points are open to doubt. Since the ones may possibly be different, it is not quite clear that there can be only one sum. We do not know whether in counting over the two groups we must take the same ones we already used in counting each individual group, or whether we may take different ones. At any rate, we are nowhere told that we must not do this, and we may thus obtain different numbers as sums, depending on whether we use, e.g., pennies or planets as ones. Since the nature of the ones is not to be disregarded, it must make a difference to the result.

Let us now consider the further problem of finding the other addend, given one number as the sum and another number as one of its two addends. Suppose the units of the first number are the stars of the first and second magnitudes of the constellation Orion and the units of the second number the stars Castor and Pollux of the constellation Gemini. The stars of the constellation Orion would then form two groups, one of which would consist of Castor and the other of Pollux. But this is impossible; the problem | is insoluble! One might try to make it soluble by correlating the two stars of the constellation Gemini one by one with, e.g., Betelgeuse and Rigel and by making the second group consist of the latter two. But should we then have made use of the second number? While the number whose units are Betelgeuse and Rigel may be equal to the number whose units are Castor and Pollux, it does not coincide with it. For after due consideration our author has explained the word 'equal' in such a way that it cannot be confused with 'identical' or 'coinciding'. While we would then be using a number equal to the given second number, we would not be using the second number itself. We should therefore not be solving our original problem, but merely substituting another one for it. It might perhaps be thought that, since we have disregarded the nature of the units, it is all the same whether we take Castor and Pollux or Betelgeuse and Rigel as units of the second number. While this is indeed a very clever idea, I should like to issue an urgent warning against taking this way out. If we did, somebody might suspect that it was no more than idle talk to speak, e.g., of the units of the number 2 or of the units of the number 9 since we ourselves had no idea what things we meant by it; for the units of a number would then not be determined at all by the number itself. Mr. Schubert is indeed very careful to talk in generalities about, e.g., 'the units of *a*', which is obviously quite a different case; but being less nimble-witted, we might find ourselves pushed into talking about the units of the number 1, and in this case it would be safer not take that way out so that we could at least assume the right airs: as if we knew what things we meant by it. It must, however, be admitted that our example will not fit when we are dealing with numbers as such, and it must be assumed that this is what we are dealing with here. Since Castor | and Pollux have a nature, just like Betelgeuse and Rigel, we   16 cannot choose them as units of a number as such. I have fallen into this temptation because I am familiar with the names of fixed stars, but not with the names of natureless things. To construct a correct example of subtraction, we must therefore take units from the class of natureless things. But since natureless things are, as we have seen, just as separate from one another as fixed stars, and since every number as such contains very definite natureless things as its units, it is just as possible to have a case where the units of the subtrahend do not occur among those of the minuend. If that is so, then a problem of subtraction cannot always be regarded as soluble even when the minuend is greater than the subtrahend.

Concerning arithmetical designations we find the following pronouncements:

> For equal, greater and smaller we use in arithmetic the signs =, > and < respectively, which we place between the numbers we have compared.

> To indicate that two numbers *a* and *b* have given rise to a third number *s* by addition, we place the sign + (plus) between the two addenda.

We have learned that a number is mental in nature and that it is probably a mental state. Now how do we manage to place an equals sign, which we can write with chalk on a blackboard, between mental states? At first one naturally supposes that our author does not mean that we are to place it between numbers, but that we are to place it between number signs. He would thus be using an imprecise expression. If I had read no further, I might well have accepted this supposition, even though Mr. Schubert's customary precision should really have made it improbable from the first. Nor would it be doing full justice to 17 the profundity of his thought. We are obviously | dealing here with an early application of a principle whose great scope will be recognized only later on. It seems that this principle has already been used repeatedly by mathematicians, but to my knowledge it has never been clearly expressed in words and it has never been given a name. I should like to call it the *principle of the non-differentiation of the different*. It stipulates – to put it briefly – *that a sign is not to be distinguished from what it designates*. It is easy to see how this principle casts light on the present obscurity. Instead of the author's explanation of the plus sign and its use, some might perhaps have preferred the following:

> A combination of signs consisting of two number signs and a plus sign standing between them designates the sum of the numbers designated on the left- and right-hand sides of the plus sign.

According to this, '2 + 3' for example is a number sign, and if we take the formula cited on p. 7 of the encyclopedia:

$$a + b = b + a$$

and replace the letters by the number signs '2' and '3', then the equals sign would come to stand between the number signs. But this is wrong, for '2 + 3' only indicates that a number, which is here neither designated nor indicated, has arisen from the addition of 2 and 3. The equals sign therefore connects such historical indications. Having adopted this point of view, we are excused from having to answer questions which might otherwise come to bother us. If 2 + 3 were a number, namely the sum of 2 and 3, then it might be asked: Which things are units of 2 + 3? Are the same things units of 2 + 3 and of 5? Is 2 + 3 the same number as 5? Or are 2 + 3 and 5 different but equal numbers? The short answer 18 to all these questions is that 2 + 3 is not a number at all; | by '2 + 3' we merely indicate the historical fact that a number – which we are under no obligation to name – has arisen from the addition of 2 and 3.

We come now to the most interesting part of Mr. Schubert's account: how to obtain zero. On p. 11 we read:

> Since according to the definition of subtraction the minuend is a sum, one of whose addenda is the subtrahend, it makes no sense to join two equal numbers by the minus sign. While such a string has the *form* of a difference, it does not represent a number in the sense of no. 1.

If one is struck by the fact that in this case the minus sign appears to join numbers instead of number signs, it is only because one has not yet fully assimilated the principle of the non-differentiation of the different. In order to remedy the defect he mentions, Mr. Schubert has recourse to the principle of permanence which according to him consists of four parts:

> First, of assigning to each string of signs which does not represent any of the numbers previously defined a sense such that the string may be manipulated according to the same rules as if it represented one of the previously defined numbers.[4]

So the string of signs is supposed to be assigned a sense, and it is supposed to follow from this sense that the string may be manipulated according to certain rules. This is clear enough: the rules according to which the string is to be manipulated depend on the sense of the signs. Nothing could be simpler, except that it is diametrically opposed to a certain formalist doctrine according to which signs have no sense, or at least | need not have a sense, but are to be conceived as similar to chess   19 figures, where the rules of manipulation can be established quite arbitrarily and irrespective of a sense. This is not Mr. Schubert's point of view; for he takes the sense at least to be necessary. True, he also takes the rules to be present beforehand, but he does not say: 'These rules shall hold also for the manipulation of signs that have as yet no sense; I do not care whether you can later find a sense for them that would fit these rules.' This is not what Mr. Schubert says; instead, he wants to give to the strings of signs a sense such that the desired rules for manipulating the strings of signs follow from their sense. The domain of objects is itself governed by certain laws, and it is clear enough how these laws are mirrored in the form of rules regulating the use of the corresponding signs. This might lead us to expect that our author would point to some object subject to the same laws as the previously defined numbers and assign to this object the sign '1–1'. However, this expectation would in no way do justice to the profundity of Mr. Schubert's thought. His procedure is indeed completely different from what one might have expected given that superficial conception. Nowhere does he demonstrate the existence of such an object; what is in store for us is a much more magnificent spectacle: we are about to witness an original creation. And this brings us to a decisive turning-point in our appreciation of the principle of the non-differentiation of

---

[4]It may not be superfluous to remark that the author has previously defined, neither the number 1 nor the number 2 nor for that matter any other number.

the different. I can well imagine that up to now some of my readers may have been eying this principle with doubts and suspicions, wondering whether we are really dealing with a principle or simply with an imprecise expression. And I must admit that this possibility has 20 not been excluded by what has been said up to now. | But we are now approaching a point where a magnificent view is about to open up before us and reveal to us the truly dominant position of our principle. But before we reach this point, we must go a little further back.

It is well known that geometry often uses auxiliary lines in its proofs. Why do we call such a line an 'auxiliary' one? Because the proposition to be proved does not treat of it even though it is used in the proof. Such a proof would collapse upon itself if there were no lines at all of the desired kind. Euclid relies in such cases on his postulates, which are actually nothing but axioms saying that there are configurations – points, lines, planes – constituted in a certain way. Thus the postulate about drawing a straight line from any point to any other says that for any two points there is a straight line connecting them. When we draw a line, we direct our attention to it, so that it is actually there before we draw it. The objective possibility of drawing a line is actually the same as the objective existence of that line. If some one took the expression 'the straight line passing through points A, B, C' and made use of it in a proof without having proved beforehand that the points A, B, C lie in a straight line, he would be practising a cheap form of make-believe. Now the kind of case where we use in a proof what a proposition does not treat of occurs not only in geometry but equally in arithmetic; indeed, we can find examples of it in all branches of mathematics. In using the theorem of De Moivre to express the cosine of m times Θ by means of the exponents of the cosine and the sine of Θ, one makes use of the square root of -1 as an auxiliary number, and the proof would collapse upon itself if there were nothing which, when multiplied by 21 itself, would yield -1. In | number theory one proves several propositions by using a primitive root as an auxiliary number. If there were no number with this property, such a proof would be a logical juggling-trick. This is why Gauss thought it necessary to prove that there were primitive roots.[5] In analysis it often happens that in order to prove a proposition one needs a positive number whose double is smaller than a certain positive number. Zero too occurs quite often as an auxiliary number, e.g., when in the course of a proof one writes down an equation with a zero sign standing alone on the right-hand side,

[5]He would have had an easier time of it if he had been as familiar with the principle of the non-differentiation of the different as some of the more recent mathematicians have been.

whereas there is no mention of zero in the proposition to be proved. If there were nothing with the properties we ascribe to zero and make use of in our calculations, such a proof would collapse upon itself. We are thus in the awkward predicament of having to prove that there is something with these properties. And we can get into similar predicaments with regard to negative, fractional, irrational and complex numbers. Now if we did not succeed in proving that there were such numbers, part of arithmetic would fall away, and while it is hard to estimate how extensive it would be, we may suppose that it would not be insignificant. Now it would not be desirable to have to conduct the requisite demonstration by relying on geometry, for this would be to introduce arguments into arithmetic that would seem to be alien to it. But to conduct such a proof in purely arithmetical terms seems at first sight very difficult. At this point the principle of the non-differentiation of the different comes to our rescue, which makes it easy to recognize its enormous scope. Indeed, what would be left of arithmetic if it were not for its assistance? | It is precisely the most beautiful parts that 22 would be doomed to destruction. Thus, far from being an imprecise expression, it is on the contrary the pillar that upholds the most glorious teachings. But how does it do this? By helping to create all the numbers that might eventually be used as auxiliary numbers in proofs. What is this act of creation like? We shall try to find out by spying on the creation of zero.

Since the principle of permanence seems to be important in the creation of zero, we first want to get to know it better. According to Mr. Schubert, it consists, 'secondly, in defining such a string as a number in the extended sense of the word and in thus extending the concept of number'.

According to what used to be the dominant view, which may perhaps still have some scattered adherents, it is not permissible to extend a concept after it has been defined, since this overturns the first definition and causes the same word to be used with different meanings, which might give rise to a *quaternio terminorum*. However, science has long ago recognized that these objections are not just trifling but also harmful impediments to its progress. On the contrary, it is very convenient that the boundaries of the concept of number should have begun to shift back and forth, since this allows us to contract them or expand them depending on the need we happen to feel at the moment.

The principle of permanence is supposed to consist, thirdly, 'in proving that the same propositions that hold for numbers in the not-yet-extended sense also hold for numbers in the extended sense'.

It might at first be asked: Is it certain that this proof will always succeed? And what happens if it does not succeed? We can clear the matter up if we look at the relationship between this component of the principle of permanence | and its first component, that of assigning to a string of signs a sense such that it may be manipulated according to the same rules as if it represented one of the previously defined numbers. A reader who has still not familiarized himself sufficiently with the principle of the non-differentiation of the different may perhaps stumble over this and say:

23

> While individual numbers have not, strictly speaking, been previously defined, we have nevertheless been given a certain concept of number such that the numbers falling under this concept, in so far as they exist, are not signs or strings of signs. Now according to the second component of the principle of permanence, the concept of number is extended in such a way that certain strings of signs fall under this concept. Accordingly, there are numbers that are, and numbers that are not, strings of signs. To those that are not belongs, e.g., the number one, which Mr. Schubert speaks of even though he has not defined it. This number one is neither a sign nor a string of signs; but its sign '1' can be a component of a string of signs ('$1 - 1$') which is a number. Such strings of signs have been assigned a sense such that they may be manipulated according to the same rules as if they represented one of the previously defined numbers. And from this it follows immediately that the rules according to which these new numbers are to be manipulated coincide with the rules for the signs of numbers in the non-extended sense; but these rules are not laws that hold for these numbers; they are merely what corresponds to those laws in the domain of signs. It does not therefore follow that the same propositions hold for numbers both in the extended sense and in the non-extended sense, but only that both the new numbers and the signs of the old numbers are to be manipulated according to the same rules. |

24   This reasoning contains an obvious fallacy. Signs are distinguished from what they designate, from which it follows that the rules to be observed in manipulating signs are to be distinguished from the laws that hold for what they designate. This is all wrong according to our principle of the non-differentiation of the different. According to it, what is designated is not to be distinguished from its sign, nor are the laws governing what is designated to be distinguished from the rules for the manipulation of signs. Once we get clear enough on this point, we

see that the third component of the principle of permanence was actually reached simultaneously with the first. We are merely dealing with a test to determine whether we have really done what the first component required us to do.

According to our author, the principle of permanence consists, fourthly, 'in defining what is called equal, greater, and smaller in the extended number domain'.

It may seem at first as if we had to know this already before we could prove that the same propositions that hold for numbers in the not-yet-extended domain also hold for numbers in the extended domain, since these propositions probably contain the words 'equal', 'greater', and 'smaller'. If we did not know the sense of these words, we would not know what thoughts were contained in these propositions and could not therefore prove these thoughts to be true. The first thing to be said against this is that it remains very doubtful whether a proposition whose thought content is unknown cannot be proved, and even whether a proof must always presuppose the existence of such a content. It is on the contrary probable that this content does not carry much weight and that the important thing is the form of the expression, whether it is in words or in arithmetical signs. This is borne out by the following reflection. It is known that | mathematicians do not agree in   25 the least on the sense in which they use the word 'equal'. It is known, further, that this word or the corresponding sign occurs in nearly all mathematical propositions. Now if the thought content of these propositions were of any importance, whether for their proof or for anything else, then the most urgent task of mathematicians would be to come to an understanding about the sense of the word 'equal'. But mathematicians generally assume the contrary: it may well be said that any other task is thought to be more urgent than this one. Although it is known that there is no agreement in mathematics regarding the sense to be assigned to the word 'equal', many authors do not even think it necessary to enunciate what sense they themselves want to assign to it; from which it can be seen that this sense is perfectly incidental. For this reason I do not fully comprehend why our author attaches some weight to the matter, as he does in footnote 19. Of course, he does it more in theory than in actual practice. I at least have not found a passage anywhere where he states explicitly what sense is to be assigned to the equals sign in an equation such as

$$1-1=2-2.$$

We keep coming back to the point that we must take heed not to overestimate thought, as is still perhaps too frequently done.

We now go on to apply this to our case. We should be mistaken in assuming that the four components of the principle of permanence would be applied in the order in which they had been presented. We must assume instead that these four components appear inseparably united with one another. Mr. Schubert continues: 'Accordingly, the string of signs $a-a$ becomes subject to the two fundamental laws of addition and the defining formula of subtraction, and we thus reach

26 |our goal: the formulae of No. 4 must also hold for the string of signs $a-a$.'

After what has been said above in general about the consequences flowing from principle of the non-differentiation of the different, it will be understood without further explanation how a string of signs can become subject to the fundamental laws of addition, and how formulae can hold for a string of signs which is itself a component of those formulae. But one might perhaps have expected something else, namely, that Mr. Schubert would first have given a sense to one of the strings of signs under consideration, that he would then have developed from its sense the rules according to which such a string of signs was to be manipulated, and that he would finally have pointed out the perfect agreement between these rules and those established for the manipulation of the original number signs. We do not find him doing any of this; what we find instead is that the very same action by which a string of signs $a-a$ becomes subject to the fundamental laws of addition and to the defining formula of subtraction also gives it a sense such that it may now be manipulated according to the same rules as if it represented one of the previously defined numbers. Perhaps it is not superfluous to show how the principle of the non-differentiation of the different proves its creative potential at this point. The string of signs $a-a$ exists, as anybody can see with his own eyes. Now according to our principle, it is not to be distinguished from what it designates; consequently, what it designates also exists. Thus according to our principle, the meaning develops from the sign all by itself. We have thus accomplished an act of creation, and there can be no doubt that the very same propositions that hold for numbers in the not-yet-extended

27   sense hold also for what we have created; only | we must not demand that these propositions have a sense or express a thought: that is not the point.

Mr. Schubert continues: 'By applying the formula $a-b=(a-n)-(b-n)$ to $a-a$, we recognize that all forms of differences in which the minuend is equal to the subtrahend are equal to one another.'

Here it should be noted that we are not given an explicit definition of what is called 'equal' in the extended number domain. But we also learn from this example that this is quite unnecessary: one can very well prove a proposition about equality without attaching a sense to the word 'equal' or the equals sign. As already noted, it is also quite unnecessary that a proposition to be proved express a thought. But if some one should have a burning desire for a sense, he can be taken care of as well. It is obvious that the same action which (1) assigns a sense to the form of difference $a - a$ and which (2) proves that the same propositions that hold for numbers in the not-yet-extended sense also hold for numbers in the extended sense also (3) defines what is to be called 'equal' in the extended number domain. Thus the same action which subjects the string of signs $a - a$ to the two fundamental laws of addition and to the definitional formula of subtraction contains somehow within itself a proof and two definitions and even more: it contains at the same time (4) a definition of what (a) the plus sign and (b) the minus sign are supposed to mean in the extended number domain. This brings out another virtue of Mr. Schubert's teachings, a virtue which I should like to call their pregnancy: their ability to kill many birds with a single stone.

Mr. Schubert continues: 'This justifies us | in introducing a common   28 constant for all those strings of signs that are equal to one another. This constant is the sign 0 (zero).'

In former times it would certainly have been objected that this procedure makes the sign 0 equivocal, since it is evidently supposed to mean such different forms of differences as $2 - 2$, $3 - 3$ and $(4 - 2) - (5 - 3)$. It should be obvious that Mr. Schubert's procedure cannot be defended by saying that these forms of differences which appear so different to the eye are not different at all but coincide in reality, and that this is what Mr. Schubert has just proved. This would be to conceive the equals sign as the sign of identity, which would be all wrong.[6] It would be asking too much even of a firm believer to take things to coincide in spite of the evidence of his senses when their difference is easily recognized even by an untrained eye. The following way out seems to be just as impassable. Mr. Schubert's utterance might be interpreted to mean that the sign 0 is not supposed to designate the different forms of differences, but to be used in their place. It would then mean what they meant. But if following our principle of the non-differentiation of the different we replace the meaning of the forms of differences by the forms of differences themselves, we get back again to our first interpretation, namely, that the sign 0 means those forms of

---

[6]Mr. Dedekind – not to mention any lesser minds – still seems unfortunately to hold on to this peculiar conception.

differences. In this case too we would have to take the equals sign for the sign of identity if we wanted to avoid equivocation. The equation $1 - 1 = 2 - 2$ cannot be saying that the meaning of the form of difference on the left-hand side of the equals sign coincides with the meaning of the one on its right-hand side; for this would imply that the equals sign | was used as the sign of identity, which would, to repeat, be wrong. From the principle of the non-differentiation of the different we can instead infer with certainty that those meanings are different because the forms of differences, as anybody can see, are different. The true justification of Mr. Schubert's procedure is the following: the principle that signs must be unequivocal is to be abandoned altogether, because there is no way to justify it on rational grounds and because to follow it would be to needlessly impede the progress of science. 0/0 has been introduced into science long ago as an equivocal string of signs and is doing an excellent job as such.

Mr. Schubert goes on to write: 'What this sign states is also called a 'number', and this 'number' is also called zero.'

The word 'state' is here presumably used in the sense of 'mean'. What a sign states is therefore the meaning of the sign. That the meaning of the sign as well as the sign itself is called zero follows immediately from our principle of the non-differentiation of the different. We can therefore do as we please and call the sign 0 as well as its meanings – for it has more than one – a number, thus extending the concept of number – to use Mr. Schubert's words.

Anyone who has followed the story of the creation of zero, entered into the spirit of this method and overcome the doubts that may have assailed him at first will have no difficulty with the creation of negative numbers: he will understand immediately how numbers can be provided with plus or minus signs, and how numbers that have arisen from numbers can also arise from relative numbers by omission of the plus or minus sign. For it is easy to understand how one and the same object can arise more than once and in different ways. | There is therefore no need to go further into this.

When we come to multiplication, we learn about another interesting property of numbers. We are now taught that many addends can represent one and the same number. As we know, addends are themselves numbers; therefore many numbers can represent one and the same number.[7] This is not to be wondered at, for many actresses, who are themselves persons, have represented one and the same person, e.g.,

---

[7]A product too is a number. This number can represent a senseless string of signs (cf. p. 15).

Mary Stuart. It may likewise be assumed that one and the same number can represent many others, as the same actress can appear in different parts. When we are later told (in footnote 22) that negative and fractional numbers are only symbols as L. Kronecker has shown, this is obviously not meant to deny that these symbols have the capacity to represent something; on the contrary, they are capable in various ways both of representing numbers and, in turn, of being represented by numbers – besides being numbers themselves. These histrionic abilities of numbers are probably intimately connected with the principle of the non-differentiation of the different. But I have not yet concluded my investigations into this matter.

In conclusion I should like to voice a doubt, in the hope that Mr. Schubert will find an opportunity to respond to it, since I have not yet succeeded in getting perfectly clear about it. According to the third component of the principle of permanence, we are supposed to prove that the same propositions that hold for numbers in the not-yet-extended sense also hold for numbers in the extended sense. But there are many who doubt that these propositions continue to hold without exception. Take for example the proposition that the sum of two numbers is greater than either one of the two, or the proposition that, of two products with the same multiplicand, the greater one is the one with the greater multiplicator: these propositions are thought to hold only in the non-extended sense. If this view were well-founded, and it does at least have a certain initial probability, we would find ourselves in the awkward predicament of having to prove something that was not true. Would it not then be advisable to give the string of signs $a-a$ a sense such that it was to be manipulated also in this respect as if it represented a previously defined number? It would not be very nice if the principle that there were to be no exceptions admitted of exceptions. Does anyone perhaps scent a logical impossibility here? But what is impossible, given our principles? The propositions that hold for the original numbers and hence the rules according to which their signs are to be manipulated – for this comes to the same thing according to our much-cited principle – are proved with respect to these numbers and do not therefore contain a contradiction in this particular case. But from this it follows that they do not contain a contradiction in the general case. Number signs[8] are merely things that submit passively to rules; it makes no difference whether they look like this or somewhat different. Remember two games of chess with pawns that look somewhat different. If the rules are free from contradiction with respect to

[8] Or 'numbers' – to use an equivalent term.

one game, they will also be free from contradiction with respect to the other. We can obviously subject some sign or some arbitrary string of signs to rules or laws which we already know to be mutually consistent. To this may be added the following. If the principle of permanence or the principle that there were to be no exceptions were subject to some restrictions | requiring some precaution in its application, Mr. Schubert would certainly not have neglected to point them out and would have shown, in each case of its application, that he had observed the restrictions on its application. Since this is not the case, we may be certain that no such restrictions exist and that there is no need for a special demonstration to prove that certain conditions are satisfied. Accordingly, there is nothing to prevent us from bestowing a sense on the string of signs $a - a$ such that it may be manipulated according to the same rules as if it represented one of the previously defined numbers. It is then also easy to prove that the propositions that hold for numbers in the not-yet-extended sense hold also, without exception, for numbers in the extended sense; for according to our principle, the laws that hold for numbers are not to be distinguished from the rules according to which their signs are to be manipulated. The propositions mentioned above by way of example will therefore hold in the extended number domain, and mathematics will become a much more harmonious whole.

What keeps me from wholly surrendering myself to the joy this vision inspires in me is the fear that the string of signs 0:0 would then lose its equivocal nature, which would surely be regrettable and besides, would contradict one of Mr. Schubert's clear pronouncements (on p. 17). It may also perhaps have consequences so far-reaching that they cannot yet be foreseen.

No one would be better qualified to cast light on these problems than Mr. Schubert himself. May he soon rid science of these doubts!

On the Foundations of Geometry: First Series

I

319 Mr. Hilbert's Festschrift concerning the foundations of geometry[1] prompted me to write to the author, setting forth my own divergent views; and out of this grew an exchange of letters which unfortunately was soon terminated. Believing that the questions dealt with therein might be of more general interest, I contemplated its future publication. However, Mr. Hilbert has some reservations about agreeing to this, since in the meantime his own views have changed. I regret this stand, since by means of this correspondence the reader would most conveniently have been familiarized with the state of the question, and I would have been spared a new composition.[2] However, it seems to me that the views in this area are still so divergent and still so far removed from any clarification that a public discussion for the purpose of bringing about an understanding would be quite justified. Therefore I should here like to consider some questions of fundamental importance, and I should like to do so in the form of a discussion of Mr. Hilbert's essay. And for this purpose it may be irrelevant whether at present the distinguished author still maintains those of his views that are being questioned here.

To begin with, let us deal with these questions: What is an axiom? What is a definition? In what relations might these stand to one another?

Traditionally, what is called an axiom is a thought whose truth is certain without, however, being provable by a chain of logical inferences. The laws of logic, too, are of this nature. Some people may nevertheless be inclined to refrain from ascribing the name 'axiom' to these general laws of inference, but rather wish to reserve it for the basic laws of a more restricted field, e.g. geometry. But this is a question of less consequence. Here we shall not go into the question of what might justify our taking these axioms to be true. In the case of geometrical ones, intuition is generally given as a source.

[1] Festschrift for the festival marking the unveiling of the Gauss–Weber Memorial in Göttingen (Leipzig, 1899).

[2] [The surviving letters between Frege and Hilbert are included in G. Frege, *Philosophical and Mathematical Correspondence* (Oxford, 1980). (*Ed.*)]

Jahresbericht der Deutschen Mathematiker-Vereinigung 12 (1903), pp. 319–24, 368–75.
(*Tr.* E.-H. W. Kluge)

In mathematics, what is called a definition is usually the stipulation
320 of the meaning of a word or sign. A definition | differs from all other
mathematical propositions in that it contains a word or sign which
hitherto has had no meaning, but which now acquires one through it.
All other mathematical propositions (axiomatic ones and theorems)
must contain no proper name, no concept-word, no relation-word, no
function-sign whose meaning has not previously been established.[3]
Once a word has been given a meaning by means of a definition, we
may form self-evident propositions from this definition, which may then
be used in constructing proofs in the same way in which we use principles.[4] For example, let us suppose that the meanings of the plus-sign,
the three-sign, and the one-sign are known; we can then assign a meaning
to the four-sign by means of the definitional equation '$3 + 1 = 4$'. Once
this has been done, the content of this equation is true of itself and
no longer needs proof. Nevertheless, it would be inappropriate to count
definitions among principles. For to begin with, they are arbitrary
stipulations and thus differ from all assertoric propositions. And even if
what a definition has stipulated is subsequently expressed as an
assertion, still its epistemic value is no greater than that of an example
of the law of identity $a = a$. By defining, no knowledge is engendered;
and thus one can only say that definitions that have been altered into
assertoric propositions formally play the role of principles but really are
not principles at all. For although one could just possibly call the law
of identity itself an axiom, still one would hardly wish to accord the
status of an axiom to every single instance, to every example, of the
law. For this, after all, greater epistemic value is required. No definition
extends our knowledge. It is only a means for collecting a manifold
content into a brief word or sign, thereby making it easier for us to
handle. This and this alone is the use of definitions in mathematics.[5]

---

[3]With few exceptions ('π', 'e'), letters do not, as a rule, have a meaning; they do not
designate anything, but only indicate in order to lend generality to the thought. As with
certain form-words, we cannot require a meaning from them; but the manner in which
they contribute to the expression of the thoughts must be definite. I have given a
protracted treatment of the usage of letters in my *Grundgesetze der Arithmetik* I (Jena, 1893)
[partial English translation, *The Basic Laws of Arithmetic* (Berkeley, Ca., 1964)],
§§8, 9, 17, 24, 25.

[4]What I here call a principle is a proposition whose sense is an axiom.

[5]One might also represent as a use of a definition that through it one becomes more
clearly aware of the content of what one has connected, albeit only half-consciously, with
a certain word. This may occur but is less a use of the definition than of defining. Once a
definition has been set up, it is irrelevant for what follows whether the explained word or
sign has just been newly invented, or whether previously some sense or other had been
connected with it.

Never may a definition strive for more. And | if it does, if it wants to   321
engender real knowledge, to save us a proof, then it degenerates into
logical sleight of hand. In the case of some of the definitions which one
finds in mathematical writings, one would like to write in the margin,

> If you can't quite give a demonstration,
> Consider it an explanation.

Never may something be represented as a definition if it requires proof
or intuition to establish its truth. On the other hand, one can never
expect principles or theorems to settle the reference of a word or sign.
It is absolutely essential for the rigour of mathematical investigations,
not to blur the distinction between definitions and all other
propositions.

Axioms do not contradict one another, since they are true; this does
not stand in need of proof. Definitions must not contradict one
another. We must set up such guidelines for giving definitions, that no
contradiction can occur. Here it will essentially be a matter of
preventing multiple explanations of one and the same sign.[6] The usage
of the words 'axiom' and 'definition' as presented in this paper is, I
think, the traditional and also the most expedient one.

As to Mr. Hilbert's Festschrift, it confronts us with a peculiar
confusion of usage. When it is said in the introduction, 'Geometry
requires ... for its consequential construction only a few simple basic
facts, These basic facts are called axioms of geometry', then this is quite
in keeping with what has just been set forth; similarly when it is said in
section 1, p. 4, 'The axioms of geometry fall into five groups; each one
of these groups expresses certain basic and interconnected facts of our
intuition.'[7]

A completely different view appears to lie at the basis of the
following pronouncement (section 3): 'The axioms of this group define
the concept "between".' How can axioms define something? Here
axioms are saddled with something that is the function of definitions.
The same remark obtrudes itself when in section 6 we read, 'The
axioms of this group define the concept of congruence or of motion.' |

Due to Mr. Hilbert's kindness I am now in a position to say in what   322
sense he has used the word 'axiom'. For him, the axioms are components of his definitions.[8] So, for example, axioms II.1 to II.5 are

---

[6]Compare my *Basic Laws of Arithmetic* II, §§56–7.

[7]In the first of the propositions quoted, the axioms are thoughts, to be sure; in the
second, they are expressions of thoughts: propositions.

[8]The time at which he held this view must be assumed to be that of the writing of the
Festschrift and of the date of his letter (29.12.99).

components of the definition of *between*. *Between*, therefore, is a
relation of those points of a straight line to which axioms II.1 to II.5
apply. In the Festschrift, II.1 reads like this:

> If *A*, *B*, *C* are points of a straight line and *B* lies between *A*
> and *C*, then *B* also lies between *C* and *A*.

The axioms state the characteristics that would otherwise be missing
from the explanations. Similarly, the explanation in section 1 of the
Festschrift also contains the definitions of the concepts point, straight
line, and plane if one adds to it all of the axiom-groups I to V, whose
presentation takes up the whole first chapter. The first definition, then,
extends thus far. Other definitions are encapsulated in it, for example
that of *between*; as well as theorems, for example congruence-theorems.
On the basis of this it is not altogether easy to see which parts of the
first chapter belong to that definition. At least it is difficult to believe
that the theorems should also be considered as such components. This
explains Mr. Hilbert's statement that axioms define something. But is it
compatible with this, that axioms express basic facts of our intuition? If
they do, then they assert something. But then, every expression that
occurs in them must already be fully understood. However, if axioms
are components of definitions, then they will contain expressions such
as 'point' and 'straight line' whose references are not yet settled but are
still to be established. And then each single axiom is something
dependent, something that cannot be thought without the other axioms
that belong to the very same definition. It is only on p. 19 of the
Festschrift that the reference of the word 'point' is established according
to Mr. Hilbert's intentions. It is only now that the axioms presented so
far express thoughts that are true in virtue of the definition; but for that
very reason they do not express basic facts of our intuition, since then
their validity would be based precisely on this intuition. Let us take the
following simple example. We may rewrite the definition 'A rectangle is
a parallelogram with a right angle' thus:

> EXPLANATION: Conceive of plane figures which we call
> rectangles.
>
> AXIOM 1. All rectangles are parallelograms. |
>
> AXIOM 2. In every rectangle there is a pair of sides that stand
> perpendicular to each other.

323

These two axioms must be regarded as inseparable components of
the explanation. If, for example, we were to leave out the first axiom,
then the word 'rectangle' would acquire a different reference; and if

upon completing the definition we went on to posit the remaining second axiom as an assertoric proposition, it too would thereby acquire a different sense from the one it now has through its connection with the first. That is, it would not even be the same proposition; not, at least, if one considers the thought expressed in it essential to the proposition.

Once the explanation including the two axioms has been posited, the latter may be asserted as true; however, their truth will not be founded on an intuition, but on the definition. And it is precisely because of this that no real knowledge is contained in them – something which undoubtedly is the case with axioms in the traditional sense of the word.

Now in chapter 2, Mr. Hilbert considers the questions whether or not the axioms contradict one another, and whether or not they are independent of one another. Now, how is this independence to be understood? After all, each of the two axioms needs the other just to be what it is. Similarly in other cases. It is only through all of the axioms that according to Mr. Hilbert belong to, for example, the definition of a point, that the word 'point' acquires its sense; and consequently it is also only through the totality of these axioms that each single axiom in which the word 'point' occurs acquires its full sense. A separation of the axioms in such a way that one considers some as valid and others as invalid is inconceivable because thereby even those that are taken to be valid would acquire a different sense. Those axioms that belong to the same definition are therefore dependent on each other and do not contradict one another; for if they did, the definition would have been postulated unjustifiedly. However, neither can one investigate before they are postulated, whether these axioms contradict one another, since they acquire a sense only through the definition. There simply cannot be any question of contradiction in the case of senseless propositions.

How, then, are we to understand Mr. Hilbert's formulation of the question? We may assume that it does not concern the whole axioms[9] but only those of their parts that express characteristics of the concepts to be defined. In the case of our example, the characteristics | are   324 *parallelogram* and *having two sides standing perpendicular to each other.* If these did contradict one another, no object having these two properties could be found; in other words, there would be no rectangle. Conversely: if one can produce a rectangle, then this means that these characteristics do not contradict one another; and in fact this is just

[9]As one can see, here, as in the preceding, I accommodate myself to Mr. Hilbert's usage.

about the way in which Mr. Hilbert proves the consistency of his axioms. In reality, however, this is merely a matter of the consistency of the characteristics. Similarly concerning independence. If from the fact that an object has a first property it may generally be inferred that it also has a second, then one may call the second dependent upon the first. And if these properties are characteristics of a concept, then the second characteristic is dependent upon the first. This is just about the way in which Mr. Hilbert proves the independence of his axioms (more correctly, of the characteristics). For the time being, the matter may be thought of in this way. And yet, it really is not quite as simple as it may appear to be according to the preceding. If we want to get to the bottom of this, we shall have to consider the peculiaries of Mr. Hilbert's definitions more closely; and that will be done in a subsequent essay.

II

368   Mr. Hilbert's definitions and explanations appear to be of two kinds. The first explanation of section 4 explains the expressions that points lie in a straight line and on the same side of a point, and that points lie in a straight line but on different sides of a point. Once the expressions 'point of a straight line *a*' and 'a point lies between a point *A* and a |

369   point *B*' are understood, then given this explanation, one knows precisely what the expressions explained mean. The explanation of section 9 is of an entirely different kind. Here we read:

> The points of a straight line stand in a certain relation to one another which we describe by using above all the word '*between*'.

From this we obviously do not get to know the meaning of the word 'between'. However, the explanation is still incomplete. It is to be completed by the following axioms:

> II.1.   If *A*, *B*, *C* are points of a straight line, and *B* lies between *A* and *C*, then *B* also lies between *C* and *A*.
>
> II.2.   If *A* and *C* are two points of a straight line, then there is always at least one point *B* that lies between *A* and *C*, and at least one point *D* such that *C* lies between *A* and *D*.
>
> II.3.   For any three points of a straight line there is always one and only one point that lies between the other two.

II.4. Any four points *A*, *B*, *C*, *D* of a straight line can always be ordered in such a way that *B* lies between *A* and *C* as well as between *A* and *D*, and also that *C* lies between *A* and *D* as well as between *B* and *D*.

But do we learn from this, when the relation of lying-in-between obtains? No, rather the reverse: we recognize the truth of the axioms once we have grasped this relation. If we posit the Gaussian definition of the congruence of numbers, we can easily decide whether 2 and 8 are congruent modulo 3, or what investigations we must conduct in order to find out. All we have to know are the expressions that occur in the definition ('difference', 'a number divides evenly into a number'). Now with this let us compare the following explanation, which has been constructed according to Mr. Hilbert's pattern:

Whole numbers stand in certain relations to each other which we describe by using above all the word 'congruent.'

AXIOM 1. Every number is congruent to itself under any modulus whatever.

AXIOM 2. If a number is congruent to a second, and the latter is congruent to a third under the same modulus, then the first is also congruent to the third under this modulus.

AXIOM 3. If a first number is congruent to a second, and a third is congruent to a fourth under the same modulus, then the sum of the first and third is also congruent to the sum of the second and fourth under this modulus.

And so on. |

Could one gather from such a definition that 2 is congruent to 8   370
modulo 3? Hardly! And here matters lie still more favourably than in the case of Mr. Hilbert's definition, in which occur the words 'point' and 'line', whose references are as yet unknown to us. But even if we were to understand these words in the sense of Euclidean geometry, given our definition we could not decide which of three points lying in a straight line lies between the other two.

If we survey the total of Mr. Hilbert's explanations and axioms, it seems comparable to a system of equations with several unknowns; for as a rule, an axiom contains several unknown expressions such as 'point', 'straight line', 'plane', 'lie' 'between', etc.; so that only the totality of axioms, not single axioms or even groups of axioms, suffices for the determination of the unknowns. But does even the total suffice? Who says that this system is solvable for the unknowns, and that these are uniquely determined? If a solution were possible, what would it look like? Each of the expressions 'point', 'straight line', etc. would have to be explained separately in a proposition in which all other words are known. If such a solution of Mr. Hilbert's system of definitions and axioms were possible, it ought to be given; but surely it is impossible. If we want to answer the question whether an object, for example my pocket watch, is a point, then in the case of the first axiom[10] we are already faced with the difficulty that here two points are being talked about. Therefore we should already have to know an object as a point in order to decide the question of whether my pocket watch together with this point determines a straight line. Not only that: we should also have to know how to understand the word 'determine' and what a straight line is. This axiom, then, gets us no further. And so it goes with every one of these axioms; and when we have finally arrived at the last one, we still do not know whether these axioms apply to my pocket watch in such a way that we are justified in calling it a point. Equally little do we know what sorts of investigations would have to be conducted to decide this equestion.

In axiom I.7 it is said, 'There are at least two points on every straight line.' With this, compare the following:

EXPLANATION: We conceive of objects which we call gods.

AXIOM 1. Every god is omnipotent.

AXIOM 2. There is at least one god. |

371   If this were admissible, then the ontological proof for the existence of God would be brilliantly vindicated. And herewith we come to the crux of the matter. Whoever has seen quite clearly the error contained in this proof will also be aware of the fundamental mistake in Mr. Hilbert's definitions. It is that of confounding what I call first- and second-level concepts. I was probably the first to draw this distinction in all its sharpness; and at the time he was writing his Festschrift, Mr. Hilbert evidently was not yet familiar with my papers on this topic.[11] And undoubtedly many others will still be in that position. On the other hand, since without this distinction a deeper insight into mathematics and logic is impossible, I shall try to indicate briefly what this is all about.

Take the proposition 'Two is a prime number'. Linguistically we

---

[10]'Two distinct points, *A* and *B*, always determine a straight line *a*.'

[11]*Die Grundlagen der Arithmetik* [*The Foundations of Arithmetic*] (Breslau, 1884), §53, where instead of 'level', I said 'order'; *Funktion und Begriff* [*Function and Concept*] (Jena, 1891), p. 26 [this volume p. 137]; *Basic Laws of Arithmetic* I, §§21ff.

distinguish here between a subject, 'two', and a predicative constituent, 'is a prime number'. One usually associates an assertive force with the latter. However, this is not necessary. When an actor on the stage utters assertoric propositions, surely he does not really assert anything, nor is he responsible for the truth of what he utters. Let us therefore remove its assertive force from the predicative part, since it does not necessarily belong to it! Even so, the two parts of the proposition are still essentially different; and it is important to realize that this difference cuts very deep and must not be blurred. The first constituent, 'two', is a proper name of a certain number; it designates an object, a whole that no longer requires completion.[12] The predicative constituent 'is a prime number', on the other hand, does require completion and does not designate an object. I also call the first constituent saturated; the second, unsaturated. To this difference in the signs there of course corresponds an analogous one in the realm of meanings: to the proper name there corresponds the object; to the predicative part, something I call a concept. This is not supposed to be a definition; for the decomposition into a saturated and an unsaturated part must be considered a logically primitive phenomenon which must simply be accepted and cannot be reduced to something simpler. | I am well aware that expressions like 'saturated' and 'unsaturated' are metaphorical and only serve to indicate what is meant – whereby one must always count on the co-operative understanding of the reader. Nevertheless, it may perhaps be made a little clearer why these parts must be different. An object, e.g. the number 2, cannot logically adhere to another object, e.g. Julius Caesar, without some means of connection. This, in turn, cannot be an object but rather must be unsaturated. A logical connection into a whole can come about only through this, that an unsaturated part is saturated or completed by one or more parts. Something like this is the case when we complete 'the capital of' by 'Germany' or 'Sweden'; or when we complete 'one-half of' by '6'.[13]

372

Now it follows from the fundamental difference of objects from concepts that an object can never occur predicatively or unsaturatedly;

[12]Propositions including 'all', 'every', 'some' are of a completely different nature and will not be considered here.

[13]From the linguistic point of view, what is to be considered the subject is determined by the form of the proposition. The situation is different when considered from the logical point of view. We may decompose the proposition '$8 = 2^3$' either into '8' and 'is the third power of 2', or into '2' and 'is something whose third power is 8', or into '3' and 'is something which, when the power of 2, yields 8'.

and that logically, a concept can never stand in for an object.[14] One could express it metaphorically like this: There are different logical places; in some only objects can stand and not concepts, in others only concepts and not objects.

Let us now consider the proposition 'There is a square root of 4'. Clearly we are not here talking about a particular square root of 4 but rather are concerned with the concept. Here, too, the latter has preserved its predicative nature. For of course instead of the preceding, one can say, | 'There is something which is a square root of 4', or 'It is false that whatever *a* may be, *a* is not a square root of 4'. In this case, of course, we cannot divide the proposition in such a way that one part is this unsaturated concept and the other is an object. If we compare the proposition 'There is something that is a prime number' with the proposition 'There is something that is a square root of 4', we recognize a common constituent: 'there is something that'. It contains the assertion proper, whereas the constituents that they do not have in common, their predicative and unsaturated nature notwithstanding, play a role analogous to that of the subject in other cases. Here something is asserted of a concept. But clearly there is a great difference between the logical place of the number 2 when we assert of the latter that it is a prime number, and the concept prime number when we say that there is something that is a prime number. Only objects can stand in the former place; only concepts in the latter. Not only is it linguistically inappropriate to say 'there is Africa' or 'there is Charlemagne'; it is also nonsensical. We may indeed say, 'there is something which is called Africa', and the words 'is called Africa' signify a concept. The *there is something which*, therefore, is also unsaturated, but in a manner quite different from that of *is a prime number*. In the former case,

373

---

[14] In §49 of his book, *The Principles of Mathematics* I (Cambridge, 1903), Mr. B. Russell does not want to concede that a concept is essentially different from an object; concepts, too, are always supposed to be *terms*. He supports his argument here with the contention that we find it necessary to use a *concept* substantively as a *term* if we want to say anything about it, e.g. that it is not a *term*. In my opinion, this necessity is grounded solely in the nature of our language and therefore is not a properly logical one. But at the bottom of p. 508, Mr. Russell once more appears to incline to my opinion. I have treated of this difficulty in my essay, 'Über Begriff und Gegenstand' ['On Concept and Object'], *Vierteljahrsschrift für wissenschaftliche Philosophie* 16 (1892) [this volume pp. 182–94]. It is clear that we cannot present a concept as independent, like an object; rather it can occur only in connection. One may say that it can be distinguished within, but that it cannot be separated from the context in which it occurs. All apparent contradictions that one may encounter here derive from the fact that we are tempted to treat a concept like an object, contrary to its unsaturated nature. This is sometimes forced upon us by the nature of our language. Nevertheless, it is merely a linguistic necessity.

completion can occur only through a concept; in the latter, only through an object. We take the similarity and the difference of the two cases into account by means of the following mode of expression: In the proposition '2' is a prime number' we say that an object (2) falls *under* a first-level concept (prime number); whereas in the proposition 'there is a prime number' we say that a first-level concept (prime number) falls *within* a certain second-level concept. First-level concepts can therefore stand in a relation to second-level concepts that is similar to the one in which objects can stand to first-level concepts.

What applies to concepts also applies to characteristics; for the characteristics of a concept are concepts that are logical parts of the latter. Instead of saying 'Two is a square root of 4, and 2 is positive', we may say, 'Two is a positive square root of 4'; and we have two component concepts – *is a square root of 4* and *is positive* – as characteristics of the concept *is a positive square root of 4*. We may also call these properties of the number 2 and accordingly say: A characteristic of a concept is a property an object must have if it is to fall under that concept. We have something analogous in the case of second-level concepts. It is easy to infer from the above that first-level concepts can have only first-level characteristics and that second-level concepts can have only second-level characteristics. | A mixture of characteristics of   374 the first and second levels is impossible. This follows from the fact that the logical places for concepts are unsuitable for objects, and that the logical places for objects are unsuitable for concepts. From this it follows further that the definition beginning with the words 'we conceive of objects which we call gods' is inadmissible; for the characteristic contained in the first axiom is of the first level, whereas a characteristic of the second level is given in the second axiom.

Now, how do things stand with Mr. Hilbert's definitions? Apparently every single point is an object. From this it follows that the concept of a point (*is a point*) is of the first level, and consequently that all of its characteristics must be of the first level. If we now go through Mr. Hilbert's axioms, considering them as parts of the definition of a point, we find that the characteristics stated in them are not of the first level. That is, they are not properties an object must have in order to be a point. Rather, they are of the second level. Therefore, if any concept is defined by means of them, it can only be a second-level concept. It must of course be doubted whether any concept is defined at all, since not only the word 'point' but also the words 'straight line' and 'plane' occur. But let us disregard this difficulty and assume that through his axioms, Mr. Hilbert has defined a concept of the second level. No doubt the relationship of the Euclidean point-concept, which is of the first level, to Mr. Hilbert's concept, which is of the second level, will then have to be expressed by saying that according to the convention we adopted above, the former falls within the latter. It is then conceivable – in fact probable – that this does not apply to the Euclidean point-concept alone. And this agrees with what is said on p. 20 of the Festschrift: 'Consider a pair of numbers (x, y) of the domain Ω to be a point', etc. If previously the word 'point' had already been given a meaning by means of the definition and the axiom belonging to it. then at this juncture it could not be defined once again. We should probably construe the matter thus: The first-level concept *is a pair of numbers of the domain* Ω, just like the Euclidean concept of a point, is supposed to fall within Mr. Hilbert's second-level concept (supposing there is one). The use of the word 'point' in both cases is, of course, irritating; for obviously the word has distinct references in the two cases.

According to the preceding, Euclidean geometry presents itself as a special case of a more inclusive system which allows for innumerable other special cases – innumerable geometries, if that word is still admissible. And in every one of these | geometries there will be a (first-level) concept of a point and all of these concepts will fall within the very same second-level concept. If one wanted to use the word 'point' in each of these geometries, it would become equivocal. To avoid this, we should have to add the name of the geometry, e.g. 'point of the A-geometry', 'point of the B-geometry', etc. Something similar will hold for the words 'straight line' and 'plane'. And from this point of view, the questions of the consistency of the axioms and of their independence from one another (that is, of the unprovability of certain propositions from certain presuppositions) will require re-examination. One could not simply say 'the axiom of parallels', for the different geometries would have distinct axioms of parallels. If the wording of each of these were the same, this would mistakenly have been brought about by the fact that one had simply said, for example, 'straight line' instead of 'straight line of the A-geometry'. This way of talking may veil the difference of the thought-contents, but it certainly cannot remove it.

But herewith we have already reached the beginning of a path that leads to greater depths. Perhaps I shall be allowed to pursue it at some future date.

What is a Function?

It is even now not beyond all doubt what the word 'function'[1] means 656
in Analysis, although it has been in continual use for a long time. In
definitions, we find two expressions constantly recurring, sometimes in
combination and sometimes separately; 'mathematical expression' and
'variable'. We also notice a fluctuating usage: the name 'function' is
given sometimes to what determines the mode of dependence, or
perhaps to the mode of dependence itself, and sometimes to the
dependent variable.

In recent times the word 'variable' is predominant in the definitions.
But this is itself very much in need of explanation. Any variation occurs
in time. Consequently Analysis would have to deal with a process in
time, since it takes variables into consideration. But in fact it has
nothing to do with time; its applicability to occurrences in time is
irrelevant. There are also applications of Analysis to geometry; and
here time is left quite out of account. This is one of the main difficulties,
one that we encounter again and again when once we try to get away
from examples to the root of the matter. For as soon as we try to
mention a variable, we shall hit upon something that varies in time and
thus does not belong to pure Analysis. And yet it must be possible to
point to a variable that does not involve something alien to arithmetic,
if variables are objects of Analysis at all. |

If variation thus already raises a difficulty, we encounter a fresh one 657
when we ask what varies. The answer one immediately gets is: a
magnitude. Let us look for an example. We may call a rod a magnitude
in respect of its being long. Any variation in the rod as regards its
length, such as may result, e.g., from heating it, occurs in time; and
neither rods nor lengths are objects of pure Analysis. This attempt to
point to a variable magnitude within Analysis is a failure; and in just
the same way, many others must fail; for the magnitudes of lengths,
surfaces, angles, masses, are none of them objects of arithmetic. Among
all magnitudes, only numbers belong to arithmetic; and it just because
this science leaves it wholly indefinite what magnitudes were measured

[1]Our discussion will be confined to functions of a single argument.

In *Festschrift Ludwig Boltzmann gewidmet zum sechzigsten Geburtstage 20. Februar 1904*
(Leipzig: Ambrosius Barth, 1904), pp. 656–666. (*Tr.* Peter Geach)

in particular cases so as to get numbers, that it admits of the most
various applications. Our question is, then: Are the variables of
Analysis variable numbers? What else could they be, if they are to
belong to Analysis at all? But why is it that people hardly ever say
'variable number' but on the other hand often say 'variable magnitude'?
The latter expression sounds more acceptable than 'variable number';
for as regards that there arises the doubt: are there variable numbers?
Surely every number retains its properties, without varying. 'Of course',
someone may say, '3 and π are obviously invariable numbers, constants; but there are also variable numbers. For example, when I say
"the number that gives the length of this rod in millimetres" I am
naming a number; and this is variable, because the rod does not always
keep the same length; so by using this expression I have designated a
variable number'. Let us compare this example with the following one.
'When I say "the King of this realm" I am designating a man. Ten
years ago the King of this realm was an old man; at present the King
of this realm is a young man. So by using this expression I have
designated a man who was an old man and is now a young man'.
There must be something wrong here. The expression 'the King of this
realm' does not designate any man at all, if the time is not mentioned;
as soon, however, as mention of a time is added, it can designate one
658   man unambiguously; | but then this mention of time is a necessary
constituent of the expression, and we get a different expression if we
mention a different time. Thus in our two sentences we just have not
the same subject of predication. Similarly, the expression 'the number
that gives the length of this rod in millimetres' does not designate any
number at all if the time is not mentioned. If mention of a time is
added, a number may thus be designated, e.g. 1,000; but then this is
invariable. If a different time is mentioned, we get a different expression,
which may thus also designate a different number, say 1,001. If we say
'Half an hour ago the number that gave the length of this rod in
millimetres was a cube; at present the number that gives the length of
this rod in millimetres is not a cube', we just have not got the same
subject of predication. The number 1,000 has not somehow swollen up
to 1,001, but has been replaced by it. Or is the number 1,000 perhaps
the same as the number 1,001, only with a different expression its face?
If anything varies, we have in succession different properties, states, in
the same object. If it were not the same one, we should have no subject
of which we could predicate variation. A rod grows longer through
being heated; while this is going on, it remains the same one. If instead
it were taken away and replaced by a longer one, we could not say it
had grown longer. A man grows older; if we could not nevertheless

recognize him as the same man, we should have nothing of which we could predicate growing older. Let us apply this to number. What remains the same when a number varies? Nothing! Hence a number does *not* vary; for we have nothing of which we could predicate the variation. A cube never turns into a prime number; an irrational number never becomes rational.

Thus there are no variable numbers; and this is confirmed by the fact that we have no proper names for variable numbers. We failed in our attempt to use the expression 'the number that gives the length of this rod in millimetres' as a designation of a variable number. But do we not use 'x', 'y', 'z' to designate variable numbers? | This way of speaking 659 is certainly employed; but these letters are not proper names of variable numbers in the way that '2' and '3' are proper names of constant numbers; for the numbers '2' and '3' differ in a specified way, but what is the difference between the variables that are said to be designated by 'x' and 'y'? We cannot say. We cannot specify what properties x has and what different properties y has. If we associate anything with these letters at all, it is the same vague image for both of them. When apparent differences do show themselves, it is a matter of applications; but we are not here talking about these. Since we cannot conceive of each variable as an individual, we cannot attach any proper names to variables.

Mr. E. Czuber has attempted to avoid some of the difficulties I have mentioned.[2] In order to eliminate time, he defines a variable as an indefinite number. But are there indefinite numbers? Must numbers be divided into definite and indefinite? Are there indefinite men? Must not every object be definite? 'But is not the number n indefinite?' I am not acquainted with the number n. 'n' is not the proper name of any number, definite or indefinite. Nevertheless, we do sometimes say 'the number n'. How is this possible? Such an expression must be considered in a context. Let us take an example. 'If the number n is even, the $\cos n\pi = 1$.' Here only the whole has a sense, not the antecedent by itself nor the consequent by itself. The question whether the number n is even cannot be answered; no more can the question whether $\cos n\pi = 1$. For an answer to be given, 'n' would have to be the proper name of a number, and in that case this would necessarily be a definite one. We write the letter 'n' in order to achieve generality. This presupposes that, if we replace it by the name of a number, both antecedent and consequent receive a sense.

---

[2] *Vorlesungen über Differential- und Integralrechnung* (Teubner, Leipzig) 1, §2.

660   Of course we may speak of indefiniteness here; but | here the word 'indefinite' is not an adjective of 'number', but 'indefinitely' is an adverb, e.g., of the verb 'to indicate'. We cannot say that 'n' designates an indefinite number, but we *can* say that it indicates numbers indefinitely. And so it is always when letters are used in arithmetic, except for the few cases (π, e, i) where they occur as proper names; but then they designate definite, invariable numbers. There are thus no indefinite numbers, and this attempt of Mr. Czuber's is a failure.

The second deficiency that he tries to remedy is that we cannot conceive of any variable so as to distinguish it from others. He calls the totality of the values that a variable may assume, the range of the variable, and says: 'The variable x counts as having been defined when it can be determined as regards any assigned real number whether it belongs to the range or not'. It counts as having been defined; but *has* it? Since there are no indefinite numbers, it is impossible to define any indefinite number. The range is represented as distinctive for the variable; so with the same range we should have the same variable. Consequently in the equation '$y = x^2$' y would be the same variable as x if the range of x is that of positive numbers.

We must regard this attempt as having come to grief; in particular, the expression 'a variable assumes a value' is completely obscure. A variable is to be an indefinite number. Now how does an indefinite number set about assuming a number? For the value is obviously a number. Does, e.g., an indefinite man likewise assume a definite man? In other connections, indeed, we say that an object assumes a property; here the number must play both parts; as an object it is called a variable or a variable magnitude, and as a property it is called a value. That is why people prefer the word 'magnitude' to the word 'number'; they have to deceive themselves about the fact that the variable magnitude and the value it is said to assume are essentially the same thing, that in this case we have *not* got an object assuming different properties in succession, and that therefore there can be no question of a variation.

661   As regards variables our results are as follows. | Variable magnitudes may certainly be admitted, but do not belong to pure Analysis. Variable numbers do not exist. The word 'variable' thus has no justification in pure Analysis.

Now how do we get from variables to functions? This will probably be done always in essentially the same way; so we follow Mr. Czuber's way of putting it. He writes (§3): 'If every value of the real variable x that belongs to its range has correlated with it a definite number y, then in general y also is defined as a variable, and is called *a function of the real variable x*. This relation is expressed by an equation of the form $y = f(x)$'.

It is at once noticeable that y is called a definite number, whereas on the other hand, being a variable, it would have to be an indefinite number. y is neither a definite nor an indefinite number; but the sign 'y' is attached incorrectly to a plurality of numbers, and then afterwards he talks as if there were only a single number. It would be simpler and clearer to state the matter as follows. 'With every number of an x-range there is correlated a number. I call the totality of these numbers the y-range.' Here we certainly have a y-range, but we have no y of which we could say that it was a function of the real variable x.

Now the delimitation of its range appears irrelevant to the question what a function essentially is. Why could we not at once take the range to be the totality of real numbers, or the totality of complex numbers, including real numbers? The heart of the matter really lies in quite a different place, viz. hidden in the word 'correlated'. Now how do I tell whether the number 5 is correlated with the number 4? The question is unanswerable unless it is somehow completed. And yet with Mr. Czuber's explanation it looks as though it were already determined, for any two numbers, whether the first is correlated with the second or not. Fortunately Mr. Czuber adds the remark: | 'The above definition 662 involves no assertion as to the *law* of correlation, which is indicated in the most general way by the *characteristic f*; this can be set up in the most various ways.

Correlation, then, takes place according to a law, and different laws of this sort can be thought of. In that case, the expression 'y is a function of x' has no sense, unless it is completed by mentioning the law of correlation. This is a mistake in the definition. And surely the law, which this definition treats as not being given, is really the main thing. We notice that now variability has dropped entirely out of sight; instead, generality comes into view, for that is what the word 'law' indicates.

Distinctions between laws of correlation will go along with distinctions between functions; and these cannot any longer be regarded as quantitative. If we just think of algebraic functions, the logarithmic function, elliptic functions, we convince our selves immediately that here it is a matter of qualitative differences; a further reason for not defining functions as variables. If they were variables, elliptic functions would be elliptic variables.

Our general way of expressing such a law of correlation is an equation, in which the letter 'y' stands on the left side whereas on the right there appears a mathematical expression consisting of numerals, mathematical signs, and the letter 'x', e.g.:

$$`y = x^2 + 3x`.$$

Functions have indeed been defined as being such mathematical expressions. In recent times this concept has been found too narrow. However, this difficulty could easily be avoided by introducing new signs into the symbolic language of arithmetic. Another objection has more weight: viz. that a mathematical expression, as a group of signs, does not belong in arithmetic at all. The formalist theory, which regards signs as the subject matter of this science, is one that I may 663   well consider to be definitively refuted by my | criticism in the second volume of my *Grundgesetze der Arithmetik*. The distinction between sign and thing signified has not always been sharply made, so 'mathematical expression' (*expressio analytica*) has been half understood as what the expression means. Now what does '$x^2 + 3x$' designate? Properly speaking, nothing at all; for the letter 'x' only indicates numbers, and does not designate them. If we replace 'x' by a numeral, we get an expression that designates a number, and so nothing new. Like 'x' itself, '$x^2 + 3x$' only indicates. This may be done for the sake of expressing generality, as in the sentences

$$`x^2 + 3x = x(x + 3)`$$

$$`\text{if } x > 0 \text{ then } x^2 + 3x > 0`.$$

But now what has become of the function? It looks as though we could not take it to be either the mathematical expression itself or the meaning of the expression. And yet we have not gone very far off the right track. Each of the expressions 'sin 0', 'sin 1', 'sin 2' means some particular number; but we have a common constituent 'sin', and here we find a designation for the essential peculiarity of the sine-function. This 'sin' perhaps corresponds to the 'f' that Mr. Czuber says indicates a law; and the transition from 'f' to 'sin', just like that from 'a' to '2', is a transition from a sign that indicates to one that designates. In that case what 'sin' means would be a law. Of course that is not quite right. The law seems rather to be expressed in the equation '$y = \sin x$'; the symbol 'sin' is only part of this, but the part that is distinctive for the essential peculiarity of the law. And surely we have here what we were looking for – the function. 'f' too will then, strictly speaking, indicate a function. And here we come upon what distinguishes functions from numbers. 'sin' requires completion with a numeral, which, however, does not form part of the designation of the function: This holds good in general; the sign for a function is 'unsaturated'; it needs to be completed with a numeral, which we then call the argument-sign. We see this also with the root-sign, with the logarithm-sign. A functional sign | cannot occur on one side of an equation by itself, but only when 664 completed by a sign that designates or indicates a number. Now what does such a complex stand for consisting of a functional sign and a numeral, e.g. 'sin 1', '$\sqrt{1}$', 'log 1'? A number each time. We thus get numerical signs composed of two dissimilar parts, an 'unsaturated' part being completed by the other one.

This need of completion may be made apparent by empty brackets, e.g. 'sin( )' or '( )$^2 + 3$. ( )'. This is perhaps the most appropriate notation, and the one best calculated to avoid the confusion that arises from regarding an argument-sign as part of a functional sign; but it will probably not meet with any acceptance.[3] A letter may also be employed for this purpose. If we choose 'ξ,' then 'sin ξ' and '$\xi^2 + 3 . \xi$' are functional signs. But in that case it must be laid down that the only thing 'ξ' does here is to show the places where the completing sign has to be inserted. It will be well not to employ this letter for any other purpose, and so, e.g., not instead of the 'x' in our examples that serves to express generality.

It is a defect of the ordinary symbolism for differential quotients that in it the letter 'x' has to serve both to show the places for the argument and to express generality, as in the equation:

$$\frac{\mathrm{d}\cos\dfrac{x}{2}}{\mathrm{d}x} = -\tfrac{1}{2}\sin\frac{x}{2}$$

From this there arises a difficulty. According to the general principles for the use of letters in arithmetic we should have to get a particular case by substituting a numeral for 'x'. But the expression

$$\frac{\mathrm{d}\cos\dfrac{2}{2}}{\mathrm{d}2} \quad |$$

is unintelligible, because we cannot recognize the function. We do not 665 know whether it is

$$\cos\frac{(\ )}{2}, \text{ or } \cos\frac{2}{(\ )}, \text{ or } \cos\frac{(\ )}{(\ )}.$$

[3] In any case it is meant only for the exceptional case where we want to symbolize a function in isolation. In 'sin 2', 'sin' by itself already symbolizes the function.

So we are forced to use the clumsy notation

$$\left(\frac{d\cos\frac{x}{2}}{dx}\right)_{x=2}$$

But the greater disadvantage is that it is thus made more difficult to see the nature of a function.

The peculiarity of functional signs, which we here called 'unsaturatedness', naturally has something answering to it in the functions themselves. They too may be called 'unsaturated', and in this way we mark them out as fundamentally different from numbers. Of course this is no definition; but likewise none is here possible.[4] I must confine myself to hinting at what I have in mind by means of a metaphorical expression, and here I rely on my reader's agreeing to meet me half-way.

If a function is completed by a number so as to yield a number, the second is called the value of the function for the first as argument. People have got used to reading the equation '$y = f(x)$' as 'y is a function of x'. There are two mistakes here: first, rendering the *equals*-sign as a copula; secondly, confusing a function with its value for an argument. From these mistakes has arisen the opinion that a function is a number, although a variable or indefinite one. We have seen, on the contrary, that there are no such numbers at all, and that functions are fundamentally different from numbers.

The endeavour to be brief has introduced many inexact expressions into mathematical language, and these have reacted by obscuring 666 thought and producing faulty definitions. | Mathematics ought properly to be a model of logical clarity. In actual fact there are perhaps no scientific works where you will find more wrong expressions, and consequently wrong thoughts, than in mathematical ones. Logical correctness should never be sacrificed to brevity of expression. It is therefore highly important to devise a mathematical language that combines the most rigorous accuracy with the greatest possible brevity. To this end a symbolic language would be best adapted, by means of which we could directly express thoughts in written or printed symbols without the intervention of spoken language.

---

[4]H. Hankel's definition, in his *Untersuchungen über die unendlich oft oszillierenden und unstetigen Funktionen* (Tübingen, 1870), §1, is useless, because of a vicious circle; it contains the expression '$f(x)$', and this makes his definition presuppose the thing that is to be defined.

On the Foundations of Geometry: Second Series

I

I am only too pleased to enter into a direct interchange with men who 293
have directed their thoughts to the same questions as I. And therefore I
at first welcomed Mr. Korselt's essay 'On the Foundations of Geometry' (this journal, 12, p. 402). And I also had the pleasure of
discovering some points of contact between us. Let me first emphasize
these. Mr. Korselt uses my expressions 'truth-value', 'the True', 'the
False' – and, as it seems, in my sense. However I should like to ask
that he say 'the truth-value a' instead of 'the truth-value of a'. The
explanation which Mr. Korselt gives the sign-complex '$a \neq b$' almost
agrees with my explanation of the corresponding sign in my *Begriffsschrift*; and it is better than that of E. Schröder, who apparently introduced the sign, and than that of Peano for his 'Ɔ'.

As for the rest, I have of course been disappointed by Mr. Korselt's
criticism. It does not offer as suitable a foundation for understanding
and fruitful development as I had wished.

If Mr. Korselt wanted to prove that my reservations concerning Mr.
Hilbert's presentation are unjustified, then he should have examined all
of my objections. This he did not do. And yet, a single irrefutable
objection can bring the whole theory to ruin.

Mr. Hilbert's theorems concern axioms, their independence and their
consistency. It is therefore imperative to leave no doubt concerning the
sense of the word 'axiom'. And consequently it is a fault of Mr.
Hilbert's paper, that it leaves this concept nebulous. I have been at
pains to draw sharp boundaries; Mr. Korselt, it seems, diligently blurs
them once again. How is this to be explained? Perhaps by a drive for
self-preservation on the part of Hilbert's doctrine, for which an
obscuring of the issue may | well be a condition of survival. If this is 294
correct, then a saviour of the doctrine must of course seek to prevent
clarification. I do not believe that Mr. Korselt has done this on

Jahresbericht der Deutschen Mathematiker-Vereiningung 15 (1906), pp. 293–309,
377–403, 423–30. (*Tr.* E.-H. W. Kluge)

purpose; but by his procedure he has made it inordinately difficult for me to reply to his essay. Mr. Hilbert, so far as I know, does not reply to my arguments at all. Perhaps in him too there is at work a secret fear, deeply shrouded in darkness, that his edifice might be endangered by closer investigation of my arguments. On the surface, of course, there will probably float the opinion that my arguments are simply not worthy of closer consideration. However, if Mr. Hilbert should ever come to illuminate the nether regions with the light of his understanding, he will perhaps allow the point that ultimately what is false in his doctrine cannot be maintained, but that it is useful and honourable to repudiate it, so that what is true and valuable may stand out all the more clearly and indisputably.

In my opinion, it was the task of a critic to take a stand *vis-à-vis* my premises; in which case the question would have been attacked at its roots and everything that followed would have been sharply illuminated. In my first essay on the present subject I considered it necessary to talk at some length about axioms and definitions, since it appeared to me that Mr. Hilbert's Festschrift threatened a great confusion. Mr. Korselt should first have addressed himself to my remarks on this point, since they constitute my point of departure and everything that follows is closely connected with them. To definitions that stipulate something, I opposed principles and theorems that assert something. The former contain a sign (word, expression) that is intended to receive a meaning by their agency; the latter contain no such sign. Does Mr. Korselt not admit the essential difference between these two types of propositions? Why not? He continues to talk of axioms that define something, as if this offered no difficulties at all. But what is an axiom really supposed to do? Is it supposed to assert something, or is it supposed to stipulate something? Why do we have two words, 'axiom' and 'definition', if axioms too are supposed to define? Merely in the interest of greater obscurity?

In the second edition of Mr. Hilbert's work as well, axioms merrily go on defining as though nothing had happened. Evidently Mr. Hilbert himself does not know what he means by the word 'axiom'; and consequently it also becomes quite doubtful whether he knows what thoughts he connects with his propositions; and still more doubtful whether Mr. Korselt knows this. Or do these gentlemen perhaps
295   consider the thought-content | of propositions to be superfluous? Words! Words! Words! I have indicated a confusion of usage in Mr. Hilbert's Festschrift with respect to the word 'axiom'. Does Mr. Korselt admit this conflict, or does he believe that he can smooth it over? He ought to have talked about this clearly, at the very beginning.

At the beginning of my second essay, I draw attention to the fact that Mr. Hilbert's explanations and definitions appear to be of two kinds. As examples of the first kind, I adduce the explanation for points of a straight line lying on the same side of a point, and for points of a straight line lying on different sides of a point. Gauss's definition of number-congruence also belongs to this kind. As an example of an explanation of the second kind, I adduce that of the word 'between'. I construct another definition of number-congruence on the model of the latter. Now if Mr. Korselt wanted to dispute in a constructive manner, he ought to have addressed himself to this. Does he admit that the explanations and definitions of Mr. Hilbert are of two kinds? What justifies the choice of the same word, 'axiom' or 'explanation', for both? Does Mr. Korselt see the enormous difference between the Gaussian definition of number-congruence and the one which I constructed on the Hilbertian model? This ought to have been made clear; otherwise we lack any solid basis for a fruitful discussion.

I believe that with my exposition about the use of the words 'axiom' and 'definition' I move within the bounds of traditional usage, and that I may justifiably demand that one not cause confusion by a completely new usage. Still, I am willing to consider a completely new usage of these words; only I must demand that it be uniform, and that it be presented intelligibly and unequivocally, prior to any consideration of particular questions. This I miss in Mr. Korselt's exposition.

Nevertheless, I do accord a value to his treatise, which makes it appear advisable to consider it more closely. For it seems to me that Mr. Korselt wants to give a peculiar turn to Mr. Hilbert's doctrine in that he understands it as a formal theory, as a purely formal system. Whether this explication quite corresponds to Mr. Hilbert's intentions is another question; for all that, a lot speaks in favour of it.

In turning to a closer examination of Mr. Korselt's treatise, I shall first collect what we find scattered throughout it concerning axiom, definition, and meaning. |

There we read the proposition, 296

> If we call a true but logically unprovable thought an axiom, then 'definitions' (nominal definitions, impositions of names) are not axioms.

What Mr. Korselt presents here in the antecedent clause as the meaning of the word 'axiom' may no doubt be called the traditional, Euclidean meaning. Axioms differ from theorems in that they are unprovable. The reasons given by Mr. Korselt for his contention approximate to those given by me and also show that conversely, no axiom can define anything. If the word 'axiom' is taken in this sense, then the expression of an axiom must contain no unknown sign, for otherwise it would express no thought at all. Letters intended to lend generality to the content of a principle may of course occur in it, since it is known how they contribute to the expression of the thought even though they designate nothing. Herewith we have an answer to Mr. Korselt's question, 'Why should not axioms contain signs whose references have not previously been settled?'

Initially, it appears as though Mr. Korselt accepts this Euclidean meaning, and indeed nowhere does he explicitly reject it. But almost all of his later statements stand in direct contradiction to it. Thus, he recognizes, for example, the possibility of invalid axioms. If he wanted to write clearly, then he ought to have said something like this: 'However, I do not accept this traditional sense of the word "axiom", but rather use it in the following sense'. And then he ought to have presented the latter as clearly as possible.

In contradiction to the Euclidean meaning, Mr. Korselt assumes that axioms contain hitherto unknown signs and that they define or determine a concept. But the fundamental difference between axioms and definitions, which he himself initially emphasizes, makes it quite impossible that axioms define anything. One must be clear on this point: Is a principle supposed to stipulate something, or is it supposed to express a thought and assert it to be true? And whatever one decides here, one must adhere to it and not continually waver back and forth between different conceptions.

Mr. Korselt also has the unfortunate idea of blending Heine's formal theory of arithmetic with Hilbert's doctrine, and of understanding an axiom as a rule for the use of the signs occurring in it. This is a third conception of axioms. |

297   In saying that modern[1] mathematics no longer designates certain facts of experience with its axioms but at best indicates them, Mr. Korselt brings the axioms of modern mathematics into contrast with those of Euclid; and doubtless we may assume that he counts himself among the modern mathematicians. Clearly, he also counts Mr. Hilbert among them and believes that with this proposition he has hit upon the latter's usage of the word 'axiom'. If this is correct, then it is a gross error to assume that Mr. Hilbert has shown anything at all about the dependence or independence of the Euclidean axioms; or that when he talks about the axiom of parallels it is the Euclidean axiom. Accordingly, by an axiom we apparently are to understand something which

[1]Are we still not out of this ghastly modern era?

looks like a proposition that is supposed to express a thought, but which actually is not a real proposition at all since it does not express a thought but merely indicates it; just as for example the letter '*a*' in arithmetic is not a number-sign, since it does not designate a number but merely indicates one. This is a fourth conception of axioms. But it is not the last, for according to Mr. Korselt, axioms also describe the manner in which objects of experience can be combined. But how these conceptions are to be reconciled with one another, in what relations they might perhaps stand to one another – about this there hovers a mysterious darkness. And now consider that everything hinges on understanding the word 'axiom', if one wants to understand Mr. Hilbert's propositions concerning the independence of these axioms. Clarity! Clarity! Clarity! Does Mr. Korselt think that it is a pleasure to be led through these thickets by him?

We can probably characterize the situation by means of the following analogy: Mr. Hilbert chops both definitions and axioms very fine, carefully blends them, and makes a sausage out of this. Mr. Korselt is not satisfied with this mixture. He also minces Mr. Thomae's rules concerning the use of signs, adds a pinch of indication supplied by me with, from his own resources, a description of the manner in which objects of experience can be combined, mixes it all up very thoroughly, and makes a sausage out of this. At least there is no dearth of ingredients; and I have no doubt but that something good will result for the fancier of such delicacies.

Let us take an example:

Every anej bazes at least two ellah. |

'How could anyone write such hair-raising nonsense! What is an 298 anej? What is an ellah?' So I hear it being asked with indignation. At your service! That is an axiom, not of the Euclidean, but of the modern, kind. It defines the concept *anej*. What an anej might be is a very impertinent question. We should first have to discuss under what circumstances an answer would be acceptable. If we don't find a thought in this axiom, that matters little. The proposition does not claim to be a description of known facts; at best it indicates them, and that, moreover, only very delicately. For example the well-known empirical fact that every sausage has at least two ends, or that every child has waved at least two streamers – It is obviously the description of a way in which objects of experience – the streamers – can be combined with one another. The domain of application of this axiom extends precisely as far as objects of experience can be assigned to the axiom.

Mr. Korselt discusses the word 'meaning' by attacking my thesis that axiomatic propositions must contain no proper names, concept-words, or relation-words whose meaning has not previously been settled. I here use the word 'axiom' in the old Euclidean sense; Mr. Korselt, however, uses it in a modern one. Consequently there is not the slightest conflict between us, since what Mr. Korselt denies is completely different from what I maintain. But with this, another divergence becomes apparent. I had thought the matter to be much simpler, namely thus: In scientific use, a proper name has the purpose of designating an object; and in the case this purpose is achieved, this object is the meaning of the proper name. The same thing holds for concept-signs, relation-signs, and function-signs. They designate concepts, relations, and functions respectively, and what they designate then is their meaning. According to Mr. Korselt, however, the matter is not quite so simple. According to him, the assertion that the meaning of a sign is settled means either that should the sign occur, it will be recognized as the same sign for the same object; or that one will always recognize all or at least certain simple propositions using the sign as being true, false, or definitions. Let us ask whether, according to this, the reference of the word 'anej' is settled. At the present time, only one proposition using the word is known, namely the axiom adduced above. Is the latter, then, true, false, or a definition? True? That does not seem to be quite right. False? Equally little. But a definition! That's it: it is a defining axiom, and I dare say we may be confident that we shall always recognize it again as such. Therefore the meaning of the 299 word 'anej' is settled. |

According to Mr. Korselt, the words 'principle', 'axiom', and 'definition' have the same meaning as far as a purely formal system is concerned, namely that of direct objects (propositions); and opposed to these stand the indirect objects (propositions). This illuminates the close relationship which according to his usage obtains between axioms and definitions. A difference is not mentioned. As with Mr. Hilbert, the definitions probably consists of axioms, whereby it is not ruled out that a definition may contain only a single axiom.

We get to know little about what constitution a proposition must have in order to be an axiom, a definition, or a rule about the use of signs. Actually, we get to know no more than that it must contain unknown signs. Of course there is still this puzzling assertion:

> Those interpretations of the signs of a purely formal system that are assertions, must not lead to contradictions with accepted propositions. Otherwise we have at best defined not the *desired* concepts, but different ones.

I really find all of this quite unintelligible. At first it looks as if the above were intended to limit the interpretations; in the end it looks like a rule for giving definitions. I do not quite see how the fact that the defined concept is one we wanted can prevent a contradiction that would emerge if the concept were not one we wanted. Even the example does not clarify the matter for me. What is the definition here? Where is the desired concept? What interpretation do we have? With what accepted proposition does a contradiction ensue? Can the latter not be avoided by a different interpretation? Does the mistake lie in the interpretation or in the definition?

With respect to defining, Mr. Korselt detects a difficulty. Mr. Korselt says that the answer to the question of what something is must always be given in words, concerning whose meaning we can once again ask; and thus there would be no end of asking. And similarly, he further states, 'We simply have to begin our investigation with some simple concepts that cannot be analysed any further'. Very well! But what is this supposed to prove? To begin with, it surely shows no more than that it is unreasonable to want to define everything. But it almost looks as if the question concerning meaning were thereby to be denied justification altogether, and as if defining, or at least a particular manner of defining, were to be presented as worthless. It cannot be allowed that only a particular manner of defining would be affected by this; for no matter of what type a definition may be, it will always have to | presuppose certain words or signs as known. Initially one may 300 think that Mr. Korselt wants to stop defining with simple concepts that cannot be analysed any further, since otherwise there would be no end of defining. But he continues: 'The simple concepts that are taken as basic can be determined only by propositions in which such a concept occurs several times or several such concepts occur simultaneously'.

Simple concepts, then, are to be determined as well. And is this not a definition? In which case is there any end to defining? Later, of course, it emerges that such propositions do not determine the concepts: 'It is both inexpedient and unfair to demand of a formal theory that it give a *determinate* meaning to the "figures" 'names) – e.g., "point" – which it has constructed on the model of proper names or concept-names'.

Mr. Korselt says, 'The above example of the Euclidean point shows that we cannot, in concert with Mr. Frege, demand that every system of principles be solvable for the unknowns (basic concepts) that occur in them; we certainly cannot demand an unambiguous solution. That would amount to unlimited defining'.

The danger of having to define *ad infinitum* arises if and only if one demands that everything be defined. But who forces us to do this? On the other hand, this danger has nothing to do with the demand that a system of principles be capable of unambiguous solution. My demand holds only in that case where such a system is supposed to be a definition by which certain concepts or relations are to be determined. Without the possibility of an unambiguous solution, we simply do not have a determination. My demand stems from the very nature of the matter; and if it cannot be met, then it does not follow that it must be dropped. Rather, it follows that concepts and relations cannot be determined in this manner; and that therefore Mr. Hilbert's so-called definitions, which are of this kind, do not meet the requirements we must place on definitions. When Mr. Korselt proves that in the case of the definition of a point, the requirements a definition must meet cannot be met – I do not want to embark on an examination of this proof – then from this it follows that we should abstain from defining; not, however, that we should do as we please and call the result a definition of a point. If it has been proved that a leap across a given ditch is impossible, then from this it follows that we had better not attempt it; not, however, that we should limp and call this limping | a leap across the ditch. Whoever wilfully deviates from the traditional sense of a word and does not indicate in what sense he wants to use it, whoever suddenly begins to call red what otherwise is called green, should not be astonished if he causes confusion. And if this occurs deliberately in science, it is a sin against science.

301

What is actually the purpose and nature of Hilbertian definition? And to what laws is it subject? For surely not even Mr. Korselt himself believes that every system of propositions that contain certain unknown words like 'anej' and 'bazes' constitutes an explanation of these words. We are agreed in this, that an explanation or definition generally need not point to a perception – a model. However, we must come to an understanding not only about what an explanation does not need to achieve, but also, and mainly, about what we must require of it.

My opinion is this: We must admit logically primitive elements that are indefinable. Even here there seems to be a need to make sure that we designate the same thing by the same sign (word). Once the investigators have come to an understanding about the primitive elements and their designations, agreement about what is logically composite is easily reached by means of definition. Since definitions are not possible for primitive elements, something else must enter in. I call it explication. It is this, therefore, that serves the purpose of mutual understanding among investigators, as well as of the communication of the science to others. We may relegate it to a propaedeutic. It has no place in the system of a science; in the latter, no conclusions are based on it. Someone who pursued research only by himself would not need it. The purpose of explications is a pragmatic one; and once it is achieved, we must be satisfied with them. And here we must be able to count on a little goodwill and cooperative understanding, even guessing; for frequently we cannot do without a figurative mode of expression. But for all that, we can demand from the originator of an explication that he himself know for certain what he means; that he remain in agreement with himself; and that he be ready to complete and emend his explication whenever, given even the best of intentions, the possibility of a misunderstanding arises.

Since mutual cooperation in a science is impossible without mutual understanding of the investigators, we must have confidence that such an understanding can be reached through explication, although theoretically the contrary is not excluded. | 302

Are Hilbertian definitions, then, elucidations? Elucidations will generally be propositions that contain the expression in question, perhaps even several such expressions; and herein they agree with what Mr. Korselt states with the following words: 'The simple concepts that are taken as basic can be determined only through propositions in which such a concept occurs several times or several such concepts occur simultaneously.' If Hilbertian definitions were to serve only the mutual understanding of the investigators and the communication of the science, not its construction, then they could be considered elucidations in the sense noted above and could be accorded all the consideration to which as such they could lay claim. But they are intended to be more. It is not intended that they belong to the propaedeutic but rather that they serve as corner-stones of the science: as premises of inferences. And given these demands, they cannot be accorded the leniency of judgement which they could have demanded as mere elucidations. Moreover, even as elucidations they miss their mark: namely to make sure that all who use them henceforth also associate the same sense with the elucidated word. We are easily misled by the fact that the words 'point', 'straight line', etc. have already been in use for a long time. But just imagine the old words completely replaced by new ones especially invented for this purpose, so that no sense is as yet associated with them. And now ask whether everyone would understand the Hilbertain axioms and definitions in this form. It would amount to pure guesswork. Some would perhaps not be able to guess anything at all; some this, others that.

Let us turn to proper definitions! They, too, serve mutual understanding, but they achieve it in a much more perfect manner than the elucidations in that they leave nothing to guess-work; nor need they count on co-operative understanding and goodwill. Of course they do presuppose knowledge of certain primitive elements and their signs. A definition correctly combines a group of these signs in such a way that the meaning of this group is determined by the meanings of the signs used. From a purely theoretical point of view, this might suffice; but such sign-groups often become too unwieldy and are too time-consuming to utter or to write out. We need a simple sign for them. And it is the task of the definition to give this new sign to the content determined by the familiar signs. Now it may happen that this sign (word) is not altogether new, but has already been used in ordinary discourse or in a scientific treatment that precedes the truly systematic one. | As a rule, this usage is too vacillating for pure science. But if we assume that in a given case it satisfies the most stringent demands, then one might think that in that case a definition would be unnecessary. And if, like an elucidation, a definition were to serve only mutual understanding and the communication of the science, then in this case it would indeed be superfluous. But that is an advantage gained only incidentally. The real importance of a definition lies in its logical construction out of primitive elements. And for that reason we should not do without it, not even in a case like this. The insight it permits into the logical structure is not only valuable in itself, but also is a condition for insight into the logical linkage of truths. A definition is a constituent of the system of a science. As soon as the stipulation it makes is accepted, the explained sign becomes known and the proposition explaining it becomes an assertion. The self-evident truth it contains will now appear in the system as a premise of inferences.

The mental activities leading to the formulation of a definition may be of two kinds: analytic or synthetic. This is similar to the activities of the chemist, who either analyses a given substance into its elements or lets given elements combine to form a new substance. In both cases, we come to know the composition of a substance. So here, too, we can achieve something new through logical construction and can stipulate a sign for it.

But the mental work preceding the formulation of a definition does not appear in the systematic structure of mathematics; only its result, the definition, does. Thus it is all the same for the system of mathematics, whether the preceding activity was of an analytic or a synthetic kind; whether the definiendum had already somehow been given before, or whether it was newly derived. For in the system, no sign (word) appears prior to the definition that introduces it. Therefore so far as the system is concerned, every definition is the giving of a name, regardless of the manner in which we arrived at it.

It is self-evident that what is given a name (sign) must be determined by the definition. A word without a determinate meaning has no meaning so far as mathematics is concerned.

Now in my second essay I have shown that for the most part, Mr. Hilbert's definitions miss their mark; at least they do so if we assume that they are to assign meaning to the words 'point', 'straight line', 'between'. | Mr. Korselt is basically of my opinion, for he says, 'The 304 signs of a formal theory have no meaning at all'.

Now clearly, he takes Mr. Hilbert's theory to be a formal one. Accordingly, there can occur in it no explanations of signs such that by means of these the signs are given meanings. Therefore if – as I claim – there is no concept that is assigned as meaning to the word 'point' by Mr. Hilbert's definition, then this is quite in accord with the fact that according to Mr. Korselt, in a formal theory no meaning whatever corresponds to the word 'point', and that by the very nature of a formal theory none could correspond to it. In agreement with this, Mr Korselt states, 'It is both inexpedient and unfair to demand of a formal theory that it give a *determinate* meaning to the "figures" (names) – e.g. "point" – which it has constructed on the model of proper names or concept-names'.

What is asserted here seems to be a bit weaker than what was said at the place mentioned previously; but as a matter of fact, it is one and the same, for a sign without determinate meaning is a sign without meaning. Therefore complete agreement obtains! But then, why does Mr. Korselt quarrel with me, e.g. over my example of the pocket watch? If the word 'point' does not designate a concept for Mr. Hilbert, then it goes without saying that the question of whether my pocket watch is a point cannot be answered. Mr. Korselt could simply have pointed out that so far as the formal theory is concerned, it isn't even the purpose of the word 'point' to refer to something. Then of course he would have had to say what the purpose of Hilbertian explanations and definitions really is, since it cannot be the one of giving meaning to signs. It may surely be taken as established once and for all that Hilbertian pseudo-definitions do not give meanings to the words 'point', 'straight line', 'between', etc. that seem to be explained by them. And herewith we have achieved one of the aims I have pursued. While agreeing with me in this conclusion, Mr. Korselt appears to raise objections against the way in which I have reached it. This may seem unimportant; nevertheless, it will not be superfluous to examine the matter a little more closely.

I demand from a definition of a point that by means of it we be able to judge of any object whatever – e.g. my pocket watch – whether it is a point. Mr. Korselt, however, misunderstands this to mean that I demand that the question be decidable from the definition alone, without the | help of perceptions; and he maintains that this is impossible. Quite right! The question of whether a given stone is a diamond cannot be answered by the mere explanation of the word 'diamond' itself. But we can demand of the explanation that it settle the question objectively, so that by means of it everyone well acquainted with the stone in question will be able to determine whether or not it is a diamond. Therefore if it is merely on account of our incomplete knowledge of the object that we cannot answer the question, then the explanation is not to blame. If, however, the question must remain unanswered no matter how complete our knowledge, then the explanation is faulty. And that is the present case. The very same difficulty that arises with the question of whether my pocket watch is a point arises for every object, whether it be sensibly apprehensible or not. For example, if we take the number two or even a Euclidean point, we shall always encounter the same obstacle, namely that we shall already have to know of another object that it is a point before we could even begin to decide whether the statement of Mr. Hilbert's first axiom applies. And no knowledge of the presented object, be it ever so complete, can help us overcome ,this difficulty. Therefore even if I agree with Mr. Korselt that the mere definition does not suffice to answer the question whether an object falls under the defined concept but that a sufficient knowledge of the object, acquired somewhere, is also necessary, I must nevertheless insist that a complete knowledge of the object together with the definition must suffice. A repair of the watch does not help in the present case, for the fault does not lie in it but in the Hilbertian definition, which provides neither sense nor meaning for the grammatical predicate 'is a point', so that every proposition with this predicate is senseless, no matter what its subject may be.

The situation is exactly the same with the example from number-theory. The Gaussian definition of number-congruence fulfils its purpose because it reduces the meaning of the word 'congruent' to the meanings of the expressions 'different' and 'a number divides evenly into a number', which are already known: It constructs the meaning logically out of known building blocks. What I miss in Hilbertian definitions, for example in that of the word 'between', is by no means the indication of a model – of the perception – but rather the logical construction. I hear the reply, 'A reduction to what is known is not possible here'. Well, in that case no definition is possible. In that case we shall simply have to recognize a primitive element and be satisfied with an elucidation. The latter, however, | cannot appear in the system but rather must precede it. Within the system, one will just have to presuppose the word 'between' as known; just as one can never circumvent the necessity of assuming some words to be known.

If a relation is correctly defined, then this definition together with an adequate knowledge of any given object must suffice to decide whether these objects stand in the defined relation to each other. This knowledge is naturally expressed in propositions that do not presuppose an acquaintance with the relation-sign in question, and that therefore contain neither it nor an expression that would have to be explained in terms of it. I have never demanded that the decision be possible on the basis of the definition alone, without the aid of other propositions. If Mr. Korselt wants to refute me, he has only to deduce from my definition of number-congruence which I constructed on Mr. Hilbert's model, that 2 is congruent to 8 modulo 3; and here he may use any propositions of arithmetic for whose understanding the word 'congruent' is not necessary. Let him try it, and he will see that it does not work. Mr. Korselt may take whatever propositions about points on a straight line he pleases, as long as these do not presuppose an acquantance with the word 'between': using these propositions, he will still be unable to prove from Hilbert's definition of lying-between that one or the other of three points on a straight line lies between the other two.

However, if we posit the Gaussian definition of number-congruence, then in order to recognize that 2 is congruent to 8 modulo 3, we need only the propositions

$$8 - 2 = 3 + 3$$

and

$$3 \text{ goes evenly into } 3 + 3$$

which neither contain the sign for congruence nor presuppose knowledge of it.

We saw that a definition which is to assign a meaning to a word must determine this meaning. Mr. Hilbert's pseudo-definition does not achieve this. There is no relation that would be designated by the word 'between' in accordance with this pseudo-definition. And here we find ourselves once more in complete agreement with Mr. Korselt, who does not want to accord any reference whatever to this word in a formal theory. Or might it perhaps have different references?

Herewith we come to a discussion of the requirement of unambiguous signs which, it seems, is ignored by some newer mathematicians – in contradistinction to the venerable Goethe, who, although |

307   not a mathematician, was nevertheless no fool. In the ninth book of his *Fiction and Truth* he says, 'Just as, after all, anything can be asserted if we permit ourselves to use and apply words quite indeterminately, now in a wider, now in a narrower, in a more closely or a more distantly related sense'.

Indeed, if it were a matter of deceiving oneself and others, there would be no better means than ambiguous signs.

Mr. Korselt declares that it is not risky to talk of 'the theorem *a*' (e.g. the axiom of parallels) if *a* has an identical or similar wording in all geometries, as if the sense did not matter at all. I had given grounds to the contrary; Mr. Korselt ignores them and simply opposes his authority to them. Does this suffice? Well, his manner of talking is indeed practical if it is a question of imagining that what one has proved of axioms taken in the modern sense also holds of them when taken in the Euclidean sense.

Generally speaking, the sciences, too, are really moving in the opposite direction. They seek to make their language ever more precise by formulating technical expressions with the greatest possible precision, so as to escape the vacillations of ordinary usage. It is only the modern mathematicians who sometimes seem to seek their strength in ambiguity; and indeed it is decidedly convenient, inviting to flights of fancy. And yet the dangers arising for the certitude of the proofs associated with this ambiguity, cannot be ignored. Are they to be deemed nothing, then? One would think that the friends of ambiguity of signs would first indicate and fully justify precautionary rules that could safeguard against the dangers arising from this ambiguity. To my knowledge this has not occurred, and indeed would be a useless labour; for the appearance that ambiguous signs are necessary arises from unclear thinking and insufficient logical insight.

If one wants to defend the ambiguity of signs, one may in the first instance think of the use of letters in mathematics. But these letters are of a nature completely different from that of the number-signs '2', '3', etc., or the relation signs '=', '>'. They are not at all intended to designate numbers, concepts, relations, or some function or other; rather, they are intended only to indicate so as to lend generality of content to the propositions in which they occur. Thus it is only in the context of a proposition that they have a certain task to fulfil, that they are to contribute to the expression of the thought. But outside of this

308   context, they say nothing. | It is quite wrong to think that the proposition '$(a+b) \times c = a \times c + b \times c$' expresses different thoughts, among others also the one contained in the proposition '$(2+3) \times 7 = 2 \times 7 + 3 \times 7$'. Rather, the first proposition expresses only a single

thought which, however, is different from that of the second proposition. It is equally wrong to think that the letter a now designates the number 2, now another number, or even several numbers at once. It simply does not have the purpose of designating a number, as does a number-sign; or for that matter, of designating anything at all. Rather, it has the sole purpose of lending generality of content to the proposition '$(a+b) \times c = a \times c + b \times c$', and it is precisely this generality that differentiates this proposition from the second one.

Concept-words offer another occasion where it may seem that ambiguous signs are necessary. If we think that the word 'planet' designates at one time the Earth, at another Jupiter, then we should take it to be ambiguous. But in fact it does not stand to the Earth in the relation of sign to thing signified. Rather, it designates a concept, and the Earth falls under it. No ambiguity is to be found here. Let us suppose that the word 'planet' is unknown and that we wanted to designate the appropriate concept. We might then perhaps hit upon the idea of using the proper name 'Mars' for it, and might find unreasonable the demand that the word 'Mars' be given a determinate meaning: as wide a range of interpretations as possible ought to be kept open for this name. But as a concept-word, 'Mars' would have to be just as unambiguous as it would have been as a proper name. Do not say that as a concept-word it has no determinate meaning, or that it refers to an indeterminate object. Every object is determinate; 'indeterminate object' is contradictory, and wherever this expression occurs, we can be quite certain that a concept is what is really meant. We cannot say that the proposition '$x > 0$' assigns an indeterminate object, an indeterminate number, to the letter 'x' as its meaning. Rather, what is designated here is a concept: *positive number*; nor is 'x' introduced as a sign for this concept; it merely takes the place of the proper names (number-signs) of objects that may perhaps be subsumed under the concept. Thus the appearance of ambiguity arises only out of an insufficient understanding, in that proper names and concept-words are not distinguished sharply enough.

A similar thing may occur one level higher, when talking of an indeterminate concept or the indeterminate meaning of a concept-word, where what one really has in mind is a concept of the second level. | This is probably the case when Mr. Korselt finds it inexpedient and unreasonable to give a determinate meaning to the word 'point'; and when he wants to leave open to names as wide a range of interpretations as possible. He apparently does not mean by this that a concept with as wide an extension as possible is to be correlated with the word 'point'; for the latter still would be – indeed, would have to be –

309

completely determinate. Rather, he has in mind a second-level concept within which, aside from the Euclidean *point-concept*, still other concepts fall. Of course this second-level concept must also be a completely determinate one; but it behaves toward the first-level concepts falling within it in a way similar to that in which a first-level concept behaves toward the object falling under it. When we consider the multiplicity of these concepts of the first level (point-concepts), we get the notion that we are faced with an indeterminacy or ambiguity. This need not be the case here any more than it is in the case of the first-level concept *prime number*, where not only 2 but also 3 falls under the latter.

In no way is it necessary to have ambiguous signs, and consequently such ambiguity is quite unacceptable. What can be proved only by means of ambiguous signs cannot be proved at all.

II

Before discussing the turn which Mr. Korselt gives to Hilbert's doctrine by calling it a formal theory or a purely formal system, I should like to adduce some considerations whose upshot is important for the understanding and appraisal of this very turn.

Mr. Korselt does not always appear to distinguish a proposition as what is sensibly perceptible, from the thought which is its sense. What I call a proposition *tout court* or a real proposition is a group of signs that expresses a thought; however, whatever has only the grammatical form of a proposition I call a pseudo-proposition. Examples of the latter are often to be found as antecedent and consequent propositions of conditional propositional complexes. We frequently encounter the conception of a conditional judgement as something by means of which judgements (propositions) are brought into relation with each other. But this only rarely applies, even if we say 'thought' instead of 'judgement'; for it is frequently the case that we have a thought in neither the antecedent nor the consequent proposition in themselves, but only in the propositional complex as a whole. Let us consider the proposition 'If something is greater than 1, then it is a positive number'. 'Something' and 'it' refer to one another. If we break this connection by separating the propositions, each of them becomes senseless. 'It is a positive number' says nothing. To be sure, we can find a thought expressed in the proposition 'Something is greater than 1'; namely, that there is something which is greater than 1. But it is not in this sense that the grammatical proposition occurs as antecedent of the propositional complex. We can also express this thought by utilizing the letter '*a*' as in arithmetic:

If $a > 1$, then $a > 0$.

Here the letter '*a*' only indicates, as did the words 'something' and 'it' above. The generality extends to the content of the whole propositional complex, not to the antecedent proposition by itself nor the consequent proposition by itself. Since neither the former nor the latter by itself expresses a thought, neither of them is a real proposition. The whole propositional complex is one; it expresses a single thought | which cannot be divided into component thoughts. We can also express this thought thus:

Whatever is greater than 1 is a positive number.

The first grammatical proposition actually takes the place of the subject, and the second contains the predicate belonging to it. From this it is also clear that logically speaking we have only a single proposition. Here we do not have a relation between thoughts, but the relation of subordination of the concept *greater than 1* under the concept *positive number*.

If the square of something is 1, then its fourth power is also 1

we can also express like this:

If $a^2 = 1$, then $a^4 = 1$

or also as

Whatever is a square root of 1 is also a fourth root of 1

or also as

Every square root of 1 is also a fourth root of 1

Here the subordination of concepts is once more discernible, so that even here we have only a single thought. Here, too, the grammatical component-propositions are merely pseudo-propositions without thought-content. For the letter '*a*' in '$a^2 = 2$' refers to '*a*' in '$a^4 = 1$' just as, for example, in Latin the word *quot* occurring in an antecedent refers to *tot* in the appropriate consequent. And just as the separation of such propositions renders both of them senseless, so in this case as well, what is contributed by the letter '*a*' to the expression of the thought is lost by the dissolution of the propositional complex. The letter is supposed to lend generality of content to the whole proposition, not to the component pseudo-propositions. And thus it comes about that the whole propositional complex expresses a true thought,

378

even though it contains a letter that signifies nothing; while the component pseudo-propositions have no sense because they contain the letter '*a*', which neither has a sense nor lends generality of content to even one of these components. If it were supposed to do the latter, then '$a^2 = 1$' would indeed express a thought, albeit a false one; to wit, that every object is a square root of 1. But it is not in this sense that '$a^2 = 1$' occurs as a part of the thought-complex. From this we see that a proposition can express a true thought even though it contains words

379 ('something', 'it') or letters that do not mean anything | but merely indicate whenever these words or letters have the purpose of lending generality of content to the proposition. On the other hand, we see that a grammatical component-proposition that contains such words or letters does not express a thought if the generality brought about by them is not supposed to be restricted to this component-proposition. In such a case, the grammatical component-proposition does not say anything; it is merely a pseudo-proposition. We can say neither that it is valid nor that it is invalid – in so far as we call a proposition invalid when it expresses a false thought.

To be sure, '$a^2 = 1$' contains something having a meaning, and its meaning is the concept *square root of 1*. However, what designates this concept is not the whole '$a^2 = 1$', but only that part of it which remains when we detach '*a*'. Similarly for '$a^4 = 1$'.

In general, we may say that neither an antecedent nor a consequent pseudo-proposition expresses a thought or sense, although both are parts of a propositional complex that does express a thought, and though both may have components that have a sense.

Moreover, the use of the letter '*a*' in such cases is fundamentally the same as that in the proposition

$$a^2 - 1 = (a - 1) \times (a + 1)$$

Here, too, it is supposed to lend generality of content to the proposition. The fact that in the first case we have two grammatical propositions whereas here we have only one is merely an inconsequential difference of form.

Insight into the logical nature of a mathematical theory is frequently made more difficult by the fact that what really ought to be represented as a unitary propositional complex is torn apart into apparently independent grammatical propositions. This often happens for stylistic reasons, in order to avoid a propositional monstrosity; but this cannot be permitted to obstruct one's insight into the nature of the case. For example, one begins like this: 'Let *a* be ...' – a locution in place of which the incorrect 'Let *a* refer to ...' is of course frequently preferred.

Such propositions with different letters may in part precede the derivation, in part be inserted into it. Thus one finally arrives at a conclusion that is expressed in one proposition containing the letters that had apparently been explained previously; for propositions like 'Let a refer to ...' look like explanations that are supposed to give references to the letters. This appearance, however, vanishes upon closer examination. Let us take an example! The propositional complex 'If a is a whole number, then $(a \times (a-1))$ is an even number' can be divided into two apparently independent propositions: | 'Let a be a whole 380 number. $(a \times (a-1))$ is an even number.' But the first proposition cannot be considered an explanation of the letter 'a' such that this 'a' together with the meaning thus acquired occurs in the second proposition; for this 'a' occurs in both propositions in place of a proper name. Therefore if it were to be given a meaning, it could only be that of a proper name, i.e. an object. This, however, cannot come about by means of the proposition 'Let a be a whole number', because this is not an identity-proposition but rather a subsumption-proposition. We cannot even say that although 'a' is not given a determinate meaning, nevertheless it is given an indeterminate one – for an indeterminate meaning is not a meaning. There must be no ambiguous signs. The following consideration also shows that an antecedent pseudo-proposition should not be taken as an explanation of a letter occurring in it. For the proposition above can be brought into the form 'If $(a \times (a-1))$ is not an even number, then a is not a whole number.' If we were to treat this proposition as before, we should end up considering the proposition 'Let $(a \times (a-1))$ not be an even number' as an explanation of the latter 'a'; and this would contradict our first explanation. Therefore we must not let ourselves be deceived by the fact that for stylistic reasons, an antecedent pseudo-proposition occasionally occurs in such a form that upon cursory examination it appears to be an explanation of one or more letters. For in fact neither these putative explanations nor the proposition in which the conclusion is asserted are real propositions. Rather, being antecedent and consequent pseudo-propositions, they belong inseparably together, so that only the whole constituted of them is a real proposition. It would greatly facilitate insight into logical structure if what is a single real proposition according to its subject matter were also a unitary propositional complex according to its grammar and did not break down into independent propositions. To be sure, in our word-languages such a propositional complex would sometimes attain a monstrous length, whereas, because of its perspicuous nature, conceptual notation is better suited to the representation of the logical fabric.

The use of letters is actually the same in all of these cases, however different it may seem. They are always supposed to lend generality of content to the whole, even when this whole consists of apparently independent propositions. Of course, words like 'something' and 'it' may also occur in place of these letters.

A system of general theorems that coincide in their antecedent pseudo-propositions may be called a theory. Since the consequent pseudo-propositions may be conjoined into a single one by the use of 381   'and', at least theoretically there exists the possibility | of changing the theory into a single theorem consisting of antecedent pseudo-propositions and one – generally composite – consequent pseudo-proposition. This theorem can be given generality of content by letters or appropriate words. The antecedent pseudo-propositions are what are sometimes called presuppositions.

Now we can pass from the general to the particular by means of an inference. So, for example, we can get from the proposition

$$a^2 - 1 = (a - 1) \times (a + 1)$$

to the proposition

$$5^2 - 1 = (5 - 1) \times (5 + 1);$$

and from the proposition

$$\text{If } a^2 = 1, \text{ then } a^4 = 1$$

to the proposition

$$\text{If } 1^2 = 1, \text{ then } 1^4 = 1$$

or even to the proposition

$$\text{If } 2^2 = 1, \text{ then } 2^4 = 1$$

As we can see, the external procedure here is to replace the letter that merely indicates by a sign with meaning. And similarly in other cases: in an inference from the general to the particular, the indicating letters or words are replaced by ones with meaning. General affirmative or negative propositions must first be brought into the conditional form. From the second example we see that the pseudo-propositions '$a^2 = 1$' and '$a^4 = 1$' thus yield the real propositions '$1^2 = 1$' and '$1^4 = 1$', or even the real propositions '$2^2 = 1$' and '$2^4 = 1$'. That the latter are invalid is another matter. In the conditional context in which they occur, neither of them is asserted – even if the whole propositional complex should be expressed with assertive force. Thus we see that to the pseudo-propositions that are parts of a general theorem – of a theory – there correspond real propositions which occur in a proposition derived from the theorem by an inference from the general to the particular. If one of the propositions that occurs as an antecedent proposition is already recognized as valid, it may be omitted. Thus in the proposition 'If $1^2 = 1$, then $1^4 = 1$', the antecedent proposition may be left out once it is recognized as valid, so that we are left only with the consequent proposition '$1^4 = 1$'. In words, the transition may be expressed like this: 'Since $1^2 = 1$, therefore $1^4 = 1$'. By means of such inferences we can get from a general theorem – a theory – to a particular proposition containing fewer antecedent-propositions. This procedure is of course called | the application of a general theorem – a theory – to a 382 particular case.

Perhaps, then, what Mr. Korselt calls a formal theory or purely formal system is a general theorem or theory in the sense in which I have just used these words. It would seem that Mr. Korselt has at least something like this in mind. I venture to say that much of his exposition will seem clearer if, when reading it, we bear in mind what has just been said. He writes: 'But modern mathematics, which more and more shades into exact logic, no longer designates by its axioms (base assertions) certain empirical facts – but at best *indicates* them; just as in algebra, a letter does not determine a number but merely indicates it.'

It seems that Mr. Korselt has borrowed this usage of the word 'indicate' from me. The comparison of axioms with letters is unfortunate, since in pure mathematics it is all one whether I use the letters '*a*', '*b*', '*c*' or the letters '*r*', '*s*', '*t*': each of the letters is considered to be simple. On the other hand, each Hilbertian axiom is apparently supposed to have its own peculiarity which is based on its particular construction out of simple signs that can also occur in other combinations. On the other hand, the comparison of one Hilbertian axiom with a pseudo-proposition such as '$a^2 = 1$' does not seem to be inappropriate. What Mr. Korselt probably has in mind I should express in the following way:

Present-day mathematics – or let us just say, Mr. Hilbert – understands by an axiom not a real proposition which expresses a thought, but a pseudo-proposition from which, by an inference from the general to the particular, several real propositions can emerge which then do express thoughts.

My 'expressing of thoughts' here corresponds to Mr. Korselt's 'designating certain empirical facts'. Thus Hilbertian axioms are parts of a general theorem that has a sense, although the parts themselves do not. And it is only as parts of a whole having a sense that those axioms

L

are justified. They appear as antecedent propositions, or as we may also say, as presuppositions. And with this the following assertion by Mr. Korselt agrees very nicely:

> Nor is it the case that 'the ontological argument for the existence of God is brilliantly vindicated' by the axiom 'On every straight line there are at least two points'. For the former is intended to *prove* existence; the axiom *presupposes* it for all or at least some of the propositions that follow from it. In fact, the 'existence-propositions' of exact logic and mathematics are no more than | presuppositions of certain conditional propositions in whose 'assertion' certain concepts mentioned in the existence-propositions no longer occur.

383

While not agreeing with every word, I nevertheless can detect in this some corroboration of what I have just conjectured. An axiom presupposes existence for all or some of the propositions that follow from it. Very well! Then it is inseparable from them. Neither the axiom nor the propositions that follow have a sense of their own; rather, the axiom is an antecedent pseudo-proposition and these propositions that follow are consequent pseudo-propositions; and these pseudo-propositions together form one or several real propositions whose parts they are. For even Mr. Korselt himself talks about antecedent propositions – these are the antecedent and consequent pseudo-propositions.

Of course, no refutation of my earlier view can be found in this. When Mr. Korselt deviates in his usage of the words 'axiom' and 'definition' from mine and attempts to construct a refutation on the basis of this, then he refutes something I have not said. One can give the appearance of refuting any proposition whatever if one takes the liberty of understanding the words in such a way that the proposition loses its import.

My train of thought was the following: If in the definition of a concept of the first level it is permitted to mention existence as a characteristic, then this may also be done in the definition of the concept *God* which is of the first level; in which case the existence of God would immediately follow. Now according to Mr. Hilbert's understanding of the matter, the axiom in question is part of the definition of a point, and existence is mentioned in it as a characteristic. Consequently *that* right is claimed, which in another case would permit the ontological argument. By pointing this out, I intended to induce Mr. Hilbert to reflect about what he calls a definition. I assumed that he would recognize that his use of the word is completely different from the customary one, and that he would perhaps go the way on which

Mr. Korselt seems to have embarked, albeit without a clear understanding. Of course, this clarification and development for which I wanted to provide the impetus apparently did not come about at all in the case of Mr. Hilbert, and only incompletely in the case of Mr. Korselt. A definition in the traditional sense does not presuppose anything, but rather stipulates something. What I have said holds true if we understand the word 'definition' as it has traditionally been understood in mathematics, and even if an axiom is part of a definition, | as Mr. Hilbert wants it.[2] Now it is possible that Mr. Hilbert's 384 procedure is nevertheless justified for a different sense of the word 'definition'; but which sense are we to assume here? Let us try to get clear about this with the help of Mr. Korselt's pronouncements! To begin with, what Mr. Hilbert calls the definition of a point is certainly not a definition in the old sense of the word. Furthermore, the definition consists of axioms. These presuppose something and therefore undoubtedly are antecedent propositions, and pseudo-propositions at that. This close connection into which the words 'axiom' and 'definition' have thus been forced is quite foreign to their original usage. Therefore a definition, when understood in this sense, is no more than a whole consisting of several axioms connected by 'and', where the latter themselves are pseudo-propositions (antecedent propositions). But then, no longer is there any real difference between a definition and an axiom. In which case a definition, too, would be an antecedent pseudo-proposition consisting of several pseudo-propositions connected by 'and'. It is immaterial whether several of the antecedent propositions are first combined into a whole which is then taken as an antecedent proposition, or whether the antecedent propositions are left uncombined. We can see that in such a case, the so-called definitions are superfluous.

But let us investigate whether our conjecture about the nature of purely formal systems is further confirmed! Mr. Korselt writes, '"Arithmeticized", or better, "rationalized" mathematics merely arranges its principles in such a way that certain known interpretations are not excluded.'

Here the principles will again be the antecedent pseudo-propositions of the general theorem. The word 'interpretation' is objectionable, for when properly expressed, a thought leaves no room for different interpretations. We have seen that ambiguity simply has to be rejected and how it may appear to be necessary because of insufficient logical

---

[2] Of course a principle in the old sense of the term neither presupposes nor stipulates something; rather, it asserts something. I use the term 'principle' for any proposition that expresses an axiom.

insight. I merely recall what I have said about the use of letters above, on p. 377. On the basis of our understanding of the nature of Mr. Korselt's purely formal system it is easy to guess what Mr. Korselt means by 'interpretation'. When we proceed from the general theorem 'If $a>1$, then $a^2>1$' to the particular one 'If $2>1$, then $2^2>1$' by means of an inference, then the pseudo-proposition '$a>1$' corresponds to the proper proposition '$2>1$'. According to Mr. Korselt's usage, '$2>1$' or the | thought of this proposition will be an interpretation of '$a>1$'. As if the general proposition were a wax nose which we could turn now this way, now that. In reality, we have not an interpretation but an inference.[3]

In a pseudo-proposition there must occur signs that do not designate anything but merely indicate. Which signs are these in the present case? Clearly the words 'point', 'straight line', 'lies in ', 'lies on', 'lies between', etc. Therefore if, as Mr. Korselt would have it, Hilbertian geometry is a purely formal system, and if we have grasped the meaning of this expression correctly, then in Hilbertian geometry these words do not designate anything at all. And in fact, Mr. Korselt actually does say that the signs of formal theories have no meaning whatever. Therefore the words 'point', 'plane', etc. are supposed to serve the purpose of lending generality of content to the theorem, as do the letters in algebra. And this once more agrees very well with what we determined above, namely that Hilbertian so-called definitions do not give meanings to these words. We also see it confirmed that these so-called definitions are not definitions, any more than the pseudo-proposition '$a>1$' in the proposition 'If $a>1$, then $a^2>1$' is a definition. Letters intended to lend generality of content to a proposition receive no explanation, for they are not supposed to designate but merely to indicate. Since letters are not supposed to be given meanings, defi-

385

---

[3]We may take this opportunity to illuminate the following pronouncement by Mr. Korselt: 'Propositions having the same wording should, if possible, be proved only once, even if they appear in different disciplines'.

As if it were permissible to have different propositions with the same wording! This contradicts the rule of unambiguousness, the most important rule that logic must impose on written or spoken language. If propositions having the same wording differ, they can do so only in their thought-content. Just how could there be a single proof of different thoughts? This looks as though what is proved is the wording alone, without the thought-content; and as though afterwards different thoughts were then supposed to be correlated with this wording in the different disciplines. Rubbish! A mere wording without a thought-content can never be proved. What Mr. Korselt has in mind is, of course, the case where what is to be proved is a general proposition from which the propositions belonging to the different disciplines are derived by means of an inference from the general to the particular (or the less general). Here, too, we must expect to hear Mr. Korselt talk of interpretation.

nitions, whose purpose would be to given them, are here out of place. Sometimes what looks like an explanation of letters is really an antecedent proposition. And likewise in the present case. The words 'point' 'plane', etc. are used here like letters. | What looks like an 386 explanation of these words is an antecedent pseudo-proposition. Considered as a definition, it does not meet even the most modest requirements which a definition must meet. Since the term 'antecedent proposition' is quite sufficient, I cannot see why the misleading words 'definition' and 'axiom', which traditionally have a different usage, should be used instead. What Mr. Hilbert calls a definition will in most cases be an antecedent pseudo-proposition, a dependent part of a general theorem.

Given this conception, it is not only pointless and inappropriate to demand of a formal theory that it give a determinate meaning to its figures, which are formed on the model of proper names and concept-words; it is nonsensical to demand any meaning of them at all. For they are not supposed to be designating, but merely indicating signs.

I do demand the solvability of a system of principles as to the unknowns occurring in it, and an unambiguous solution, if this system of so-called principles is supposed to be a definition that assigns references to the unknown signs. For this purpose can be achieved only when this demand is met. But in no way do I require that one should define everything. I certainly do not require that in order to define something, one construct a system of so-called principles. Least of all do I require that one explain signs which, like letters, are used only in an indicating capacity and not as having meaning; for that would be to demand nonsense.

Now when proceeding from a general theorem to a particular one by means of an inference, to every pseudo-proposition which is part of the former there corresponds a real one in the latter. These real propositions may indeed be principles – expressions of axioms – in the old and proper sense of that word. Since the axioms of Euclidean geometry are true, we may omit them wherever they occur as conditions. We then have made an application of the general theorem and have thus arrived at a proposition of Euclidean geometry. But other applications are also possible; Mr. Korselt mistakenly calls them interpretations.

We now understand how Mr. Hilbert's peculiar confusion in the use of the word 'axiom' came about. The expression was transferred from real propositions to the pseudo-propositions which correspond to them. Through this misuse and that | of the word 'definition', insight into the 387 logical nature of Hilbertian geometry has been made inordinately more difficult.

Let us continue in our investigation of Mr. Korselt's pronouncements! There we read, 'In this way, *one* sequence of formal inferences can sometimes be "interpreted" in *different* ways'.

What can be interpreted is perhaps a sign or a group of signs, although the univocity of the signs – which we must retain at all cost – excludes different interpretations. But an inference does not consist of signs. We can only say that in the transition from one group of signs to a new group of signs, it may look now and then as though we are presented with an inference. An inference simply does not belong to the realm of signs; rather, it is the pronouncement of a judgement made in accordance with logical laws on the basis of previously passed judgements. Each of the premises is a determinate thought recognized as true; and in the conclusion, too, a determinate thought is recognized as true. There is here no room for different interpretations.

What is a formal inference? We may say that in a certain sense, every inference is formal in that it proceeds according to a general law of inference; in another sense, every inference is non-formal in that the premises as well as the conclusions have their thought-contents which occur in this particular manner of connection only in that inference. But perhaps the word 'formal' is here supposed to be understood differently. Perhaps a series of formal inferences is not supposed to be a proper inference-chain but only the schema of one. Its interpretation would then consist in indicating an inference-chain that would proceed according to this schema. Now of what use is such a schema? Perhaps this, that in a given case we do not have to go through the whole inference-chain, but instead can pass directly from the first premises to the last consequent proposition. But then we no longer have a mere schema, but a general theorem.

Consider, for example, the following schema:

a is a *b*; every *b* is a *c*; therefore *a* is a *c*; therefore there is a *c*!

Here we obviously do not have an inference, for we do not have real propositions – no thoughts. But a chain of inferences can proceed according to this schema, and in accordance with the double occurrence of 'therefore' it would consist of two inferences. The schema itself says nothing, but it provides the occasion for constructing propositions that do say something. To begin with the following: |

388   If *a* is a *b*, and if every *b* is a *c*, then *a* is a *c*; If *a* is a *c*, then there is a *c*.

By means of an inference, we obtain from these the general theorem,

If *a* is a *b*, and if every *b* is a *c*, then there is a *c*.

In a given case, instead of proceeding in accordance with the schema of the inference-chain, we can use the general theorem in such a way that by means of an inference from the general to the particular we deduce from it a proposition which we can free from the conditions that have now been fulfilled. That, after all, is generally the use of a theorem: It keeps the result of a series of inferences ready for use whenever we wish. In this way we have again been led to something which Mr. Korselt probably calls a formal theory or a purely formal system.

But let us leave these abstract considerations and see how all this manifests itself in the Hilbertian theory itself. If, as we have assumed, the words 'point', 'straight line', etc. do not designate but merely are to lend generality, like the letters in arithmetic, then it will be conducive to our insight into the true state of affairs to actually use letters for this purpose. Let us therefore stipulate the following: Instead of 'the point A lies in the plane α', let us say, 'A stands in the p-relation to α'. Instead of 'the point A lies on the straight line a', let us say 'A stands in the q-relation to a.' Instead of 'A is a point', let us say, 'A is a Π'.

Hilbert Axiom I.1 can now be expressed like this:

If A is a Π and if B is a Π, then there is something to which both A and B stand in the q-relation.

We must distinguish here between two generalities. The one engendered by the letters 'A' and 'B' is confined to this pseudo-axiom;[4] while the one engendered by 'Π' and 'q' extends to a general theorem (purely formal system, formal theory) of which this pseudo-axiom is only a dependent part that is without meaning on its own. |

Hilbert Axiom I.6 (I.5)[5] can be expressed like this: 389

If A is different from B, if A and B stand in the p-relation to α, and if A, B, and C stand in the q-relation to a, then C stands in the p-relation to α.

The generality engendered by the letters 'A', 'B', 'C', 'a', and 'α' is limited to this pseudo-axiom.

Hilbert Axiom I.7 (I.6)[5] now looks like this.

[4]This expression may occasion objections. One could say that generality, after all, belongs to the thought-content of a proposition; hence how can there be talk of it here, in the case of a pseudo-proposition that does not even express a thought? It is to be understood in this way: the generality engendered by 'A' and 'B' is supposed to apply to the content of every real proposition arising out of this pseudo-axiom by replacing the letters 'Π' and 'q', which merely indicate, by determinate signs.

[5]What is in parentheses refers to the first edition.

If A stands in the p-relation to both α and β, then there exists something distinct from A which stands in the p-relation to both α and β.

The generality engendered by the letters 'A', 'α', and 'β' is limited to this pseudo-axiom.

We still need a pseudo-axiom Σ, which Mr. Hilbert does not have and which we express like this:

Σ. If A stands in the p-relation to α, then A is a Π.

Here the generality engendered by the letters 'A' and 'α' is limited to this pseudo-axiom. The letters 'Π', 'p', and 'q' neither mean anything, nor are they supposed to lend generality to the content of the particular pseudo-axioms; wherefore the latter, taken in themselves, do not express thoughts but are without sense. It is because of this that I add the 'pseudo'. For in the case of proper principles we must have thoughts. To be sure, the letters 'Π', 'p', and 'q' are supposed to engender generality, but the latter is supposed to extend over a theorem whose antecedent pseudo-propositions are these pseudo-axioms.

It seems to me that one advantage in recasting the Hilbert pseudo-axioms in this way is immediately apparent; namely, that no one will imagine that he understands such a pseudo-axiom, or that he finds a thought expressed in it. In reality, however, nothing essential has been changed by the use of letters in place of the expressions 'point', 'lies in', 'lies on'. At least, not as long as these expressions do not mean anything, but like the letters, merely lend generality to the purely formal system, to use Mr. Korselt's phrase.[6] Therefore if these pseudo-axioms, when recast in the Hilbertian form, give the appearance of having a sense, then clearly this is because being familiar with Euclidean geometry, we are | used to associating a sense with the words 'point', 'lies in', etc., and because we do not forget the latter as we should when concerning ourselves with Mr. Hilbert's 'Foundations'. As a matter of fact, we must here assume the outlook of someone who has never heard anything of points, planes, etc.; and in this we are not very successful. We have much better success with signs with which we in fact have not as yet associated a sense. The two cases are, however, essentially the same.

From the fact that the pseudo-axioms do not express thoughts, it further follows that they cannot be premises of an inference-chain. Of

390

[6]But even if Mr. Hilbert's axioms were supposed to give meanings to the words 'point', etc., nothing essential would be changed, for these very meanings would now be given to the letters 'Π', etc. If these letters do not obtain a reference by this move, then neither do the words.

course, one really cannot call propositions – groups of audible or visible signs – premises anyway, but only the thoughts expressed by them. Now in the case of the pseudo-axioms, there are no thoughts at all, and consequently no premises. Therefore when it appears that Mr. Hilbert nevertheless does use his axioms as the premises of inferences and apparently bases proofs on them, these can be inferences and proofs in appearance only.

Now we could try the following move. The inferences may be conducted purely formally, as if the letters 'Π', '*p*', and '*q*' did have meaning; for after all, what they might mean is all one so far as the correctness of the inference is concerned. If for these letters we now substitute signs that actually have meaning of such a kind that true propositions thereby emerge from the pseudo-axioms, then a true proposition will emerge from the so-called consequent proposition as well.

Let us try this with an example. First, from our pseudo-axioms I.1 and Σ we derive the pseudo-proposition

> If A as well as B stands in the p-relation to α, then there is something to which A as well as B stands in the q-relation.   (A)

Furthermore, by combining I.6 with itself, we derive the pseudo-proposition

> If A is different from B, and if A as well as B stands in the p-relation to α as well as to β; and if A, B, and C stand in the q-relation to a, then C stands in the p-relation to α as well as to β.   (B)

From this we further derive the pseudo-proposition

> If A is different from B, and A as well as B stands in the p-relation to α as well as to β, and if there exists something to which A as well as B stands in the q-relation, then there is an object such that whatever stands in the q-relation | to it stands in the p-relation to α as well as to β.   (Γ)   391

From this and (A), which was just derived above, we then obtain the pseudo-proposition

> If A is different from B, and A as well as B stands in the p-relation to α as well as to β, then there is an object such that whatever stands in the q-relation to it stands in the p-relation to α as well as to β.   (Δ)

From this we further infer the pseudo-proposition

If *A* stands in the *p*-relation to α as well as to β, and if there is something distinct from *A* such that it stands in the *p*-relation to α as well as to β, then there is an object such that whatever stands in the *q*-relation to it stands in the *p*-relation to α as well as to β.   (E)

When we combine our pseudo-axiom I.7 with this, we obtain

If *A* stands in the *p*-relation to α as well as to β, then there is an object such that whatever stands in the *q*-relation to it stands in the *p*-relation to α as well as to β.   (Z)

And from this we further obtain the pseudo-proposition

If there is something that stands in the *p*-relation to both α and β, then there is an object such that whatever stands in the *q*-relation to it stands in the *p*-relation to α as well as to β.   (H)

In Mr. Hilbert's writings, we find the following wording for the above:

Two planes have either no point or a straight line in common.

Without becoming exercised over the fact that our wording is significantly longer than Hilbert's, let us ask whether what we have just constructed is really an inference-chain. Clearly not; for the links are only pseudo-propositions, as is the consequent proposition. Not one of them contains a thought. But if instead of our letters we were to use Hilbert's words 'point', 'lies in', etc., the propositions we should thus obtain would not have a sense either – assuming, of course, that these words are to have no more sense than do our letters. But then, what is the point of all these merely apparent inferences? What is the point of going through all these pseudo-propositions if the proposition that we finally arrive at is as much without sense as the preceding ones? Well, let us recall that although pseudo-propositions by themselves do not express thoughts, nevertheless they may be constituents of a whole that does have a sense. We cannot treat our pseudo-axioms as independent propositions that contain true thoughts and hence can serve as the foundations of our logical constructions; rather, we must carry them along as antecedent | pseudo-propositions. Therefore, instead of our pseudo-proposition (*A*), we now have to write:

392

If it holds universally of *A* and α that if *A* stands in the *p*-relation to α, then *A* is a Π;

and if it holds universally of *A* and *B* that

> if *A* is a Π and if *B* is a Π, then there is something to which both *A* and *B* stand in the *q*-relation;

then it holds universally of *A*, *B*, and α that

> if *A* as well as *B* stands in the *p*-relation to α, then there is something to which *A* as well as *B* stands in the *q*-relation.

The preceding is a proposition that does express a thought; nor do we find more than one thought in it. Those parts of it that present themselves grammatically as propositions are merely pseudo-propositions. The letters 'Π', '*p*', '*q*' lend generality of content to the whole proposition, while the generality effected by the letters '*A*', '*B*', 'α' is always restricted to one of the indented component pseudo-propositions.[7] From this it becomes apparent how the component pseudo-propositions, although senseless in and by themselves, nevertheless can form a proposition that expresses a thought.

Similarly, in order to obtain real propositions we shall have to supplement the remaining pseudo-propositions that occur in the apparent inference-chain with our pseudo-axioms as antecedent propositions. From our merely apparent inference-chain, we obtain a real one. Only then do we have real premises and real consequent propositions. Thus in the end our consequent pseudo-proposition (H) will also have to be supplemented by our four pseudo-axioms, which will appear here as antecedent pseudo-propositions. And thus we shall obtain a consequent proposition that really does contain a thought. To be sure, this consequent proposition will be rather lengthy, but it is only through such supplementation that we obtain complete insight into the logical connection. Therefore let us not be distressed by the amount of effort involved in constructing such a proposition, for it appears that many confusions in mathematics are caused by an unnecessary economy with printer's ink and by false elegance. The principle of achieving as much as possible with the least possible means, if correctly understood, is certainly to be applauded; only the means must not be gauged by the consumption of printer's ink. In place of our previous pseudo-proposition (H), we now obtain the following consequent proposition: |

If it holds universally of *A* and α that   393

> if *A* stands in the *p*-relation to α, then *A* is a Π,

---

[7]Cf. note 4 above.

and if it holds universally of *A* and *B* that

> If *A* is a Π and *B* is a Π, then there is something to which both *A* and *B* stand in the *q*-relation;

also, if it holds universally of *A*, *B*, *C*, *a*, and α that

> if *A* is distinct from *B*, if *A* and *B* stand in the *p*-relation to α, and if *A*, *B*, and *C* stand in the *q*-relation to *a*, then *C* stands in the *p*-relation to α;

furthermore, if it holds universally of *A*, α and *β* that

> if *A* stands in the *p*-relation to α as well as *β*, then there is something distinct from *A* that stands in the *p*-relation to both α and *β*;

then it holds universally of α and *β* that

> if there is something that stands in the *p*-relation to both α and *β*, then there is an object such that whatever stands in the *q*-relation to it stands in the *p*-relation to both α and *β*.

The indented pseudo-propositions are in part our pseudo-axioms and in part our previous consequent pseudo-proposition, and we can see they are merely dependent parts of the real consequent proposition which alone expresses a thought. The generality effected by the letters '*A*', '*B*', '*C*', '*a*', 'α', and '*β*' is in each case restricted to the indented component pseudo-proposition in which they occur; while the generality effected by 'Π', '*p*' and '*q*' extends to the whole proposition. We now see what really has been proved. This is not at all evident from Mr. Hilbert's consequent proposition:

> Two planes have either no point or a straight line in common.

For here, unless we are to understand the words in the Euclidean sense, just about everything is unknown.

Let us continue to examine Mr. Korselt's expositions as to whether or not they agree with our conception of his formal theory. Thus, on p. 403 we read, 'We must therefore distinguish between those formal theories ("purely formal systems") that can be related to other experiences and those for which as yet no such correlation is known.'

What Mr. Korselt here calls 'relating to other experiences' and 'correlation' is evidently the same as what he previously had called 'interpreting' and 'interpretation', and is nothing but an inference | from the general to the particular. Therefore, if by means of such an inference it is possible to go from a general theorem to a particular one of such a kind that the antecedent propositions in it which correspond to the antecedent pseudo-propositions of the general proposition are real and indeed valid propositions, then Mr. Korselt will say that the formal theory (our general theorem) can be related to other experiences; that it can be correlated to other experiences. This would also seem to be the objectiveness of which he speaks in the following: 'The "object-iveness" and above all the consistency of a purely formal system is always and necessarily demonstrated by exhibiting objects of which the basic assertions hold.'

We can now understand this somewhat. For example, let the following be a general theorem (a formal theory, a formal system):

If *a* is a square root of 1, then *a* is a fourth root of 1.

By means of an inference from the general to the particular, we derive from it the following:

If 1 is a square root of 1, then 1 is a fourth root of 1.

And according to Mr. Korselt's manner of speaking, we are herewith presented with an object, to wit 1, of which the basic assertion holds. For after all, 1 is a square root of 1. And in Mr. Korselt's words, with this the objectiveness and, even more, the consistency of our purely formal system has been proved. In the previously considered example taken from Hilbert's geometry, matters are of course not quite so simple, since not just one but several antecedent pseudo-propositions occur, and because not just one but three letters ('Π', '*p*', '*q*') appear. Furthermore we have this difference, that these letters do not indicate objects – or, as we could also say, stand in for proper names – but partly concepts, partly relations. Consequently, since these so-called basic assertions cannot fit objects, it cannot be objects that are presented here but only a concept and relations. However, an inference from the general to the particular is possible in this way: that 'point' stands in the place of 'Π', 'lies in the plane' stands in the place of 'stands in the *p*-relation to', 'lies on the straight line' stands in the place of 'stands in the *q*-relation to', where these expressions are to be understood in the Euclidean sense. From our pseudo-axioms we thus derive real principles which do express axioms; | and this is the 395 presentation of a concept and relations by means of which, in Mr. Korselt's words, the objectiveness[8] of our purely formal system (general theorem) is proved. At this point however, it must be emphasized that our theorem has been proved and is true quite independently of the

[8]Of course, this word is not quite appropriate in the present context.

proof of this so-called objectiveness. What Mr. Korselt says is therefore quite correct: we should not from the very start demand objectiveness of a purely formal system. The following statement also somehow hits the mark, even though in it there seems to have occurred a confusion to which we shall have to return later: 'Even if we then call the latter (the purely formal system) "an empty playing with words, signifying nothing" and the like, as a strictly lawlike connection of propositions, it has no further need of any special "dignity".'

Indeed, a general theorem needs no greater dignity than that accruing to it because it expresses a true thought. The only thing to which I take exception here is the expression 'of propositions'. By a real proposition I understand the expression of a thought, and therefore something sensible: a sequence of words that can be heard, or a group of signs that can be seen. This last holds true even of pseudo-propositions. A concatenation of real and pseudo-propositions will belong to a grammar. Mr. Korselt does not distinguish strictly between the external or sensible, and the thought-content. In the present case, he probably means a concatenation of thoughts. But even this cannot be what is presently at issue; for here we have pseudo-propositions, none of which have a sense. Therefore what is meant here needs still more accurate expression, where it would of course be necessary to coin a new phrase.

As for the rest, I agree with it, particularly with the claim that objectiveness in the sense previously indicated is not necessary to ensure a thought-content for the proposition. Matters would of course lie differently if the words 'point', 'lying in', etc. were not to be used indicatively to lend generality to the content of a proposition, as are letters, but rather were to be used as concept- and relation-words with a meaning. In that case, of course, there would have to be a concept that would be designated by the word 'point' and a relation that would be designated by the expression 'lies in'.

But it seems to me that here a confusion obtains. The charge of being an empty playing with signs may justifiably be levelled against certain formal theories; these, however, are quite different from general | theorems of the kind considered here. For in the latter we always have a sense. Those other formal theories, however, proceed after the manner of Dr. Ironbeard.[9] Since the sense occasions difficulties now and then, it is simply exorcised. What remains is of course the inanimate sign. The originator of such a theory does not want to express thoughts with his

396

---

[9][Dr. Ironbeard – *Eisenbart* in German – is the traditional German figure of a quack who effects cures no matter what, even at the price of killing the patient. Hence the expression, 'nach der Methode des Dr. Eisenbarts verfahren'. (*Tr.*)]

signs, but merely wants to play with them according to certain rules. Consequently, it cannot be truth that is here at issue. The word 'theory' is really quite inappropriate; we ought to say 'game'. At least, it would be so if the execution of the enterprise were consistent. But this is never the case: the theorists want to have their cake and eat it too. They empty the signs so as to escape inconvenient questions; but then they refuse to acknowledge that the signs are really empty. Thus they become entangled in a thicket of contradictions. What we have hitherto called a formal theory is something quite different. To be sure, we also use signs that have no meaning, but they contribute to the expression of thoughts in the familiar way. To express a thought by using letters alone and not using any signs with meaning is impossible. In those unacceptable so-called formal theories, signs like '1/2', '$\sqrt[3]{5}$' neither are proper names with meaning, as is usually the case, nor serve to lend generality of content to a proposition, as do the letters. They are not means of understanding and communication; rather, they are objects with which one plays according to certain rules. Mr. Korselt confounds these two quite distinct cases because he has not clearly understood the peculiarity of either. He finds a thought expressed in an arrangement of chess pieces. Perhaps he has some mental equipment for grasping thoughts that I lack. Does a whole new realm of thoughts here open up before us? Very interesting! But I cannot quell certain misgivings. If Mr. Korselt means that an arrangement of chess pieces expresses a thought merely because of the rules of chess, then I question this and shall continue to question it until I am presented with this thought as expressed in ordinary language and am shown how, in virtue of the rules of chess, this thought is expressed by that arrangement. After all, laying down rules for the use of chess pieces and stipulating the meaning of a sign are at first glance two quite distinct things. If someone really thinks that under certain conditions the former could be combined with the latter, then he has to prove this. To my knowledge, however, no one has as yet even tried to do so. |

If an axiom contains a hitherto unknown sign, then according to Mr. 397 Korselt it is a rule for the use of this sign. If we cannot agree on the meaning of a sign, then we should acquire one or several more propositions about the sign or using the sign. From this Mr. Korselt concludes that '"The sign has no meaning" will therefore mean "We are not acquainted with any propositions regulating the use of this sign in general or for a given domain".' How he arrives at this conclusion escapes me, since nowhere in the preceding has there been any talk of regulating the use of a sign. But this much is clear: that in some admittedly mysterious way, such regulating is supposed to give a meaning to the sign. Let us take an example. The axiom 'Every anej bazes at least two ellah' regulates the use of the words 'anej', 'base', and 'ellah'. If in spite of this we nevertheless did not agree on the meaning of the word 'anej', this would be an indication that one of us should acquire more propositions about or using the word 'anej'. In such a case I should be more than happy to provide more propositions using the word 'anej'; and if necessary, even propositions about this word.

The rule 'Every anej bazes at least two ellah' deserves to be followed most conscientiously by all modern mathematicians. But I perceive a voice from the lower depths: 'How can that be a rule! After all, in a rule something must be demanded, ruled out, or permitted, I expect imperatives, or words like "must", "ought", "may", "is ruled out", etc. Nothing of the kind do I find in this so-called rule. It certainly seems as if what is being talked about is a concept designated by the word "anej". But if a rule about the use of the word "anej" is supposed to be found in this peculiar, proposition-like construction, then it is the word itself which is the subject of the discussion. Principles and theorems are propositions using a sign; rules are propositions about a sign.'

To this I should like to reply, 'How do you know, kind sir, that the word "rule" is being used here in the sense familiar to you? And even if it is, it is quite understandable that in a sausage mixture such as the one we have before us, the peculiarity of a particular constituent is no longer clearly recognizable.'

At times Mr. Korselt takes unnecessary pains, e.g. in the case of the domain of application of the axioms. If an axiom is a rule about the use of the unknown signs occurring in it, then | the latter naturally form the domain of application of the rule and therefore of the axiom. Thus the question has been answered in the simplest terms.

If we use 'axiom' in the Euclidean sense, then contrary to what Mr. Korselt assumes, there cannot be invalid axioms. In the case before us, however, an invalid axiom containing unknown signs will be an invalid rule for the use of these signs. It would be impertinent to ask what purpose such a rule might serve.

Herewith we shall leave these so-called rules and what is connected with them. If we strike it from Mr. Korselt's expositions, we free them of confusions.

As far as consistency and independence are concerned, it is Mr. Hilbert's opinion that they are to be proved of the axioms. Here there arises the question whether he means his pseudo-axioms or the axioms in the old Euclidean sense.

Mr. Korselt writes:

It is irrelevant whether it is the axioms or the characteristics of the concepts introduced that are said to be consistent. The former corresponds more closely to ordinary usage, according to which two propositions are called 'independent' of one another if under certain circumstances both, under other circumstances not both, obtain; whereas they are called 'incompatible' if there are no conditions under which both are satisfied together.

What does 'the proposition obtains' mean? Surely that the proposition expresses a true thought. Now a real proposition expresses a thought. The latter is either true or false: *tertium non datur*.[10] Therefore that a real proposition should obtain under certain circumstances and not under others could only be the case if a proposition could express one thought under certain circumstances and a different one under other circumstances. This, however, would contravene the demand that signs be unambiguous – a demand to which we must adhere under all circumstances, as has been argued at length above. A pseudo-proposition does not express a thought at all; consequently we cannot say that it obtains. Therefore it simply cannot happen that a proposition obtains under certain circumstances but not under others, whether it be a real proposition or a pseudo-proposition.[11] Still, we can guess | what Mr. Korselt means. It can concern only pseudo- 399 propositions, and here comes Mr. Korselt once again with his interpretations. He interprets a proposition like this, and it obtains; he interprets it otherwise, and it does not obtain. He turns the wax nose now to the right, now to the left, just as he pleases. For example, let us take the proposition 'On a straight line there are at least two points!' Now let us interpret the word 'point' as foot, the words 'straight line' as worm, and the words 'there are' as has. We then interpret our proposition thus: A worm has at least two feet. Almost as easily as we have here obtained something false, can we obtain something true from this proposition by means of different interpretations. We now see how right Mr. Korselt is when he says that a proposition may hold under some circumstances, but not under others; it simply all depends upon

---

[10]For we are here in the realm of science. In myth and fiction, of course, there may occur thoughts that are neither true nor false but just that: fiction.

[11]Even when Mr. Korselt says, 'But on the other hand, a formal theory may be applied to a given domain only if we have assured ourselves of the correctness of the principles for that domain', he seems to mean that one and the same proposition could hold in one domain but not in another. What Mr. Korselt means is expressed more precisely like this: 'If we have derived a particular proposition from a general one by an inference from the general to the particular, then we may omit the antecedent propositions in it if and only if these are valid.'

the interpretation. But let us stop joking. A proposition that holds only under certain circumstances is not a real proposition. However, we can express the circumstances under which it holds in antecedent propositions and add them as such to the proposition. So supplemented, the proposition will no longer hold only under certain circumstances but will hold quite generally. The original proposition appears in it as a consequent proposition; and as a pseudo-proposition at that. Well, however we may consider the matter, the upshot is one and the same: If we suppose that a proposition can hold under certain circumstances but not under others, then we allow ourselves to be led by the nose by self-induced inexactitudes of expression.

In the passage cited, Mr. Korselt says, 'It is irrelevant whether it is the axioms or the characteristics of the concepts introduced that are said to be consistent.'

To be sure, irrelevant for one who cares nothing for precision of expression and who is not concerned to get a deeper insight into the state of affairs. Axioms are simply not characteristics of concepts. Therefore from the very first the consistency of the axioms must be distinguished from the consistency of the concepts introduced. Whoever maintains that there is no difference must prove it. The mere assertion of Mr. Korselt does not suffice to establish this lack of difference as an assured tenet of science. '4^2' and '2^4' must first be distinguished; only after the coincidence of their references has been proved can they be interchanged. |

400   Mr. Korselt continues, 'The former corresponds more closely to ordinary usage, according to which two propositions are called "independent" of one another if under certain circumstances both, under other circumstances not both, obtain.'

Really? Is this ordinary usage? In the propositional complex 'If $a > 1$, then $a > 0$' we have two pseudo-propositions, '$a > 1$' and '$a > 0$'. Are these called independent of one another in ordinary usage? And yet according to Mr. Korselt's manner of speaking – which must of course be rejected – we have circumstances under which both hold ($2 > 1$ and $2 > 0$, $3 > 1$ and $3 > 0$), and other circumstances under which it is not the case that both hold ($1 > 1$ and $1 > 0$, $0 > 1$ and $0 > 0$). This much may perhaps be admitted, that according to ordinary usage '$a > 1$' is called independent of '$a > 0$'. But ordinary usage cannot decide anything for one who does not want to let himself be deceived by words but rather wants to get to the bottom of the matter. For there is always this question: Is ordinary usage appropriate to the occasion?

Therefore we cannot agree with Mr. Korselt's explanation of the independence of propositions for a variety of reasons. But this much is clear – that the former is only supposed to concern pseudo-propositions. Therefore according to the opinion of Mr. Korselt, the question of independence will concern not axioms in the Euclidean sense, but rather the pseudo-axioms of Mr. Hilbert. And in this he is probably quite correct, since real axioms very likely do not have a place in Mr. Hilbert's presentation at all.

What, then, are we really talking about when, for example, we call the propositions '$a>0$' and '$a>1$' independent of one another? Is it the groups of signs, irrespective of whether these signs have a sense? Of course not! On the other hand, neither the group of signs '$a>0$' '$a>1$' has a sense. Still, '$a>0$' is not completely divorced from all sense, since it can belong to a larger whole that does express a thought, and also because it itself contains a part with meaning. The largest part of '$a>0$' that still refers is the predicative one, and its meaning is the concept of a positive number. Similarly, the meaning of the largest part of '$a>1$' that still has meaning is the concept of a number smaller than 1. Now it may be conjectured that when it is apparently asserted of these propositions that they are independent of one another, something is really being said about these concepts. And indeed, one generally supposes that the first concept is not subordinate to the second, nor the second to the first. The point may also be expressed like this: 'Some positive numbers are not smaller than 1, and some numbers that are smaller than 1 are | not positive.' From this we can clearly see that we   401 are here concerned with relations between concepts.

A proposition in which, following Mr. Korselt's unquestionably imprecise usage, one proposition is presented as being dependent upon others, consists of a consequent pseudo-proposition and one or more antecedent pseudo-propositions. They are pseudo-propositions because in them occur constituents that do not designate anything but only indicate so as to lend generality of content to the whole proposition. This proposition, in so far as it holds true, will be what according to Mr. Korselt should be called a purely formal system or formal theory. But when this proposition does not hold and therefore independence rather than dependence obtains, the thought of the whole proposition is to be denied. Therefore a proposition in which an independence of this kind is asserted denies the validity of such a general proposition. Therefore the antecedent pseudo-propositions are not brought into relation with the consequent pseudo-propositions by a general proposition such as the preceding; nor even the thoughts that they might express, for there are none. Rather, what is brought into relation are the meanings of parts of the pseudo-propositions; and these parts do not express thoughts. What has just been said about general propositions also holds of their negations, i.e. of propositions in which, according to Mr. Korselt's usage, what is supposed to be asserted is the independence of one proposition from others. Therefore even this sort of proposition relates neither propositions nor thoughts, but instead relates the meanings of the parts of pseudo-propositions. It is these pseudo-propositions that are the pseudo-axioms of Mr. Hilbert's independence-proofs. From this it follows that the independence proved by Mr. Hilbert does not concern these pseudo-axioms.

When one uses the phrase 'prove a proposition' in mathematics, then by the word 'proposition' one clearly means not a sequence of words or a group of signs, but a thought; something of which one can say that it is true. And similarly, when one is talking about the independence of propositions or axioms, this, too, will be understood as being about the independence of thoughts. It is therefore not at all unnecessary to say that this conception is false and to reject the manner of speaking that gives rise to this misunderstanding.

We have to distinguish between the external, audible, or visible which is supposed to express a thought, and the thought itself. It seems to me that the usage prevalent in logic, according to which only the former is called a proposition, is preferable. Accordingly, we simply cannot say that one proposition is independent of other propositions; | for after all, no one wants to predicate this independence of what is audible or visible. Since pseudo-propositions, and hence also pseudo-axioms, have no thought-content, something can be asserted of them only when they are understood in the last sense recommended above; but it is precisely independence that cannot be predicated of them.

Summarizing our result, we may say this: Hilbert's independence-proofs concern neither the independence of propositions in the sense just recommended, nor the independence of thoughts. Rather, they concern the independence of the meanings of the parts of pseudo-propositions. These parts are the largest that still refer. But they are not propositions, and therefore do not express thoughts. We lack a short designation for the references of such parts, a designation covering all cases. In the simpler cases, we have concepts (*positive number, number smaller than 1*). Toward the end of my first essay[12] I accommodated my usage to one suggested in a letter by Mr. Hilbert and called them characteristics, although this does not quite agree with my own usage.

It must be noted that Mr. Hilbert's independence-proofs simply are not about real axioms, the axioms in the Euclidean sense; for these, surely, are thoughts. Now nowhere in Mr. Hilbert's writings do we find

402

---

[12]*Jahresbericht der Deutschen Mathematiker-Vereinigung* 12 (1903), pp. 323 and 324 [this volume pp. 277–8].

a differentiation that might correspond to our own between real and pseudo-propositions, between real and pseudo-axioms. Instead, Mr. Hilbert appears to transfer the independence putatively proved of his pseudo-axioms to the axioms proper, and that without more ado, because he simply fails to notice the difference between them. This would seem to constitute a considerable fallacy. And all mathematicians who think that Mr. Hilbert has proved the independence of the real axioms from one another have surely fallen into the same error. They do not see that in proving this independence, Mr. Hilbert is simply not using the word 'axiom' in the Euclidean sense. The fault here lies in the double usage of the words 'point', 'straight line', etc., which on the one hand, like letters, are to lend generality to the whole theory, in which case they do not designate anything; and on the other hand have their traditional references in the Euclidean axioms. In the former case his axioms are merely pseudo-axioms without sense, since only the whole (the formal theory, the purely formal system of Mr. Korselt) whose | dependent parts they are, has a sense – in which case the Euclidean 403 axiom of parallels simply does not occur, and consequently nothing is proved of it. In the other case real axioms do occur. But then these independence-proofs are inappropriate, since it is impossible to substitute other concept-words for 'point', 'straight line', etc. But surely it is on this very possibility that such a proof depends.

Even Mr. Korselt seems to have overlooked this complementary side of the matter when he emphasizes the difference of the axioms of modern mathematics from the Euclidean ones. This difference, after one has used its advantages in the beginning, cannot be denied in the final result.

The twilight which rules over Mr. Hilbert's presentation must first give way to uniform illumination before the matter can become clear. And then the mixing of axioms and definitions will also come to an end.

III

Now the question may still be raised whether, taking Mr. Hilbert's 423 result as a starting point, we might not arrive at a proof of the independence of the real axioms.

We must first ask what is here to be understood by 'independence'; for what is called independence in the case of pseudo-propositions – even if this is an inexactitude – cannot enter into consideration here. If we take the words 'point' and 'straight line' in Mr. Hilbert's so-called

Axiom II.1 in the proper Euclidean sense, and similarly the words 'lie' and 'between', then we obtain a proposition that has a sense, and we can acknowledge the thought expressed therein as a real axiom. Let us designate it by '[II.1]'. Let [II.2] emerge in a similar way from Mr. Hilbert's II.2. Now if one has acknowledged [II.1] as true, one has grasped the sense of the words 'point', 'straight line', 'lie', 'between'; and from this the truth of [II.2] immediately follows, so that one will be unable to avoid acknowledging the latter as well. Thus one could call [II.2] dependent upon [II.1]. Of course, we do not have an inference here; and it seems inexpedient to use the word 'dependent' in this way, even though linguistically it might be possible to do so.

What I understand by independence in the realm of thoughts may become clear from the following. I here use the word 'thought' instead of 'proposition', since surely it is only the thought-content of a proposition that is relevant, and the former is always present in the case of real propositions – and it is only with these that we are here concerned. What I call a group of thoughts will be apparent from the fact that I say: The linguistic expression of a group of thoughts consists of real propositions connected by 'and'. We can think of a group of thoughts as one thought constituted out of other thoughts.

Let Ω be a group of true thoughts. Let a thought G follow from one or several of the thoughts of this group by means of a logical inference such that apart from the laws of logic, no proposition not belonging to Ω is used. Let us now form a new group of thoughts by adding the
424   thought G to | the group Ω. Call what we have just performed a logical step. Now if through a sequence of such steps, where every step takes the result of the preceding one as its basis, we can reach a group of thoughts that contains the thought A, then we call A dependent upon group Ω. If this is not possible, then we call A independent of Ω. The latter will always occur when A is false.

In section 10 of his 'Foundations of Geometry', Mr. Hilbert raises the question whether axioms are independent of one another, and then continues: 'Indeed, it turns out that none of the axioms can be deduced from the remaining ones by means of logical inferences.' According to this, he appears to use the word 'independent' just as has been stipulated above. But apparently it only seems that way, since in our case we are concerned with thoughts; Mr. Hilbert's axioms, however, are pseudo-propositions which therefore do not express thoughts. This may be seen from the fact that according to Mr. Hilbert an axiom now holds, and now does not. A real proposition, however, expresses a thought, and the latter is either true or false; *tertium non datur.*[13] A

---
[13]Cf. note 10 above.

false axiom – where the word 'axiom' is understood in the proper sense – is worthy of exhibition in Kastan's Waxworks,[14] alongside a square circle. Moreover, it appears that Mr. Hilbert's usage vacillates. If something is supposed to express now this thought, now that, then in reality it expresses no thought at all. Mr. Hilbert's pseudo-axioms are of this nature. They are groups of sounds or written signs which are apparently intended to express thoughts without, however, actually doing so. Now it is clear that such groups cannot be premises of inferences, for inferring is not an activity within the realm of the sensible. Therefore – strictly speaking – not even real propositions can be premises of inferences, but at best the thoughts expressed by them. Deducing something by logical inferences from Mr. Hilbert's pseudo-axioms is about as possible as cultivating a garden plot by means of mental arithmetic. In this case, therefore, Mr. Hilbert cannot be using the word 'axiom' in the usual way. With such vacillations in usage, it cannot be ascertained how he understands the word 'dependent'. He himself probably knows this as little as he knows what he means by 'axiom'.

By way of elucidating my explanation, let me add a few remarks. |

In taking a logical step from the thought-group Ω, we are applying a 425 logical law. The latter is not to be counted among the premises and therefore need not occur in Ω. Thus there are certain thoughts, namely the laws of logic, which are not to be considered when dealing with questions concerning the dependence of a thought.

Only true thoughts can be premises of inferences. Therefore if a thought is dependent upon a thought-group Ω, then all the thoughts in Ω that are used in the proofs must be true. But, one might perhaps object, surely one can make deductions from certain thoughts purely hypothetically without adjudging the truth of the latter. Certainly, purely hypothetically! But then it is not these thoughts that are the premises of such inferences. Rather, the premises are certain hypothetical thoughts that contain the thoughts in question as antecedents. Even in the final result, the thoughts in question must occur as conditions; whence it follows that they were not used as premises, for otherwise they would have disappeared in the final result. If one has left them out, one has simply made a mistake. Only after one of the thoughts in question has been admitted as true can one omit it as an antecedent. This occurs through an inference having as one of its premises the thought now admitted as true.

We cannot from the very start exclude the case where every thought of group Ω' is dependent upon group Ω, while at the same time every

14[A waxworks similar to Mme. Tussaud's. (*Tr.*)]

thought of group Ω is dependent upon group Ω'. Therefore from the fact that all thoughts of group Ω' are dependent upon Ω, it cannot be concluded without more ado that the thoughts of group Ω are independent of Ω'.

Another case that cannot be ruled out *a priori* is that in which a thought A is dependent upon both a group Ω and also upon a group Ω_1, whereby no thought of group Ω is dependent on Ω_1, nor any thought of group Ω_1 dependent upon Ω. In this case, therefore, A can be proved from group Ω_1 without the thoughts of group Ω even being known. In spite of this we could not call A independent of group Ω.

We now return to our question: Is it possible to prove the independence of a real axiom from a group of real axioms? This leads to the further question: How can one prove the independence of a thought from a group of thoughts? First of all, it may be noted that with this question we enter into a realm that is otherwise foreign to mathematics. For although like all other disciplines | mathematics, too, is carried out in thoughts, still, thoughts are otherwise not the object of its investigations. Even the independence of a thought from a group of thoughts is quite distinct from the relations otherwise investigated in mathematics. Now we may assume that this new realm has its own specific, basic truths which are as essential to the proofs constructed in it as the axioms of geometry are to the proofs of geometry; and that we also need these basic truths especially to prove the independence of a thought from a group of thoughts.

To lay down such laws, let us recall that our definition reduced the dependence of thoughts to the following of a thought from other thoughts by means of an inference. This is to be understood in such a way that all these other thoughts are used as premises of the inference and that apart from the laws of logic no other thought is used. The basic truths of our new discipline which we need here will be expressed in sentences of the form:

> If such and such is the case, then the thought G does not follow by a logical inference from the thoughts A, B, C.

Instead of this, we may also employ the form:

> If the thought G follows from the thoughts A, B, C by a logical inference, then such and such is the case.

In fact, laws like the following may be laid down:

> If the thought G follows from the thoughts A, B, C by a logical inference, then G is true.

Further,

If the thought G follows from the thoughts A, B, C by a logical inference, then each of the thoughts A, B, C is true.

For we have seen that only true thoughts can be the premises of inferences. But our aim is not to be achieved with these basic truths alone. We need yet another law which is not expressed quite so easily. Since a final settlement of the question is not possible here, I shall abstain from a precise formulation of this law and merely attempt to give an approximation of what I have in mind. One might call it an emanation of the formal nature of logical laws.

Imagine a vocabulary: not, however, one in which words of one language are opposed to corresponding ones of another, but where on both sides there stand words of the same language but having different senses. Let this occur in such a way that proper names are once again opposed to proper | names and concept-words again to concept-words. 427 Furthermore, let this occur with preservation of level,[15] so that to words for first-level concepts on the left there correspond similar ones on the right. Likewise for the second level. Let something similar hold of relation-words as well. We may say in general that words with the same grammatical function are to stand opposite one another. Each word occurring on the left has its determinate sense – at least we assume this – and likewise for each one occurring on the right. Now by means of this opposition the senses of the words on the left are also correlated with the senses of the words on the right. Let this correlation be one-to-one, so that on neither the left nor the right is the same thing expressed twice. We can now translate; not, however, from one language to another, whereby the same sense is retained; but into the very same language, whereby the sense is changed. We can now ask whether, in such a translation, there once more results from a proposition on the left a proposition on the right. Since a real proposition must express a thought, for this to be the case it will be necessary that to a thought on the left there again corresponds a thought on the right. If we make one

---

[15]I have treated of concepts of the first and second level in my *Grundgesetze der Arithmetik* [*The Basic Laws of Arithmetic*] I (Jena, 1893), §§ 21 and 22. Here I confine myself to the following remarks. The subsumption of an object under a concept (Plato is a human being. Two is a prime number.) is familiar. Here we have only first-level concepts. First-level concepts can stand to second-level concepts in a relation similar to the one in which objects stand to first-level concepts. But here we must not think of subordination, because in the latter case, both concepts are of the same level. Consider the proposition 'There is a prime number'. Here we see the first-level concept *prime number* stand to a second-level concept in a relation similar to that in which 2 stands to the concept *prime number*.

of the spoken natural languages the basis of our considerations, this is of course doubtful. But let us here presuppose a logically perfect language. Then indeed, to every thought expressed on the left, there will correspond one expressed on the right. Even if one doubts this, at least it will be admitted that it may so in some cases. Now let the premises of an inference be expressed on the left. We then ask whether the thoughts corresponding to them on the right are the premises of an inference of the same kind; and whether the proposition corresponding to the conclusion-proposition on the left is the appropriate conclusion-proposition of the inference on the right. In any case, the thoughts expressed on the right must be true in order to be premises. Let us assume that this condition is met. One may now be tempted to answer our question in the affirmative, thereby appealing to the formal nature of the laws of logic according to which, as far as logic itself is 428   concerned, each object is as good as any other, and each concept | of the first level as good as any other and can be replaced by it; etc. But this would be excessively hasty, for logic is not as unrestrictedly formal as is here presupposed. If it were, then it would be without content. Just as the concept *point* belongs to geometry, so logic, too, has its own concepts and relations; and it is only in virtue of this that it can have a content. Toward what is thus proper to it, its relation is not at all formal. No science is completely formal; but even gravitational mechanics is formal to a certain degree, in so far as optical and chemical properties are all the same to it. To be sure, so far as it is concerned, bodies with different masses are not mutually replaceable; but in gravitational mechanics the difference of bodies with respect to their chemical properties does not constitute a hindrance to their mutual replacement. To logic, for example, there belong the following: negation, identity, subsumption, subordination of concepts. And here logic brooks no replacement. It is true that in an inference we can replace Charlemagne by Sahara, and the concept *king* by the concept *desert*, in so far as this does not alter the truth of the premises. But one may not thus replace the relation of identity by the lying of a point in a plane. Because for identity there hold certain logical laws which as such need not be numbered among the premises, and to these nothing would correspond on the other side. Consequently a lacuna might arise at that place in the proof. One can express it metaphorically like this: About what is foreign to it, logic knows only what occurs in the premises; about what is proper to it, it knows all. Therefore in order to be sure that in our translation, to a correct inference on the left there again corresponds a correct inference on the right, we must make certain that in the vocabulary to words and expressions that might occur on the left and whose references belong to logic, identical ones are opposed on the right. Let us assume that the vocabulary meets this condition. Then not only will a conclusion again correspond to a conclusion, but also a whole inference-chain to an inference-chain, i.e. to a proof on the left there will correspond a proof on the right – always presupposing that the initial propositions on the right hold just as do those on the left.

Let us now consider whether a thought G is dependent upon a group of thoughts Ω. We can give a negative answer to this question if, according to our vocabulary, to the thoughts of group Ω there corresponds a group of true thoughts Ω', while to the thought G there corresponds a false thought G'. For if G were dependent upon Ω, then, since the thoughts of Ω' are true, G' would also have to be dependent upon Ω' and consequently G' would be true. |

With this we have an indication of the way in which it may be possible to prove independence of a real axiom from other real axioms. Of course, we are far from having a more precise execution of this. In particular, we will find that this final basic law which I have attempted to elucidate by means of the above-mentioned vocabulary still needs more precise formulation, and that to give this will not be easy. Furthermore, it will have to be determined what counts as a logical inference and what is proper to logic.

If, following the suggestions given above, one then wanted to apply this to the axioms of geometry, one would still need propositions that state, for example, that the concept *point*, the relation of a point's lying in a plane, etc. do not belong to logic. These propositions will probably have to be taken as axiomatic. Of course, such axioms are of a very special kind and cannot otherwise be used in geometry. But we are here in unexplored territory.

One can easily see that these questions cannot be settled briefly; and therefore I shall not attempt to carry this investigation any further here.

To whoever might wish to answer my expositions, I should like to recommend strongly that he begin by stating as clearly as possible what he calls an axiom, when he calls an axiom independent of others, and how he delimits the meaning of the word 'axiom' from that of the word 'definition'. Of course, if one asks only for the sake of asking, then, as Mr. Korselt fears, one can go on asking forever. But it would never occur to any reasonable individual to continue asking when there is simply no danger of misunderstanding. In scientific dispute, one must seek to find out as precisely as possible wherein the difference of opinion consists, so as to avoid a mere dispute over words. In the present case, one must decide whether an axiom is something audible, perhaps a sequence of words which grammar calls a proposition, and if

429

such is the case, whether it is a pseudo-proposition or a real one; or whether perhaps an axiom is a thought, the sense of a real proposition. As long as the word 'axiom' was used as a heading only, a fluctuation in its meaning could be tolerated. Now, however, since the question of whether an axiom is independent of others has been raised, the word 'axiom' has been introduced into the text itself and something is asserted or proved about what it is supposed to designate. It is now necessary to bring about complete agreement on its meaning. In the first edition of his essay, Mr. Hilbert should already have given a definition of an | axiom; or, if that seemed impossible, an elucidation. But perhaps at that time he had not yet become aware of his departure from the Euclidean usage of the word. But then he ought to have filled this gap in the second edition. As it stands, we remain completely in the dark as to what he really believes he has proved and which logical and extralogical laws and expedients he needs for this. It cannot even be recognized for certain whether Mr. Korselt's use of the word 'axiom' agrees with Mr. Hilbert's. Therefore when I press for clarity, this is not to be shrugged off as useless questioning. If anyone wanted to continue this dispute further without first making a serious effort to answer the questions just posed, he would only be making hot air – an enterprise in which I do not care to participate.

Reply to Mr. Thomae's Holiday *Causerie*

On pp. 80–153 of volume 2 of my *Basic Laws of Arithmetic*,[1] I gave a 586
critical analysis of the best-known theories of irrational numbers. The
task was anything but pleasant. After all, destruction is always less
satisfying than construction and also finds less recognition; for at least
at first it almost exclusively creates enemies. I made a serious effort to
understand unfamiliar modes of expression and trains of thought, since
I recognized that | such a work could be valuable only on the condition 587
that it be most thorough and that it strive to be fair to even the most
unfamiliar of theories. It required great renunciation on my part to
pursue paths which from the very start I recognized as blind alleys,
merely in order to prove in particular cases that they are blind alleys,
and to do this without even the hope of learning something valuable
from this occupation with unfamiliar thoughts. Nevertheless, I under-
took this task for the sake of science, since the desire for what is true
can arise only after the worthlessness of all surrogates has been
recognized. I should like to hope not merely for my own sake, but also
for that of science, that as many as possible try to understand my
writings, my trains of thought, with equal thoroughness and with the
same desire to be fair to them.

I am convinced that with my critique of Thomae's formal arithmetic,
I have destroyed it once and for all, and this conviction is merely
confirmed by Mr. Thomae's holiday *causerie*.[2] Even if Mr. Thomae
were correct in everything he said there, enough would remain of my
critique to bring his formal theory to ruin. And how does he proceed in
this *causerie*? He repeats his claims without even mentioning my
counter-arguments. My distinctions – e.g. between a figure and a sign,

---

[1] Jena, 1903.

[2] [J. Thomae 'Ferienplauderei', pp. 434–8 of the same periodical: English translation in
G. Frege, *On the Foundations of Geometry* (New Haven and London, 1971), pp. 115–20.
(*Ed.*)]

Jahresbericht der Deutschen Mathematiker-Vereinigung 15 (1906), pp. 586–90.
(*Tr.* E.-H. W. Kluge)

between a game and the theory of a game – he suppresses, thus obscuring once more what I had illuminated. He adduces my propositions in such a way that the reader cannot know how I intended them or what reasons I had for holding them.[3] The matter is very simple! I think that those readers who care to take the trouble to compare Thomae's holiday *causerie* with my expositions on pp. 96–139 of the second volume of my *Basic Laws* will find that there I have already refuted everything which Mr. Thomae adduces against me, with the possible exception of one point which I shall consider in more detail. Since this can be done briefly, let me adduce something from my Table of Contents. There, on p. ix, we read,

§ 93. There are neither theorems nor proofs nor definitions in a number-game, though there are such in the theory of the game.

This shows that part of Mr. Thomae's exposition is off target. Sometimes one might almost think that Mr. Thomae did not even read what he was attacking.

I do not know what value one might see in such a polemic. I wonder if there is anyone at all besides Mr. Thomae himself and Mr. Korselt[4] who believes in Thomae's number-game? I should less regret having sacrificed so much time and effort in this matter if Mr. Thomae had said something about whether for example my surmise about addition and abstraction in the number-game is correct. I raised many such questions. An answer to them would at least | further the development somewhat, and some small utility for science might arise from this. But Mr. Thomae surely knows why he is silent on this point. For his major mistake consists precisely in this, that he continually abandons his role as a formal arithmetician and imports many things from non-formal to formal arithmetic that fit into the latter like square pegs into round holes; and he does so without noticing that formal arithmetic is superfluous if it has to presuppose non-formal arithmetic. In fact, if we abstract from formal arithmetic everything it has derived from non-formal arithmetic, almost nothing remains except a few incredible assertions. Mr. Thomae calls numbers signs, where by the latter he obviously means spatial, material things; but he never acts accordingly,

588

---

[3]Mr. Thomae, it seems, did not understand my propositions.

[4]Compare his essay 'Concerning the Foundations of Mathematics' (this journal, 14 (1905)). From this it is obvious that he believes in Mr. Thomae's number-game only within limits. He says (p. 382) that the rules of Mr. Thomae's game can only be considered as suggestions for the formulation of a truly formal theory. Well, I shall wait until Mr. Korselt has produced one. Then we shall see further.

and resents it when someone else does. On this point, compare what he says in his holiday *causerie* about the growing of three. In his case, the disease seems to be incurable.

What Mr. Thomae says on p. 436 about the word 'identical' may be very useful for a defence attorney in a murder trial who has to invalidate the prosecuting attorney's proof of identity. I have prepared a speech appropriate for just such an occasion but shall refrain from presenting it, since I am sure that the reader himself is capable of preparing far nicer speeches of this sort. However, Mr. Thomae has brought out in me not only the lawyer but the poet as well. After reading what he said about abstraction, I vented my feelings in this verse:

> Abstraction's might a boon is found
> While man does keep it tamed and bound;
> Awful its heav'nly powers become
> When that its stops and stays are gone.

Yes, Mr. Thomae's abstraction is surely dangerous. For example, consider the case where the human mind, sovereign in its creative power, prescribing laws to nature, forms the concept *white powder* and arranges this concept in such a way that sodium bicarbonate is the same white powder as arsenic. We would do well to be very careful about abstracting. But we should also not forget its beneficial effects! We abstract from the difference between figure and sign, and immediately figures are signs and signs figures. We abstract from that by which the relation of a figure to its role in the game differs from the relation of a sign to its meaning, and right away the two coincide. We abstract from the difference between a sign and what is signified, and immediately they coalesce. We abstract from the difference between rule and theorem and lo! they are identical. We abstract from the difference between formal and non-formal arithmetic, between game and science, and no one can keep them apart any longer. All this is very important; especially as regards Mr. Thomae's formal arithmetic. If abstraction did not perform these miracles, it could not survive a second longer.

But let us stop joking and once again be serious! All of us probably agree that time designations belong to a predicate, and that an | object 589 may have a property at one time which it does not have at another. At one time a person may have no knowledge at all of the multiplication tables, and at another time he may know them. Still, he is the same person, and for this we do not need abstraction.

Now Mr. Thomae continues thus:

Similarly, someone learning how to count abstracts from the differences, if any, of the counting blocks which he uses to learn this and equates them with one another. I believed that I had discerned the fruitfulness of the equality-sign in this possibility or capability of the human mind to abstract from the differences of certain things and to equate them with one another.

Really now! Again and again this superficiality and weakness of thought which does not know whether by the word 'equal' it wants to designate identity or something else. On the basis of what he said before, it seems that Mr. Thomae wants to achieve identity by means of abstraction. Very well! If through this the counting blocks become identical, then we now have only one counting block; counting will not proceed beyond 'one'. Whoever cannot distinguish between things he is supposed to count, cannot count them either. Even someone learning how to count must distinguish between the counting blocks; for example on the basis of their different distances from the edge of the table. The counting blocks must differ, and this difference must also be recognized. If abstraction caused all differences to disappear, it would do away with the possibility of counting. On the other hand, if the word 'equal' is not supposed to designate identity, then the objects that are the same will therefore differ with respect to some properties and will agree with respect to others. But to know this, we do not have to abstract from their differences. Since the objects will have to differ anyway, it really matters little whether they differ a bit more or a bit less, as long as they are distinguishable at all. To see, either physically or mentally, is to distinguish. Mr. Thomae's abstraction is non-distinguishing or non-seeing; it is not a power of insight or of clarity but one of obscurantism and confusion. If by the word 'equal' we do not mean identity but merely agreement in some respect or other, then either we must state in what respect sameness obtains – e.g. equal in colour, equal in odour, etc. – or this must be evident from the context. The word 'equal' in itself says nothing if it is not somehow explained more precisely. And if the human mind can equate any objects whatever, it is especially meaningless, and the meaning of equating will also remain obscure. But don't let us imagine that by means of abstracting and equating we can achieve greater agreement than obtains in reality. We do not thereby alter anything in the things themselves. The only thing we can thus achieve is error with respect to these things. If the equality-sign in arithmetic were to have as nebulous and ungraspable a meaning as this, it would be useless. We find that thinkers of Mr. Thomae's kidney want the one thing as well as the other, which latter, however, is incompatible with the first. What do they want to achieve by abstracting? They want – well, what they really want is identity; for of what use is partial agreement, since that already obtains even without abstraction! | But do they really want to become serious 590 about this identity? No: that they certainly do not! Things are supposed to become identical by being equated – as if that mattered to the things themselves. But distinguishable: yes, that they must remain. And to use Mr. Thomae's phrase the external sign of this feeble behaviour is the word 'equal'.

But why must I always repeat the same arguments? Twenty-two years ago, in my *Foundations of Arithmetic*, §§ 34–48.[5] I presented at length what must be considered when dealing with this question; and in § 48 in particular I indicated the reason why one is tempted to derive numbers via abstraction. Is my whole effort, then, to have been in vain? Is my attempt to discuss this question as thoroughly and penetratingly and understandably as possible, weighing arguments and counter-arguments – is all this effort simply to have been wasted? Is all this to have been written into the wind? At that time, twenty-two years ago and even afterwards, even someone like Weierstrass could utter a farrago of balderdash when talking about the present subject. But now, surely, it is time to think more carefully about the matter before writing about it. If someone can confute my arguments, let him do so; if not, let him spare me — but I don't want to become unparliamentary. It seems that there are people from whom logical arguments run off like water from a duck's back. And apparently there also are opinions which, although repeatedly confuted[6] and although no serious attempt is ever made to refute this confutation, nevertheless continue to maintain themselves as though nothing had happened. I regret that I know of no admissible means, be they parliamentary or literary, of shooing these opinions back into their haunts, so that they never again dare emerge into the light of day.

---

[5] Breslau, 1884.
[6] Cf. my essay *On Mr. H. Schubert's Numbers* (Jena, 1899) [this volume pp. 249–72].

M

Renewed Proof of the Impossibility of Mr. Thomae's Formal Arithmetic

Opposed to formal arithmetic, there stands non-formal arithmetic. The two differ as follows: In non-formal arithmetic, numerals really are signs: mere tools of research, intended to designate numbers, where the latter are the non-sensible objects of the science. In formal arithmetic, it is the numerals themselves that are the numbers; they are not mere tools but rather the very objects of the investigation.

The basic idea of Thomae's formal arithmetic may be expressed briefly as follows:

Mr. Thomae compares formal arithmetic to chess. To the chess pieces whose use is governed by the rules of the game, there correspond certain spatial and visible figures, produced by writing or printing, which Mr. Thomae calls signs. With respect to their use, too, rules are to be laid down. These are the rules of the computing game. However, we immediately encounter a difficulty. The beginner at chess is initially introduced to the chess board and chess pieces as the things on and with which the game is played. Let us call such things game-pieces. The first question then, is this: What are the game-pieces of the computing game? Mr. Thomae writes,

> The system of signs of the computing-game is produced in the familiar way from
>
> 0 1 2 3 4 5 6 7 8 9.[1]

Had he merely said that these numerals are the game-pieces of the computing game, we should have been satisfied. But now he apparently wants to say that the game-pieces are first produced from these numerals, and in the familiar way at that. How could this matter be familiar to us, since we still want to learn the computing game? Mr. Thomae here makes the mistake he commits time and again: He

[1]This journal, 15, p. 435 [English translation, G. Frege, *The Foundations of Geometry* (New Haven and London, 1971), p. 115].

Jahresbericht der Deutschen Mathematiker-Vereinigung 17 (1908), pp. 52–5.
(*Tr*. E.-H. W. Kluge)

assumes as known that for which he still wants to lay the groundwork. For we certainly cannot know whether he counts

$$\text{'23'}, \text{'}\tfrac{2}{3}\text{'}, \text{'}2-3\text{'}, \text{'}2{:}(5+3)\text{'}, \text{'}\sqrt[3]{3}\text{'},$$

$$\text{'}3>2\text{'}, \text{'}2\times 2=4\text{'}, \text{'}\int_0^1 \frac{\mathrm{d}\xi}{1+\xi}\text{'}, \quad |$$

$$\text{'}2\times a\text{'}, \text{'}1-(\tfrac{1}{3})+(\tfrac{1}{5})-(\tfrac{1}{7})\dots\text{'}^2 \qquad\qquad 53$$

among the signs about which he is here talking, and which therefore are comparable to chess pieces. Anyone familiar with arithmetic certainly knows that such groups do occur. To that extent we can say that they were constructed out of these numerals in the familiar way. But surely, given this we still do not know whether Mr. Thomae considers them game-pieces. For aside from the numerals, other figures also occur: fraction-stroke, division-sign, root-sign, equality-sign, brackets, dots, letters, etc. Are these figures, then, not to occur in the computing game at all? Or are they, too, supposed to be game-pieces? Or is it that only certain groups in which they occur together with numerals are to be comparable to chess pieces? We don't know. And yet Mr. Thomae says, 'in the familiar way'! This uncertainty in which we are left is the mental fog that evidently is quite conducive to the success of the computing game. For now, let us console ourselves with the thought that, after all, we shall get to know the rules of the computing game. And of course given these, we shall presumably see with what sorts of things the latter are concerned.

The second question concerns the actions involved in playing the game. We are all familiar with the kind of action involved in playing chess. A piece is transferred from one square of the chessboard to another, or is completely removed from the board, etc. The rules of chess relate to these actions. The question as to the nature of the actions in the computing game is more difficult to answer. Perhaps they consist in this, that by means of writing, certain figures are formed or those already written are again erased. But how in the world can this be in doubt? After all, this must be evident from the rules of the computing game!

The first of the formulae which according to Mr. Thomae are supposed to contain the rules of this game, looks like this:

$$a+a'=a'+a$$

---

[2] I here use quotation-marks because I mean not what is designated by these groups in non-formal arithmetic, but rather these figures themselves as visible, corporeal signs.

This formula, when understood in the sense of non-formal arithmetic, belongs to the latter as one of its theorems; it does not, however, belong to formal arithmetic. But it must not be understood that way, since non-formal arithmetic must not be presupposed. In formal arithmetic, however, nowhere previously has this formula been assigned a sense. It has been assigned a sense neither as a whole nor by separately explaining each of its parts. The vertical cross has not yet occurred at all. Therefore so far as formal arithmetic is concerned, this formula is quite senseless; as senseless as a configuration of chess pieces before it has somehow been accorded a sense or before any rule of chess has even been laid down. Now the rules of the computing game are of course supposed to give something like a content to the game-pieces – to the 'signs'. Whether this is possible or not is irrelevant: in neither case is this content | already present before a rule has been laid down. Rules either command, forbid, or permit. But nowhere in formal arithmetic has a sign been explained by commanding, forbidding, or permitting something with respect to it. Thus, from the start, the first rule of the computing game vanishes into thin air, and with it the computing game itself.

One might perhaps attempt to avoid this conclusion by construing not the whole formula but merely parts of it – e.g. the equality-sign – in the sense of non-formal arithmetic. But exactly what sense is this? The equality-sign occurs only between signs or groups of signs; and here we must distinguish between two cases. In the first, as for example in

$$\tfrac{2}{3}+\tfrac{3}{5}=\tfrac{19}{15},$$

a simple or a complex sign designating something stands on the left; similarly on the right. What a sign designates, I call its meaning. Now the equality-sign designates a certain relation and is our means of expressing the fact that this relation obtains between the meaning of the sign on the left and that of the sign on the right.

In the other case, as in

$$a+b=b+a,$$

we have letters. Of these we cannot say that they designate something, as do the numbers '2' and '$\tfrac{1}{2}$'. But although they have no meaning, nevertheless they do contribute something to the sense of the proposition I use the locution: They indicate so as to lend generality to the content of the proposition. By this I mean to say that no matter what numbers we understand by the letters,[3] we always get something true.

[3][The German has the singular; the plural rendering is in keeping with the whole context. (*Tr.*)]

Therefore, if our formula is to have a sense in non-formal arithmetic, we must once more return to the first case when replacing the letters by numerals.

However, if in combination with the equality-sign there occur written or printed figures that neither have a sense in non-formal arithmetic nor are letters – as is the case with

$$\S\S = \pounds$$

then the sense which the equality-sign otherwise has in non-formal arithmetic cannot come into play. Such a combination has no sense.

A case that must be classed with the preceding is this: Where all the signs that occur can otherwise be understood in the sense of non-formal arithmetic but here are not to be understood in this way; as when in

$$\tfrac{2}{3} + \tfrac{3}{5} = \tfrac{3}{5} + \tfrac{2}{3}$$

'$\tfrac{2}{3}$' and '$\tfrac{3}{5}$' are not to be understood as numerals in the sense of non-formal arithmetic, but perhaps as game-pieces in the computing game. |

Therefore, the equality-sign can be understood in the sense of non-   55
formal arithmetic only when the whole formula of which it is a part is to be understood in the sense of non-formal arithmetic. Hence either the formula.

$$a + a' = a' + a$$

is a theorem of non-formal arithmetic, or it is quite senseless. In neither case do we have a rule.

Mr. Thomae falls into error because he chooses as his game-pieces figures that look like the numerals of non-formal arithmetic. As far as the game itself is concerned, it should really be quite irrelevant what the game-pieces look like, as long as those that are distinguished in the rules are in fact clearly distinct, and as long as the actions of the game remain possible. In chess, for example, instead of castles, knights, bishops, queens, and kings, we could use pieces representing cannons, lancers, lieutenants, colonels, and generals, and could play with these just as well as with the traditional pieces. Similarly, it should be possible to play the computing game with figures that look quite different from the signs of arithmetic; e.g. these:

$$\rightharpoonup \quad = \quad > \quad < \quad \times \quad \S \quad \cap \quad \cup \quad \cap \quad \cup \quad \eth \quad \mathcal{C} \quad \pounds \quad \S^4$$

But that doesn't work. Why doesn't it work? Why must the game-pieces agree with the signs of non-formal arithmetic? Because formal

---

[4]Of course it would not occur to anyone to see a rule of the game in $< \quad \S \quad \eth \quad \times \quad \eth \quad \S \quad <.$

arithmetic cannot do without the sense which its objects have in non-formal arithmetic. It is comparable to a creeper twining around non-formal arithmetic, losing all hold once its support and source of sustenance are removed. Accordingly, formal arithmetic presupposes the non-formal one; its pretension of replacing the latter herewith falls to the ground.

Therefore, so far as the computing game is concerned, we have established the following:

1. We are not fully told with which game-pieces we are dealing.

2. We are left completely in the dark as to wherein the actions of this game consist.

We easily ought to be able to get clear on these two points if we were told the rules of the game; but

3. What we are offered as the rules of the game does not remove the above doubts. In formal arithmetic these formulae are senseless. In order to give them a sense, we should have to adduce non-formal arithmetic as extended to cover negative, fractional, etc. numbers – which in the first place is inadmissible, and in the second would not yield any rules.

CONCLUDING REMARKS[5]

In the preceding essay, I have combated a theory objectively and seriously. If Mr. Thomae knows something that can be opposed to it, then it is his duty to present it. There is no valid reason for keeping it back, except perhaps for continuing weakness. If, when seriously attacked, a doctrine is no longer defended, then by all general principles of scientific enterprise it must be considered refuted.

[5][From *Jahresbericht der Deutschen Mathematiker-Vereinigung*, 17 (1908), 56. (*Tr.* E.-H. W. Kluge)]

Logical Investigations

PART I

THOUGHTS

Just as 'beautiful' points the ways for aesthetics and 'good' for ethics, 58
so do words like 'true' for logic. All sciences have truth as their goal;
but logic is also concerned with it in a quite different way: logic has
much the same relation to truth as physics has to weight or heat. To
discover truths is the task of all sciences; it falls to logic to discern the
laws of truth. The word 'law' is used in two senses. When we speak of
moral or civil laws we mean prescriptions, which ought to be obeyed
but with which actual occurrences are not always in conformity. Laws
of nature are general features of what happens in nature, and occurrences in nature are always in accordance with them. It is rather in this
sense that I speak of laws of truth. Here of course it is not a matter of
what happens but of what is. From the laws of truth there follow
prescriptions about asserting, thinking, judging, inferring. And we may
very well speak of laws of thought in this way too. But there is at once
a danger here of confusing different things. People may very well
interpret the expression 'law of thought' by analogy with 'law of nature'
and then have in mind general features of thinking as a mental
occurrence. A law of thought in this sense would be a psychological law.
And so they might come to believe that logic deals with the mental
process of thinking and with the psychological laws in accordance with
which this takes place. That would be misunderstanding the task of
logic, for truth has not here been given its proper place. Error and
superstition have causes just as much as correct cognition. Whether
what you take for true is false | or true, your so taking it comes about 59
in accordance with psychological laws. A derivation from these laws, an
explanation of a mental process that ends in taking something to be
true, can never take the place of proving what is taken to be true. But

---

In three parts in *Beiträge zur Philosophie des deutschen Idealismus* I (1918–19), pp. 58–
77, 143–57; III (1923–26), pp. 36–51. (*Tr.* Peter Geach and R. H. Stoothoff)

may not logical laws also have played a part in this mental process? I do not want to dispute this, but if it is a question of truth this possibility is not enough. For it is also possible that something non-logical played a part in the process and made it swerve from the truth. We can decide only after we have come to know the laws of truth; but then we can probably do without the derivation and explanation of the mental process, if our concern is to decide whether the process terminates in *justifiably* taking something to be true. In order to avoid any misunderstanding and prevent the blurring of the boundary between psychology and logic, I assign to logic the task of discovering the laws of truth, not the laws of taking things to be true or of thinking. The meaning of the word 'true' is spelled out in the laws of truth.

But first I shall attempt to outline roughly how I want to use 'true' in this connection, so as to exclude irrelevant uses of the word. 'True' is not to be used here in the sense of 'genuine' or 'veracious'; nor yet in the way it sometimes occurs in discussion of artistic questions, when, for example, people speak of truth in art, when truth is set up as the aim of art, when the truth of a work of art or true feeling is spoken of. Again, the word 'true' is prefixed to another word in order to show that the word is to be understood in its proper, unadulterated sense. This use too lies off the path followed here. What I have in mind is that sort of truth which it is the aim of science to discern.

Grammatically, the word 'true' looks like a word for a property. So we want to delimit more closely the region within which truth can be predicated, the region in which there is any question of truth. We find truth predicated of pictures, ideas, sentences, and thoughts. It is striking that visible and audible things turn up here along with things which cannot be perceived with the senses. This suggests that shifts of meaning have taken place. So indeed they have! Is a picture considered as a mere visible and tangible thing really true, and a stone or a leaf not true? Obviously we could not call a picture true unless there were an intention involved. A picture is meant to represent something. (Even an idea is not called true in itself, but only with respect to an intention that the idea should correspond to something.) It might be supposed from this that truth consists in a correspondence of a picture to what it depicts. Now a correspondence is a relation. But this goes against the use of the word 'true', which is not a relative term and contains no indication of anything else to which something is to correspond. If I do not know that a picture is meant to represent Cologne Cathedral then I
60   do not know | what to compare the picture with in order to decide on its truth. A correspondence, moreover, can only be perfect if the

corresponding things coincide and so just are not different things. It is supposed to be possible to test the genuineness of a bank-note by comparing it stereoscopically with a genuine one. But it would be ridiculous to try to compare a gold piece stereoscopically with a twenty-mark note. It would only be possible to compare an idea with a thing if the thing were an idea too. And then, if the first did correspond perfectly with the second, they would coincide. But this is not at all what people intend when they define truth as the correspondence of an idea with something real. For in this case it is essential precisely that the reality shall be distinct from the idea. But then there can be no complete correspondence, no complete truth. So nothing at all would be true; for what is only half true is untrue. Truth does not admit of more and less. – But could we not maintain that there is truth when there is correspondence in a certain respect? But which respect? For in that case what ought we to do so as to decide whether something is true? We should have to inquire whether it is *true* that an idea and a reality, say, correspond in the specified respect. And then we should be confronted by a question of the same kind, and the game could begin again. So the attempted explanation of truth as correspondence breaks down. And any other attempt to define truth also breaks down. For in a definition certain characteristics would have to be specified. And in application to any particular case the question would always arise whether it were *true* that the characteristics were present. So we should be going round in a circle. So it seems likely that the content of the word 'true' is *sui generis* and indefinable.

When we ascribe truth to a picture we do not really mean to ascribe a property which would belong to this picture quite independently of other things; we always have in mind some totally different object and we want to say that the picture corresponds in some way to this object. 'My idea corresponds to Cologne Cathedral' is a sentence, and now it is a matter of the truth of this sentence. So what is improperly called the truth of pictures and ideas is reduced to the truth of sentences. What is it that we call a sentence? A series of sounds, but only if it has a sense (this is not meant to convey that *any* series of sounds that has a sense is a sentence). And when we call a sentence true we really mean that its sense is true. And hence the only thing that raises the question of truth at all is the sense of sentences. Now is the sense of a sentence an idea? In any case, truth does not consist in correspondence of the sense with something else, for otherwise the question of truth would get reiterated to infinity.

Without offering this as a definition, I mean by 'a thought' something for which the question of truth can arise at all. So I count what is false

61 | among thoughts no less than what is true.[1] So I can say: thoughts are senses of sentences, without wishing to assert that the sense of every sentence is a thought. The thought, in itself imperceptible by the senses, gets clothed in the perceptible garb of a sentence, and thereby we are enabled to grasp it. We say a sentence *expresses* a thought.

A thought is something imperceptible: anything the senses can perceive is excluded from the realm of things for which the question of truth arises. Truth is not a quality that answers to a particular kind of sense-impressions. So it is sharply distinguished from the qualities we call by the names 'red', 'bitter', 'lilac-smelling'. But do we not see that the Sun has risen? and do we not then also see that this is true? That the Sun has risen is not an object emitting rays that reach my eyes; it is not a visible thing like the Sun itself. That the Sun has risen is recognized to be true on the basis of sense-impressions. But being true is not a sensible, perceptible, property. A thing's being magnetic is also recognized on the basis of sense-impressions of the thing, although this property does not answer, any more than truth does, to a particular kind of sense-impressions. So far these properties agree. However, we do need sense-impressions in order to recognize a body as magnetic. On the other hand, when I find it is true that I do not smell anything at this moment, I do not do so on the basis of sense-impressions.

All the same it is something worth thinking about that we cannot recognize a property of a thing without at the same time finding the thought *this thing has this property* to be true. So with every property of a thing there is tied up a property of a thought, namely truth. It is also worth noticing that the sentence 'I smell the scent of violets' has just the same content as the sentence 'It is true that I smell the scent of violets'. So it seems, then, that nothing is added to the thought by my ascribing to it the property of truth. And yet is it not a great result when the scientist after much hesitation and laborious researches can finally say 'My conjecture is true'? The meaning of the word 'true' seems to be altogether *sui generis*. May we not be dealing here with something which cannot be called a property in the ordinary sense at

---

[1]So, similarly, people have said 'a judgement is something which is either true or false'. In fact I use the word 'thought' more or less in the sense 'judgement' has in the writings of logicians. I hope it will become clear in the sequel why I choose 'thought'. Such an explanation has been objected to on the ground that it makes a division of judgements into true and false judgements – perhaps the least significant of all possible divisions among judgements. But I cannot see that it is a logical fault that a division is given along with the explanation. As for the division's being significant, we shall perhaps find we must hold it in no small esteem, if, as I have said, it is the word 'true' that points the way for logic.

all? In spite of this doubt I will begin by expressing myself in accordance with ordinary usage, | as if truth were a property, until   62 some more appropriate way of speaking is found.

In order to bring out more precisely what I mean by 'a thought,' I shall distinguish various kinds of sentences.[2] We should not wish to deny sense to a command, but this sense is not such that the question of truth could arise for it. Therefore I shall not call the sense of a command a thought. Sentences expressing wishes or requests are ruled out in the same way. Only those sentences in which we communicate or assert something come into the question. But here I do not count exclamations in which one vents one's feelings, groans, sighs, laughs – unless it has been decided by some special convention that they are to communicate something. But how about interrogative sentences? In a word-question[3] we utter an incomplete sentence, which is meant to be given a true sense just by means of the completion for which we are asking. Word-questions are accordingly left out of consideration here. Propositional questions[4] are a different matter. We expect to hear 'yes' or 'no'. The answer 'yes' means the same as an assertoric sentence, for in saying 'yes' the speaker presents as true the thought that was already completely contained in the interrogative sentence. This is how a propositional question can be formed from any assertoric sentence. And this is why an exclamation cannot be regarded as a communication: no corresponding propositional question can be formed. An interrogative sentence and an assertoric one contain the same thought; but the assertoric sentence contains something else as well, namely assertion. The interrogative sentence contains something more too, namely a request. Therefore two things must be distinguished in an assertoric sentence: the content, which it has in common with the corresponding propositional question; and assertion. The former is the thought or at least contains the thought. So it is possible to express a thought without laying it down as true. The two things are so closely joined in an assertoric sentence that it is easy to overlook their separability. Consequently we distinguish:

    (1)   the grasp of a thought – thinking,

[2] I am not using the word 'sentence' here in quite the same sense as grammar does, which also includes subordinate clauses. An isolated subordinate clause does not always have a sense about which the question of truth can arise, whereas the complex sentence to which it belongs has such a sense. [Elsewhere in this volume *Satz* has usually been rendered as 'proposition'. (*Ed.*)]

[3] [Frege means a question introduced by an interrogative word like 'who?' (*Tr.*)]

[4] [I.e. yes–no questions: German *Satzfragen*. (*Tr.*)]

(2)   the acknowledgement of the truth of a thought – the act of judgement,[5]

(3)   the manifestation of this judgement – assertion.

We have already performed the first act when we form a propositional question. An advance in science usually takes place in this way: first a thought is grasped, and thus may perhaps be expressed in a propositional question; after appropriate investigations, this thought is finally 63   recognized to be true. | We express acknowledgement of truth in the form of an assertoric sentence. We do not need the word 'true' for this. And even when we do use it the properly assertoric force does not lie in it, but in the assertoric sentence-form; and where this form loses its assertoric force the word 'true' cannot put it back again. This happens when we are not speaking seriously. As stage thunder is only sham thunder and a stage fight only a sham fight, so stage assertion is only sham assertion. It is only acting, only fiction. When playing his part the actor is not asserting anything; nor is he lying, even if he says something of whose falsehood he is convinced. In poetry we have the case of thoughts being expressed without being actually put forward as true, in spite of the assertoric form of the sentence; although the poem may suggest to the hearer that he himself should make an assenting judgement. Therefore the question still arises, even about what is presented in the assertoric sentence-form, whether it really contains an assertion. And this question must be answered in the negative if the requisite seriousness is lacking. It is unimportant whether the word 'true' is used here. This explains why it is that nothing seems to be added to a thought by attributing to it the property of truth.

An assertoric sentence often contains, over and above a thought and assertion, a third component not covered by the assertion. This is often meant to act on the feelings and mood of the hearer, or to arouse his imagination. Words like 'regrettably' and 'fortunately' belong here. Such constituents of sentences are more strongly prominent in poetry, but are seldom wholly absent from prose. They occur more rarely in mathematical, physical, or chemical expositions than in historical ones. What are called the humanities are closer to poetry, and are therefore

---

[5]It seems to me that thought and judgement have not hitherto been adequately distinguished. Perhaps language is misleading. For we have no particular bit of assertoric sentences which corresponds to assertion; that something is being asserted is implicit rather in the assertoric form. We have the advantage in German that main and subordinate clauses are distinguished by the word-order. However in this connection we must observe that a subordinate clause may also contain an assertion, and that often neither main nor subordinate clause expresses a complete thought by itself but only the complex sentence does.

less scientific, than the exact sciences, which are drier in proportion to being more exact; for exact science is directed toward truth and truth alone. Therefore all constituents of sentences not covered by the assertoric force do not belong to scientific exposition; but they are sometimes hard to avoid, even for one who sees the danger connected with them. Where the main thing is to approach by way of intimation what cannot be conceptually grasped, these constituents are fully justified. The more rigorously scientific an exposition is, the less the nationality of its author will be discernible and the easier it will be to translate. On the other hand, the constituents of language to which I here want to call attention make the translation of poetry very difficult, indeed make perfect translation almost always impossible, for it is just in what largely makes the poetic value that languages most differ.

It makes no difference to the thought whether I use the word 'horse' or 'steed' or 'nag' or 'prad'. The assertoric force does not cover the ways in which these words differ. What is called mood, atmosphere, illumination in a poem, what is portrayed by intonation and rhythm, does not belong to the thought. |

Much in language serves to aid the hearer's understanding, for   64 instance emphasizing part of a sentence by stress or word-order. Here let us bear in mind words like 'still' and 'already'. Someone using the sentence 'Alfred has still not come' actually says 'Alfred has not come', and at the same time hints – but only hints – that Alfred's arrival is expected. Nobody can say: Since Alfred's arrival is not expected, the sense of the sentence is false. The way that 'but' differs from 'and' is that we use it to intimate that what follows it contrasts with what was to be expected from what preceded it. Such conversational suggestions make no difference to the thought. A sentence can be transformed by changing the verb from active to passive and at the same time making the accusative into the subject. In the same way we may change the dative into the nominative and at the same time replace 'give' by 'receive'. Naturally such transformations are not trivial in every respect; but they do not touch the thought, they do not touch what is true or false. If the inadmissibility of such transformations were recognized as a principle, then any profound logical investigation would be hindered. It is just as important to ignore distinctions that do not touch the heart of the matter, as to make distinctions which concern essentials. But what is essential depends on one's purpose. To a mind concerned with the beauties of language, what is trivial to the logician may seem to be just what is important.

Thus the content of a sentence often goes beyond the thought expressed by it. But the opposite often happens too; the mere wording, which can be made permanent by writing or the gramophone, does not suffice for the expression of the thought. The present tense is used in two ways: first, in order to indicate a time; second, in order to eliminate any temporal restriction, where timelessness or eternity is part of the thought – consider for instance the laws of mathematics. Which of the two cases occurs is not expressed but must be divined. If a time-indication is conveyed by the present tense one must know when the sentence was uttered in order to grasp the thought correctly. Therefore the time of utterance is part of the expression of the thought. If someone wants to say today what he expressed yesterday using the word 'today', he will replace this word with 'yesterday'. Although the thought is the same its verbal expression must be different in order that the change of sense which would otherwise be effected by the differing times of utterance may be cancelled out. The case is the same with words like 'here' and 'there'. In all such cases the mere wording, as it can be preserved in writing, is not the complete expression of the thought; the knowledge of certain conditions accompanying the utterance, which are used as means of expressing the thought, is needed for us to grasp the thought correctly. Pointing the finger, hand gestures, glances may belong here too. The same utterance containing the word 'I' in the mouths of different men will express different thoughts of which some may be true, others false. |

65   The occurrence of the word 'I' in a sentence gives rise to some further questions.

Consider the following case. Dr. Gustav Lauben says, 'I was wounded', Leo Peter hears this and remarks some days later, 'Dr. Gustav Lauben was wounded'. Does this sentence express the same thought as the one Dr. Lauben uttered himself? Suppose that Rudolph Lingens was present when Dr. Lauben spoke and now hears what is related by Leo Peter. If the same thought was uttered by Dr. Lauben and Leo Peter, then Rudolph Lingens, who is fully master of the language and remembers what Dr. Lauben said in his presence, must now know at once from Leo Peter's report that he is speaking of the same thing. But knowledge of the language is a special thing when proper names are involved. It may well be the case that only a few people associate a definite thought with the sentence 'Dr. Lauben was wounded'. For complete understanding one needs in this case to know the expression 'Dr. Gustav Lauben'. Now if both Leo Peter and Rudolph Lingens mean by 'Dr. Gustav Lauben', the doctor who is the only doctor living in a house known to both of them, then they both understand the sentence 'Dr. Gustav Lauben was wounded' in the same way; they associate the same thought with it. But it is also possible that

Rudolph Lingens does not know Dr. Lauben personally and does not know that it was Dr. Lauben who recently said 'I was wounded.' In this case Rudolph Lingens cannot know that the same affair is in question. I say, therefore, in this case: the thought which Leo Peter expresses is not the same as that which Dr. Lauben uttered.

Suppose further that Herbert Garner knows that Dr. Gustav Lauben was born on 13 September, 1875 in N.N. and this is not true of anyone else; suppose, however, that he does not know where Dr. Lauben now lives nor indeed anything else about him. On the other hand, suppose Leo Peter does not know that Dr. Lauben was born on 13 September 1875, in N.N. Then as far as the proper name 'Dr. Gustav Lauben' is concerned, Herbert Garner and Leo Peter do not speak the same language, although they do in fact refer to the same man with this name; for they do not know that they are doing so. Therefore Herbert Garner does not associate the same thought with the sentence 'Dr. Gustav Lauben was wounded' as Leo Peter wants to express with it. To avoid the awkwardness that Herbert Garner and Leo Peter are not speaking the same language, I shall suppose that Leo Peter uses the proper name 'Dr. Lauben' and Herbert Garner uses the proper name 'Gustav Lauben'. Then it is possible that Herbert Garner takes the sense of the sentence 'Dr. Lauben was wounded' to be true but is misled by false information into taking the sense of the sentence 'Gustav Lauben was wounded' to be false. So given our assumptions these thoughts are different.

Accordingly, with a proper name, it is a matter of the way that the object so designated is presented. This may happen in different ways, and | to every such way there corresponds a special sense of a sentence   66 containing the proper name. The different thoughts thus obtained from the same sentences correspond in truth-value, of course; that is to say, if one is true then all are true, and if one is false than all are false. Nevertheless the difference must be recognized. So we must really stipulate that for every proper name there shall be just one associated manner of presentation of the object so designated. It is often unimportant that this stipulation should be fulfilled, but not always.

Now everyone is presented to himself in a special and primitive way, in which he is presented to no-one else. So, when Dr. Lauben has the thought that he was wounded, he will probably be basing it on this primitive way in which he is presented to himself. And only Dr. Lauben himself can grasp thoughts specified in this way. But now he may want to communicate with others. He cannot communicate a thought he alone can grasp. Therefore, if he now says 'I was wounded', he must use 'I' in a sense which can be grasped by others, perhaps in the sense of 'he who is speaking to you at this moment'; by doing this he makes the conditions accompanying his utterance serve towards the expression of a thought.[6]

Yet there is a doubt, Is it at all the same thought which first that man expresses and then this one?

A man who is still unaffected by philosophy first of all gets to know things he can see and touch, can in short perceive with the senses, such as trees, stones and houses, and he is convinced that someone else can equally see and touch the same tree and the same stone as he himself sees and touches. Obviously a thought does not belong with these things. Now can it, nevertheless, like a tree be presented to people as identical?

Even an unphilosophical man soon finds it necessary to recognize an inner world distinct from the outer world, a world of sense-impressions, of creations of his imagination, of sensations, of feelings and moods, a world of inclinations, wishes and decisions. For brevity's sake I want to use the word 'idea' to cover all these occurrences, except decisions.

Now do thoughts belong to this inner world? Are they ideas? They are obviously not decisions. |

67 How are ideas distinct from the things of the outer world?

First: ideas cannot be seen, or touched, or smelled, or tasted, or heard.

I go for a walk with a companion. I see a green field, I thus have a visual impression of the green. I have it, but I do not see it.

Secondly: ideas are something we have. We have sensations, feelings, moods, inclinations, wishes. An idea that someone has belongs to the content of his consciousness.

The field and the frogs in it, the Sun which shines on them, are there no matter whether I look at them or not, but the sense-impression I have of green exists only because of me, I am its owner. It seems absurd to us that a pain, a mood, a wish should go around the world without an owner, independently. A sensation is impossible without a sentient being. The inner world presupposes somebody whose inner world it is.

[6]I am not here in the happy position of a mineralogist who shows his audience a rock-crystal: I cannot put a thought in the hands of my readers with the request that they should examine it from all sides. Something in itself not perceptible by sense, the thought, is presented to the reader – and I must be content with that – wrapped up in a perceptible linguistic form. The pictorial aspect of language presents difficulties. The sensible always breaks in and makes expressions pictorial and so improper. So one fights against language, and I am compelled to occupy myself with language although it is not my proper concern here. I hope I have succeeded in making clear to my readers what I mean by 'a thought'.

Thirdly: ideas need an owner. Things of the outer world are on the contrary independent.

My companion and I are convinced that we both see the same field; but each of us has a particular sense-impression of green. I glimpse a strawberry among the green strawberry leaves. My companion cannot find it, he is colour-blind. The colour-impression he gets from the strawberry is not noticeably different from the one he gets from the leaf. Now does my companion see the green leaf as red, or does he see the red berry as green, or does he see both with one colour which I am not acquainted with at all? These are unanswerable, indeed really nonsensical, questions. For when the word 'red' is meant not to state a property of things but to characterize sense-impressions belonging to my consciousness, it is only applicable within the realm of my consciousness. For it is impossible to compare my sense-impression with someone else's. For that, it would be necessary to bring together in one consciousness a sense-impression belonging to one consciousness and a sense-impression belonging to another consciousness. Now even if it were possible to make an idea disappear from one consciousness and at the same time make an idea appear in another consciousness, the question whether it is the same idea would still remain unanswerable. It is so much of the essence of any one of my ideas to be a content of my consciousness, that any idea someone else has is, just as such, different from mine. But might it not be possible that my ideas, the entire content of my consciousness, might be at the same time the content of a more embracing, perhaps Divine consciousness? Only if I were myself part of the Divine Being. But then would they really be my ideas, would I be their owner? This so far oversteps the limits of human understanding that we must leave this possibility out of account. In any case it is impossible for us men to compare other people's ideas with our own. I pick the strawberry, I hold | it between my fingers. Now my companion sees it too, this same strawberry; but each of us has his own idea. Nobody else has my idea, but many people can see the same thing. Nobody else has my pain. Someone may have sympathy with me, but still my pain belongs to me and his sympathy to him. He has not got my pain, and I have not got his feeling of sympathy.

Fourthly: every idea has only one owner; no two men have the same idea.

For otherwise it would exist independently of this man and independently of that man. Is that lime-tree my idea? By using the expression 'that lime-tree' in this question I am really already anticipating the answer, for I mean to use this expression to designate what I see and other people too can look at and touch. There are now two possibilities. If my intention is realized, if I do designate something with the expression 'that lime-tree', then the thought expressed in the sentence 'That lime-tree is my idea' must obviously be denied. But if my intention is not realized, if I only think I see without really seeing, if on that account the designation 'that lime-tree' is empty, then I have wandered into the realm of fiction without knowing it or meaning to. In that case neither the content of the sentence 'That lime-tree is my idea' nor the content of the sentence 'That lime-tree is not my idea' is true, for in both cases I have a predication which lacks an object. So then I can refuse to answer the question, on the ground that the content of the sentence 'That lime-tree is my idea' is fictional. I have, of course, got an idea then, but that is not what I am using the words 'that lime-tree' to designate. Now someone might really want to designate one of his ideas with the words 'that lime-tree'. He would then be the owner of that to which he wants to designate with those words, but then he would not see that lime-tree and no one else would see it or be its owner.

I now return to the question: is a thought an idea? If other people can assent to the thought I express in the Pythagorean theorem just as I do, then it does not belong to the content of my consciousness, I am not its owner; yet I can, nevertheless, acknowledge it as true. However, if what is taken to be the content of the Pythagorean theorem by me and by somebody else is not the same thought at all, we should not really say '*the* Pythagorean theorem', but '*my* Pythagorean theorem', '*his* Pythagorean theorem', and these would be different, for the sense necessarily goes with the sentence. In that case my thought may be the content of my consciousness and his thought the content of his. Could the sense of my Pythagorean theorem be true and the sense of his false? I said that the word 'red' was applicable only in the sphere of my consciousness if it was not meant to state a property of things but to characterize some of my own sense-impressions. Therefore the words 'true' and 'false', as I understand them, might also be applicable only in 69   the realm of my consciousness, if they were not | meant to apply to something of which I was not the owner, but to characterize in some way the content of my consciousness. Truth would then be confined to this content and it would remain doubtful whether anything at all similar occurred in the consciousness of others.

If every thought requires an owner and belongs to the contents of his consciousness, then the thought has this owner alone; and there is no science common to many on which many could work, but perhaps I have my science, a totality of thoughts whose owner I am, and another person has his. Each of us is concerned with contents of his own consciousness. No contradiction between the two sciences would then be possible, and it would really be idle to dispute about truth; as idle, indeed almost as ludicrous, as for two people to dispute whether a hundred-mark note were genuine, where each meant the one he himself had in his pocket and understood the word 'genuine' in his own particular sense. If someone takes thoughts to be ideas, what he then accepts as true is, on his own view, the content of consciousness, and does not properly concern other people at all. If he heard from me the opinion that a thought is not an idea he could not dispute it, for, indeed, it would not now concern him.

So the result seems to be: thoughts are neither things in the external world nor ideas.

A third realm must be recognized. Anything belonging to this realm has it in common with ideas that it cannot be perceived by the senses, but has it in common with things that it does not need an owner so as to belong to the contents of his consciousness. Thus for example the thought we have expressed in the Pythagorean theorem is timelessly true, true independently of whether anyone takes it to be true. It needs no owner. It is not true only from the time when it is discovered; just as a planet, even before anyone saw it, was in interaction with other planets.[7]

But I think I hear an odd objection. I have assumed several times that the same thing as I see can also be observed by other people. But what if everything were only a dream? If I only dreamed I was walking in the company of somebody else, if I only dreamed that my companion saw the green field as I did, if it were all only a play performed on the stage of my consciousness, it would be doubtful whether there were things of the external world at all. Perhaps the realm of things is empty and I do not see any things or any men, but only have ideas of which I myself am the owner. An idea, being something which can no more exist independently of me than my feeling of fatigue, cannot be a man, cannot | look at the same field together with me, cannot see the strawberry I am holding. It is quite incredible that I really have only my inner world, instead of the whole environment in which I supposed myself to move and to act. And yet this is an inevitable consequence of the thesis that only what is my idea can be the object of my awareness. What would follow from this thesis if it were true? Would there then be other men? It would be possible, but I should know nothing of them.   70

---

[7]A person sees a thing, has an idea, grasps or thinks a thought. When he grasps or thinks a thought he does not create it but only comes to stand in a certain relation to what already existed – a different relation from seeing a thing or having an idea.

For a man cannot be my idea; consequently, if our thesis were true, he cannot be an object of my awareness either. And so this would undercut any reflections in which I assumed that something was an object for somebody else as it was for myself, for even if this were to happen I should know nothing of it. It would be impossible for me to distinguish something owned by myself from something I did not own. In judging something not to be my idea I would make it into the object of my thinking and, therefore, into my idea. On this view, is there a green field? Perhaps, but it would not be visible to me. For if a field is not my idea, it cannot, according to our thesis, be an object of my awareness. But if it is my idea it is invisible, for ideas are not visible. I can indeed have the idea of a green field; but this is not green, for there are no green ideas. Does a missile weighing a hundred kilogrammes exist, according to this view? Perhaps, but I could know nothing of it. If a missile is not my idea then, according to our thesis, it cannot be an object of my awareness, of my thinking. But if a missile were my idea, it would have no weight. I can have an idea of a heavy missile. This then contains the idea of weight as a constituent idea. But this constituent idea is not a property of the whole idea, any more than Germany is a property of Europe. So the consequence is:

Either the thesis that only what is my idea can be the object of my awareness is false, or all my knowledge and perception is limited to the range of my ideas, to the stage of my consciousness. In this case I should have only an inner world and I should know nothing of other people.

It is strange how, in the course of such reflections, opposites turn topsy-turvy. There is, let us suppose, a physiologist of the senses. As is proper for someone investigating nature scientifically, he is at the outset far from supposing the things that he is convinced he sees and touches to be his own ideas. On the contrary, he believes that in sense-impressions he has most reliable evidence of things wholly independent of his feeling, imagining, thinking, which have no need of his consciousness. So little does he consider nerve-fibres and ganglion-cells to be the content of his consciousness that he is on the contrary inclined to regard his consciousness as dependent on nerve-fibres and ganglion-cells. He establishes that light-rays, refracted in the eye, strike the visual nerve-endings and there bring about a change, stimulus. From this something is transmitted through nerve-fibres to ganglion-cells. Further 71 processes in the nervous system perhaps follow upon this, and | colour-impressions arise, and these perhaps combine to make up what we call the idea of a tree. Physical, chemical and physiological occurrences get in between the tree and my idea. Only occurrences in my nervous system are immediately connected with my consciousness – or so it seems – and every observer of the tree has his particular occurrences in his particular nervous system. Now light-rays before they enter my eye, may be reflected by a mirror and diverge as if they came from places behind the mirror. The effects on the visual nerves and all that follows will now take place just as they would if the light-rays had come from a tree behind the mirror and had been propagated undisturbed to the eye. So an idea of a tree will finally occur even though such a tree does not exist at all. The refraction of light too, with the mediation of the eye and nervous system, may give rise to an idea to which nothing at all corresponds. But the stimulation of the visual nerves need not even happen because of light. If lightning strikes near us, we believe we see flames, even though we cannot see the lightning itself. In this case the visual nerve is perhaps stimulated by electric currents occurring in our body as a result of the flash of lightning. If the visual nerve is stimulated by this means in just the way it would be stimulated by light-rays coming from flames, then we believe we see flames. It just depends on the stimulation of the visual nerve, no matter how that itself comes about.

We can go a step further. Properly speaking this stimulation of the visual nerve is not immediately given; it is only an hypothesis. We believe that a thing independent of us stimulates a nerve and by this means produces a sense-impression; but strictly speaking we experience only that end of the process which impinges on our consciousness. Might not this sense-impression, this sensation, which we attribute to a nerve-stimulation, have other causes also, just as the same nerve-stimulation may arise in different ways? If we call what happens in our consciousness an idea, then we really experience only ideas, not their causes. And if the scientist wants to avoid all mere hypothesis, then he is left just with ideas; everything dissolves into ideas, even the light-rays, nerve-fibres and ganglion-cells from which he started. So he finally undermines the foundations of his own construction. Is everything an idea? Does everything need an owner without which it could have no existence? I have considered myself as the owner of my ideas, but am I not myself an idea? It seems to me as if I were lying in a deck-chair, as if I could see the toes of a pair of polished boots, the front part of a pair of trousers, a waistcoat, buttons, parts of a jacket, in particular the sleeves, two hands, some hair of a beard, the blurred outline of a nose. Am I myself this entire complex of visual impressions, this aggregate idea? It also seems to me as if I saw a chair over there. That is an idea. I am not actually much different from the chair myself, | for am I not myself just a complex of sense-impressions, an idea? But where then is

72

the owner of these ideas? How do I come to pick out one of these ideas and set it up as the owner of the rest? Why need this chosen idea be the idea I like to call 'I'? Could I not just as well choose the one that I am tempted to call a chair? Why, after all, have an owner for ideas at all? An owner would anyhow be something essentially different from ideas that were just owned; something independent, not needing any extraneous owner. If everything is idea, then there is no owner of ideas. And so now once again I experience opposites turning topsy-turvy. If there is no owner of ideas then there are also no ideas, for ideas need an owner and without one they cannot exist. If there is no ruler, there are also no subjects. The dependence which I found myself induced to ascribe to the sensation as contrasted with the sentient being, disappears if there no longer is any owner. What I called ideas are then independent objects. No reason remains for granting an exceptional position to that object which I call 'I'.

But is that possible? Can there be an experience without someone to experience it? What would this whole play be without a spectator? Can there be a pain without someone who has it? Being felt necessarily goes with pain, and furthermore someone feeling it necessarily goes with its being felt. But then there *is* something which is not my idea and yet can be the object of my awareness, of my thinking; I myself am such a thing. Or can I be one part of the content of my consciousness, while another part is, perhaps, an idea of the Moon? Does this perhaps take place when I judge that *I* am looking at *the Moon*? Then this first part would have a consciousness, and part of the content of this consciousness would be I myself once more. And so on. Yet it is surely inconceivable that I should be inside myself like this in an infinite nest of boxes, for then there would not be just one I but infinitely many. I am not my own idea; and when I assert something about myself, e.g. that I am not feeling any pain at the moment, then my judgement concerns something which is not a content of my consciousness, is not my idea, namely myself. Therefore that about which I state something is not necessarily my idea. But someone perhaps objects: if I think I have no pain at the moment, does not the word 'I' answer to comething in the content of my consciousness? and is that not an idea? That may be so. A certain idea in my consciousness may be associated with the idea of the word 'I'. But then this is one idea among other ideas, and I am its owner as I am the owner of the other ideas. I have an idea of myself, but I am not identical with this idea. What is a content of my consciousness, my idea, should be sharply distinguished from what is an object of my thought. Therefore the thesis that only what belongs to the content of my consciousness can be the object of my awareness, of my thought, is false. |

Now the way is clear for me to acknowledge another man likewise as 73 an independent owner of ideas. I have an idea of him, but I do not confuse it with him himself. And if I state something about my brother, I do not state it about the idea that I have of my brother.

The patient who has a pain is the owner of this pain, but the doctor who is treating him and reflects on the cause of this pain is not the owner of the pain. He does not imagine he can relieve the pain by anaesthetizing himself. There may very well be an idea in the doctor's mind that answers to the patient's pain, but that is not the pain, and is not what the doctor is trying to remove. The doctor might consult another doctor. Then one must distinguish: first, the pain, whose owner is the patient; secondly, the first doctor's idea of this pain; thirdly, the second doctor's idea of this pain. This last idea does indeed belong to the content of the second doctor's consciousness, but it is not the object of his reflection; it is rather an aid to reflection, as a drawing may be. The two doctors have as their common objective of thought the patient's pain, which they do not own. It may be seen from him this that not only a thing but also an idea may be a common object of thought for people who do not have the idea.

In this way, it seems to me, the matter becomes intelligible. If man could not think and could not take as the object of his thought something of which he was not the owner, he would have an inner world but no environment. But may this not be based on a mistake? I am convinced that the idea I associate with the words 'my brother' corresponds to something that is not my idea and about which I can say something. But may I not be making a mistake about this? Such mistakes do happen. We then, against our will, lapse into fiction. Yes, indeed! By the step with which I win an environment for myself I expose myself to the risk of error. And here I come up against a further difference between my inner world and the external world. I cannot doubt that I have a visual impression of green, but it is not so certain that I see a lime-leaf. So, contrary to widespread views, we find certainty in the inner world, while doubt never altogether leaves us in our excursions into the external world. But the probability is nevertheless in many cases hard to distinguish from certainty, so we can venture to judge about things in the external world. And we must make this venture even at the risk of error if we do not want to fall into far greater dangers.

As the result of these last considerations I lay down the following: not everything that can be the object of my acquaintance is an idea. I, being owner of ideas, am not myself an idea. Nothing now stops me from acknowledging other men to be owners of ideas, just as I am

74   myself. And, once given the possibility, the probability | is very great, so great that it is in my opinion no longer distinguishable from certainty. Would there be a science of history otherwise? Would not all moral theory, all law, otherwise collapse? What would be left of religion? The natural sciences too could only be assessed as fables like astrology and alchemy. Thus the reflections I have set forth on the assumption that there are other men besides myself, who can make the same thing the object of their consideration, their thinking, remain in force without any essential weakening.

Not everything is an idea. Thus I can also acknowledge thoughts as independent of me; other men can grasp them just as much as I; I can acknowledge a science in which many can be engaged in research. We are not owners of thoughts as we are owners of our ideas. We do not *have* a thought as we have, say, a sense-impression, but we also do not *see* a thought as we see, say, a star. So it is advisable to choose a special expression; the word 'grasp' suggests itself for the purpose.[8] To the grasping of thoughts there must then correspond a special mental capacity, the power of thinking. In thinking we do not produce thoughts, we grasp them. For what I have called thoughts stand in the closest connection with truth. What I acknowledge as true, I judge to be true quite apart from my acknowledging its truth or even thinking about it. That someone thinks it has nothing to do with the truth of a thought. 'Facts, facts, facts' cries the scientist if he wants to bring home the necessity of a firm foundation for science. What is a fact? A fact is a thought that is true. But the scientist will surely not acknowledge something to be the firm foundation of science if it depends on men's varying states of consciousness. The work of science does not consist in creation, but in the discovery of true thoughts. The astronomer can apply a mathematical truth in the investigation of long past events which took place when – on Earth at least – no one had yet recognized that truth. He can do this because the truth of a thought is timeless. Therefore that truth cannot have come to be only upon its discovery.

Not everything is an idea. Otherwise psychology would contain all the sciences within it, or at least it would be the supreme judge over all the sciences. Otherwise psychology would rule even over logic and mathematics. But nothing would be a greater misunderstanding of mathematics than making it subordinate to psychology. Neither logic

[8]The expression 'grasp' is as metaphorical as 'content of consciousness'. The nature of language does not permit anything else. What I hold in my hand can certainly be regarded as the content of my hand; but all the same it is the content of my hand in quite another and a more extraneous way than are the bones and muscles of which the hand consists or again the tensions these undergo.

nor mathematics has the task of investigating minds and contents of consciousness owned by individual men. Their task could perhaps be represented rather as the investigation of *the* mind; of *the* mind, not of minds. |

The grasp of a thought presupposes someone who grasps it, who 75 thinks. He is the owner of the thinking, not of the thought. Although the thought does not belong with the contents of the thinker's consciousness, there must be something in his consciousness that is aimed at the thought. But this should not be confused with the thought itself. Similarly Algol itself is different from the idea someone has of Algol.

A thought belongs neither to my inner world as an idea, nor yet to the external world, the world of things perceptible by the senses.

This consequence, however cogently it may follow from the exposition, will nevertheless perhaps not be accepted without opposition. It will, I think, seem impossible to some people to obtain information about something not belonging to the inner world except by sense-perception. Sense-perception indeed is often thought to be the most certain, even the sole, source of knowledge about everything that does not belong to the inner world. But with what right? For sense-perception has as necessary constituents our sense-impressions and these are a part of the inner world. In any case two men do not have the same sense-impressions though they may have similar ones. Sense-impressions alone do not reveal the external world to us. Perhaps there is a being that has only sense-impressions without seeing or touching things. To have visual impressions is not to see things. How does it happen that I see the tree just there where I do see it? Obviously it depends on the visual impressions I have and on the particular sort which occur because I see with two eyes. On each of the two retinas there arises, physically speaking, a particular image. Someone else sees the tree in the same place. He also has two retinal images but they differ from mine. We must assume that these retinal images determine our impressions. Consequently the visual impressions we have are not only not the same, but markedly different from each other. And yet we move about in the same external world. Having visual impressions is certainly necessary for seeing things, but not sufficient. What must still be added is not anything sensible. And yet this is just what opens up the external world for us; for without this non-sensible something everyone would remain shut up in his inner world. So perhaps, since the decisive factor lies in the non-sensible, something non-sensible, even without the co-operation of sense-impressions, could also lead us out of the inner world and enable us to grasp thoughts. Outside our inner world we should have to distinguish the external world proper of sensible, perceptible things and the realm of what is non-sensibly perceptible. We should need something non-sensible for the recognition of both realms; but for the sense-perception of things we should need sense-impressions as well, and these belong entirely to the inner world. So the distinction between the ways in which a thing and a thought are given mainly consists in something which is assignable, not to either of the two realms, but to the inner world. Thus I cannot find this distinction to be so great as to make impossible the presentation of a thought that does not belong to the inner world. |

76   A thought, admittedly, is not the sort of thing to which it is usual to apply the term 'actual'. The world of actuality is a world in which this acts on that and changes it and again undergoes reactions itself and is changed by them. All this is a process in time. We will hardly admit what is timeless and unchangeable to be actual. Now is a thought changeable or is it timeless? The thought we express by the Pythagorean theorem is surely timeless, eternal, unvarying. But are there not thoughts which are true today but false in six months' time? The thought, for example, that the tree there is covered with green leaves, will surely be false in six months' time. No, for it is not the same thought at all. The words 'This tree is covered with green leaves' are not sufficient by themselves to constitute the expression of thought, for the time of utterance is involved as well. Without the time-specification thus given we have not a complete thought, i.e. we have no thought at all. Only a sentence with the time-specification filled out, a sentence complete in every respect, expresses a thought. But this thought, if it is true, is true not only today or tomorrow but timelessly. Thus the present tense in 'is true' does not refer to the speaker's present; it is, if the expression be permitted, a tense of timelessness. If we merely use the assertoric sentence-form and avoid the word 'true', two things must be distinguished, the expression of the thought and assertion. The time-specification that may be contained in the sentence belongs only to the expression of the thought; the truth, which we acknowledge by using the assertoric sentence-form, is timeless. To be sure the same words, on account of the variability of language with time, may take on another sense, express another thought; this change, however, relates only to the linguistic realm.

    And yet what value could there be for us in the eternally unchangeable, which could neither be acted upon nor act on us? Something entirely and in every respect inactive would be quite unactual, and so far as we are concerned it would not be there. Even the timeless, if it is to be anything for us, must somehow be implicated with the temporal.

What would a thought be for me if it were never grasped by me? But' by grasping a thought I come into a relation to it, and it to me. It is possible that the same thought as is thought by me today was not thought by me yesterday. Of course this does away with strict timelessness. But we may be inclined to distinguish between essential and inessential properties and to regard something as timeless if the changes it undergoes involve only inessential properties. A property of a thought will be called inessential if it consists in, or follows from, the fact that this thought is grasped by a thinker.

How does a thought act? By being grasped and taken to be true. This is a process in the inner world of a thinker which may have further consequences in this inner world, and which may also encroach on the sphere of the will and make itself noticeable in the outer world as well. If, for example, I grasp the thought we express by the theorem of Pythagoras, the consequence may be that I | recognize it to be true, 77 and further that I apply it in making a decision, which brings about the acceleration of masses. This is how our actions are usually led up to by acts of thinking and judging. And so thoughts may indirectly influence the motion of masses. The influence of man on man is brought about for the most part by thoughts. People communicate thoughts. How do they do this? They bring about changes in the common external world, and these are meant to be perceived by someone else, and so give him a chance to grasp a thought and take it to be true. Could the great events of world history have come about without the communication of thoughts? And yet we are inclined to regard thoughts as unactual, because they appear to do nothing in relation to events, whereas thinking, judging, stating, understanding, in general doing things, are affairs that concern men. How very different the actuality of a hammer appears, compared with that of a thought! How different a process handing over a hammer is from communicating a thought! The hammer passes from one control to another, it is gripped, it undergoes pressure, and thus its density, the disposition of its parts, is locally changed. There is nothing of all this with a thought. It does not leave the control of the communicator by being communicated, for after all man has no power over it. When a thought is grasped, it at first only brings about changes in the inner world of the one who grasps it; yet it remains untouched in the core of its essence, for the changes it undergoes affect only inessential properties. There is lacking here something we observe everywhere in physical process – reciprocal action. Thoughts are not wholly unactual but their actuality is quite different from the actuality of things. And their action is brought about by a performance of the thinker; without this they would be inactive, at least as far as we can see. And yet the thinker does not create them but must take them as they are. They can be true without being grasped by a thinker; and they are not wholly unactual even then, at least if they *could* be grasped and so brought into action.

PART II

NEGATION

A propositional question contains a demand that we should either 143
acknowledge the truth of a thought, or reject it as false. In order that
we may meet this demand correctly, two things are requisite: first, the
wording of the question must enable us to recognize without any doubt
the thought that is referred to; secondly, this thought must not belong
to fiction. I always assume in what follows that these | conditions are 144
fulfilled. The answer to a question[9] is an assertion based upon a
judgement; this is so equally whether the answer is affirmative or
negative.

Here, however, a difficulty arises. If a thought has being by being
true, then the expression 'false thought' is just as self-contradictory, as
'thought that has no being'. In that case the expression 'the thought:
three is greater than five' is an empty one; and accordingly in science it
must not be used at all – except between quotation-marks. In that case
we may not say 'that three is greater five is false'; for the grammatical
subject is empty.

But can we not at least ask if something is true? In a question we
can distinguish between the demand for a judgement and the special
content of the question, the point as to which we must judge. In what
follows I shall call this special content simply the content of the
question, or the sense of the corresponding interrogative sentence. Now
has the interrogative sentence

'Is 3 greater than 5?'

a sense, if the being of a thought consists in its being true? If not, the
question cannot have a thought as its content; and one is inclined to
say that the interrogative sentence has no sense at all. But this surely
comes about because we see the falsity at once. Has the interrogative
sentence

'Is $(21/20)^{100}$ greater than $^{10}\sqrt{10^{21}}$?'

got a sense? If we had worked out that the answer must be affirmative,

[9]Here and in what follows I always mean a propositional question when I just write
'question'.

we could accept the interrogative sentence as making sense, for it would have a thought as its sense. But what if the answer had to be negative? In that case, on our supposition, we should have no thought that was the sense of the question. But surely the interrogative sentence must have some sense or other, if it is to contain a question at all. And are we really not asking for something in this sentence? May we not be wanting to get an answer to it? In that case, it depends on the answer whether we are to suppose that the question has a thought as its content. But it must be already possible to grasp the sense of the interrogative sentence before answering the question; for otherwise no answer would be possible at all. So that which we can grasp as the sense of the interrogative sentence before answering the question – and only this can properly be called the sense of the interrogative sentence – cannot be a thought, if the being of a thought consists in being true. 'But is it not a truth that the Sun is bigger than the Moon? And does not the being of a truth just consist in its being true? Must we not therefore recognize after all that the sense of the interrogative sentence:

'Is the Sun bigger than the Moon?'

is a truth, a thought whose being consists in its being true?' No! Truth cannot go along with the sense of an interrogative sentence; that would contradict the very nature of a question. The content of a question is that as to which we must judge. | Consequently truth cannot be counted as going along with the content of the question. When I raise the question whether the Sun is bigger than the Moon, I am seeing the sense of the interrogative sentence

'Is the Sun bigger than the Moon?'

Now if this sense were a thought whose being consisted in its being true, then I should at the same time see that this sense was true,. Grasping the sense would at the same time be an act of judging; and the utterance of the interrogative sentence would at the same time be an assertion, and so an answer to the question. But in an interrogative sentence neither the truth nor the falsity of the sense may be asserted. Hence an interrogative sentence has not as its sense something whose being consists in its being true. The very nature of a question demands a separation between the acts of grasping a sense and of judging. And since the sense of an interrogative sentence is always also inherent in the assertoric sentence that gives an answer to the question, this separation must be carried out for assertoric sentences too. It is a matter of what we take the word 'thought' to mean. In any case, we need a short term for what can be the sense of an interrogative sentence. I call this a thought. If we use language this way, not all thoughts are true. The being of a thought thus does not consist in its being true. We must recognize that there are thoughts in this sense, since we use questions in scientific work; for the investigator must sometimes content himself with raising a question, until he is able to answer it. In raising the question he is grasping a thought. Thus I may also say: The investigator must sometimes content himself with grasping a thought. This is anyhow already a step towards the goal, even if it is not yet a judgement. There must, then, be thoughts, in the sense I have assigned to the word. Thoughts that perhaps turn out later on to be false have a justifiable use in science, and must not be treated as having no being. Consider indirect proof; here knowledge of the truth is attained precisely through our grasping a false thought. The teacher says 'Suppose *a* were not equal to *b*.' A beginner at once thinks 'What nonsense! I can see that *a is* equal to *b*'; he is confusing the senselessness of a sentence with the falsity of the thought expressed in it.

Of course we cannot infer anything from a false thought; but the false thought may be part of a true thought, from which something can be inferred. The thought contained in the sentence:

'If the accused was in Rome at the time of the deed, he did not commit the murder'[10]

may be acknowledged to be true by someone who does not know if the accused was in Rome at the time of the deed nor if he committed the murder. Of the two component thoughts contained in the whole, neither the antecedent nor the consequent is being uttered assertively when the whole | is presented as true. We have then only a single act of judgement, but three thoughts, viz. the whole thought, the antecedent, and the consequent. If one of the clauses were senseless, the whole would be senseless. From this we see what a difference it makes whether a sentence is senseless or on the contrary expresses a false thought. Now for thoughts consisting of an antecedent and a consequent there obtains the law that, without prejudice to the truth, the opposite of the antecedent may become the consequent, and the opposite of the consequent the antecedent. In English this procedure is called *contraposition.*

According to this law, we may pass from the proposition

146

[10]Here we must suppose that these words by themselves do not contain the thought in its entirety; that we must gather from the circumstances in which they are uttered how to supplement them so as to get a complete thought.

'If $(21/20)^{100}$ is greater than $\sqrt[10]{10^{21}}$, then $(21/20)^{1000}$ is greater than 10^{21}'

to the proposition

'If $(21/20)^{1000}$ is not greater than 10^{21}, then $(21/20)^{100}$ is not greater than $\sqrt[10]{10^{21}}$'.

And such transitions are important for indirect proofs, which would otherwise not be possible.

Now if the first complex thought has a true antecedent, viz, $(21/20)^{100}$ *is greater than* $\sqrt[10]{10^{21}}$, then the second complex thought has a false consequent, viz. $(21/20)^{100}$ *is not greater than* $\sqrt[10]{10^{21}}$. So anybody that admits the legitimacy of our transition from *modus ponens* to *modus tollens* must acknowledge that even a false thought has being; for otherwise either only the consequent would be left in the *modus ponens* or only the antecedent in the *modus tollens*; and one of these would likewise be abolished as a nonentity.

The being of a thought may also be taken to lie in the possibility of different thinkers' grasping the thought as one and the same thought. In that case the fact that a thought had no being would consist in several thinkers' each associating with the sentence a sense of his own; this sense would in that case be a content of his particular consciousness, so that there would be no *common* sense that could be grasped by several people. Now is a false thought a thought that in this sense has no being? In that case investigators who had discussed among themselves whether bovine tuberculosis is communicable to men, and had finally agreed that such communicability did not exist, would be in the same position as people who had used in conversation the expression 'this rainbow', and now came to see that they had not been designating anything by these words, since what each of them had had was a phenomenon of which he himself was the owner. The investigators would have to realize that they had been deceived by a false appearance; for the presupposition that could alone have made all their activity and talk reasonable would have turned out not to be fulfilled; they would not have been giving the question that they discussed a sense common to all of them.

But it must be possible to put a question to which the true answer is negative. The content of such a question is, in my terminology, a thought. It must be possible for several people who hear the same interrogative sentence to grasp the same sense and recognize the falsity of it. Trial by jury would assuredly be a silly arrangement if it could not be assumed that each of the jurymen could understand the question at issue in the same sense. So the sense of an interrogative sentence, even when the question has to be answered in the negative, is something that can be grasped by several people.

What else would follow if the truth of a thought consisted in the possibility of its being grasped by several people as one and the same thing, whereas a sentence that expressed something false had no sense common to several people?

If a thought is true and is a complex of thoughts of which one is false, then the whole thought could be grasped by several people as one and the same thing, but the false component thought could not, Such a case may occur. E.g. it may be that the following assertion is justifiably made before a jury: 'If the accused was in Rome at the time of the deed, he did not commit the murder'; and it may be false that the accused was in Rome at the time of the deed. In that case the jurymen could grasp the same thought when they heard the sentence 'If the accused was in Rome at the time of the deed, he did not commit the murder,' whereas each of them would associate a sense of his own with the *if*-clause. Is this possible? Can a thought that is present to all the jurymen as one and the same thing have a part that is not common to all of them? If the whole needs no owner, no part of it needs an owner.

So a false thought is not a thought that has no being – not even if we take 'being' to mean 'not needing an owner.' A false thought must be admitted, not indeed as true, but as sometimes indispensable: first, as the sense of an interrogative sentence; secondly, as part of a hypothetical thought-complex; thirdly, in negation. It must be possible to negate a false thought, and for this I need the thought; I cannot negate what is not there. And by negation I cannot transform something that needs me as its owner into something of which I am not the owner, and which can be grasped by several people as one and the same thing.

Now is negation of a thought to be regarded as dissolution of the thought into its component parts? By their negative verdict the jury can in no way alter the make-up of the thought that the question presented to them expresses. The thought is true or false quite independently of their giving a right or a wrong verdict in regard to it. And if it is false it is still a thought. If after the jury's verdict there is no thought at all, but only fragments of thought, then the same was already the case before the verdict; in what looked like a question, the jury were not presented with any thought at all, but only with fragments of thought; they had nothing to pass a verdict on.

Our act of judgement can in no way alter the make-up of a thought. We can only acknowledge what is there. A true thought cannot | be   148 affected by our act of judgement. In the sentence that expresses the

N

thought we can insert a 'not'; and the sentence we thus get does not contain a non-thought (as I have shown) but may be quite justifiably used as antecedent or consequent in a hypothetical sentence complex. Only, since it is false, it may not be uttered assertively. But this procedure does not touch the original thought in any way; it remains true as before.

Can we affect a false thought somehow by negating it? We cannot do this either; for a false thought is still a thought and may occur as a component part of a true thought. The sentence

'3 is greater than 5',

uttered non-assertively, has a false sense; if we insert a 'not,' we get

'3 is not greater than 5',

a sentence that may be uttered assertively. There is no trace here of a dissolution of the thought, a separation of its parts.

How, indeed, could a thought be dissolved? How could the interconnection of its parts be split up? The world of thoughts has a model in the world of sentences, expressions, words, signs. To the structure of the thought there corresponds the compounding of words into a sentence; and here the order is in general not indifferent. To the dissolution or destruction of the thought there must accordingly correspond a tearing apart of the words, such as happens, e.g., if a sentence written on paper is cut up with scissors, so that on each scrap of paper there stands the expression for part of a thought. These scraps can then be shuffled at will or carried away by the wind; the connection is dissolved, the original order can no longer be recognized. Is this what happens when we negate a thought? No! The thought would undoubtedly survive even this execution of it in effigy. What we do is to insert the word 'not,' and, apart from this, leave the word-order unaltered. The original wording can still be recognized; the order may not be altered at will. Is this dissolution, separation? Quite the reverse! it results in a firmly-built structure.

Consideration of the law *duplex negatio affirmat* makes it specially plain to see that negation has no separating or dissolving effect. I start with the sentence

'The Schneekoppe is higher than the Brocken'.

By putting in a 'not' I get:

'The Schneekoppe is not higher than the Brocken'.

(Both sentences are supposed to be uttered non-assertively.) A second negation would produce something like the sentence

> 'It is not true that the Schneekoppe is not higher than the Brocken'.

We already know that the first negation cannot effect any dissolution of the thought; but all the same let us suppose for once that after the first negation we had only | fragments of a thought. We should then have to   149 suppose that the second negation could put these fragments together again. Negation would thus be like a sword that could heal on again the limbs it had cut off. But there the greatest care would be wanted. The parts of the thought have lost all connection and inter-relation on account of its being negated the first time. So by carelessly employing the healing power of negation, we might easily get the sentence:

> 'The Brocken is higher than the Schneekoppe'.

No non-thought is turned into a thought by negation, just as no thought is turned into a non-thought by negation.

A sentence with the word 'not' in its predicate may, like any other, express a thought that can be made into the content of a question; and this, like any propositional question, leaves open our decision as to the answer.

What then are these objects, which negation is supposed to separate? Not parts of sentences: equally, not parts of a thought. Things in the outside world? They do not bother about our negating. Mental images in the interior world of the person who negates? But then how does the juryman know which of his images he ought to separate in given circumstances? The question put before him does not indicate any to him. It may evoke images in him. But the images evoked in the jurymen's inner worlds are different; and in that case each juryman would perform his own act of separation in his own inner world, and this would not be a verdict.

It thus appears impossible to state what really is dissolved, split up, or separated by the act of negation.

With the belief that negation has a dissolving or separating power there hangs together the view that a negative thought is less useful than an affirmative one. But still it cannot be regarded as wholly useless. Consider the inference:

> 'If the accused was not in Berlin at the time of the murder, he did not commit the murder; now the accused was not in Berlin at the time of the murder; therefore he did not commit the murder',

and compare it with the inference:

'If the accused was in Rome at the time of the murder, he did
not commit the murder; now the accused was in Rome at the
time of the murder; therefore he did not commit the murder'.

Both inferences proceed in the same form, and there is not the least
ground in the nature of the .case for our distinguishing between
negative and affirmative premises when we are expressing the law of
inference here involved. People speak of affirmative and negative
judgements; even Kant does so. Translated into my terminology, this
would be a distinction between affirmative and negative thoughts. For
logic at any rate such a distinction is wholly unnecessary; its ground
must be sought outside logic. I know of no logical principle whose
150   verbal expression makes it necessary, or | even preferable, to use these
terms.[11] In any science in which it is a question of conformity to laws,
the thing that we must always ask is: What technical expressions are
necessary or at least useful, in order to give precise expression to the
laws of this science? What does not stand this test cometh of evil.[12]

What is more, it is by no means easy to state what is a negative
judgement (thought). Consider the sentences 'Christ is immortal',
'Christ lives for ever', 'Christ is not immortal', 'Christ is mortal', 'Christ
does not live for ever'. Now which of the thoughts we have here is
affirmative, which negative?

We usually suppose that negation extends to the whole thought
when 'not' is attached to the verb of the predicate. But sometimes the
negative word grammatically forms part of the subject, as in the
sentence 'no man lives to be more than a hundred.' A negation may
occur anywhere in a sentence without making the thought indubitably
negative. We see what tricky questions the expression 'negative judgement (thought)' may lead to. The result may be endless disputes, carried
on with the greatest subtlety, and nevertheless essentially sterile.
Accordingly I am in favour of dropping the distinction between
negative and affirmative judgements or thoughts until such time as we
have a criterion enabling us to distinguish with certainty in any given
case between a negative and an affirmative judgement. When we have

---

[11]Accordingly, in my essay 'Thoughts', *Beiträge zur Philosophie des deutschen Idealismus*
I, p. 58 [p. 351 above], I likewise made no use of the expression 'negative thought.' The
distinction between negative and affirmative thoughts would only have confused the
matter. At no point would there have been occasion to assert something about affirmative
thoughts, excluding negative ones, or to assert something about negative thoughts,
excluding affirmative ones.

[12][An apparent allusion to Matthew v. 37! (*Tr.*)]

such a criterion we shall also see what benefit may be expected from this distinction. For the present I still doubt whether this will be achieved. The criterion cannot be derived from language; for languages are unreliable on logical questions. It is indeed not the least of the logician's tasks to indicate the pitfalls laid by language in the way of the thinker.

After refuting errors, it may be useful to trace the sources from which they have flowed. One source, I think, in this case is the desire to give definitions of the concepts one means to employ. It is certainly praiseworthy to try to make clear to oneself as far as possible the sense one associates with a word. But here we must not forget that not everything can be defined. If we insist at any price on defining what is essentially indefinable, we readily fasten upon inessential accessories, and thus start the inquiry on a wrong track at the very outset. And this is certainly what has happened to many people, who have tried to explain what a judgement is and so have | hit upon compositeness.[13] 151 The judgement is composed of parts that have a certain order, an interconnection, stand in mutual relations; but for what whole we do not get this?

There is another mistake associated with this one: viz. the view that the judging subject sets up the connection or order of the parts in the act of judging and thereby brings the judgement into existence. Here the act of grasping a thought and the acknowledgement of its truth are not kept separate. In many cases, of course, one of these acts follows so directly upon the other that they seem to fuse into one act; but not so in all cases. Years of laborious investigations may come between

---

[13]We are probably best in accord with ordinary usage if we take a judgement to be an act of judging, as a leap is an act of leaping. Of course this leaves the kernel of the difficulty uncracked; it now lies in the word 'judging'. Judging, we may say, is acknowledging the truth of something; what is acknowledged to be true can only be thought. The original kernel now seems to have cracked in two; one part of it lies in the word 'thought' and the other in the word 'true'. Here, for sure, we must stop. The impossibility of an infinite regress in definition is something we must be prepared for in advance.

If a judgement is an act, it happens at a certain time and thereafter belongs to the past. With an act there also belongs an agent, and we do not know the act completely if we do not know the agent. In that case, we cannot speak of a synthetic judgement in the usual sense. If we call it a synthetic judgement that through two points only one straight line passes, then we are taking 'judgement' to mean, not an act performed by a definite man at a definite time, but something timelessly true, even if its being true is not acknowledged by any human being. If we call this sort of thing a truth, then we may perhaps with advantage say 'synthetic truth' instead of 'synthetic judgement'. If we do nevertheless prefer the expression 'synthetic judgement', we must leave out of consideration the sense of the verb 'to judge'.

grasping a thought and acknowledging its truth. It is obvious that here the act of judging did not make the thought or set its parts in order; for the thought was already there. But even the act of grasping a thought is not a production of the thought, is not an act of setting its parts in order; for the thought was already true, and so was already there with its parts in order, before it was grasped. A traveller who crosses a mountain-range does not thereby make the mountain-range; no more does the judging subject make a thought by acknowledging its truth. If he did, the same thought could not be acknowledged as true by one man yesterday and another man to-day; indeed, the same man could not recognize the same thought as true at different times – unless we supposed that the existence of the thought was an intermittent one.

If someone thinks it within his power to produce by an act of judgement that which, in judging, he acknowledges to be true, by setting up an interconnection, an order, among its parts; then it is easy for him to credit himself also with the power of destroying it. As destruction is opposed to construction, to setting up order and interconnection, so also negating seems to be opposed to judging; | and people easily come to suppose that the interconnection is broken up by the act of negation just as it is built up by the act of judgement. Thus judging and negating look like a pair of polar opposites, which, being a pair, are coordinate; a pair comparable, e.g., to oxidation and reduction in chemistry. But when once we see that no interconnection is set up by our judging; that the parts of the thought were already in their order before our judging; then everything appears in a different light. It must be pointed out yet once more that to grasp a thought is not yet to judge; that we may express a thought in a sentence without asserting its truth; that a negative word may be contained in the predicate of a sentence, in which case the sense of this word is part of the sense of the sentence, part of the thought; that by inserting a 'not' in the predicate of a sentence meant to be uttered non-assertively, we get a sentence that expresses a thought, as the original one did. If we call such a transition, from a thought to its opposite, negating the thought, then negating in this sense is not coordinate with judging, and may not be regarded as the polar opposite of judging; for what matters in judging is always the truth, whereas we may pass from a thought to its opposite without asking which is true. To exclude misunderstanding, let it be further observed that this transition occurs in the consciousness of a thinker, whereas the thoughts that are the *termini a quo* and *ad quem* of the transition were already in being before it occurred; so that this psychical event makes no difference to the make-up and the mutual relations of the thoughts.

152

Perhaps the act of negating, which maintains a questionable existence as the polar opposite of judging, is a chimerical construction, formed by a fusion of the act of judging with the negation that I have acknowledged as a possible component of a thought, and to which there corresponds in language the word 'not' as part of the predicate – a chimerical construction, because these parts are quite different in kind. The act of judging is a psychical process, and as such it needs a judging subject as its owner; negation on the other hand is part of a thought, and as such, like the thought itself, it needs no owner, must not be regarded as a content of a consciousness. And yet it is not quite incomprehensible how there can arise at least the illusion of such a chimerical construction. Language has no special word or syllable to express assertion; assertive force is supplied by the form of the assertoric sentence, which is specially well-marked in the predicate. On the other hand the word 'not' stands in intimate connection with the predicate and may be regarded as part of it. Thus a connection may seem to be formed between the word 'not' and the assertoric force in language that answers to the act of judging.

But it is a nuisance to distinguish between the two ways of negating. Really my only aim in introducing the polar opposite of judging was to accommodate myself to a way of thinking that is foreign to me. I now return to my previous | way of speaking. What I have just been designating as the polar opposite of judging I will now regard as a second way of judging – without thereby admitting that there is such a second way. I shall thus be comprising both polar opposites under the common term 'judging'; this may be done, for polar opposites certainly do belong together. The question will then have to be put as follows:

Are there two different ways of judging, of which one is used for the affirmative, and the other for the negative, answer to a question? Or is judging the same act in both cases? Does negating go along with judging? Or is negation part of the thought that underlies the act of judging? Does judging consist, even in the case of a negative answer to a question, in acknowledging the truth of a thought? In that case the thought will not be the one directly contained in the question, but the opposite of this.

Let the question run, e.g., as follows: 'Did the accused intentionally set fire to his house?' How can the answer take the form of an assertoric sentence, if it turns out to be negative? If there is a special way of judging for when we deny, we must correspondingly have a special form of assertion. I may, e.g., say in this case 'it is false that...' and lay it down that this must always have assertoric force attached to it. Thus the answer will run something like this: 'It is false that the accused intentionally set fire to his house.' If on the other hand there is only one way of judging, we shall say assertorically: 'The accused did not intentionally set fire to his house.' And here we shall be presenting as something true the opposite thought to the expressed in the question. The word 'not' here belongs with the expression of this thought. I now refer back to the two inferences I compared together just now. The second premise of the first inference was the negative answer to the question 'was the accused in Berlin at the time of the murder?' – in fact, the answer that we fixed upon in case there is only one way of judging. The thought contained in this premise is contained in the *if*-clause of the first premise, but there it is uttered non-assertively. The second premise of the second inference was the affirmative answer to the question. 'Was the accused in Rome at the time of the murder?' These inferences proceed on the same principle, which is in good agreement with the view that judging is the same act whether the answer to a question is affirmative or negative. If on the other hand we had to recognize a special way of judging for the negative case – and correspondingly, in the realm of words and sentences, a special form of assertion – the matter would be otherwise. The first premise of the first inference would run as before:

> 'If the accused was not in Berlin at the time of the murder, he did not commit the murder'.

Here we could not say 'If it is false that the accused was in Berlin at the time of the murder'; for we have laid it down that to the words 'it is false that' assertoric force must always be attached; but in acknowledg-
154 ing the truth of this first premise we are not | acknowledging the truth either of its antecedent or if its consequent. The second premise on the other hand must now run: 'It is false that the accused was in Berlin at the time of the murder'; for being a premise it must be uttered assertively. The inference now cannot be performed in the same way as before; for the thought in the second premise no longer coincides with the antecedent of the first premise; it is now the thought that the accused *was* in Berlin at the time of the murder. If nevertheless we want to allow that the inference is valid, we are thereby acknowledging that the second premise contains the thought that the accused was *not* in Berlin at the time of the murder. This involves separating negation from the act of judging, extracting it from the sense of 'it is false that...', and uniting negation with the thought.

Thus the assumption of two different ways of judging must be rejected. But what hangs on this decision? It might perhaps be regarded as valueless, if it did not effect an economy of logical primitives and their expressions in language. On the assumption of two ways of judging we need:

1. assertoric force for affirmatives;
2. assertoric force for negatives, e.g. inseparably attached to the word 'false';
3. a negating word like 'not' in sentence uttered non-assertorically.

If on the other hand we assume only a single way of judging, we only need:

1. assertoric force;
2. a negating word.

Such economy always shows that analysis has been pushed further, which leads to a clearer insight. There hangs together with this an economy as regards a principle of inference; with our decision we can make do with one where otherwise we need two. If we *can* make do with one way of judging, then we *must*; and in that case we cannot assign to one way of judging the function of setting up order and connection, and to another, the function of dissolving this.

Thus for every thought there is a contradictory[14] thought; we acknowledge the falsity of a thought by admitting the truth of its contradictory. The sentence that expresses the contradictory thought is formed from the expression of the original thought by means of a negative word.

The negative word or syllable often seems to be more closely united to part of the sentence, e.g. the predicate. This may lead us to think that what is negated is the content, not of the whole sentence, but just of this part. We may call a man uncelebrated and thereby indicate the falsity of the thought that he is celebrated. This may be regarded as the negative | answer to the question 'is the man celebrated?'; and hence we   155 may see that we are not here just negating the sense of a word. It is incorrect to say: 'Because the negative syllable is combined with part of the sentence, the sense of the whole sentence is not negated.' On the contrary: it is by combining the negative syllable with a part of the sentence that we do negate the content of the whole sentence. That is to say: in this way we get a sentence in which there is a thought contradicting the one in the original sentence.

I do not intend by this to dispute that negation is sometimes restricted just to a part of the whole thought.

---

[14]We could also say 'an opposite thought'.

P

If one thought contradicts another, then from a sentence whose sense is the one it is easy to construct a sentence expressing the other. Consequently the thought that contradicts another thought appears as made up of that thought and negation. (I do not mean by this, the act of denial.) But the words 'made up of,' 'consist of,' 'component,' 'part' may lead to our looking at it the wrong way. If we choose to speak of parts in this connection, all the same these parts are not mutually independent in the way that we are elsewhere used to find when we have parts of a whole. The thought does not, by its make-up, stand in any need of completion; it is self-sufficient. Negation on the other hand needs to be completed by a thought. The two components, if we choose to employ this expression, are quite different in kind and contribute quite differently towards the formation of the whole. One completes, the other is completed. And it is by this completion that the whole is kept together. To bring out in language the need for completion, we may write 'the negation of...', where the blank after 'of' indicates where the completing expression is to be inserted. For the relation of completing, in the realm of thoughts and their parts, has something similar corresponding to it in the realm of sentences and their parts. (The preposition 'of', ['*von*'], followed by a substantive can also be replaced [in German] by the genitive of the substantive; this may as a rule be more idiomatic, but does not lend itself so well to the purpose of expressing the part that needs completion.) An example may make it even clearer what I have here in mind. The thought that contradicts the thought:

$$(21/20)^{100} \text{ is equal to } \sqrt[10]{10^{21}}$$

is the thought:

$$(21/20)^{100} \text{ is not equal to } \sqrt[10]{10^{21}}.$$

We may also put this as follows:

'The thought:

$$(21/20)^{100} \text{ is not equal to } \sqrt[10]{10^{21}}$$

is the negation of the thought:

$$(21/20)^{100} \text{ is equal to } \sqrt[10]{10^{21}}\text{'.} \mid$$

156   In the last expression (after the penultimate 'is') we can see how the thought is made up of a part that needs completion and a part that completes it. From now on I shall use the word 'negation' (except, e.g.,

within quotation marks) always with the definite article. The definite article '*the*' in the expression

'*the* negation of the thought that 3 is greater than 5'

shows that this expression is meant to designate a definite single thing. This single thing is in our case a thought. The definite article makes the whole expression into a singular name, a proxy for a proper name.

The negation of a thought is itself a thought, and can again be used to complete *the negation*.[15] If I use, in order to complete *the negation,*[15] the negation of the thought that $(21/20)^{100}$ is equal to $^{10}\sqrt{10^{21}}$, what I get is:

the negation of the negation of the thought that $(21/20)^{100}$ is equal to $^{10}\sqrt{10^{21}}$.

This is again a thought. Designations of thoughts with such a structure are got according to the pattern:

'the negation of the negation of *A*',

where '*A*' takes the place of the designation of a thought. Such a designation is to be regarded as directly composed of the parts:

'the negation of ——'
and 'the negation of *A*'.

But it may also be regarded as made up of the parts:

'the negation of the negation of ——'
and: '*A*'.

Here I have first combined the middle part with the part that stands to the left of it and then combined the result with the part '*A*' that stands to the right of it; whereas originally the middle part was combined with '*A*,' and the designation so got, viz.

'the negation of *A*',

was combined with what stood to the left of it

'the negation of ——'.

---

[15][I.e. to complete the thought-component whose verbal expression is '*the negation (of)*...', so as to get a complete thought; just as, in the realm of language, we get a complete designation of a thought by inserting a designation of a thought in the blank of 'the negation of——'. (The italics in the text are ours, not Frege's.) (*Tr.*)]

The two different ways of regarding the designation have answering to them two ways of regarding the structure of the thought designated.[16]

If we compare the designations:

'the negation of the negation of: $(21/20)^{100}$ is equal to $\sqrt[10]{10^{21}}$' and 'the negation of the negation of: 5 is greater than 3'

we recognize a common constituent:

'the negation of the negation of ——': |

157　this designates a part common to the two thoughts – a thought-component that stands in need of completion. In each of our two cases, it is completed by means of a thought: in the first case, the thought that $(21/20)^{100}$ is equal to $\sqrt[10]{10^{21}}$; in the second case, the thought that 5 is greater than 3. The result of this completion is in either case a thought. This common component, which stands in need of completion, may be called double negation. This example shows how something that needs completion can be amalgamated with something that needs completion to form something that needs completion. Here we are presented with a singular case; we have something – the negation of... – amalgamated with itself. Here, of course, metaphors derived from the corporeal realm fail us; for a body cannot be amalgamated with itself so that the result is something different from it. But then neither do bodies need completion, in the sense I intend here. Congruent bodies *can* be put together; and in the realm of designations we have congruence in our present case. Now what corresponds to congruent designations is one and the same thing in the realm of designata.

Metaphorical expressions, if used cautiously, may after all help towards an elucidation. I compare that which needs completion to a wrapping, e.g. a coat, which cannot stand upright by itself; in order to do that, it must be wrapped round somebody. The man whom it is wrapped round may put on another wrapping, e.g. a cloak. The two wrappings unite to form a single wrapping. There are thus two possible ways of looking at the matter; we may say either that a man who already wore a coat was now dressed up in a second wrapping, a cloak, or, that his clothing consists of two wrappings – coat and cloak. These ways of looking at it have absolutely equal justification. The additional wrapping always combines with the one already there to form a new wrapping. Of course we must never forget in this connection that

---

[16][*Bezeichnenden* is here surely a misprint for *bezeichneten* or *zu bezeichnenden*. (*Tr.*)]

dressing up and putting things together are processes in time, whereas what corresponds to this in the realm of thoughts is timeless.

If A is a thought not belonging to fiction, the negation of A likewise does not belong to fiction. In that case, of the two thoughts: A and the negation of A: there is always one and only one that is true. Likewise, of the two thoughts: the negation of A, and the negation of the negation of A: there is always one and only one that is true. Now the negation of A is either true or not true. In the first case, neither A nor the negation of the negation of A is true. In the second case, both A and the negation of the negation of A are true. Thus of the two thoughts: A, and the negation of the negation of A: either both are true or neither is. I may express this as follows:

Wrapping up a thought in double negation does not alter its truth-value.

PART III

COMPOUND THOUGHTS

36 It is astonishing what language can do. With a few syllables it can express an incalculable number of thoughts, so that even if a thought has been grasped by an inhabitant of the Earth for the very first time, a form of words can be found in which it will be understood by someone else to whom it is entirely new. This would not be possible, if we could not distinguish parts in the thought corresponding to the parts of a sentence, so that the structure of the sentence can serve as a picture of the structure of the thought. To be sure, we really talk figuratively when we transfer the relation of whole and part to thoughts; yet the analogy is so ready to hand and so generally appropriate that we are hardly even bothered by the hitches which occur from time to time.

If, then, we look upon thoughts as composed of simple parts, and take these, in turn, to correspond to the simple parts of sentences, we can understand how a few parts of sentences can go to make up a great multitude of sentences, to which, in turn, there correspond a great multitude of thoughts. But the question now arises how a thought comes to be constructed, and how the parts are so combined together that the whole amounts to something more than the parts taken separately. In my article 'Negation'[17] I considered the case where a

37 thought seems to be composed of | a part needing completion (the unsaturated part, as one may call it) which corresponds in language to the negating word, and a thought. There can be no negation without something negated, and this is a thought. The unity of the whole comes about through the fact that the thought saturates the unsaturated part or, as we can also say, completes the part needing completion. And it is natural to suppose that, for logic in general, combination into a whole always comes about by the saturation of something unsaturated.[18]

But here a special case of such combination is to be considered, namely that in which two thoughts are combined to form a single thought. In the realm of language, this corresponds to the combination of two sentences into a whole which likewise is a sentence. On the

---

[17][pp. 373ff. above.]

[18]Here, and in what follows, it must always be remembered that this saturation and combination are not temporal processes.

analogy of the grammatical term 'compound sentence', I shall employ the expression 'compound thought', without wishing to imply by this that every compound sentence has a compound thought as its sense, or that every compound thought is the sense of a compound sentence. By 'compound thought' I shall understand a thought consisting of thoughts, but not of thoughts alone. For a thought is complete and saturated, and needs no completion in order to exist. For this reason, thoughts do not cleave to one another unless they are connected together by something that is not a thought, and it may be taken that this connective is unsaturated. The compound thought must itself be a thought: that is, something either true or false (*tertium non datur*).

Not every sentence composed, linguistically speaking, of sentences will provide us with a serviceable example; for grammar recognizes sentences which logic cannot acknowledge as sentences proper because they do not express thoughts. This is illustrated in relative clauses; for in a relative clause detached from its main clause, we cannot tell what the relative pronoun is supposed to refer to. Such a clause contains no sense whose truth can be investigated; in other words, the sense of a detached relative clause is not a thought. So we must not expect a compound sentence consisting of a main and a relative clause to have as its sense a compound thought.

FIRST KIND OF COMPOUND THOUGHT

In language, the simplest case seems to be that of two main clauses conjoined by 'and'. But the matter is not so simple as it first appears, for in an assertoric sentence we must distinguish between two things: the thought expressed and the assertion. Only the former is in | question here, for it is not acts of judgement that are to be conjoined.[19]   38 I therefore take the sentences conjoined by 'and' to be uttered without assertoric force. Assertoric force can most easily be eliminated by changing the whole into a question; for one can express the same thought in a question as in an assertoric sentence, only without asserting it. If we use 'and' to conjoin two sentences, neither of which is uttered with assertive force, then we have to ask whether the sense of the resultant whole is a thought. For not only each of the component

---

[19]Logicians often seem to mean by 'judgement' what I call 'thought'. In my terminology, one judges by acknowledging a thought as true. This act of acknowledgement I call 'judgement'. judgement is made manifest by a sentence uttered with assertive force. But one can grasp and express a thought without acknowledging it as true, i.e. without judging.

sentences, but also the whole, must have a sense which can be made the content of a question. Suppose witnesses are asked: 'Did the accused deliberately set fire to the pile of wood, and deliberately start a forest-fire?'; the problem then arises whether two questions are involved here, or only one. If the witnesses are free to reply affirmatively to the question about the pile of wood, but negatively to that about the forest-fire, then we have two questions, each containing a thought, and there is no question of a single thought compounded out of these two. But if – as I shall suppose – the witnesses are permitted to answer only 'yes' or 'no', without dividing the whole into sub-questions, then this whole is a single question which should be answered affirmatively only if the accused acted deliberately both in setting fire to the pile of wood and also in starting the forest-fire; and negatively in any other case. Thus, a witness who thinks that the accused certainly set fire to the pile of wood on purpose, but that the fire then spread further and set the forest alight without his meaning it to, must answer the question in the negative, For the thought in the whole question must be distinguished from the two component thoughts: it contains, as well as the component thoughts, that which combines them together; and this corresponds in language to the word 'and'. This word is used here in a particular way; we are concerned only with its use as a conjunction between two sentences proper. I call any sentence a sentence proper if it expresses a thought. But a thought is something which must be either true or false, *tertium non datur*. Furthermore, the 'and' now under discussion can conjoin only sentences which are uttered without assertoric force. I do not mean by this to exclude the act of judgement; but if it occurs, it must relate to the compound thought as a whole. If we wish to present a compound of this first kind as true, we may use the phrase 'It is true that ... and that ...'.

Our 'and' is not meant to conjoin interrogative sentences, any more than assertoric sentences. In our example the witnesses are confronted with only one question. | But the thought proposed for judgement by this question is composed of two thoughts. In his reply, however, the witness must give only a single judgement. Now this may certainly seem an artificial refinement; for doesn't it really come to the same thing, whether the witness first replies affirmatively to the question 'Did the accused deliberately set fire to the pile of wood?' and then to the question 'Did the accused deliberately start a forest-fire?', or rather replies affirmatively at one stroke to the whole question? This may well seem so, in case of an affirmative reply, but the difference shows up more clearly where the answer is negative. For this reason it is useful to express the thought in a single question, since then both negative and affirmative cases will have to be considered in order to understand the thought correctly.

The 'and' whose mode of employment is more precisely delimited in this way seems doubly unsaturated: to saturate it we require both a sentence preceding and another following. And what corresponds to 'and' in the realm of sense must also be doubly unsaturated: inasmuch as it is saturated by thoughts, it combines them together.[20] As a mere thing, of course, the group of letters 'and' is no more unsaturated than any other thing. It may be called unsaturated in respect of its employment as a symbol meant to express a sense, for here it can have the intended sense only when situated between two sentences: its purpose as a symbol requires completion by a preceding and a succeeding sentence. It is really in the realm of sense that unsaturatedness is found, and it is transferred from there to the symbol.

If 'A' and 'B' are both sentences proper, uttered with neither assertoric nor interrogative force, then 'A and B' is likewise a sentence proper, and its sense is a compound thought of the first kind. Hence I also say that 'A and B' expresses a compound thought of the first kind.

That 'B and A' has the same sense as 'A and B' we may see without proof by merely being aware of the sense. Here we have a case where two linguistically different expressions correspond to the same sense. This divergence of expressive symbol and expressed thought is an inevitable consequence of the difference between spatio-temporal phenomena and the world of thoughts.[21]

Finally, we may point out an inference that holds in this connection:

A is true;[22]
B is true; therefore
(A and B) is true. |

SECOND KIND OF COMPOUND THOUGHT

The negation of a compound of the first kind between one thought and   40
another is itself a compound of the same two thoughts. I shall call it a compound thought of the second kind. Whenever a compound thought of the first kind out of two thoughts is false, the compound of the second kind out of them is true, and conversely. A compound of the

---

[20]*Cf.* p. 37 above [of the original].

[21]Another case of this sort is that 'A and A' has the same sense as 'A'.

[22]When I write 'A is true', I mean more exactly 'the thought expressed in the sentence "A" is true'. So too in analogous cases.

second kind is false only if each compounded thought is true, and a compound of the second kind is true whenever at least one of the compounded thoughts is false. In all this it is assumed throughout that the thoughts do not belong to fiction. By presenting a compound thought of the second kind as true, I declare the compounded thoughts to be incompatible.

Without knowing whether

$$(21/20)^{100} \text{ is greater than } \sqrt[10]{10^{21}},$$

or whether

$$(21/20)^{100} \text{ is less than } \sqrt[10]{10^{21}},$$

I can still recognize that the compound of the first kind out of these two thoughts is false. Accordingly, the corresponding compound of the second kind is true. Apart from the thoughts compounded, we have something that connects them, and here too the connective is doubly unsaturated: the connection comes about in that the component thoughts saturate the connective.

To express briefly a compound thought of this kind, I write

'not [A and B]',

where 'A' and 'B' are the sentences corresponding to the compound thoughts. The connective stands out more clearly in this expression: it is the sense of whatever occurs in the expression apart from the letters 'A' and 'B'. The two gaps in the expression

'not [and]'

bring out the two-fold unsaturatedness. The connective is the doubly unsaturated sense of this doubly unsaturated expression. By filling the gaps with expressions of thoughts, we form the expression of a compound thought of the second kind. But we really should not talk of the compound thought as originating in this way, for it is a thought and thoughts have no origin.

In a compound thought of the first kind, the two thoughts may be interchanged. The same interchangeability must also hold for the negation of a compound thought of the first kind, hence for a compound thought of the second kind. If, therefore, 'not [A and B]' expresses a compound thought, then 'not [B and A]' express the same compound of the same thoughts. This interchangeability should no more be regarded as a theorem here than for compounds of the first kind, for there is no difference in sense between these expressions. It is

therefore self-evident | that the sense of the second compound sentence 41
is true if that of the first is true – for it is the same sense.

An inference may also be mentioned for the present case:

not [A and B] is true;
A is true; therefore
B is false.

THIRD KIND OF COMPOUND THOUGHT

A compound of the first kind, formed from the negation of one thought
conjoined with the negation of another thought, is also a compound of
these thoughts themselves. I call it a compound of the third kind out of
the first thought and the second. Let the first thought, for example, be
that Paul can read, and the second that Paul can write; then the
compound of the third kind out of these two thoughts is the thought
that Paul can neither read nor write. A compound thought of the third
kind is true only if each of the two compounded thoughts is false, and
it is false if at least one of the compounded thoughts is true. In
compound thoughts of the third kind, the component thoughts are also
interchangeable. If 'A' expresses a thought, then 'not A' must express
the negation of this thought, and similarly for 'B'. Hence, if 'A' and 'B'
are sentences proper, then the sense of

'(not A) and (not B)',

for which I also write

'neither A nor B'

is the compound of the third kind out of the two thoughts expressed by
'A' and 'B'.

Here the connective is the sense of everything in these expressions
apart from the letters 'A' and 'B'. The two gaps in

'(not) and (not)',

or in

'neither , nor ',

indicate the twofold unsaturatedness of these expressions which corresponds to the two fold unsaturatedness of the connective. When the
latter is saturated by thoughts, there comes about the compound of the
third kind out of these thoughts.

Once again we may mention an inference:

A is false;
B is false; therefore
(neither A nor B) is true.

The brackets are to make it clear that what they contain is the whole whose sense is presented as true.

FOURTH KIND OF COMPOUND THOUGHT

The negation of a compound of the third kind between two thoughts is likewise a compound of these two thoughts: it may be called a compound thought | of the fourth kind. A compound of the fourth kind out of two thoughts is a compound of the second kind out of the negations of these thoughts. In presenting such a compound thought as true, we thereby assert that at least one of the compounded thoughts is true. A compound thought of the fourth kind is false only if each of the compounded thoughts is false. Given once again that 'A' and 'B' are sentences proper, the sense of

'not [(not A) and (not B)]'

is a compound thought of the fourth kind between the thoughts expressed by 'A' and 'B'. The same holds of

'not [neither A nor B]',

which may be written more briefly

'A or B'.

Taken in this sense, 'or' occurs only between sentences – indeed only between sentences proper. By recognizing the truth of such a compound thought, I do not rule out the truth of both compounded thoughts: we have in this case the non-exclusive 'or'. The connective is the sense of whatever occurs in 'A' or 'B' apart from 'A' and 'B', that is, the sense of

'(or   )'

where the gaps on both sides of 'or' indicates the twofold unsaturatedness in the connective. The sentences conjoined by 'or' should be regarded merely as expressions of thoughts, and not therefore as individually endowed with assertoric force. The compound thought as a whole, on the other hand, may be acknowledged as true. The linguistic expression does not make this clear: each component sentence of the assertion '5 is less than 4, or 5 is greater than 4' has the linguistic form which it would also have if it were uttered separately with assertoric force, whereas really only the whole compound is meant to be presented as true.

Perhaps it will be found that the sense here assigned to the word 'or' does not always agree with ordinary usage. On this point it should first be noted that in determining the sense of scientific expressions we cannot undertake to concur exactly with the usage of ordinary life; this, indeed, is for the most part unsuited to scientific purposes, where we feel the need for more precise definition. The scientist must be allowed to diverge, in his use of the word 'or',[23] from what is otherwise the custom. In the field of logic, the overtones of subsidiary thoughts may be distracting. In virtue of what has been said about our use of 'or', it can truly be asserted 'Frederick the Great won the battle of Rossbach, or two is greater than three'. This leads someone to think: 'Good Heavens! What does the battle of Rossbach have to do with the nonsense that two is greater than three?' But 'two is greater than three' is false, not nonsense: it makes no difference to logic whether the falsity of a thought is easy or difficult to discern. In sentences conjoined by 'or', we usually suppose that the sense of the one has something to do with that of the other, that there is some sort of relationship between them. | Such a relationship may well indeed be specifiable for a given   43 case, but for different cases there will be different relationships, and it will therefore be impossible to specify a relationship of sense which would always be attached to 'or' and could accordingly count as going with the sense of this word. 'But why does the speaker add the second sentence at all? If he wants to assert that Frederick the Great won the battle of Rossbach, then surely the first sentence would be sufficient. We may certainly assume that he does not want to claim that two is greater than three; and if he had been satisfied with just the first sentence, he would have said more with fewer words. Why, therefore, this waste of words?' These questions, too, only distract us into side-issues. Whatever may be the speaker's intentions and motives for saying just this and not that, our concern is not with these at all, but solely with what he says.

Compound thoughts of the first four kinds have this in common, that their component thoughts may be interchanged.

Here, too, follows another inference:

---

[23][In the original '*Ohr*' ('ear'), probably a misprint for '*oder*' ('or'). (*Ed.*)]

(A or B) is true;
A is false; therefore
B is true.

FIFTH KIND OF COMPOUND THOUGHT

By forming a compound of the first kind out of the negation of one thought and a second thought, we get a compound of the fifth kind out of these two thoughts. Given that 'A' expresses the first thought and 'B' expresses the second, the sense of

'(not A) and B'

is such a compound thought. A compound of this kind is true if, and only if, the first compounded thought is false while the second is true. Thus, for example, the compound thought expressed by

'(not $3^2 = 2^3$) and $(2^4 = 4^3)$'

viz. the thought that 3^2 is not equal to 2^3 and 2^4 is equal to 4^2, is true. After seeing that 2^4 is equal to 4^2, someone may think that in general the exponent of a number raised to a power can be interchanged with the number itself. Someone else may then try to correct this mistake by saying '2^4 equals 4^2 but 2^3 does not equal 3^2'. If it is asked what difference there is between conjunction with 'and' and with 'but', the answer is: with respect to what I have called the 'thought' or the 'sense' of the sentence, it is immaterial whether the idiom of 'and' or that of 'but' is chosen. The difference comes out only in what I call the illumination of the thought (cf. my article – 'Thoughts' p. 63 in the original) and does not belong to the province of logic.

The connective in a compound thought of the fifth kind is the doubly incomplete sense of the doubly incomplete expression

'(not   ) and (   )'. |

44 Here the compounded thoughts are not interchangeable, for

(not B) and A'

does not express the same as

'(not A) and B'.

The first thought does not occupy the same kind of position in the compound as the second thought. Since I hesitate to coin a new word,

I am obliged to use the word 'position' with a transferred meaning. In speaking of written expressions of thoughts, 'position' may be taken to have its ordinary spatial meaning. But a position in the expression of a thought must correspond to something in the thought itself, and for this I shall retain the word 'position'. In the present case we cannot simply make the two thoughts exchange their position, but we can set the negation of the second thought in the position of the first, and at the same time the negation of the first in the position of the second. (Of course, this too must be taken with a grain of salt, for an operation in space and time is not intended.) Thus from

'(not A) and B'

we obtain

'(not (not B)) and (not A)'.

But since 'not (not B)' has the same sense as 'B', we have here

'B and (not A)',

which expresses the same as

'(not A) and B'.

SIXTH KIND OF COMPOUND THOUGHT

By negating a compound of the fifth kind out of two thoughts, we get a compound of the sixth kind out of the same two thoughts. We can also say that a compound of the second kind out of the negation of one thought and a second thought is a compound of the sixth kind out of these two thoughts. A compound of the fifth kind is true if and only if its first component thought is false, but the second is true. From this it follows that a compound of the sixth kind out of two thoughts is false if and only if its first component is false, but the second is true. Such a compound thought is therefore true given only the truth of its first component thought, regardless of whether the second is true or false. It is also true given only the falsehood of its second component thought, regardless of whether the first is true or false.

Without knowing whether

$((21/20)^{100})^2$ is greater than 2^2,

or whether

$(21/20)^{100}$ is greater than 2,

45 I can still recognize as true the compound of the sixth kind | out of these two thoughts. The negation of the first thought excludes the second thought, and *vice versa*. We can put it as follows:

'If $(21/20)^{100}$ is greater than 2,
then $((21/20)^{100})^2$ is greater than 2^2.'

Instead of 'compound thought of the sixth kind', I shall also speak of 'hypothetical compound thought', and I shall refer to the first and second components of a hypothetical compound thought as 'consequent' and 'antecedent' respectively. Thus, a hypothetical compound thought is true if its consequent is true; it is also true if its antecedent is false, regardless of whether the consequent is true or false. The consequent must always be a thought.

Given once again that 'A' and 'B' are sentences proper, then

'not (not A) and B'

expresses a hypothetical compound with the sense (thought-content) of 'A' as consequent and the sense of 'B' as antecedent. We may also write instead:

'If B, then A'.

But here, indeed, doubts may arise. It may perhaps be maintained that this does not square with linguistic usage. In reply, it must once again be emphasized that science has to be allowed its own terminology, that it cannot always bow to ordinary language. Just here I see the greatest difficulty for philosophy: the instrument it finds available for its work, namely ordinary language, is little suited to the purpose, for its formation was governed by requirements wholly different from those of philosophy. So also logic is first of all obliged to fashion a usable instrument from those already to hand. And for this purpose it initially finds but little in the way of usable instruments available.

Many would undoubtedly declare that the sentence

'If 2 is greater than 3, then 4 is a prime number'

is nonsense; and yet, according to my stipulation it is true because the antecedent is false. To be false is not yet to be nonsense. Without knowing whether

$$\sqrt[10]{10^{21}} \text{ is greater than } (21/20)^{100},$$

we can see that

If $\sqrt[10]{10^{21}}$ is greater than $(21/20)^{100}$,

then $(^{10}\sqrt{10^{21}})^2$ is greater than $(21/20)^{100})^2$;

and nobody will see any nonsense in that. But it is false that

$^{10}\sqrt{10^{21}}$ is greater than $(21/20)^{100}$, |

and it is equally false that

$(^{10}\sqrt{10^{21}})^2$ is greater than $((21/20)^{100})^2$.

If this could be seen as easily as the falsity of '2 is greater than 3', then the hypothetical compound thought of the present example would seem just as nonsensical as that of the previous one. Whether the falsity of a thought can be seen with greater or less difficulty is of no matter from a logical point of view, for the difference is a psychological one.

The thought expressed by the compound sentence

'If I own a cock which has laid eggs today, then Cologne Cathederal will collapse tomorrow morning'

is also true. Someone will perhaps say: 'But here the antecedent has no inner connection at all with the consequent'. In my account, however, I required no such connection, and I ask that 'If B, then A' should be understood solely in terms of what I have said and expressed in the form

'not [(not A) and B]'.

It must be admitted that this conception of a hypothetical compound thought will at first be thought strange. But my account is not designed to square with ordinary linguistic usage, which is generally too vague and ambiguous for the purposes of logic. Questions of all kinds arise at this point, e.g. the relation of cause and effect, the intention of a speaker who utters a sentence of the form 'If B, then A', the grounds on which he holds its content to be true. The speaker may perhaps give hints in regard to such questions arising among his hearers. These hints are among the adjuncts which often surround the thought in ordinary language. My task here is to remove the adjuncts and thereby to pick out, as the logical kernel, a compound of two thoughts, which I have called a hypothetical compound thought. Insight into the structure of thoughts compounded of two thoughts must provide the foundation for consideration of multiple compound thoughts.

What I have said about the expression 'If B, then A' must not be so understood as to imply that every compound sentence of this form expresses a hypothetical compound thought. If either 'A' or 'B' by itself does not completely express a thought, and is not therefore a sentence proper, the case is altered. In the compound sentence,

'If someone is a murderer, then he is a criminal',

neither the antecedent-clause not the consequent-clause, taken by itself, expresses a thought. Without some further clue, we cannot determine whether what is expressed in the sentence 'He is a criminal' is true or false when detached from this compound; for the word 'he' is not a proper name, and in the detached sentence without that further clue it designates nothing. It follows that the consequent-clause expresses no thought, and is therefore not a sentence proper. This holds of the
47 antecedent-clause as well, for it | likewise has a non-designating component, namely 'someone'. Yet the compound sentence can none the less express a thought. The 'someone' and the 'he' refer to each other. Hence, and in virtue of the 'If—, then—', the two clauses are so connected with one another that they together express a thought; whereas we can distinguish three thoughts in a hypothetical compound thought, namely the antecedent, the consequent, and the thought compounded of these. Thus, compound sentences do not always express compound thoughts, and it is very important to distinguish the two cases which arise for compound sentences of the form

'If B, then A'.

Once again I append an inference:

[If B, then A] is true;
B is true; therefore
A is true.

In this inference, the characteristic feature of hypothetical compound thoughts stands out, perhaps in its clearest form.

The following mode of inference is also noteworthy:

[If C, then B] is true;
[If B, then A] is true; therefore
[If C, then A] is true.

I should like here to call attention to a misleading way of speaking. Many mathematical writers express themselves as if conclusions could be drawn from a thought whose truth is still doubtful. In saying 'I infer A from B', or 'I conclude from B that A is true', we take B for one of the premises or the sole premise of the inference. But before acknowledging its truth, one cannot use a thought as premise of an inference, nor can one infer or conclude anything from it. If anyone still thinks this can be done, he is apparently confusing acknowledgement of the truth of a hypothetical compound thought with performing an inference in which the antecedent of this compound is taken for a premise. Now recognition of the truth of the sense of

'If C, then A'

can certainly depend on an inference, as in the example given above, while there may yet be a doubt about the truth of C.[24] But in this case, the thought expressed by 'C' is by no means a premise of the inference; the premise, rather, was the sense of the sentence

'If C, then B'.

If the thought-content of 'C' were a premise of the inference, then it would not occur in the conclusion: for that is just how inference works. |

We have seen how, in a compound thought of the fifth kind, the first   48
thought can be replaced by the negation of the second, and the second simultaneously by the negation of the first, without altering the sense of the whole. Now since a compound thought of the sixth kind is the negation of a compound thought of the fifth kind, the same also holds for it: that is, we can replace the antecedent of a hypothetical compound by the negation of the consequent, and the consequent simultaneously by the negation of the antecedent, without thereby altering its sense. (This is contraposition, the transition from *modus ponens* to *modus tollens*.)

SUMMARY OF THE SIX COMPOUND THOUGHTS

I.	A and B;	II.	not (A and B);
III.	(not A) and (not B);	IV.	not ((not A) and (not B));
V.	(not A) and B;	VI.	not ((not A) and B).

It is tempting to add

A and (not B).

But the sense of 'A and (not B)' is the same as that of '(not B) and A', for any 'A' and 'B' that are sentences proper. And since '(not B) and A' has the same form as '(not A) and B', we get nothing new here, but only another expression of a compound thought of the fifth kind; and in 'not (A and (not B))' we have another expression of a compound thought of the sixth kind. Thus our six kinds of compound thought

---

[24]More precisely: whether the thought expressed by 'C' is true.

form a completed whole, whose primitive elements seem here to be the first kind of compound and negation. However acceptable it may be to psychologists, this apparent pre-eminence of the first kind of compound over the others has no logical justification; for any one of the six kinds of compound thought can be taken as fundamental and can be used, together with negation, for deriving the others; so that, for logic, all six kinds have equal justification. If, for example, we start with the hypothetical compound

> If B, then C,   i.e.   not ((not C) and B)),

and replace 'C' by 'not A', then we get

> If B, then not A,   i.e.   not (A and B). |

49   By negating the whole, we get

> not (if B, then not A),   i.e.   A and B.

from which it follows that

> 'not (if B, then not A)'

says the same as

> 'A and B'.

We have thereby derived a compound of the first kind from a hypothetical compound and negation; and since compounds of the first kind and negation together suffice for the derivation of the other compound thoughts, it follows that all six kinds of compound thought can be derived from hypothetical compounds and negation. What has been said of the first and the sixth kinds of compound holds in general for all our six kinds of compound thought, so that none has any priority over the others. Each of them can serve as a basis for deriving the others, and our choice is not governed by any fact of logic.

A similar situation exists in the foundation of geometry. Two different geometries can be formulated in such a way that certain theorems of the one occur as axioms of the other, and conversely.

Let us now consider cases where a thought is compounded with itself rather than with some different thought. For any 'A' that is a sentence proper, 'A and A' expresses the same thought as 'A'; the former says no more and no less than the latter. It follows that 'not (A and A)' expresses the same as 'not A'.

Equally, '(not A) and (not A)' also expresses the same as 'not A'; and consequently 'not [(not A) and (not A)]' also expresses the same as 'not (not A)', or 'A'. Now, 'not [(not A) and (not A)]' expresses a compound of the fourth kind and instead of this we can say 'A or A'. Accordingly, not only 'A and A', but also 'A or A' has the same sense as 'A'. |

It is otherwise for compounds of the fifth kind. The compound   50 thought expressed by '(not A) and A' is false, since, of two thoughts, where one is the negation of the other, one must always be false; so that a compound of the first kind composed of them is likewise false. The compound of the sixth kind out of a thought and itself, namely that expressed by 'not [(not A) and A]' is accordingly true (assuming that 'A' is a sentence proper). We can also render this compound thought verbally by the expression 'If A, then A'; for example, 'If the Schneekoppe is higher than the Brocken, then the Schneekoppe is higher than the Brocken'.

In such a case the questions arise: 'Does this sentence express a thought? Does it not lack content? Do we learn anything new upon hearing it?' Now it may happen that before hearing it someone did not know this truth at all, and had therefore not acknowledged it. To that extent one could, under certain conditions, learn something new from it. It is surely an undeniable fact that the Schneekoppe is higher than the Brocken if the Schneekoppe is higher than the Brocken. Since only thoughts can be true, this compound sentence must express a thought; and, despite its apparent nonsensicality, the negation of this thought is also a thought. It must always be borne in mind that a thought can be expressed without being asserted. Here we are concerned just with thoughts, and the appearance of nonsensicality arises only from the assertoric force with which one involuntarily takes the sentence to be uttered. But who says that anyone uttering it non-assertorically does so in order to present its content as true? Perhaps he is doing it with precisely the opposite intention.

This can be generalized. Let 'O' be a sentence which expresses a particular instance of a logical law, but which is not presented as true. Then it is easy for 'not O' to seem nonsensical, but only because it is thought of as uttered assertorically. The assertion of a thought which contradicts a logical law can indeed appear, if not nonsensical, than at least absurd; for the truth of a logical law is immediately evident of itself, from the sense of its expression. But a thought which contradicts a logical law may be expressed, since it may be negated. 'O' itself, however, seems almost to lack content.

Any compound thought, being itself a thought, can be compounded with other thoughts. Thus, the compound expressed by '(A and B) and

'C' is composed of the thoughts expressed by 'A and B' and 'C'. But we
51 can also treat it as composed of | the thoughts expressed by 'A' and 'B'
and 'C'. In this way compound thoughts containing three thoughts can
originate.[25] Other examples of such compounds are expressed by:

'not [(not A) and (B and C)]', and
'not [(not A) and ((not B) and (not C))]'.

So too it will be possible to find examples of compound thoughts
containing four, five, or more thoughts.

Compound thoughts of the first kind, and negation, are together
adequate for the formation of all these compounds, and any other of
our six kinds of compound can be chosen instead of the first. Now the
question arises whether every compound thought is formed in this way.
So far as mathematics is concerned, I am convinced that it includes no
compound thoughts formed in any other way. It will scarcely be
otherwise in physics, chemistry, and astronomy as well; but final clauses
call for caution and seem to require more precise investigation. Here I
shall leave this question open. Compound thoughts thus formed with
the aid of negation from compounds of the first kind seem, at all
events, to merit a special title. They may be called mathematical
compound thoughts. This should not be taken to mean that there are
compound thoughts of any other type. Mathematical compound
thoughts seem to have something else in common; for if a true
component of such a compound is replaced by another true thought,
the resultant compound thought is true or false according to whether
the original compound is true or false. The same holds if a false
component of a mathematical compound thought is replaced by
another false thought. I now want to say that two thoughts have the
same truth-value if they are either both true or both false. I maintain,
therefore, that the thought expressed by 'A' has the same truth-value as
that expressed by 'B' if either 'A and B' or else '(not A) and (not B)'
expresses a true thought. Having established this, I can phrase my
thesis in this way:

'If one component of a mathematical compound thought is replaced
by another thought having the same truth-value, then the resultant
compound thought has the same truth-value as the original.'

---

[25]This origination must not be regarded as a temporal process.

Index

The mathematical writings (pp. 1–107) are not covered. ~ signifies
repetition of the catchword or of that part of it preceding /.

abstraction, 203, 204, 205, 231, 233,
   254, 343, 345
addition, 259–61, 268
affirmative) (negative
   unnecessary distinction, 380
'all', 'some'
   prefixed to concept-words, 187
   predicative, 216
   not part of subject, 239
analysis, mathematical, 138, 144, 153,
   169, 194, 285, 286, 288
arithmetic
   foundations of 111, 253
   modes of inference reducible to
      those of logic, 113
   and logic, 112, 145
article, definite, 117, 139, 170, 387
) (indefinite, 184, 185
assertion, 172, 282, 356
   ~-sign (judgement-stroke), 149,
      150, 247
assertive force, 312, 385, 391
   not necessarily attached to
      predicative part, 281
   how supplied, 383
attending to, 197, 203
axiom, 112, 113, 180, 235, 264, 273,
   275, 278, 293–8, 306, 315, 317,
   328, 330, 333, 339, 340
   never false, 335
   pseudo-~, 320, 323, 332, 333
   see also consistency

Biermann, O., 205
Boltzmann, L., 285
Boole, G., 210, 214, 240
   ~'s logic a *calculus ratiocinator*)
      (*lingua characterica*, 242

Cantor, G., 122, 179–81
characteristics, 114, 179, 283, 332

class (domain), 210, 211, 212, 213,
   216, 217, 218, 219, 220
   ~) (collection, 224, 226
   empty ~, 212, 213, 224
   = extension of a concept, 213, 240
   singular ~, 218
cognitive (epistemic) value, 157, 158
Cohen, H., 108–11
collectivity, 202, 208
   see also class, multiplicity, set
colouring, shading of sense or
   thought, 16, 185
   see also mood
common name
   confusing term, 227
   (concept word), 205
complete
   ~ expressions, 123
   function in ~, 140
   ~) (incomplete (saturated) (un-
      saturated), 154, 281, 290, 292
   negation in ~, 386
   double negation doubly in ~, 388
   parts of a thought in ~, 390, 391
concept, 114, 158, 197, 208, 211, 254,
   282, 296, 297
   bringing objects under, 198, 205
   ~) (class, 240
   must be sharply delimited, 148
   empty ~, 117, 225, 226, 228,
   extension of, see extension of a
      concept
   first-level) (second-level, 189, 190,
      280, 283, 284, 307, 308, 314, 337
   ~) (idea, 133–5
   logical, 133
   marks of, 170
   ~) (object, 182–94, 281
   'the concept "horse"' designates an
      object, 184
   objectivity of, 208

407